Mercenary Commander

Mercenary Commander

Col **Jerry Puren**
as told to
Brian Pottinger

GALAGO

©Colonel Jerry Puren and Brian Pottinger
©Front cover painting Francis Lategan

All Rights Reserved
ISBN 0 947020 21 7

First published by Galago July 1986
Galago books are published by Galago Publishing (Pty) Ltd
P O Box 404, Alberton 1450 RSA

Type computer set by Galago.
Interfaced to $10\frac{1}{2}/12$ Times Roman by Citygraphics

Colour and half tones by Citygraphics

Printed and bound by CTP Book Printers

DUST JACKET DESIGN BY FRANCIS LATEGAN

PAINTING OF JERRY PUREN AS A MERCENARY PILOT IN A T6
BY FRANCIS LATEGAN

BOOK DESIGN: FRANCIS LATEGAN AND PETER STIFF

For Julia, who was always there...

Contents

Chapter	Page

List of Illustrations

Number		Page

Maps

Photographic Credits

Some pictures are unacknowledged although the publishers have made every effort to establish their authorship. For this, the publishers apologise. The subject, it will be understood, is the chaos of independence and the rebellions in the Congo, and much of the information regarding who was who at the time, has been blown away by the dual winds of war and change. However the publishers will be glad to amend or add credits in subsequent editions and to make the necessary arrangements with those photographers who were not known at the time of going to press, or who had not been traced.

Associated Press 14, 15; Camera Press 43, 46; Lionel Lang 30; Le Soir 77, 78; Charles Masy 19, 29, 31, 35, 37, 54, 57, 59; Photo de Presse 74; Jerry Puren 9, 10, 11, 12, 13, 16, 17, 18, 21, 22, 56, 63, 66; Rapport 79, 80, 81, 82, 83, 84, 86, 87, 88, 89; Rhodesia Herald 1, 3, 4, 6, 7, 8, 20; Rizzoli Press 65; Wilf Schindler 23, 25, 32, 33, 34, 36, 38, 39, 48, 51, 52, 53; Scope 41, 65, 67, 68, 72, 74, 75, 76; UPI 27; Jan van Vreden 26, 42, 44, 45, 47, 49, 50, 55.

Foreword

The place and the time
The Belgian Congo: a verdant area spanning the central regions of Africa — giant, somnambulant, beautiful and menacing. In 1960 the Belgian authorities, who had for years ruled the Congo with a stern hand, opted to grant independence to the country's hugely diverse population.

On June 30 1960 the Congo became independent. Within five days the country had fallen into four squabbling parts: the central government in the old capital of Leopoldville, a rebel movement in the eastern capital of Stanleyville, an independent republic of Kasai in the south west and an independent Katanga in the southern regions with its capital at Elisabethville.

United Nations troops were deployed in a 'peace keeping' role and after three wars succeeded in quashing the Katangese coup. But they had hardly finished their task when rebel 'Simbas' in the eastern Congo began sweeping across the Congo with the intention of capturing Leopoldville.

Supported by the CIA, the central Congolese government recruited mercenaries and fought back. By 1954 the mercenaries had taken Stanleyville and smothered the revolt.

In 1966 and 1967 the Katangese revolted and were repressed. On two subsequent occasions, one in 1977 and the other in 1978, Katangese rebels operating from north Angola again attacked Katanga province — now called Shaba. They were defeated.

The black leaders
The story of modern Zaire can be written around the names of four black men.

The first is former colonial army sergeant, Joseph Desire Mobutu, later President Mobutu Seso Seke, a brutal dictator.

Equal in stature but vastly different in personality was Moise Tshombe, son of a wealthy Katangese trading family. He became the first president of the secessionist state of Katanga, was driven into exile after the collapse of the secession, returned as prime minister of the Congo to defeat the Simba rebels, was banished into exile and, finally, died in an Algerian prison after being kidnapped as a result of a US CIA plot.

Patrice Lumumba, a brilliant and erratic Marxist intellectual, was the first black president of the Congo after independence. He was quickly usurped, however, and was eventually murdered in Katanga at the behest of Mobutu. His name became a rallying call for the communist-supported rebels of the eastern Congo.

Christopher Gbenye united the rebel Simba forces of the eastern Congo and led them on their march across the Congo towards Leopoldville — and to their destruction.

The white mercenaries

Tied with blood and history to the troubled country were the mercenaries. Moise Tshombe first brought them to defend Katangese independence in late 1960; they were quickly dubbed *le affreux* — the frightful ones.

When Tshombe returned in 1964 he again brought his dogs of war; Belgian, French, British and, the biggest contingent, South African and Rhodesian. They stopped the Soviet-backed insurgency in the east in its tracks.

Here too mercenary history can be written with a handful of names: 'Black Jack' Jean Schramme, planter turned warlord, Bob Denard, Algerian policeman and professional buccaneer, Mike Hoare, correct but ruthless and Roger Faulques, the scarred Foreign Legion veteran of Dien Bien Phu.

And among them, dubbed early by the press as an *eminence gris* of the mercenary community in the Congo, was the shadowy Colonel Jerry Puren, mercenary commander extraordinary; Moise Tshombe's soldier extraordinary, air force commander, co-conspirator, top adviser, emissary and friend.

This story is about honest and corrupt black leaders, it is about the mercenaries, the Congo and a way of life that has disappeared in the winds of Africa's change.

Seychelles coup attempt

It also tells of one of the most audacious and yet badly planned mercenary exploits in history; the abortive coup attempt in the Seychelles in 1981 that nearly claimed the last of Colonel Puren's nine lives.

This is a true story of adventure, of politics, of love, of betrayal . . . and of death.

It is Colonel Puren's amazing story . . . and it all happened.

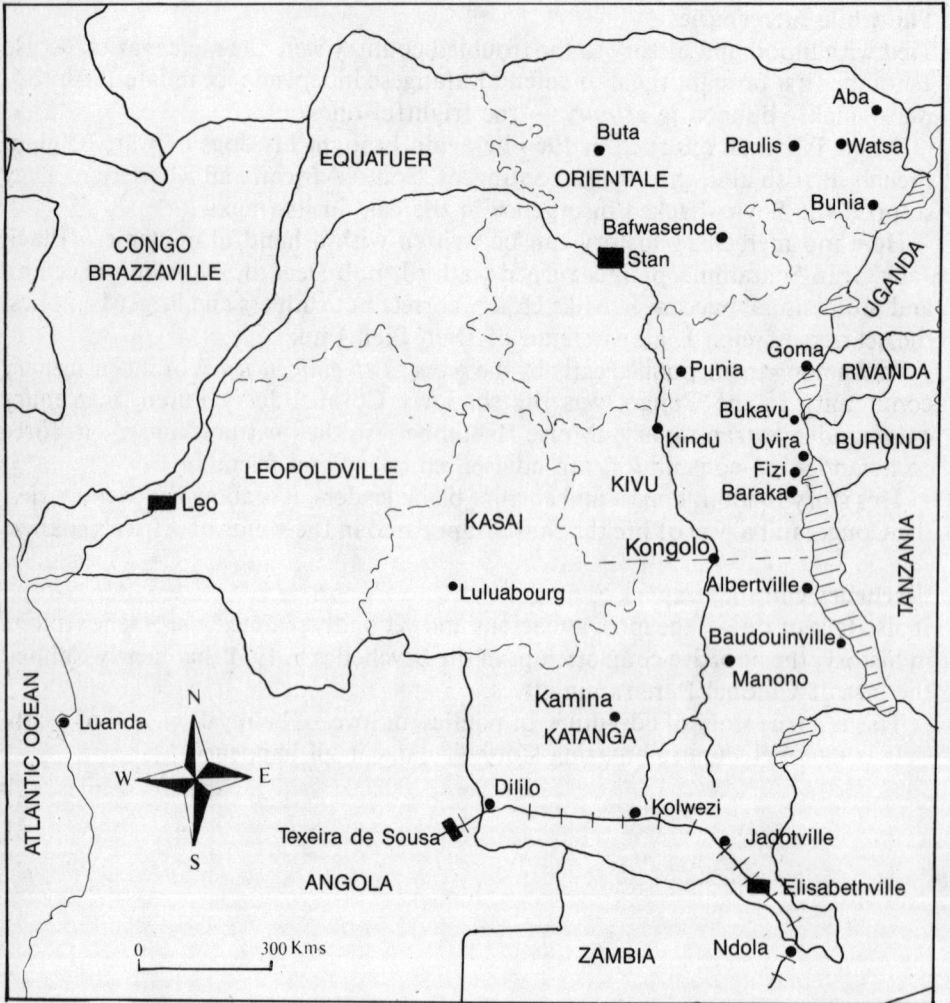

1

To Arms
Katanga : 1961 to 1963

The call to arms came casually, almost incidentally. A contact in South African Defence Force HQ mentioned in passing that a Belgian chappie was in the country recruiting for somebody called Tshombe in a place called Katanga. Would I be interested?

It was January 1961 in Springs, South Africa. I had a dead end job in commerce, my marriage had just fallen through and my thoughts were restless with the exciting years I had spent in the South African and Royal Air Forces from 1942 through to the early 1950s. North Africa, Middle East, Italy, Germany and eastern Europe in bombers; Egypt, Far East, Iraq and Malaya in RAF Transports; the names bore memories of battles won and lost, incidents and events in which I had featured as a tiny extra on the great stage of history. I was indeed interested in the Belgian chappie, Tshombe, and the Congo.

Three weeks later I was at Jan Smuts airport saying tearful farewells to my children before launching into the great unknown. The recruiter, Carlos Huyghe, had appointed me on the basis of my past military experience and commissioned me as a lieutenant in the Katangese Gendarmerie. I was to be a platoon leader and, as I looked around Jan Smuts Airport departure concourse that boiling February day, I watched the thirty other mercenaries of my command also saying their farewells.

I permitted myself a moment of self-doubt. Was I doing the right thing? Would I see my children again? I thrust the doubts away and comforted myself with the thought that the money would perhaps help set me on my way to owning a business when I returned in six months.

It was a blur of last minute kisses and hugs and then we were all settled on the Elisabethville bound aircraft. I concentrated on getting to know my men. They came from all walks . . . steady jobs, the unemployment queues, farms, mines and from other armies. But three major qualities bound them; they all had military experience, they all liked adventure and they all had a taste for money.

We had little idea of what we were heading towards. Vaguely I knew of the background to the Katanga secession; the decision of the mineral rich southern province of the Congo to declare independence after the collapse of central Government control in the wake of the Belgian-granted independence. I also knew that the Katangese President, Moise Tshombe, faced fierce opposition from all quarters; from what was left of the central Congolese Government, from the United Nations, from the United States and not least from dissident Baluba tribes within Katanga itself.

By UN resolution a number of 'peace-keeping' troops had already been deployed in Katanga with the ostensible aim of merely monitoring entry and exit of weapons and troops. Rapidly the UN forces had begun to assume a more offensive role against the Katangese people, the white 'Colons' and the Belgian mining houses.

I also knew Tshombe's first line of defence was his Gendarmerie . . . in other words, us.

We stepped from the aircraft at Elisabethville into the stifling night time heat of equatorial Africa; from the security of our homes and acquaintances in South Africa into the uncertainties of a particularly vicious African war; from boredom to excitement.

At the airport to meet us was Dick Browne; a burly, freckled Englishman whose brother was a British Tory MP.

We were quickly ushered through customs and on to a bus that was to take us to our training camp.

Barrelling along the dusty Katanga roads, I was to have my first encounter with the volatile Congo ethos. A ragged black hunter on the side of the road drew Browne's ire and it was with great difficulty that I restrained him from blowing the poor man away there and then.

Home base turned out to be a deserted mining camp at Shinkolobwe, twenty five kilometers west of Jadotville. It was here that my merry band were quickly kitted out and converted into an effective mobile fireforce operating from seven jeeps equipped with ,30 cal and ,50 cal machineguns. Together with our sidearms, FN rifles fresh from Belgium and parabellum pistols, we were supplied with Uzi submachineguns, 3,5 rocket launchers and old 60mm mortars. All in all we packed a fair punch when in battle order.

Several weeks later I had to return to Elisabethville to settle some pay matters concerning my troops. It was in this gracious tropical city, only marginally scarred by war and its accoutrements, that I was to run into many of the personalities that were to stud Congo history for the next seven years. People like Jean 'Black Jack' Schramme, the Belgian settler from the eastern Maniema areas turned mercenary leader and Bob Denard, the Gascon former Algerian policeman.

Also around was Glasspole, the gum chewing Canadian pilot who had ferried me in from Jadotville. He was to become a constant, if sometimes unfathomable companion over the years. Glasspole was ex-services and a competent pilot — but always on the wild side. And of course there were the other members of the mercenary forces; the large Belgian contingent comprising many former colonial officers, the smaller French detachment boasting predominantly Foreign Legionaires and paratroopers fresh from the Algerian war and finally the *Compagnie Internationale* which had English speaking mercenaries drawn from Britain, South Africa and Rhodesia.

Overall commander of the mercenaries was a Belgian, Colonel Crevecoeur, and his 2 IC was a Major Matisse. Under them served two seconded Belgian officers; Colonel Liegeois, formerly of the crack *Chasseurs d'Ardennes,* commanding forces in the north, and an officer called Lamouline, commanding the Kaminaville sector.

The French group was under Colonel Faulques, a Foreign Legionaire and veteran

18

of Dien Bien Phu and countless scraps with the Algerian FLN; Browne commanded the *Compagnie Internationale* in which served myself and an Irish-South African who was to make a name for himself in the Congo and elsewhere, Mike Hoare. Hoare, however, I was only to meet later.

In the field the different groups operated independently with their assigned Katangese Gendarmes which sometimes led to co-ordination problems; not eased by the antagonisms existing between the Belgians and French. The mercenary and Katangese forces were controlled by the *Etat Major* in Elisabethville and directly under the control of Moise Tshombe, his seconded Belgian officers and several independent Belgian operators.

Overall the mercenaries were a tough and effective force; the Belgians primarily because they knew the area, the French because they were fierce if sometimes temperamental fighters and the *Compagnie Internationale* because it brought discipline and professionalism to the task.

Altogether there were no more than two hundred mercenaries in Katanga at the time.

Largely because of the deliberately cultivated desperado look of the French mercenaries . . . weird hats, trinkets, personal weapons . . . we were labelled *Le Affreux* . . . the frightful ones.

While on my first visit to Elisabethville, Glasspole was not slow in introducing me to the favourite watering holes of the mercenaries; the Beaulieu Ladies Bar opposite the central post office, the Sabena Guest House, the Hotel Leopold II and the Relais.

It was here I was to meet many of the Katangese Colons, the white Congolese with roots deep in the country, many of them fearful of the events sweeping the Congo, many of them already refugees from other parts of the country where public order had collapsed.

The attitude of the civilians to the mercenaries was mixed; on the one hand gratitude for the assistance in maintaining order in Katanga, on the other hand deep suspicion of the freewheeling soldiers of fortune who acted as if tomorrow would never come.

The mercenaries accepted the civilians' reserve phlegmatically; if the fathers locked their daughters up there were always the Jungle Bunnies, and if the locals wouldn't take a drink with one there were always plenty of comrades from the units.

From the earliest days in the Congo, however, I distanced myself slightly from the other mercenaries to the extent that I made deliberate attempts to cultivate friendships among the Katangese, black and white, and made an effort to understand what was actually happening in the Congo.

In the process I made some firm friends among the Katangese, came to a deep understanding of the infant country's problems and roused not a little suspicion in my fellow mercenaries.

My first Elisabethville sojourn ended abruptly. I was still dozing in my hotel bed early one Monday morning when Glasspole came hurriedly and unannounced through the doorway. He began pulling my bed clothes off.

'For Christ's sake. What's happening?' I demanded.

'Wake up, Jerry. Rise and shine. The Gendarmes are moving out.'

2

The North

It was like old times again, preparing for a big operation. Suppressed excitement, a lot of careful planning and rumours, rumours, rumours. Shinkolobwe was a madhouse of activity.

The ninety white mercenaries of the *Compagnie Internationale* were trained, fit, equipped and raring to move. For myself, the indulgent Elisabethville life was temporarily behind and I looked forward enthusiastically to the chance of doing the job for which I had been employed.

At Shinkolobwe our vehicle park was filled with bustling activity as jerry cans of petrol were hoisted on to jeeps, ammo boxes dragged out and stacked, trucks loaded with supplies and blankets and hasty last minute adjustments made to individual kit and weapons. Excitement suffused the whole camp. Browne was in his element, striding around with his swagger stick, bellowing orders, partially drunk and abusive.

All the officers were ushered into one of the prefab huts used for briefings and we were addressed by a senior Belgian intelligence officer.

The political situation in Katanga was grave, we were told, and the time had now come for military assertiveness in defence of the secession.

While the mercenary officers remained raptly silent, the intelligence officer went on to sketch the three momentous factors which were background to the decision to go on to the offensive. From the intelligence briefing and my own knowledge gained from reading widely and holding discussions in the Beaulieu, it was easy enough to discern the pattern.

Firstly, on February 13, the Katangese Minister of Interior, Godefroid Munongo, had announced to an incredulous world the death of Patrice Lumumba, head of the Movement National Congolaise and representative of the rebellious eastern Congo, while in the custody of Katangese forces. The circumstances surrounding the death of Lumumba were heavy with the treachery and deceit of one man — Joseph Mobutu.

In December 1960, Lumumba had been arrested by Colonel Mobutu and President Kasavubu of the Leopoldville government. Held in detention, a constant headache to the shaky central government, it was decided early in January that responsibility for the detention of the burdensome Lumumba should be shifted to somebody else. Tshombe was asked and promptly refused. For Mobutu the solution was simple . . . put Lumumba on a plane and fly him to Luluabourg in Kasai and Lumumba would miraculously become the problem of Kalonje, head of the semi-independent Kasai Province.

By design or criminal error, eight Baluba guards were sent with Lumumba and his two aides, Maurice Mpolo and Joseph Okito.

At that stage the Lumumbaists were massacring the Baluba at a fearful rate and Mobutu could surely not have been unaware of the inevitable reaction from the hate-crazed and undisciplined Baluba guards. The beatings began before the plane had even taken off and continued with such mounting ferocity that several times the pilot, a South African called Dixon, was forced to come into the fuselage to warn the guards to desist for fear of causing some real structural damage to the aircraft.

Problem was that Kalonje also was no fool and, aware of the plane's poisoned cargo, refused to allow it to land in Luluabourg. Forced on to Elisabethville, the plane circled the airport steadily running lower on fuel until it was eventually allowed to land. Lumumba and his aides, by now fatally injured, were spotted by a UN picket being hustled away by Katangese Gendarmes. That was the last that is known conclusively of the incident.

On February 13, Munongo announced that Lumumba had escaped from his Katangese prison and had been killed by tribesmen. Stories circulated that he had actually been taken to a house near Elisabethville, visited by Munongo, beaten again, and eventually shot by Colonel Huyghe. I doubt it. Huyghe was not the sort who would be able to shoot a wounded man in cold blood and Munongo had sufficient political insight to know Lumumba could be useful to us.

In later years I came to know Tshombe and Munongo intimately. Only once did Tshombe mention Lumumba to me and that was in a sunny Spanish villa many years after the event. Our conversation touched on Lumumba. Tshombe crossed to a cupboard drawer. He pulled out a few snapshots and wordlessly threw them down in front of me.

They were all taken in Leopoldville shortly before Lumumba's ill-fated plane ride. The snaps showed Lumumba sitting on the ground, head erect, hands handcuffed behind him. A man towered over Lumumba threateningly holding a huge stick above the hapless man's head.

The man was Joseph Mobutu.

I can still recall the fearless way in which Lumumba looked directly at his tormentor.

The second factor influencing our operation was the United Nations' resolution on February 21 1961. With the death of Lumumba fresh in their minds the UN called for the dismissal of all foreign military troops from Katanga and gave its troops in the country the authority to use force to do so.

Paragraph A of the resolution read: *'Urges the United Nations take immediately all appropriate measures to prevent the occurrence of civil war in the Congo, including arrangements for ceasefires, the halting of all military operations, the prevention of clashes, and the use of force, if necessary in the last resort.'*

The key words were, of course, 'use of force'. The script was drafted for the tragedy to be violently played out over the next two years. Having gained entry to Katanga under the guise of a peace-keeping force the United Nations troops had overnight changed character to become a fully fledged hostile force squatting in the very heart of Katanga.

A third factor also weighing heavily in the background was the increasing activity of the ANC — *Armee Nationale Congolaise* . . . the troops of the Central Government under Mobutu . . . along the Kasai and Katangese borders.

'Gentlemen', the intelligence officer concluded his preliminary address, 'it is imperative that the rebel Baluba areas be pacified, the ANC met head on, and Tshombe's authority over the whole of Katanga conclusively cemented in the eyes of the United Nations'.

Turning to the array of large scale maps plastered around the ops room, the officer seized his pointer and rapped it three times on an area shaded dark green for dense jungle on a large scale map as the northern Katangese border.

The first phase of the planned offensive into Northern Katanga was simple enough. Dick Browne and his group were to leave for Mitwaba, about two hundred kilometers north of Jadotville, and then strike along the eastern route to Manono, capital of the Sendwe rebels. I was to follow with my group from the south on a direct route from Malemba Nkulu on Lake Upemba and RV with Browne in Manono.

Browne's group . . . about forty white mercenaries and a number of Katangese support troops pulled out of Shinkolobwe early on a March morning, a long column of olive green jeeps and trucks, packed with expectant mercenaries. Five days later my group roared out of Shinkolobwe's gates in the soft early morning light and turned on to the dirt road leading north to Mitwaba. The morale of the men was high and I was confident of their ability to deal with whatever lay ahead.

Hour after hour we bowled along in billowing clouds of dust, eyes probing the rolling bushveld on either side of the road. Although still in friendly country the prospects of action sharpened the awareness of the entire column.

Relaxed behind their machinegun pedestals and rifles, the jeep crews were inwardly taut, fingers restlessly hovering around trigger guards, safety catches off, rifles cocked.

Along the roadside, knots of African peasants walked by unconcernedly, small children stopped to gaze, a few waved, some cattle on the road. Very peaceful. I sat in the lead jeep with one leg lolling over the side, enjoying the sun and whipping breeze, the prospect of action. On my lap I cradled my FN rifle.

By the end of the first day's driving the country had begun to change from the plateau bushveld of the Kolwezi/Jadotville/Elisabethville areas to the dense bush of northern Katanga. Whereas previously we would have operated in the bushveld, here we were restricted to the road, hemmed in by the threatening jungle . . . speed, firepower and accuracy our only defences.

Tired, and dusty, we made camp in a small village near Mitwaba. We were bordering Sendwe country; villagers and mercenaries kept a wary distance.

From radio messages along the road it had become clear that Manono, capital of the Balubakat Republic of north Katanga, had fallen to the whirlwind attack spearheaded by Browne's mercenaries. A few concentrated firefights, the occasional rocket burst and Browne's force quickly drove the rebels back into the impenetrable forests. I doubt Browne lost a man.

In Manono Browne found several prisoners who had been held captive by the Balubas for some months. From the stories he was told, and the whitening skeletons lying around, he found much evidence of Balubakat *Jeunesse* cruelty.

Next day we pushed north as quickly as we could, anxious to reach Manono and reinforce Browne in case of counter attack. Late that afternoon we arrived, still without sight of a rebel.

At Manono there were now three groups in occupation . . . Browne's, mine and a Belgian group . . . each with their supporting Katangese troops. Major Matisse from *Etat Major* in Elisabethville arrived and we planned the next phase.

Browne . . . now unduly inflated by his success . . . was to take his group by air to Kongolo while the rest of us were to push for Niemba, north east of Manono, pacifying the area as we went.

If we had expected action we were sorely disappointed. Between Manono and Niemba the road was completely deserted. Our column spun through village after village, all completely empty of humans, only a few lean dogs and chickens, token representatives of what had once been bustling communities.

Our route was lined, however, with the vast silent Congo forests, hectare upon hectare of thrusting trees, vines, tangled bush and twisted branches. Within all of us lurked the fear, ridiculous as it turned out, that somewhere, perhaps just around the next corner, lay the ambush that would leave our jaunty column a smoking line of death and destruction.

On several occasions we passed burnt out villages, stark husks of buildings, blackened beams pointing crookedly skywards, huge swatches of charcoal ground with a few green blades already pushing upwards. The villages were mute testimony to the activity of the Balubakat *Jeunesse* against any tribal chiefs they believed were pro-Tshombe.

We arrived on the banks of the Lukuga River at midday. On the opposite bank, five hundred meters away, Niemba lay lazily sunning itself in the staggering Congo midday heat. My group deployed on either side of the road and standing on the bonnet of my command jeep I swept the village with my field glasses.

Nothing moved. Not a dog's whisker visible. Silent, higgledy-piggledy streets fronted by mud houses, a few corrugated iron roofs, even one or two brick structures. An open space swept back from the banks of the Lukuga directly opposite us.

The perfect site for a bridgehead.

I knew we were deep in Sendwe country. Inwardly I felt certain they would be making a stand at some point and Niemba seemed the most likely. Behind the walls of those inscrutable buildings I imagined an army of Balubakat rebels waiting for us to set foot on their side of the river.

On the far side of the river, placidly nestling against a little jetty, was a battered old ferry boat. Intelligence had said the diesel engines of the ferry were no longer functional after long disuse.

We radioed our position to HQ and waited. Within half an hour two Sikorski helicopters . . . painted in patchwork camouflage and proudly bearing the triple copper cross on a red, white and green background of the Katangese Air Force . . . clattered low over the verdant forests, violently swaying treetops and grass.

The helicopters settled near our parked jeeps and I immediately ordered two sections of my men into the bellies of the choppers. I pushed my way forward into the cockpit of one of them and introduced myself to a fair-headed man at the controls . . . Peter Wicksteed, ex-RAF. Then we were off . . . sixteen mercenaries against who knew what on the opposite bank of the Lukuga.

Scarcely had the choppers landed at the bridgehead site, then the hatches were thrown open and my sections spilled out. Expertly they fanned and went to ground behind every available scrap of cover. Behind us we heard the choppers lift off in a cloud of dust and scud back over the river.

Minutes later they were back with another two sections and several Belgian military technicians to fix the ferry. No point in waiting for the Katangese support troops. I decided to give the order to advance.

We moved into the cluster of buildings at a steady trot, rifles at port arms, safety catches off, fingers on triggers. As soon as I reached the first irregular row of buildings with my troops spread to right and left in a long line, I heard the rattle of small arms fire . . . short bursts to right and left slightly behind me, the harsh bark of FN rifles and once the chatter of a light machinegun. I moved slowly through the village and out the other side.

Within minutes the rest of the group had caught up.

'Any casualties?' was my first question. None.

'See any rebels?' None.

'What was all the firing then?' The embarrassed scuffling of feet.

'We had to fire our rifles sometime, Captain', came the hesitant reply.

Niemba was as deserted as all the other villages. Not a soul to be seen. Once again the rebels had melted into the primeval jungle . . . hospitable to them, hostile to us.

After thirty minutes furious tinkering by the Belgian technicians the ferry engine spluttered into life and, to the cheers of the mercenaries and the exaggerated bows of the Belgian mechs the ferry chugged back across the river. Quickly she began ferrying the Katangese Gendarmes and the vehicles to Niemba.

Within five hours the entire force was across the river.

If my mobile force was disappointed in not having had contact at Niemba they were soon consoled by another discovery.

An inquisitive mercenary decided to see what was inside a large warehouse-type building on the banks of the Lukuga. Kicking open the door he walked into a cavernous room stacked from floor to rafters with row upon row of dust covered elephant tusks . . . a fortune in ivory. The tusks had been lying in their shed for months, ignored by the rebels and unavailable to the authorities. By unanimous decision it was agreed that as much of the ivory as possible should be 'liberated'. Blankets were thrown off one of the trucks and one hundred of the choicest tusks loaded on. The tusks were taken to Nyunzu and then later sent back to Manono and stored in the mission station.

What happened thereafter I never found out.

The seizure of the tusks raised several moral questions at that point but I was able to justify our actions in terms of claiming an advance on our already overdue first pay cheque. We also knew that if we did not seize the tusks they would most certainly be claimed by the other mercenary and Katangese forces following us.

Next day the column made the last leg dash to Nyunzu, sixty kilometers to the west. Once again my mobile group was first into the town. At Nyunzu we found a number of tribesmen patiently awaiting our arrival.

By then we were almost in Bahembi country, among tribesmen who although not fanatically pro-Tshombe were certainly not in open revolt against him. Knowing they had little to fear from the Gendarmes the Bahembi tribesmen began flocking into Nyunzu and within five days the town was back to bustling normal, the airstrip was operating and a number of senior Katangese Gendarme officers were flying in and out.

Plans were now made for the third phase of the operation, an advance on Kabalo, about one hundred kilometers to the west, Sendwe capital after Manono, a stronghold at the confluence of the Lukuga and Lualaba rivers.

While still in Nyunzu, Colonel Liegeois, the Belgian officer commanding the operation in the north, ordered me to take my group on a two day expedition to the south towards Kahemba, 'to keep them sharp and let off a little steam'. If my men were expecting action they were again disappointed. The tribes on the way were not ardent Tshombists but were equally indifferent to our presence. We passed through village after village without any show of opposition or antagonism.

The entire operation in the north had, up to that point, been an overwhelming success. Tshombe's forces had established a strong incontrovertible presence in the area . . . only Kabalo remained. And then the United Nations stepped in.

On our return from Kahemba we had our first taste of things to come. The column of dust-clogged jeeps turned into the town's single main street and drove slowly towards the building serving as temporary HQ.

'What the hell's that?' one of the mercenaries in my jeep roared above the engine and the wind, pointing with a stick in the direction of Colonel Liegeois' HQ.

Outside the building stood a white UN jeep with the blue UN pennant hanging limply on the stifling air. Sitting impassively behind the wheel was a Malaysian in British army uniform. Even before our column came to a stop we saw a young army captain from the UN British contingent clump across the veranda, descend the stairs and leap into the passenger seat of the jeep.

The jeep slid past us. Grizzled, sun burnt mercenaries and the impeccably battle dressed British officer exchanged cool stares.

After the UN jeep had passed, one of the mercenaries swore and spat theatrically on the ground.

The appearance of the officer was soon explained. The UN forces in Northern Katanga had come to warn Liegeois that they had instructions to oppose any further operations by us and had been ordered to move into Nyunzu itself.

Our North Katanga operation had ground to a sudden end.

In retrospect the outcome of the operation was never in doubt. The mercenaries were equipped with the best weapons, were trained, disciplined and motivated. Against them stood the Balubakat . . . armed with ancient mausers, pou-pous and spears, poorly disciplined and badly led. If they had possessed only a handful of mines they would have irreparably hampered our speedy advances. Not lacking in courage, the rebels had occasionally sallied against strongpoints, road convoys and even trains. Always they were effortlessly repulsed, carrying their weapons, their wounded and their aspirations back into the enfolding arms of the jungle.

For the mercenaries the expedition at times resembled more the jolly course of a safari than a serious military operation. Our communication lines were good, c-rations plentiful, and game . . . shot with high powered rifles from the choppers . . . provided us with a healthy daily intake of fresh meat.

Although unequal to the power of sophisticated mobile firepower in the hands of experts, the Balubas could, and did, when they had the chance, retaliate with a comparably powerful weapon . . . dread, barbaric terrorism.

The Balubakat *Jeunesse,* youngsters freed of the constraints of any authority, colonial or tribal, went on rampages of calculated brutality against their enemies. Against whites and Tshombe's blacks, the *Jeunesse* were uncompromisingly bestial.

Sharpened bicycle chains . . . which could shred living human flesh from the bone with the efficacy of a modern mincing machine . . . and magic motivated cannibalism, made the prospect of falling prisoner to the Baluba inconceivable and motivated the mercenaries to a grim resolve that, should the chips be down, they would fight to the bitter end.

Perhaps one of the most frightening occupational hazards of the campaign were the poisoned arrows and spears used by the rebels. Once I saw a man felled by one of those arrows and the memory of his writhing agonies in the hands of helpless medics will live with me forever.

One ghost that needs to be conclusively laid at this point is the allegation of mass genocide on the part of the mercenaries. United Nations Special Representative in Katanga, Conor Cruise O'Brien, the dark haired Irishman with rhetoric far exceeding understanding, charged the mobile groups with employing a large scale scorched earth policy.

During a visit to the north at this period, he actually accused Liegeois of burning villages and threatened a violent UN response.

There were a vast number of burnt out villages but the evidence was overwhelming that they were the result of Balubakat *Jeunesse* activity against Tshombe's tribal chiefs during September 1960.

In the entire operation in the north no more than twenty rebels were killed by the mobile troops . . . all of them armed and threatening. At the most two villages were burnt, both in areas of intense rebel activity and from which fire had been received.

One incident I clearly remember served to emphasise the type of campaign the mercenary Gendarmes were trying to implement in the north. On one exceptionally hot Congo day, Colonel Liegeois, a junior officer, a handful of Belgian mercenaries and myself were clattering along a lonely jungle road in the back of an armoured personnel carrier. Through the open rear hatches of the carrier the young Belgian officer spotted a Baluba tribesman standing impassively alongside the road with a tall spear in his hand.

Immediately the junior officer had pulled out his pistol and a split second later snapped a shot through the rear hatches at the motionless figure.

The report crashed around the narrow and steamy confines of the carrier, shocking us all from our heat dazes. Fortunately the shot had gone wide of the tribesman who had merely bounded back into the bush.

Both Liegeois and I had seen the tribesman at precisely the moment he was spotted by the young officer, but unlike him, we had instantly realised that the tribesman presented no threat. Through inexperience or malice the young officer had completely over reacted.

I will never forget the way Colonel Liegeois lashed out at the officer's gun hand with his boot and then, before the troops, proceeded to tear strips off the officer. His theme: we were there to pacify, not murder.

Our role in the area was that of a police force.

The last operation I undertook with my mobile group was a three day trip to M'Bulula . . . again on the instructions of Colonel Liegeois. By this time, however, the UN presence in the area had greatly expanded and we operated in a strangely ambivalent situation, moving heavily armed among generally welcoming tribesmen, showing the Katangese colours, while being closely watched by the UN troops.

In the field there would be bizarre encounters of UN and Gendarme units, both manoeuvering around each other in some strange dance of distrust.

Otherwise the mini operation was in every respect that of a free-and-easy safari. For appearances' sake the group stood to defensive positions at dawn and dusk in approved military tradition.

Predictably we only found ourselves confronted with the dew or the evening breeze and the stunningly beautiful blood red sun rising or sinking behind the omnipresent jungle wall.

Again, dutifully, we posted guards and worked rosters for the night but invariably it was only the small game that disturbed a guard shift. Evening meals consisted of an impressive barbecue, Congo-style, with monstrous haunches of freshly slaughtered venison spitted over open coals. Of course there was beer and fresh vegetables and fireside talk of home, women and adventures.

Surprisingly, on my return to Nyunzu, I found the fraternization with the UN was continuing apace; so much so that on our first night back from M'Bulula we were treated to a variety concert put on by the Malaysian troops.

And then into the confused situation at Nyunzu roared Mike Hoare with his mobile group, easily comparable in discipline and turnout to the UN's best troops. His column arrived early one morning in a cloud of dust and gunning jeep engines. It was the first time I had met the energetic Irishman and we managed a few hasty words before our different duties called.

Later that same morning I was summoned to the temporary HQ where I found Colonel Liegeois sitting relaxed behind a desk.

'Many thanks for your group's help, Captain, I have been most impressed.' I bowed my acknowledgement.

'I would now like you to return to Elisabethville to sort out the pay question.'

So back to the soft life it was.

3

Demise and a New Direction

'There's no way Tshombe is going to get out of this mess without fighting the UN.'

Max Glasspole's voice was flat and assertive. Under his peaked flying cap his face was serious and, behind those dark glasses I could imagine his uncharacteristically sombre eyes surveying the Congolese jungle unfolding below us. He even chewed his bubblegum with a more serious mien.

'What makes you say that?' I asked diffidently.

Glasspole jerked a thumb to port in the direction of north Katanga.

'I fly recce ops every day up there . . . right over the UN positions. Believe me, Jerry, they're not just sitting around on their arses. You haven't seen the half of what they've got in the field. Mortars, recoilless cannon, armoured cars, APCs . . . you bloody name it.

'Christ knows how many Ethiopians the UN have got there and those guys are bad enough to shame the *Jeunesse*. Big trouble brewing. I can even pick it up having a few snorts with the UN guys in Elisabethville.'

The Canadian chomped his gum twice as if to emphasize the point.

'The problem is that with the February 21 resolution, the UN guys have now really got the mandate to act. Some of them are getting pissed off sitting around doing nothing and they are just itching to get stuck in. That bloody Irishman, Conor Cruise O'Brien, is the main one.'

And what Glasspole said was true.

While on pacification operations in the north, events in the always volatile Congo had taken several jumps forward. In late February Tshombe and other Congolese politicians . . . including Gizenga and Bomboko . . . had met at Tananarive in Madagascar to try and sort out a *modus vivendi* for the score of struggling nationalisms, tribalisms and ideologies then tearing the Congo apart.

At Tshombe's skillful insistence the leaders, led by none other than Kasavubu, agreed to a confederal form of government for the Congo with Tshombe magnanimously making several important concessions on his part. United States opposition was immediate and vocal. A return meeting was arranged for mid April at Coquilhatville in Equateur Province to ratify the accord.

In a shameful display of treachery a few days later, countenanced and indeed inspired by the US CIA, Tshombe and his advisors were detained in Coquilhatville on April 26 when Kasavubu refused to ratify the Tananarive agreement. Contrary to CIA hopes the Katanga secession did not collapse and the running of the state fell to a college of three men . . . the powerful Godefroid Munongo, Kimba and Kiwele. It was in the context of these sombre events that Glasspole and I winged our way towards Albertville, a north Katanga town, and the first stop on our return to Elisabethville.

Glasspole's railing against the UN 'bastards' continued all the way to Albertville, during our circuit, in the descent, as we taxied to the hangar and even as we drove through the streets of Albertville to a newish block of flats not far from the airfield. Whereupon Glasspole gave ample demonstration of his phenomenal ability to be all things to all men.

Pushing me up a flight of steps to the door of a flat, Glasspole rapped twice loudly on the knocker and stood back staring at me with a half smile terminated by a sly wink.

The door burst open to reveal a fair-headed young man in the uniform of the UN Swedish Air contingent. Christ, what is Glasspole up to now, I wondered apprehensively.

'Max. Goot, goot. Come in, come', the young man burst simultaneously into broken English and a broad smile.

We were introduced to another Swede and within a couple of minutes Glasspole and I were haltingly but convivially swopping stories about recce missions, contacts and the Scandinavians' experiences as chopper pilots.

Only days earlier UN troops and Katangese Gendarmes had clashed bloodily at Elisabethville airport over entry rights. Thirty two Gendarmes had been arrested, a lot of blood had flowed and bitterness had been whipped up on both sides. And here, in the cosy warmth of their flat, Glasspole and I were getting drunk with the enemy . . . albeit charming, generous and intelligent hosts . . . but nevertheless the enemy.

Glasspole and I slept the night in the pilots' quarters and next morning we parted from them on the best of terms. So much for the infinite variety of life.

Back in Elisabethville it was as if nothing had changed. Although there for only four days, I managed to re-establish contacts with my associates in the *Etat Major,* chase up our back pay and get in some serious drinking and discussing in the Beaulieu. Tshombe or not, Katanga was running confidently, proudly and peacefully. Only problem was the ominously increasing number of Irish and Gurkha troops now on the Elisabethville streets.

It was at this stage that we received information of the fiasco that had happened at Kabalo. The plan was ambitiously but soundly drawn, the only defect being the man chosen to lead the operation . . . Brawler Browne. Kabalo, as a Sendwe strongpoint, was an essential element in the complete pacification of the north. Although under UN control, it was decided that the town must be seized and placed unquestionably into Katangese hands.

Everything had been planned minutely. Browne would lead an air-borne assault on the airfield with his mobile unit and picked black gendarmes.

Simultaneously, two river steamers packed with troops would make a landing on the banks of the Lualaba River while a train load of Katangese Gendarmes would steam into the important railway junction at Kabalo with support troops.

Facing this formidable assault group of over a thousand men would be two companies of Ethiopians . . . generally accepted as the most ruffianly element of all the UN troops.

The operation was a disaster from the start. The DC4 transport carrying Browne's troops arrived from Kongolo and landed at Kabalo unopposed. Browne's platoon rushed off the aircraft in a thunder of boots and war cries, dispersed and thrust for the station where they were due to RV with the train borne group. Trailing a whiff of beery perspiration and a barrage of curses, Browne led his mercenaries down the dusty road, through several streets of the town and straight for the station.

Just short of their target they were suddenly and unpleasantly made aware they were not the only troops in Kabalo that fine day. The Ethiopians had deployed in the area surrounding the station and Browne was faced by the business ends of two hundred well placed rifle barrels. Faced with the reasonable alternatives of establishing a firebase, engaging the Ethiopians and awaiting support from the Katangese or tactically withdrawing to the airfield, Browne did neither. He meekly surrendered without a shot.

A mixed bag of thirty South African and English mercenaries fell like ripe plums into the UN's laps.

Meanwhile one of the river boats had run into intense UN fire from the banks and had eventually sunk with heavy loss of life.

The other steamer did an about turn and thrashed its way homewards. The train chugged into the area, scouts recced the position and within twenty four hours the train was racing back out of the disaster area belting out huge gouts of black smoke.

Fault for the failure of the plan lay both with Browne and the Belgians. In the first place, Browne's operation was not helped by the fact that a Belgian officer at the Katangese *Etat Major,* slipped a copy of the entire battle plan to his opposite number in Leopoldville who then promptly handed it over to the UN.

So, if Browne was surprised to see the UN at Kabalo, the UN was certainly not surprised to see him.

Yet another example of the double game the Belgians were playing. Browne's responsibility for the fiasco lies in the fact that he did not push through with the offensive — UN or not. A single success at that stage could have changed the future history of Katanga. But if anything, the sorry incident showed the glaring deficiency of unmotivated mercenary officers in sticky situations as opposed to committed nationalistic army officers.

As a soldier Browne should have ordered his men into the attack and once engaged, fought it out to the end.

As a mercenary, Browne weighed the odds, believed them unfavourable and speedily jettisoned his duty.

Browne and his merry men were later expelled and faded completely from the Congo scene. Only once was I to see that ruddy face again and that was five months later at Ndola in Northern Rhodesia (now Zambia) when Browne pleaded with me to help him return to Katanga. I refused.

Early on my fifth day at Elisabethville, Glasspole and I took off in a Katangese Air Force Tri-Pacer to return to Nyunzu. Kilometer after kilometer of rolling green forests were spread below us, creased occasionally by the broad silver band of one of the Congo's mighty rivers, or less frequently by a single trace of red earth road. We had left at first light and by the time we reached Nyunzu the sun was standing high on our starboard side, slowly bringing the Congo day to its usual white-hot boil. Already our shirts were clinging to our backs in wet patches.

While we were on our final circuit over Nyunzu airfield the sharp-eyed Glasspole suddenly grunted his surprise.

'Something fishy, Jerry', he said quietly.

'What?' I asked, trying to guess in which direction Glasspole's sunglass-shaded eyes were looking.

'There on our portside, by that belt of trees on the perimeter of the field. Can you see?'

I shook my head while my eyes continued scouting the thick bush fringing the field.

'We'll lose a little height. Hang on though', he said and slowly brought the Tri-Pacer down several hundred meters.

'There, told you so', Glasspole shouted triumphantly and thrust a stubby finger towards the foliage.

I saw them quite clearly then. Pulled up alongside the runway, well under the trees but indifferently camouflaged, were a number of UN jeeps and armoured cars. We could even see the swarthy upturned faces of the crews as they waited expectantly for our landing.

'Here we go', shouted Glasspole opening the throttle and jerking back on the stick.

The Tri-Pacer shot upwards, Glasspole and I imagining the roars of disappointment and Malaysian curses that must have greeted our sudden departure.

Glasspole's sharp eyesight and the instinct for survival that kept him alive through numerous scrapes had saved us both from a lot of unpleasantness and a possible end to our Congo soldiering.

We headed for the Gendarme camp at Nyunzu, only a short distance from the airfield. As we circled the camp we saw instantly the concentric rings of UN troops and armoured cars pulled up around the besieged camp. A number of mercenaries, among them Mike Hoare, stood up in their emplacements and waved at us not to land. What the hell was going on? A few more circuits and we headed east to find Liegeois' group, then operating with a mobile group about sixty kilometers from Nyunzu. It was two very worried people who flew low over the column of jeeps and lobbed out a message reading: 'Nyunzu surrounded by UN troops. We are heading for Albertville'.

Back at Albertville we were debriefed by several grave faced Belgian intelligence officers who refused to venture an opinion on what it all portended.

Then off for drinks with our Swedish UN chopper pilot friends.

Alice in bloody Wonderland, this place!

Our two Scandinavian counterparts warmly congratulated us on our escape as they poured stiff tots.

'But what the hell does it all mean?' I eventually exploded.

Both pilots looked uncomfortable.

'February 21 resolution, Jerry' one of them eventually said. 'Use of force to prevent clashes between the Gendarmes and the Balubakat. And that means force against you and Max if necessary. Simple as that. Just accept it, Jerry, the Congo party is over for you.'

The UN were later to claim that their actions were aimed, not at the black Katangese Gendarmes but at the mercenaries assisting them. It had almost the same effect. Stripped of the stabilizing and expert assistance of the mercenaries, the black Katangese Gendarmes operated less effectively and, once again the Baluba *Jeunesse* found unpoliced areas to wreak their horrible vengeance . . . especially against the missionaries and Tshombe loyalists.

Mike Hoare meanwhile acted responsibly and quickly in his peculiar circumstances. He ordered his men to disperse through the UN lines and the jungle and then regroup in Albertville. Taking a leaf from the rebels' handbook, Hoare's company just melted into the bush one dark night and left the UN forces facing a row of empty buildings. All the men, except two who got lost, were able to regroup at Albertville and Manono after two weeks.

For the *Compagnie Internationale* it was the end of a short but fairly adventurous road. Hoare's men eventually jetted out to share the fate of Browne's contingent. The few remaining English speaking mercenaries attached themselves to other sections. But for the majority of the men of the *Compagnie,* it was back to their home countries and to bars where wide-eyed audiences soon ensured a speedy disposal of their Congo nest eggs.

Many though, were not destined to disappear completely from the Congo scene. At a later date and under different circumstances they would be needed again. Tshombe would call and they would come with a mixture of adventurism, greed, and yes, even loyalty for the man they had served before and from whom they had received the best.

I was in a quandary. Stay or go? South Africa, routine, thankless labour for little return — or the Congo, excitement, enough money to ensure my family were well provided for, and a chance to help a tiny country through a particularly rough patch?

The choice was obvious. I would stay.

But where could I serve? Again the answer was obvious. I had already helped the Gendarmes by doing aerial mapping from a light aircraft. I was a former air force man and I knew the Katangese Air Force needed men.

It was time to spread my wings.

4

Of Bombers and Mercy Missions

Commandant Jan von Resighem was a genial former Belgian Air Force officer and, in 1961, possessor of the proud title, Commander of the Katangese Air Force's Operational Squadron. I presented myself to him at his HQ at Elisabethville airport, in a neatly starched uniform, shiny boots and an eager smile.

I didn't even need the accessories. My past track record in bombers with the South African Air Force and in transports with the Royal Air Force was commendation enough for him.

'Bomber Command you said, Captain. I am delighted you have arrived. Most fortuitous. Yes, most fortuitous', he said while looking reflectively out of the HQ window to where the Katangese Air Force aircraft squatted.

'Commandant, there is one problem though. I am still officially attached to the Gendarmes.'

'No problem at all. A 'phone call to Crevecoeur will sort that out', von Resighem said with an airy wave of the hand. 'Bombers, you said?'

I nodded.

'Captain, allow me to show you something', von Resighem said ushering me out of the door. We walked across the scorching tarmac, and towards the neatly lined Air Force aircraft.

Von Resighem showed me over the two Sikorski helicopters (I told him I had seen them in operation before) and two Fouga Magister jet fighter trainers . . . trim little single seaters. He explained that a third was in for repairs. Then on to an ageing DC 3. 'We've got another one at Kolwezi at the moment', he said.

He waved a hand at a flight of Piper Tri-Pacers with Katangese Air Force markings. We walked past several Herons and towards a point where two eight seater Doves stood surrounded by a litter of equipment . . . lathes, machining tools, boxes of bolts, screws and nuts. The aircraft were used for ferrying small groups of senior military or government officials from point to point or for light cargo deliveries. I knew them to be reliable small aircraft for that type of light work.

We stopped for a moment and von Resighem turned to me.

'Captain Puren, as you can see we're well equipped for fighter, recce and transport work. Quite well equipped. But we lack . . .' and here he paused expectantly.

'Bombers', I dutifully replied.

'Quite so, quite so. Now step this way please.'

We picked our way over the litter of tools and equipment to the side hatch of one of the Doves. Von Resighem clambered in and I followed.

With the pride of a magician producing a rabbit from a hat, von Resighem waved a hand at a rack system rigged along the fuselage of the Dove, at a hatch affair in the floor, at a big lever and at a plastic bomb sight thrusting up from the floor of the aircraft.

'You see, Captain. We do have bombers', von Resighem said with an emphatic stab of the finger at the contraption. 'And now we have an OC for the bomber section . . . you.'

I stared at him in open-mouthed amazement.

Actually the system was not nearly so hairbrained as it initially seemed. The racks were fitted so as to take bombs with a payload of 12,5kg. By pulling the lever, the bombs were despatched one at a time through the hatch in the floor. A bombing crew would thus have to consist of a pilot, a bomb aimer and a bombardier.

Our first official trial run early on a Wednesday morning attracted the attention of a number of Air Force and Gendarme officers. On a huge range not far from Elisabethville a large white cross had been laid out in an exposed position . . . the target.

At a safe (very safe) distance away, the little knot of officers headed by an excited von Resighem, gathered with field glasses. High above the plateau bushveld in the Dove I quickly ran through the drill with my pilot and bombardier. No mistakes, I warned.

We approached the target area from the east at two thousand meters, dropped to one thousand meters and rushed towards the white cross. Flat on my stomach in the Dove, I glued my eye to the bomb sight and suddenly it seemed as if all the years had fallen away. Egypt, Italy or Congo; 1942 or 1961; through the narrow confines of the sights all land looked the same — vulnerable and pregnant with the possibility of destruction.

'Steady . . . steady . . . left . . . left', I muttered over the intercom to the pilot and felt the direction of the aircraft shift subtly.

'Steady . . . steady',

I waited for the rush of brown green earth to crystallize into a pattern, waited for the large white cross to fill the sights and then raised three fingers. Three bombs. The bombardier grasped the rack and jerked furiously. Clatter, thump, clatter, thump, clatter, thump.

Then silence.

I prayed for the honour of the South African Air Force, the Royal Air Force and not least of all, my honour, that they were on target. I watched the little specks curving down at increasing speed.

The first exploded a fair distance short of the target, the second a bit closer and the third, as I held my breath, right next to the cross. Then we were past and the cross out of sight.

The Dove banked and flew back over the target. A plume of dust eddied from a point a good seventy meters from the cross, another rose forty meters away and the third was right on the edge.

Not too bad at all.

Several more runs, dropping bombs singly, in pairs or three at a time and we flew low over the target area. It was obscured by a pall of smoke and dust.

The pilot flew the Dove low over the little knot of observers, dipped our wings and then streaked back to Elisabethville airfield. I was satisfied that with practise our aim could only improve.

At a debriefing later that day von Resighem furiously pumped my hand while repeating over and over, 'You see we do have bombers . . . you see we do have bombers.'

Several weeks' hard practise later we were ready for our first operation — a strike against Baluba concentrations around Lake Upemba and along the river towards Kabalo. My crew and I were called to a briefing room where a podgy Belgian intelligence officer gesticulated with his pointer at various little spots on a map representing huge swatches of territory along the northern borders of Katanga.

'Enemy concentrations here and here', he said.

The pointer descended on two little villages with unpronounceable names.

'We require blanket bombings to disperse the *Jeunesse* concentrations and neutralize the village as an effective enemy base.'

The pointer rapped the spots with finality and the fate of the villages was sealed.

The first operation was disgustingly simple.

Lacking the normal navigational aids we had to rely on medium scale maps of the area, flying by rivers, roads and other features, dipping low over the sprawling mass of jungle and lakes with the occasional village carved into the solid jungle wall. Our directions were spot on.

A few minutes past 10h00 on a sparkling clear Congo morning we flew low over our target, a medium sized village of daub houses, thatched roofs and rutty paths.

At a thousand meters I flew a preliminary run over the houses and then back again. Below us I noticed people scrambling for cover in the jungle.

The third run we dropped our first stick of three bombs, returned twice again to drop three more bombs a time and then made a final run to drop two bombs squarely on to the largest structure in the village which I assumed accommodated the Baluba warriors.

We took a final run over the village to check the results. Huge eddies of smoke obscured large parts of it, flames occasionally shot angrily through the pall, grass flanking the village smouldered.

Highly elated, we turned our nose homeward.

With the passage of time, the missions I undertook at Upemba have appeared to me more and more reprehensible. It was not something I was proud of or would wish to repeat.

At first, in good faith, I flew missions against villages that had been described as rebel strongpoints. Routinely we made our bombing runs at a thousand meters, laying our voracious cargo of eggs in neat patterns across the villages, professionally checking the damage to the target afterwards . . . noting the flaming huts . . . the destruction and death.

I was not entirely naive though. During our operations in the North, we had never met any rebel soldiers at all. I knew that there were Baluba warriors at Kabalo, but here we were bombing their villages far to the south in an area we had never penetrated.

It became rapidly clear we were bombing soft civilian targets.

Later we received reports of tribespeople, men, women and children, crawling injured to Protin, commander of the Gendarmes in the sector, after our bombing raids.

During three years of World War-2 I took part in bombing missions against huge concentrations of civilian targets that resulted in a loss of life incomparably greater than that wrought by our primitively despatched bombs.

I have never had cause to question the morality of my actions in that conflict, but still today I think of those hounded jungle tribespeople — victims of either faulty intelligence or sheer malice. The bombing of defenceless villages was something I was never to do again.

I had far less scruples, though, about attacking the ANC troops of the Central Government, then tentatively thrusting against the Katangese border from either Stanleyville or Leopoldville. They were strange, inconclusive little affairs. Military intelligence in Elisabethville would order us to bomb up and report to one of the small airfields near the border. There we would be met by the local Gendarme commander and given exact directions on how to locate the ANC concentrations.

Into the overloaded Dove-cum-bomber we would clamber and set off tracing our course by the interminable red roads slicing through the jungle beneath us. Sometimes we would make contact, sometimes not.

At several hundred meters above the treetops we would suddenly come upon our prey — a column of olive green trucks, one or two jeeps, perhaps an armoured car. All hell would break loose below us as we shot over the column, rose steeply and wheeled for the return run. The entire ANC troop strength would disappear into the jungle before we had even wheeled. A few of the braver souls would try blasting away at us with their mounted machine guns but to little avail. At the bomb sight I would guide the pilot on to the road and we would drop a stick of bombs, ascend wheel and return. Below us furiously burning hulks of vehicles, dense plumes of oily black smoke, relieved occasionally by brilliant flashes of light as the ammunition stores exploded. For several hundred troops it meant a long walk home.

During this period I must have logged tens of thousands of miles in bombing and recce missions. Always close to the surface was the fear that, should we develop engine failure, our chances of getting back to Elisabethville were minimal. It was better not to think of the fate that awaited us if we were captured by the *Jeunesse*.

Like the mercenary ground forces the Air Force consisted of seconded Belgian military and a rag-tag of cosmopolitan adventurers filling the lower ranks. Perhaps the only common qualities linking all the pilots were that they were fiercely individualistic, all loved money and all, because of the hairy nature of their work, were damn good pilots.

Apart from that, some were extraordinarily daring and brave, others frustratingly cautious, some were consistently reliable, others very rarely so. For those days the pay was very good — never less than one thousand US dollars a month — and of course many of the mercenaries had 'deals' which netted them anything from a few dollars to tens of thousands of dollars extra.

Apart from Glasspole, one of my closest associates, and ofttimes pilot on bombing missions, there was Sandor Sputnik Gurkitz - an intense, dark little

Hungarian who had fled the street barricades of Budapest only a few years previously. Then there was the Briton, Peter Wicksteed and two South Africans, Jimmy Hedges, and a slow but loyal Afrikaner named Vosloo.

Belgium was well represented by, among others, the 'terrible twins', Libert and Bracco. Bracco was a former Air Force pilot whose family lived in Rwanda, the Congo's eastern neighbour. Libert came from a long family of aviators. Both were to prove themselves exceptionally able and loyal pilots when not diverted by complicated and highly profitable personal 'deals' of some sort. Another Belgian pilot was Magain — a small, perpetually drunk daredevil who always rose to fighting fury whenever the UN was mentioned.

Like most people whose work constantly brings them in the shadow of death, these pilots worked hard and played rough — with one another and with others. Discipline was slack and often non-existent, the motives of the men so diverse that it was difficult to mould a unified command.

It was with this background of unchecked individualism that any later failures in command and achievement in the Air Force were to be explained. What the air wing lacked in a cohesive command structure, however, it more often than not made up for in the sparkling ability and courage of the no more than a dozen pilots who flew either for the pay, for idealism or for both.

My position among this cosmopolitan collection had slowly improved during the weeks since I had joined, largely because I showed a willingness to go on operational missions. Generally the rest of the strength looked with exceedingly jaundiced eyes upon anything but transport work and only a couple of pilots consistently and loyally joined me on the more dangerous sorties.

On June 26, 1961, Tshombe was released from detention at Coquilhatville and flown home. Various theories have circulated about his release, not the least being that substantial amounts of money went into Mobutu's foreign bank accounts immediately prior to it happening.

Be that as it may, on June 25, Sandor and I were suddenly ordered to distribute pamphlets from the air over the Elisabethville townships telling of the popular president's return.

Thousands of ecstatic supporters turned up at the airport to welcome the return of Tshombe — a response that could hardly have gone unnoticed by the UN. Not unexpectedly, Tshombe renounced all pledges he had been forced to sign in detention.

One of the extracted concessions was that Mobutu's men would take command of the Gendarmerie as a first step to integration with the ANC. Thus when Tshombe arrived to his tumultuous welcome at Elisabethville, he had with him one of Mobutu's senior officers. This unfortunate gentleman was duly placed in nominal command of the Gendarmes, told he could have his authority if he proved himself, and from that point on was consistently overruled or totally ignored by the real powers at *Etat Major* — the Belgians.

Ironically the Belgian military were simultaneously advising Mobutu in Leopoldville. I never could work out how they managed to reconcile these divided loyalties and motives to their own satisfaction.

On his return Tshombe took an unequivocally hard line. Addressing the Katangese

Assembly on June 28 he struck the keynote when he said: 'We shall see to it that the Katangese nation shall endure. Let the enemies of Katanga know they have to deal with a people.'

The refrain was taken up proudly by those people.

In Elisabethville of course, social life was as frenetic as ever. Glasspole and I were now permanent residents in the Lido Hotel. Off duty we spent time circulating in the company of other Air Force officers, between the Beaulieu, the gourmet delights of Chez Felix and the numerous pubs of Elisabethville.

At times, sitting in some smoke filled bar with the rugged individualists and adventurers from all parts of the world, it seemed I had lived decades in this world of action, danger and off-duty luxury, decades since I had left my stuffy little office in South Africa. Actually I had been in the Congo less than six months. Already my French had improved, my grip on the realities of the Congo sharpened.

But I couldn't live by flying and debauchery alone. I needed a diversion and quite suddenly I stumbled on it — my old pastime of horse riding. On one of my interminable circuits over Elisabethville I had noted the neat brick structure and paddocks of a riding school. One rainy day with little to do, I presented myself at the club, explained who I was and signed as a member. From then on much of my time was spent cantering on a lively bay stallion along the bridle paths that surrounded the airfield — a release from the tensions of flying missions, a sublimation of fears in the pleasure of movement and strength in that most magnificent of creatures — the horse.

I rapidly realised that my pastime could also easily and pleasurably be combined with business.

In accordance with the original assurances made between Tshombe and the UN in August of the previous year, the UN had joint control of the airport. At key points all around the perimeter of the field the Gurkha contingent had dug in, strongpoints I passed almost daily on my horse riding jaunts.

On my first tour, the appearance of a jodhpurred and booted figure on a flying bay stallion was regarded with the greatest of suspicion. Machinegun barrels traversed as I passed and only the tips of suspicious helmets were visible above the sandbagged parapets. It was like that for a few days.

Then the coffee-skinned sentries stopped reaching for their weapons and merely regarded me impassively as I galloped past. A week more and we had started to nod greetings to each other.

Then it was a hand wave and within another week Puren and the deathly bored Gurkha sentries were often to be seen chatting idly about the weather or Rollo, the bay stallion, by then snuffling impatiently at the bit while his rider indulged in the pleasantries.

Which was ideal, as every day I kept check on the quality and quantity of the weapons appearing in the pits, the extensions of the sandbagged emplacements.

The political intrigues in the Congo worsened and it became clear that Conor Cruise O'Brien wanted the removal of Munongo from the government because of his inordinate power in Tshombe's cabinet. O'Brien — armed with the February 21 Resolution which called for the expulsion of foreign military and paramilitary forces — was determined to end the secession and stepped up the pressure. Seconded officers like Crevecoeur were easily disposed of by bringing pressure to bear on Belgium, via the UN, to recall her regular troops from Katanga. But the volunteers, and that included me, were far more difficult to get rid of.

Rumours — always voluminous in Katanga but now especially incessant — began to circulate about a black list; a carefully compiled UN document with the names of all the white mercenaries, foreign advisors, technical staff, *surete,* all those marked by the UN as of assistance to Katanga, all due for expulsion. The next step by the UN to sabotage the viability of the independent state of Katanga.

I decided to adopt a low profile and await developments.

Then in late July I was invited to accompany Moise Tshombe and his entourage on a tour of the eastern areas of Katanga. It was a trip destined to convince me of Tshombe's immense popularity among his people.

I had seen Tshombe before during inspections and in public appearances. This was the first time I had accompanied him on any trip and it was to be an experience.

He greeted us politely when he arrived and remained courteous throughout the journey. He was not physically a big man but his presence, enhanced by large and expressive eyes, made him seem larger than he was. He spoke French and a variety of Congolese dialects fluently and was never better than when addressing a large crowd. He was a passionate and convincing orator.

In later years Tshombe was to be accused of being corrupt and brutal. He was certainly not the latter and, if judged by African standards, neither the former. Tshombe had a capacity to change from the serious to the sombre to the lighthearted; a wonderful African quality.

To Tshombe loyalty counted for everything: to his own people he was fiercely devoted and many was the time he would dig deep into his own pocket to help the family of political associates or even rivals who had been bereaved by the dreadful attrition of those turbulent years.

He also lived life to the full . . . and not always discreetly. During one of his affairs he was photographed in bed with a woman. The photographer . . . a European seeking some quick financial returns . . . sent him a set of photographs with a blackmail demand note. Tshombe, by return of post, ordered six copies of each photograph for distribution among friends, and thus ended the blackmail attempt.

At all places we visited, Tshombe was greeted by huge crowds of stamping, clapping, cheering, tribesmen. Everywhere he was borne on the shoulders of his admirers. Crowds packed the venues where he spoke, listening in rapt attention to his fluent French and Swahili as he accused the UN of treachery and double standards, as he cajoled, encouraged, and assured. Occasionally his speeches were interrupted by thunderous applause. In halls, barns, marquees, on open stretches of ground, the people came from distant parts to hear their president.

It was on this trip that I met the Reverend Len Robinson, a no-nonsense, solidly built Seventh Day Adventist who, although American, had grown up in the area and spoke Swahili and the dialects better than many Congolese. He was uncompromisingly committed to the interests of his widespread and rumbustious flock and, once seized with an idea, never relinquished it.

It was while we were at Baudouinville that Robinson came storming up to me very early one morning.

'Know what, know what?' he demanded of me angrily while waving some sort of message in my face.

I desperately tried to think of what I could possibly have done wrong recently.

'Those UN people are now starving my flock in Nyunzu — starving them of simple Christian love and starving them of food. They've thrown a cordon to separate them from the Balubas but now they have also separated them from the food.'

I clucked sympathetically.

'Don't stand there, do something,' he demanded.

'What, Reverend. I can't take on the whole UN single handed.'

'No man, fly some food to these people. I've got tons of US AID stored at Elisabethville. I just need to get it to Nyunzu.'

'Reverend, I can't just use a Katangese Air Force plane for something like that. I'll have to get permission.'

'Permission from whom?'

I desperately racked my brains.

'Permission from Commandant von Resighem,' I finally blurted out.

Robinson looked at me steadily for a few seconds then turned smartly on his heel.

'Forget it. I'll ask Tshombe,' he shouted back over his shoulder.

And ask Tshombe he did. Within an hour, Sputnik, Robinson and I were winging our way back to Elisabethville to collect the supplies for the faithful. Once loaded with the cases of cooking oils, skimmed milk and maize meal, we headed back to Nyunzu, Robinson singing gospel blues in a magnificent baritone almost the whole way.

As we landed at Nyunzu, the field where Glasspole and I had narrowly escaped being captured only weeks before, a UN jeep rushed on to the strip and up to where we had stopped the Dove. I cut engines, Sputnik opened the side hatch and Robinson clambered out.

A gangling young British captain advanced uncertainly on us. He obviously knew Robinson because he stopped some distance away and essayed a hesitant smile of greeting.

'Good day, Reverend.'

Robinson nodded affably enough, shook hands and stood for a few seconds directing a beatific smile at the officer. The captain shuffled his feet nervously.

'Captain, I have brought food supplies for the members of my flock who have been inconvenienced by your troop dispositions.'

The officer cleared his throat nervously.

'I am sorry I cannot let you through to them, Reverend.'

Robinson stopped for a second as if unsure of what he had just heard.

'Pardon, Captain?'

'I can't let you through.'

'Why ever not?'

'Orders,' the officer looked as if he was about to cry.

With an apparent show of immense patience, Robinson reached out a hand and patted the man on his silver-pipped shoulder.

'I understand, Captain. Orders. But I also have orders from a higher authority than yours. If you won't let us take it to them, let them come here to collect it.'

The captain miserably shook his head.

'Can't let you do that either. Orders.'

Robinson exploded. In a ten minute outburst he delivered the finest fire and brimstone sermon I have ever heard, heaped damnation and solemn warnings on the UN and the poor officer's head until the soldier looked quite drunk with shame. Then Robinson played his trump card.

'Captain, I will return to Elisabethville with this little mercy mission. I will then send telegrams to my church in the US, the relevant authorities in the Western governments, to the UN secretariat and to certain journalists in the western media. I will tell them, Captain, that UN troops under your command have surrounded a tiny defenceless flock of Christians and are starving them to death, are refusing to allow their minister of God to join them in their travail.'

Robinson swung on his heel and made as if to leave. The captain capitulated.

Twenty minutes later the first handful of pitifully eager tribesmen arrived to collect the life giving food supplies and to rejoice in the appearance of their fiery mentor. Within an hour we had cleared the Dove and were on our way home. It was not the first mission I was to go on with the indomitable American.

But our small success with the mercy mission was soon overshadowed by the more pressing developments in Katanga. Great forces were discreetly but visibly moving. On my daily jaunts on Rollo past the airfield strongpoints I noticed the strengthening of fortifications — a new emplacement here, a heavy mortar there, a recoilless cannon somewhere else. Things were afoot. August 1961 crept uneasily on.

5

Arrest and Escape

The first flushes of pink were prickling the skyline to the east of Elisabethville when I dragged myself out of bed. Gummy-eyed, I stood at my hotel window and surveyed the silhouetted tree-lined boulevards now devoid of traffic.

It was 28th August 1961 . . . the time was 04h40.

'Too many Simba beers last night,' I reproached myself in the mirror as I scraped a razor over my stubbly chin.

Twenty minutes later I was dressed in my normal flying outfit — shorts, camouflage jacket and peaked flying cap jauntily pulled over my eyes — and on the way down in the lift. In the foyer of the hotel I shook a reclining Sputnik out of the slumber he had fallen into while waiting for me and we walked out into the chill dawn air of the deserted street.

A normal operational day — or so we thought.

That day at least we were fortunate in having persuaded Glasspole the previous night to allow us to use his private car to get to the airfield in the morning. No draughty jeep today.

I climbed behind the wheel and switched on the ignition. After a few coughs the engine turned over and we slid out from the hotel grounds into the main road. Around us the streets of the capital were rapidly lightening in the grey dawn rays. Sputnik and I remained sunk in our thoughts — an easy recce operation to the north of Elisabethville and back for breakfast. Simple.

It was at the first intersection that we noticed something out of the ordinary. A bulky UN armoured personnel carrier drawn up on the pavement, a knot of Gurkhas standing behind it, facing the road. As we drove past I noticed an officer in the turret suddenly start and point at us. Sputnik and I exchanged quizzical glances.

Down the main road towards the post office. Suddenly two UN jeeps swung out from a side street and hared past. They were packed with Irish troops in full battledress. A burly NCO shouted something as the jeeps slid away.

At the central post office we had our biggest surprise. Two Gendarme jeeps pulled up near the steps, a knot of black Katangese troops and — we rubbed our eyes — the dapper figure of President Tshombe standing with them. The President on the streets of Elisabethville at five o'clock in the morning? The usually somnambulant UN troops out of their redoubts and riding around?

Sputnik and I were still debating the strange start to the day as I turned into the Route Don Bosco and headed towards the Etat Major. And there the mystery ended.

A red and white boom across the road. Large 'Stop — UN checkpoint' signs, several armoured cars with depressed cannon, crews sitting expectantly atop the turrets, a squad of Irish soldiers with FN rifles, torches, activity.

I drew the car to a halt. Two fresh-faced soldiers took up positions on either side of the car, rifles levelled at us, faces expressionless in the grey morning light. A burly sergeant pushed his way forward, carbine dangling from his hand and glowered at us.

'Okay. Get out, get out', he shouted, shattering the morning silence. 'Get out and be quick about it.'

As if to emphasise the point he thrust his carbine muzzle in our direction. Sputnik and I exchanged glances, shrugged and slowly climbed out. Hands against the car, the Irishman frisked us with liberal and ungentlemanly cuffs in the process.

'What the hell's going on here?' Sputnik finally exploded in broken French.

The sergeant responded with a poke of his carbine butt into Sputnik's kidney. I was only glad we could not understand the stream of Hungarian swear words that followed.

Suddenly we heard the click of camera shutters and became aware of the lightning flash bulbs. I snatched a quick glance over my shoulder; a dozen or more newsmen jostling for pictures of the historic occasion when the UN arrested Sandor Sputnik Gurkitz and Jerry Puren.

'You'd think we were bloody film stars', Sputnik muttered bitterly before another butt from the carbine shut him up.

For my part I was quite calm. It was as if all the tensions and conjectures of the past months were destined to end this way. Arrest by the UN. It was almost a relief that the situation had been crystallised; the battle lines finally and irrevocably drawn. And as I stood motionless with my hands against the car roof, soft Irish brogues incongruously surrounding me, I stared across the dew-damp Elisabethville streets, the neat buildings, the tree lined boulevards and quite suddenly I determined that no matter what, I was not leaving Katanga.

The conversations of scores of concerned white settlers, black Katangese officials, the memory of the thousands of ecstatic tribesmen welcoming Tshombe flooded back and I resolved that I had indeed become a Katangese.

'Okay. Turn around but keep your hands up.'

I turned to face the sergeant, noted his finger nervously hovering around the trigger guards and decided to play it cool.

'What about the car. It belongs to a friend?'

The sergeant looked perplexed. He stared around.

Suddenly a UN jeep pulled to a stop at the checkpoint, pennant and radio aerial whipping, bodywork still crystal tipped with dew. Out leaped Colonel Bjorn Egge, Swedish UN intelligence officer in Elisabethville. A trim aquiline featured man with typically Scandinavian good manners. Not surprisingly he was a good friend of Max Glasspole. I decided to try my luck.

'What about the car? It's Max Glasspole's.'

'No problems', said Egge affably, 'I'll take it back to him'.

'Look, I'm also Katangese Air Force', I said.

Egge shrugged his shoulders and muttered something about 'all mercenary, foreign military and paramilitary forces are to be arrested', before climbing into Glasspole's car and roaring off.

Secretly I had to give Glasspole full marks for organisation — while the rest of us were being rounded up he was having his car returned to him personally by the head of the UN intelligence section in the capital. Chutzpah!

Simultaneously, throughout the whole of Katanga, similar scenes of detention were taking place in what the UN called *Operation Rumpunch* — the United Nations effort to forcibly implement the resolution of February 21. Two days previously Conor Cruise O'Brien had unsuccessfully attempted to have Tshombe attend a meeting with Cyril Addoula, now the Prime Minister of the Central Government of a loosely united Congo, but this had failed.

The arrest of the mercenaries was obviously a hard headed response to Tshombe's show of independence.

The excuse used by the UN for the operation was tenuous. From the gutters of Kamina — a largish Katangese town north of the copper plateau — they had dragged up a disreputable character called Martin Cremer, a former mercenary and a fugitive from Katangese justice.

A little skillful pressure from the United Nations and Cremer blurted out a story about being hired by Munongo to kill UN personnel in Kamina — a patently absurd story as there were few UN forces in Kamina, the vast majority being in Elisabethville and highly vulnerable.

'Okay, okay, move, move', the sergeant blustered.

Sputnik and I turned our backs and with hands in the air, were frog-marched towards an APC. The rear hatches were thrown open and we were unceremoniously bundled into it.

Slam!

The hatch closed and Sputnik and I scrabbled in the sudden darkness to find seats.

'Well, well, well', I said more to myself than anybody else.

Sputnik was more vocal and soon the armoured entrails of the APC were ringing with a torrent of swear words.

'That won't help, monsieur', a dispirited voice rose from the darkness nearby.

'Who are you?' Sputnik and I both demanded.

'Lieutenant Jean Dupont, *Etat Major*. Going for an early morning jog and seized by the UN. Ruthlessly thrown into this carrier'.

'What's going on?' I asked.

'Nothing personal, you may be assured of that, monsieur. We are far from being the only ones rounded up. It is the beginning of the end for poor Katanga and Tshombe'.

There was a big sigh.

'Like hell it is. We're just beginning Lieutenant', I shot back through the darkness.

Sputnik began muttering about the UN being worse than the Russians. He should have known.

44

The hatch opened twice again and several more people were thrown in. Then, after two hours the hatches parted and four soldiers with bayonets fixed to their rifles climbed into the steaming interior. The engines of the APC roared into life.

We drove a short distance to the *Etat Major* and were then marched through the empty corridors of the once busy building to a large room which now held ten very nervous mercenaries. There were a few wry greetings and we all settled down despondently to consider this unfortunate twist of fate.

Within an hour there were fifty mercenaries lounging around in little knots, anxious, indignant, perplexed, all loudly discussing the latest events. From the bits of information eagerly gleaned from each new batch of prisoners it became apparent that *Operation Rumpunch* was well organised and effective.

Caught off guard the mercenaries had been rounded up in the capital almost to a man without a single shot being fired.

The pattern was to be the same throughout Katanga.

Suddenly the door to our temporary prison burst open, the UN guards fell back, and a harassed looking Tshombe barged in. I have never been quite as pleased to see anybody so much in my life.

But from the deep lines on his forehead, his anxious questions and his response I knew that there was little he could do. He had lost the initiative to the UN's unscrupulous attack. We learnt later that Munongo had been placed under house arrest and Tshombe was forced to carry the entire weight of events.

At the end of that day's confinement — without any food and in a sweatbox of a prison — we were taken out and marched in heavily guarded squads to the ubiquitous APCs. Back in the cramped transports we were trundled through the now busy streets of Elisabethville to the airport.

As I stood in the motley throng at the runway, I looked out across to where the aircraft of the Katangese Air Force stood. I felt sick to my stomach as I watched perspiring UN troops unravelling rolls of barbed wire around the parcel of fourteen aircraft.

No attempt had been made to disperse the aircraft by the senior Belgian Air Force officers, no attempt to fly them out. The UN had scooped virtually the entire air wing of the Katanga Gendarmes.

A DC4 transport with the USAF markings lumbered on to the runway and we were marched off towards the concrete apron.

We were a dispirited collection of sun bronzed adventurers, some in uniform, some partly in uniform, some in civilian clothes and our poor friend in his jogging kit. As crestfallen as I felt we were, it was apparent the UN was taking no chances with the legendary Congo mercenaries. Scores of heavily armed troops dogged our footsteps at bayonet's length, fingers ceaselessly hovering over trigger guards.

Once in the air the DC4 circled the airfield then struck out on a north west course. No bets as to where we were headed. Kamina air base, the sprawling white elephant of a NATO base constructed some years previously by the Belgians to serve as some sort of bastion in Africa and now a vast domain of overgrown bush, rotting huts, cracked runways and wasted money.

By the time we arrived at Kamina it was early evening. Through the dusk we were hastened from the aircraft to a rudely constructed stockade with eight dilapidated bungalows and surrounded by feeble arc lights. And there we waited.

All that day and the next small detachments of glum faced mercenaries were brought in from points all over Katanga. Von Resighem arrived and other senior former Belgian officers. They were quite resigned and I quickly learnt why. They had actually known beforehand they were to be arrested. The Belgian connection between the two sides in Leopoldville and Elisabethville!

I buttonholed von Resighem on his arrival.

'Why didn't you arrange for the planes to be flown out from Elisabethville to Kolwezi if you knew this was about to happen? Why let the UN seize them?' I demanded heatedly.

Von Resighem shrugged his shoulders and muttered something about orders to leave the planes as they were.

'Who's orders?' I asked.

Von Resighem stared at me distantly.

'None of your business.'

'What are we going to do now?' I persisted.

'What are we supposed to do?'

'We could try and escape.'

Von Resighem gave a guffaw of laughter.

'Escape from here? Where on earth could you go. The surrounding tribes are hostile, this base alone is huge and crawling with UN troops. Besides, why escape? Just accept, the party is over.'

He swung on his heel and strode away. It was the second time I had heard the expression.

From the moment of arrest the other mercenaries had fallen into long sombre discussions, arguments and post mortems about what had happened. The great burden on everybody's mind was whether we were to be sent to Leopoldville for trial for our actions in the north. For me though, there was no time for recriminations. I was determined to get out and back into Tshombe's service. But first I needed a companion. Who? My thoughts turned to Martin.

Martin was a South African who liked to pass himself off as a Frenchman — even to pronouncing his surname in the French way and assuming a false French accent. I had originally met the lithe twenty five year old Gendarme lieutenant about four weeks earlier while on a visit to Albertville. At that stage he had introduced himself as head of a special force in Albertville. Casually he had invited me to his 'killing grounds.'

'Sure', I had answered thinking he was referring to some sort of hunting reserve.

Eagerly Martin had piled me into a jeep and we had driven several kilometers out of Albertville into the thick jungle, off the tar road, on to a dirt road and finally off again on to a dirt track. We had bumped along for a while, Martin seemingly visibly more excited as we approached his 'killing grounds'.

Eventually we had passed several official no-entry signs and had then driven into a small clearing hemmed in by the steaming jungle wall.

'Here we are', Martin said excitedly.

I had recognised the stench immediately — putrifying human flesh. Scarcely able to believe my eyes I had counted up to seven human corpses lying unburied around the clearing before utter nausea overcame me. Quietly I turned to him.

'What in God's name is this?'

'Enemies of the State of Katanga. Tried and executed by my special section,' he had replied smartly and proudly.

He had, of course, been trying to shock me. I had refused to be drawn.

'Perhaps we should return now,' I had said evenly.

The executioner had subsided into the driver's seat, very deflated. We had bumped our way out of that clearing and away from the sorry spectacle while I kept a straight face. Inwardly I had been sick at the depravity I had just seen.

Martin came easily to mind as I stood pensively in the Kamina Base stockade. He was remorseless, tough as nails and fearless. Just the man I needed as an escape companion.

I found him playing patience in the corner of one of the bungalows. He did not look up as I approached.

'I want to escape and I want you to join me,' I said quietly. He continued playing with the cards. I repeated myself.

'Forget it,' he snapped.

'Why?'

'I've had enough of this country. Enough of the blood and the heat. I want to go home.'

For the first time I noticed how his hands were shaking violently as he flipped the cards. He looked up and stared straight at me with tortured and red-rimmed eyes.

'I just want out, Jerry.'

Conscience or fear of retribution, I wondered as I walked away.

Next I spoke to Sputnik. He pulled the corners of his mouth down and cocked his head to one side.

'Look Jerry, within a short while they are going to repatriate us. Why try to escape. Rather go home first at UN expense. Besides, what if we run into that bloody Irish sergeant again?'

'Then I'll kill him with my bare hands.'

Moodily I walked to the barbed wire fence and stared across the sprawling and almost deserted camp. I heard a slight cough behind me. Turning I saw a darkly handsome Belgian pilot called Verloo I had seen around the Elisabethville base before.

'Yes?'

'Pardon, Captain, I could not but help overhearing your plan to escape. May I be permitted to join you?'

This approach from Verloo of all people quite astonished me. The thirty year old had shown himself extremely reluctant to go on any operations while in the Air Force.

'Why you?'

'Captain, I have a girl in Elisabethville. We are engaged and I cannot leave her now.'

What greater reason to escape than for love, I thought and warmly welcomed him aboard. Fortunately, as he had actually served at the Kamina base while he was still in the Belgian Air Force, his knowledge of the camp proved invaluable. We fell to plotting.

I am the first to confess that breaking out of the Kamina base was not exactly a Great Escape epic. We began noting the Irish guard's movements minutely and took a special interest in the layout of the buildings and shrubs when we were marched three times a day for meals from our compound to a nearby mess hall. Quickly we planned a route via the bushes, buildings and patches of dark. From the mess to the fence was, we estimated, about five kilometers through rough bush.

The third night in camp was D-day. That night we routinely joined the straggling column of men and made our way to the mess. Suppressing our excitement, we forced down a plate of brown stew and waited our chance.

The rows of men at the trestle tables and hard wooden benches began drifting away to stand in knots just outside the door talking to the guards — Irish brogue and French-accented English on the African night air. Others crammed in a corner around one of the Frenchmen who had slipped out a harmonica and had launched into some lively *Provencal* music to an appreciative audience.

Verloo and I looked at each other. I nodded. Casually we rose from the benches and sauntered through a side door into the adjoining toilet block. Several men were lined before the urinal, one of the three toilet cubicles was occupied, a few men gathered near the wash basin. Verloo walked into one of the cubicles and I into the other. We shut the doors and waited.

Five minutes . . . ten minutes . . . then we heard it. The whistle of the Irish sergeant major.

Through the thin doors we heard the shuffle of feet as the mercenaries moved to form up. A shouted order. From experience we knew that there would be no roll call.

Judging the moment right I slipped the bolt on the cubicle door, knocked softly on Verloo's door and then tiptoed towards a door on the far side of the toilet block that Verloo knew by experience led out into a garden. The door — we had noted earlier — was secured only by a ridiculously inadequate padlock.

Verloo produced a jemmy, slipped it into the hasp and jerked suddenly.

With what sounded like a deafening clatter, the lock shot open and skittered on to the floor. Swiftly I shovelled the broken padlock into my pocket, Verloo slipped the bolt and we walked out into the night. We were in an overgrown garden surrounded by a small hedgerow. Pale light was shed by a row of distant arc lights. We ducked down in the shadows of the toilet block wall and cast desperate glances around.

All clear.

Gently Verloo pulled the toilet door shut from the outside. On the other side of the toilet block we could hear the murmurs of the mercenaries as they formed sloppy ranks.

While still pressed against the outside wall, Verloo and I heard the clump of heavy army boots approaching from within the adjacent mess hall towards the toilet block. The footfalls strode into the toilet block.

From outside we heard the doors in the toilet cubicles being banged in turn. A few scuffles of boots on concrete and then the footfalls marched away towards the mess hall.

We breathed more easily. The sentry had not seen the broken lock, or that the outer door was ajar.

The mutter of voices had disappeared into enveloping silence before we moved; through the small garden, around a tennis court and then flat under a hedge in some shadows. I had to hand it to Verloo, he knew the way.

We peered out through the tangled branches at a tarmac service road a few meters ahead. Ten or fifteen meters to the left we spotted two sentries patrolling a stretch of the road, stopping once to swop cigarettes and a joke, oblivious to our presence.

We waited fifteen minutes and then, when the guards' attention was momentarily diverted, darted across the road and dived head first into a patch of weeds.

We rapidly leopard crawled from one patch of shadow to the next, breathlessly negotiating the two hundred meters of lighted area to the welcoming darkness.

Only meters from the lapping edge of darkness we heard a shout from behind us. Verloo and I froze, hearts pounding, tight bands of tension around our scalps. Reluctantly we turned our heads to look behind us.

False alarm!

A sentry shouting to a friend. Weak with relief we scrambled the last few meters into the shadows. I looked at the dial of my watch. Exactly an hour since we had left the mess.

We clambered to our feet and took a direct line towards the gate, hugging a road all the way. With still an hour to the moon's rising, it was pitch dark.

Occasionally we heard the rattle of an approaching bicycle, once there was the stab of a car's headlights and then the purr of its engine. Instinctively we flattened ourselves into cover and waited with pounding hearts for the intruders to pass.

An hour brought us to the thick bush and at the same time the moon rose over the trees and illuminated the road we had travelled as brightly as if a row of neon lights had been switched on.

We kept the moon behind our backs and pushed on as fast as we could, stumbling through the clinging bushes, scratched, tired and furiously perspiring in the humid air. Occasionally we heard the bark of the UN Swedish troop's dogs — not necessarily for us but still a reminder that we were not yet clear.

Two and a half hours later after leaving the mess, a puffing Verloo and myself pushed our way under the outer perimeter barbed wire fence and threw ourselves on to a soft grassed patch hemmed in by trees and scrub.

For thirty minutes we lay and looked at the moon, gathering our strength and our thoughts. Then we were on the road again — striking hard in the direction of Kaminaville, taking circuitous routes around the Baluba villages and putting all our faith in our speed, strength and sense of direction.

We were both uncomfortably aware that the villages hemming Kaminaville were anti-Tshombe and that we could expect short shrift if captured.

The grey light of dawn was just prickling the east when Verloo and I eventually struggled footsore and very weary into Kaminaville after a twenty five kilometer hike. I did not know the area very well but Verloo knew it like the back of his hand. Just after 07h00 he deftly led me to a small church on the outskirts of the town. When still some distance away we heard the rich voices of the African congregation raised in song, warm, beckoning, beautiful. Like two waifs we wandered in and sat down in the pew at the back. Weary almost beyond endurance we shut our eyes and let the pristine waves of sound wash over our tired bodies.

6

Missionary and Mercenary

'Incredible, incredible', the Belgian priest kept muttering to himself as we sat in his sacristy with boiling mugs of coffee and recounted the story of our escape.

'Incredible that you should have been able to penetrate this far and not be discovered by the villagers', he said while gravely shaking his head of cropped grey hair.

'They're all Balubas you know. Not at all friendly to Tshombe. Probably have cut your throat if they had caught you. Not that my parishioners would do a thing like that I hasten to add, but there's plenty of other heathen around who would.'

Verloo and I nodded understandingly. The priest had been extremely kind to us. Immediately after mass he had beckoned us to follow him into his sacristy, waved us to chairs and then set about boiling up a pot of coffee. He had known exactly who we were and from where we had just sprung. Tshombe's mercenaries, protectors of the missionaries, the strange nexus of mercenarism and missionarism in central Africa.

I was part way through telling the priest of the details surrounding our capture in Rumpunch when Verloo's head suddenly slumped forward on to his chest and he began slowly sliding sideways off his chair — a victim of utter exhaustion.

'Sleep now, talk later. You will be safe here', the priest said with a smile at the embarrassed Verloo. 'Follow me.'

Along a stone corridor, down some steps, around a corner then into a largish room — quite bare except for two stretcher beds with blankets and a huge crucifix on one lime-washed wall.

'Pleasant dreams', the priest said as he left, quietly closing the door behind him.

Verloo and I needed no second bidding. Under the sheltering arms of the crucifix we curled up on the stretchers and within seconds were dead to the world.

Bang! Bang! Bang!

The thumping on the door jerked us awake. I stumbled from the stretcher, disentangled myself from the blanket and made for the door. I threw it open.

It was an officer of the Katangese *Surete*. A lean, fair- haired man, neatly pressed khaki uniform, sam-brown and bulky leather pistol holster. I saw the priest behind him.

Christ, I thought desperately, what's happened in the outside world while we've been in detention. Has Tshombe capitulated? Are the *Surete* — Tshombe's *Surete* — now also to arrest mercenaries? Has the priest betrayed us?

A broad smile split the *Surete* officer's face. He thrust a hand out; 'Congratulations on your resourceful escape from the United Nations, Captain. Congratulations, congratulations.'

I breathed easily again.

The priest and the officer — who turned out to be head of the *Surete* in Kaminaville — came into the room and we fell to discussing our future. Amid a host of protestations of admiration the *Surete* chief promised all assistance in getting us back to Elisabethville and into Tshombe's service.

'This country can't afford to lose people like you,' were his parting words.

Good as his promises, we were later spirited out at night, bundled into a police car and driven by back roads to the home of a wealthy Belgian colon who lived on the outskirts of Kaminaville. There we lived in luxurious indolence for several days, attended by the colon's pretty teenage daughters who proved a source of constant temptation to the bespoken Verloo.

On the third day at the house the *Surete* chief again arrived in his official car and came bounding up the stairs.

'Ready to move, Father Marchais?' he said to me.

'Captain Puren,' I hastened to correct him.

'No, Father, you are mistaken.'

Before I could speak again he had hauled two brand new identity documents from his pocket and presented one to Verloo and one to me. I stared closely at the familiar face starting out of the paper — my photograph from the Gendarme ID card I had presented to the chief soon after our arrival. According to the appended details I was now Father Raymond Marchais, thirty seven years of age, born in Liege and now resident in Katanga. The document had the usual official stamps and signatures. Verloo had miraculously become Father Tolbert.

I looked up at the *Surete* chief and he gave me a big grin.

'All's fair in love and war.'

He handed me a brown paper packet which he had been nursing under his arm.

'Present from Father Wauthier.'

I tore the wrapping off and out fell two priest's habits, complete with dog collars.

'You can't be serious,' both Verloo and I protested.

The *Surete* chief's face became instantly grave.

'Captain, the only place where you will be relatively safe from the United Nations is in Kolwezi. That is three hundred kilometers to the south. Between here and there are untold UN checkpoints. Make no mistake; your escape has not gone unnoticed and they will be looking out for both of you, looking very carefully indeed.'

I bowed to his judgment. Verloo and I quickly changed into the unfamiliar, clinging garments. Even the taciturn Belgian host couldn't resist a smile as we strode into the sitting room in our unusual attire, Verloo clutching the bulky crucifix at his side as if it was a magnum pistol and I tripping over the hem of the cassock with my military boots.

After lengthy and most unpriestly farewells between Verloo and the two heartbroken mistresses of the house we were handed the keys to a rusty old VW Beetle by the *Surete* chief and wished Godspeed.

Our thanks were more than just sincere.

Off we set on our journey, Verloo frequently breaking into song as the kilometers between him and his fiancee diminished and his thoughts wandered in directions largely uncelibate. We hit a number of UN checkpoints but invariably our clothes earned us a polite salute and easy passage from the UN guards.

Kolwezi itself is a largish mining town situated on the vital rail link that runs from the Northern Rhodesian (now Zambian) town of Ndola in the south east, along the copper plateau of Katanga, through Elisabethville, Jadotville and Dilolo to Texeira de Sousa in Angola and then on to Lobito in the west.

We entered the town with sighs of relief for this was the only major Katangese town at that stage not garrisoned by UN troops. Following directions by the Surete chief and the priest, we located the Roman Catholic College — home of the parish priests of Kolwezi.

Obviously we had been expected. As soon as the VW wheezed to a halt a bevy of white robed priests descended on us with salutations and benedictions. We were shown to a comfortable flatlet in the grey stone building which had two beds, a record player, a heap of records and a pile of magazines.

'If this is the missionary life, I'm never taking these clothes off', Verloo whispered to me later as we ploughed our way through plates heaped with roast beef and potatoes in the priests' dining room.

But man cannot live by indolence alone and the first thing we did was try to re-establish contacts with the Katangese Government.

It was easier than we expected.

A civilian friend of Verloo with good contacts at the *Etat Major* took the glad tidings to Elisabethville that we were free and eager to re-enter Tshombe's service.

Several days went by and then we received a message from the President himself that he was delighted at our escape and telling us to remain where we were.

Two days later we received terse instructions to return to Elisabethville and enrol in the *Travaux Publics*, the Department of Public Works, as civilian employees of the Katangese Government. Another set of false papers was enclosed.

Early one Sunday morning, immediately after mass, Verloo and I, back in civilian clothes, were picked up by Verloo's pretty fiancee and driven back to Elisabethville and the action. It had been a pleasant and sometimes exciting break. No more, no less.

One of the first things I realised when I reached Elisabethville was that *Operation Rumpunch* had, after its initial success, diminished the key mercenary population very little. Several prominent mercenaries had gone into hiding during the operation and had not been caught, a number who had been jetted out at UN expense had jetted right back in at Tshombe's expense and found diverse means of getting back into service, while others still had not even been touched by the dragnet.

About the only 'foreign military' elements that had been successfully evicted were the Belgians . . . who would have gone anyway.

The mercenaries, a far more resourceful group, remained largely intact.

The situation now prevailing in Katanga was one of absolute farce. The UN accused Tshombe of having mercenaries remaining in his service; Tshombe denied it. When the visible presence of the mercenaries was pointed out to him he unabashedly described them as something else — technicians or civilian advisors.

Among the Air Force pilots I found the only significant change was that they were now all in civilian clothes. Glasspole — sporting a natty checked ensemble — seemed astonished and a little disconcerted to see me.

'Jerry, I thought you'd been sent out'.

'No such luck', I replied. 'But I've got a question for you. How come you got your car delivered back to you by the same people who were arresting the rest of us?'

Glasspole smiled mysteriously and put a finger to his lips in a sign of mock conspiracy.

I wasn't in any way reassured.

Next person I met was Peter Wicksteed, in English tweeds and showing a suspicious bulge on his hip where he hefted his ,44 Colt.

'And how did you escape?' I demanded.

'Easy, Jerry. The UN said I was Katangese Air Force and I said I wasn't — I was commercial air. He said I wasn't, I said I was. He got hysterical, I got angry and eventually he left me alone. Simple'.

Next day I drove to the offices of the *Travaux Publics* — which included the civil aviation section — and was appointed to the post of Deputy Chief of the Aerodrome. I was now in the civil and not the military service of Katanga, an official gravely explained — wink, wink.

As I was about to leave, a note was thrust into my hand. It was from the office of the President.

'Thank you for your loyalty in Katanga's hour of travail' it said. As a token of appreciation, please accept two weeks paid leave in South Africa before you begin your new post in civil aviation'.

That night was one of riotous celebration for a number of reasons. I was free of the UN, back in Tshombe's service and, most cogent of all, I had missed my birthday celebrations during the dislocations of the previous few weeks. I was now a few days past thirty seven years old.

Not slow to show their appreciation at my safe return, my riding companions at the riding school threw a rollicking party attended by riders, horses, mercenary pilots, Katangese civilians and even a curious Gurkha sentry from a UN post only meters from the club houses. Attracted by the noise I doubt he knew he was witnessing birthday celebrations of a fugitive from his colleagues.

Next day, September 12, heavy-headed but excited, I was on the aircraft to Jan Smuts Airport in Johannesburg. Warm greetings from family and friends, tears of welcome, talks of eight months in the Congo, domestic news. We drove back home to Springs and late that night I crept to bed dreaming of two weeks with family and friends.

My leave lasted one day.

Noon on September 13 we were sitting at the breakfast table with the radio blaring from the sideboard. We had already made plans for a family outing that afternoon to friends near Springs.

'Another helping, Jerry?' My mother asked as the one o'clock news broadcast began over Radio South Africa.

'Fierce fighting erupted early today in key centres of the secessionist state of Katanga following a surprise dawn attack by UN peace-keeping forces on positions held by the forces of President Moise Tshombe. Details of the fighting are still sketchy but it is believed confined to the capital, Elisabethville, and the mining town of Jadotville. Casualties are reported high as the UN troops have encountered fierce resistance from the mercenary supported forces of President Tshombe . . . regarded as an attempt to end the one year old secession . . . UN Secretary General, Dag Hammerskjöld to speak later . . .'

'Another helping Jerry?' My mother asked after the last details of the fighting were broadcast.

'I'm afraid I can't, mother. I don't have time', I said rising from the table.

7

Graveyard of Hopes

The South African Airways flight from Johannesburg put down at Ndola Airport in Northern Rhodesia at 16h00 on September 17.

My first impressions were that the whole Katangese Government had come to the Northern Rhodesian airfield to greet me. Tshombe and his entourage were in town, so were a host of UN officials, scores of officers of Rhodesian Federal forces and even a few well-known and unwanted mercenary faces — people like Dick Browne and Carlos Huyghe who, having been expelled by the UN and Tshombe, were desperately trying to regain access to Katanga, the action and the money.

I was quickly disabused of any notion that this awesome array of officialdom was in any way in my honour. With the guns still chattering in Elisabethville, Tshombe and Hammerskjöld had agreed to meet in neutral Northern Rhodesia to discuss the future of the tiny nation state of Katanga.

My arrival at the airport on that day was coincidence, one of those quirks of fate. Others were later to try and read significance into it.

At the centre of the action I found my old friends Glasspole and Gurkitz — the latter back in harness after a UN expenses paid trip home and a Tshombe paid trip back to Katanga.

Ensconced in the airport lounge, they were swapping notes with a wide circle of Katangese and Federal officials as I strode through customs and toward them. We greeted each other like long-lost friends.

'Been missing the fun,' Glasspole said jerking a thumb north in the general direction of the Katangese border.

I grinned and joined the discussion.

The fighting between the UN and the Katangese troops was inevitable. What was less foreseeable was the dramatic reversals the UN experienced — losses in its own prestige and losses in terms of its primary objectives and in all hopes of a peaceful resolution of the Congolese debacle.

Motives behind the UN assault were easy to discern. *Operation Rumpunch* had not really succeeded and a hardcore hundred mercenaries still remained loyal in Katanga. The UN were thus no nearer eviscerating the Katangese Gendarmes by taking their key personnel.

It appeared that the UN representatives in the Congo, Sture Linner and Khiary in Leopoldville and Conor Cruise O'Brien in Katanga had decided unilaterally to give teeth to the UN resolutions about the mercenaries and had embarked on drastic steps without the knowledge of Hammerskjöld.

The contradictory statements put out by UN HQ and their own representative in Katanga, O'Brien, points unwaveringly to the confusion that must have reigned in the upper reaches of the UN when the fighting first broke out.

O'Brien's ostensible reason for launching the operation was the old hoary myth of a Munongo-inspired assassination order against UN personnel — duly regurgitated by the brigand Cremer — and strong opposition to the UN attempts to strip the Gendarmes of their senior white police advisors.

The operation was code named Morthor — a Hindi word meaning smash — which has more than a touch of irony in that all it ultimately achieved was the smashing of the UN's facade of 'peace keeping' impartiality.

The die was cast.

At 04h00 on the morning of September 13 1961, the sleepy eyed UN troops thundered out of their compounds and redoubts in Elisabethville and Jadotville and trundled towards the Katangese strongpoints.

They had armoured cars, Swedish personnel carriers, ,75mm recoilless rifles and heavy mortars — a vast array of weaponry brought in by US transports in direct contravention of the agreements between Tshombe and the UN.

Their immediate objectives were to seize the strategic points of the post office, the radio tower at the College of St Francis, Radio Katanga and the railway tunnel.

Also on the agenda was the arrest of Munongo; Minister of Information, Samalenge; Minister of Finance, Kibwe; top white advisors and anybody else with leadership ability in the infant nation.

If the UN expected a walkover they were in for a series of shocks.

First one came when the three hundred Indian *Dogras* supported by armoured cars bore down on the thinly defended post office. Forty tense black Katangese, without a single mercenary officer, waited in the pre-dawn darkness.

The first row of *Dogras* came in for a withering blast of fire from the various vantage points in the post office building. Armoured cars wheeled into position and a small knot of grim-faced Indians crouched in the cover of the vehicles.

A slow advance, crash of the car's cannon, pinpoints of light in the receding dark, groans of the wounded and the *Dogras* were swarming through clouds of falling masonry and gun smoke into the belly of the building.

Step by step the Gendarmes retreated up the tower, stubbornly clinging to each floor. It took the battle hardened *Dogras* two hours of bitter fighting to drive the last living defender on to the roof of the building.

He stood, badly wounded, futilely swinging his empty rifle at the advancing Gurkhas.

Below, a crowd of Katangese civilians watched the grim pantomime being played out in the fresh morning air.

The *Dogras* used their bayonets to prod the man into a step by step retreat.

Swaying exhausted, weak from loss of blood the Gendarme stepped back into air and without a sound, fell gracefully thirty meters to his death.

56

An enraged roar from the crowd outside the building was answered by a volley of fire from the Indians atop the tower. A number of people were wounded, one man, a Belgian bank official was killed.

Bullets in return for words — an exchange that was to become standard UN procedure for many of its months ahead in the Congo.

Two lessons could be drawn from the post office tower incident. The first was that black Katangese Gendarmes could fight skillfully, determinedly and dedicatedly without mercenary help. The second was that the UN perceptions of its peace keeping role had changed radically since Hammerskjöld first arrived with his 'guard of honour' in August of the previous year.

The unexpectedly fierce resistance by the defenders of the post office tower was mirrored in countless other firefights and encounters between UN and Katangese troops in Jadotville and Elisabethville — at street strongpoints, across golf courses, from the gardens of private homes, from parks and rooftops and the vast Union Miniere workshops.

Inevitably the overwhelming firepower of the UN wrested them their key objectives — but it didn't help them find Munongo, Kibwe or indeed Tshombe who escaped from his residence in the back of an ambulance, more injured in spirit than in body.

One of the things he may well have had cause to ponder as he lay on his ambulance stretcher was the disgraceful negligence of the senior Belgian Air Force officers attached to the Gendarmes.

Despite repeated warnings — not least of all from myself — they steadfastly refused to see the dangers the Katangese Air Force was facing with the increased UN activity. No steps had been taken to move the aircraft out to UN-free Kolwezi or other bush strips.

The net result was that between *Rumpunch* and the 13th September Operation, the UN made a total haul of fourteen badly needed aircraft — two Sikorski helicopters, three Alouettes, three Dakotas, four Doves and two Herons. Millions of francs worth of aircraft lay slowly rotting behind barbed wire for more than three years because of this oversight.

The outcome of the first and the subsequent battles with the UN might have been vastly different . . . if we had had those aircraft to ferry men and material more quickly from point to point.

All that was left to the Katangese Air Force were two Fouga Magister jet trainers, two Doves in for service in Johannesburg and a Tri-pacer.

What the air force lacked in numbers, however, it made up in the spirit of one of its pilots, like the delightful, stocky little Belgian, Magain, who flew incomparably better when soundly drunk.

Day after day Magain took the lone Fouga on rocket, machinegun and bomb strikes against the UN ground forces. At that stage the UN had no air cover and Magain in his absurdly inadequate aircraft suddenly found himself holding sway across the vast blue Katangese skies.

Within days Magain and the Fouga had become a major factor in any tactical planning by the UN. It was Magain, shouting filthy Flemish curses, who frequently buzzed UN HQ in Elisabethville and once succeeded in driving none other than

O'Brien himself to earth in a foxhole.

It was Magain who deftly bombed the Gurkha transports at the bridge to Jadotville, thereby turning back the relief column pushing for the besieged Irish troops in Jadotville.

It was Magain who expertly laid a stick of bombs in the street alongside the Irish troops barracks in Jadotville, thereby gently suggesting they surrender to the encircling Katangese; a suggestion they took on September 17 when they marched out, one hundred and eighty strong, and surrendered to Munongo — a humiliating defeat for the UN and an inarguable indication of the competence of the Katangese ground and air forces.

Soon the little jet fighter trainer stalked the theatre with such arrogance that UN pilots on recce missions in light aircraft were known to fly to Northern Rhodesia to avoid him and an elaborate flight plan was filed for the transport carrying Hammerskjöld so as to elude Magain.

So while the bloodletting continued in bitter, desultory bursts one hundred and eighty kilometers north, Glasspole, Gurkitz and myself discussed the future with some of the Katangese delegation at the Ndola Airport lounge.

'It's make or break here today,' Glasspole said ominously to the little group.

A black Katangese nodded.

'We've got faith in Hammerskjöld though. He's not like O'Brien and Linner, he's more . . ? and here he waved a hand searching for the right word, 'more reasonable.'

'I don't believe he even knew about Morthor. It's come as a hell of a shock and a real test of UN credibility about its peace keeping role.'

'What are the UN's options?' I asked.

A senior white Gendarme advisor spread his hands expressively and shrugged.

'At this point in time it's clear that the UN's attempt to force a military solution has stalled. Six hours ago the Irish garrison at Jadotville surrendered and there is still fierce fighting in Elisabethville, right? The UN has got to think again.

'Either it brings in more troops, or it negotiates a ceasefire, or it pulls out entirely.'

We were all listening attentively.

'If the UN goes for the first option they are likely to be opposed by the western European powers — especially Britain and France. Tshombe has threatened to blow up the Union Miniere installations as a last resort and that's the last thing the Belgians are going to let happen.

'The third option is also unthinkable at this point. The Americans will never allow their proteges in Leopoldville to be dumped.

'No, the only thing is a negotiated ceasefire and a real attempt at some sort of compromise. Tshombe will give a little; he's also been scared by the fighting and I'll bet my bottom dollar Hammerskjöld is also set on negotiating.'

The official paused to sip his beer.

'Mark my words; there's going to be some pretty high stakes played here in dusty Ndola over the next few days and I'm damn sure it isn't Katanga that's going to come out short changed.'

Later that evening Glasspole and I wandered from our hotel towards the airstrip and joined a small knot of people before the control tower. Hammerskjöld was due that night. Excitement ran high, history was unfolding and we were right on the spot.

Initial information was that the aircraft was due at 18h00. The hour came and went. So did 19h00.

Conversation in the group died to a few gruff exchanges. Glasspole and I sloped off to the hotel for supper.

We were back at 20h00.

Rumour and counter rumour.

The aircraft was approaching, then it wasn't.

We found out that no flight plan had been filed for the aircraft.

What was going on?

Shortly after 22h00 there was a rustle of excitement among the chilled gathering. Several people claimed they heard the sound of an aircraft's engine, others said they saw lights disappearing low in the west.

We saw nothing.

Eventually Glasspole and I looked at each other, shrugged our shoulders and returned to our welcoming beds at the Savoy Hotel.

By next morning Ndola had become the focus of world attention and the graveyard of any hopes for a resolution to the Katangese independence issue.

Hammerskjöld's plane had disappeared.

The actual sequence of events leading up to the aircraft's disappearance was strange enough. In an attempt reputedly to cover their tracks from Magain's daredevilry, it was agreed that flight plans be filed for a DC4, carrying Lord Landsdowne, British Parliamentary Under Secretary of State for Foreign Affairs, and that the DC6 carrying Hammerskjöld should arrive surreptitiously later.

Accordingly, Landsdowne's plane left Leopoldville at 15h04 (GMT) on September 17 and arrived at Ndola at 20h35, keeping strictly according to its flight plan, in constant radio contact with Salisbury and in accordance with the requirements of the Salisbury Flight Information Centre into whose region they were flying.

Hammerskjöld's aircraft, however, carrying sixteen people, including a crew of five, took off from Leopoldville at 15h51 (GMT), having filed a flight plan for Luluabourg in Kasai. The aircraft kept complete radio silence until 20h00 (GMT) when it suddenly contacted Salisbury and asked for the ETA of Landsdowne's aircraft. It later told Salisbury that it was crossing Lake Tanganyika to avoid Congolese territory and that it hoped to make Ndola at 21h47. At this stage it was still unknown if Hammerskjöld was actually aboard the aircraft.

Several more radio calls. Then at 21h35 Ndola the pilot of the DC6B were in contact.

At 21h38 and 21h47 more flight information was exchanged.

At 22h10 the pilot sent the message 'lights in sight, overhead Ndola, descending'.

Nothing more was ever heard from the aircraft.

All morning 18th September, Ndola was a hive of intense activity. Royal Rhodesian Air Force aircraft launched a massive air search while ground forces were called in to help scour the thick bush surrounding the town.

It had been established beyond doubt that Hammerskjöld had been aboard the aircraft.

The Katangese delegation hung around in a fever of impatience, anxiously listening to every report that came through.

At 13h10 in the afternoon the wreckage of the aircraft was spotted about eight kilometers from the airfield. Only one man, a Sergeant Julian, escaped from the crash but he died several days later.

In the wake of Hammerskjöld's death hundreds of baseless accusations were directed at the Federal authorities and Tshombe for engineering the death of the Secretary General; prime example being the aircraft had fallen victim to the dastardly Fouga.

The presence of mercenary airmen at Ndola — myself included — was remarked upon.

It seemed as if suddenly we were part of a grand conspiracy!

Two Federal investigations and a UN one failed to to turn up a satisfactory reason for the crash.

One thing I do know is that Magain was blameless in this incident.

The Fouga did not have the range for such an operation, never flew at night and Magain was not the sort of person to keep such a singular triumph from his drinking associates.

The death of the evenhanded Hammerskjöld was a tragedy for the UN but an even greater one for Katanga which had its fate inexorably sealed on that dark Northern Rhodesian night.

8

Revenge and Promotion

Sputnik stared morosely at his big toe sticking out whitely from a hole in his sock. He was flat on his back on a creaky bed in an Ndola hotel room. I was slumped in an armchair, also morbidly studying the Great Hungarian Toe.

'Stuck here for three bloody days', Sputnik eventually exploded. 'Three days before we can collect those two Doves in South Africa, three days in bloody Ndola with bloody UN investigators and bloody Dick Browne.'

His toe quivered with frustration.

'Orders are orders. Nothing we can do about it', I replied tersely.

The Hungarian subsided into mutters.

It had been a rough day for the whole Katangese delegation. Only that morning Tshombe and his delegation had left Ndola in a frame of bitter despondency over the death of Hammerskjöld the day before.

Ndola itself was now crowded with UN personnel, civil aviation investigators from both the UN and the Federation, Federal troops and a swarm of journalists. Intermittent contact with the UN investigators convinced us that we — Tshombe's mercenary pilots — were the number one suspects in the crash of the DC6 carrying the Secretary General.

Such political naivety was little short of breathtaking.

So for Sputnik and I, time revolved around the dual ends of keeping out of the way of the UN investigators and ducking the importunings of Browne and Huyghe who were in Ndola trying to talk their way back into Katanga and the money.

Sputnik's big toe jerked into life.

'I have to go down to the airfield to arrange something. Want to come?'

I shrugged my acquiescence, Sputnik pulled on his boots and we walked out of the hotel and towards the airfield through a bright and sunny day.

It was while we were at the airfield that we were to find the chance to get our own back on the UN — definitively, pleasurably and poetically.

My Hungarian comrade and I were standing in the warm sun before the airport control tower, idly watching the comings and goings of aircraft and people. Warily we eyed the little groups of UN troops and officials interspersed around the airport.

A small Piper Cub flitted into the circuit above the airfield. Sputnik and I squinted upwards. The little aircraft made its approach run, dropped daintily from the sky and landed at the far side of the airfield.

Sputnik grabbed my arm and pointed at the KAT registration, now clearly visible on the aircraft. It wasn't difficult to identify as one of the Katangese Air Force aircraft that had been impounded by the United Nations at Elisabethville.

The Piper Cub taxied up to the apron not far from us, the hatch swung open and out clambered a young pilot in Swedish Air Force overalls wearing captain's pips.

'Christ, they not only throw us out of Katanga but now they also steal our aircraft,' Sputnik hissed in broken but forceful French.

I didn't waste time talking. We pushed our way into the control tower building and marched to the office of the airport manager; a middle-aged man with iron grey hair and a sardonic twist to the mouth. We identified ourselves and told him the story.

'That aircraft belongs to the Katangese Air Force of which I am a representative. It has been stolen by the UN and I demand that it be impounded and returned.'

The Federal official smiled broadly, pulled out a statement form and pushed it towards me.

'Write it all down,' he said.

At this period in time, it must be borne in mind, the Federation under Sir Roy Welensky was foursquare behind Tshombe, obviously preferring an ordered and stable country on their northern borders to the chaos then prevalent in the rest of the Congo. Most Federal officials thus had little sympathy for the UN aims of crippling Katanga.

I was about to find tangible proof of that.

I pushed my statement across the desk to the official. He glanced quickly through it, raised his head and gave us a big wink accompanied by a circular thumb and index finger signal of approval.

Sputnik and I left his office in high spirits and wended our way through the UN personnel in the building's concourse and back to the Savoy Hotel.

Two hours later we were sitting in the dining room of the hotel at lunch when my old adversary, Colonel Egge, came striding through the swing door, his aquiline features creased with concern. It was not at all the same jovial face he had displayed when sending me into detention three weeks earlier.

Egge stopped in his tracks and peered intently at the collection of uniformed officials, businessmen and travellers packing the tables in the room; obviously looking for somebody. I nudged Sputnik and pointed in Egge's direction.

Egge's roving eye settled on us at our corner table. He raised a finger in recognition and threaded his way across the dining room to our table.

'Good morning, Mister Puren. I'm pleased to see you escaped *Rumpunch,*' he said in clipped and very correct English.

I nodded affably.

'We seem to have a minor problem. I understand you have laid a complaint with the Federal authorities that one of my men has stolen an aircraft. Well, apparently the aircraft has been impounded and the pilot, Captain Sorgensen, arrested.'

Sputnik and I looked at each other in mock shock.

'A senior Swedish Air Force officer arrested. Horrors! What shame, what a terrible thing.' Sputnik said in hushed tones.

I shook my head and clucked sympathetically.

Egge pressed on regardless.

'I am asking you, Mister Puren, to withdraw your charge and allow us to fly the aircraft back to Elisabethville so it can be left with the other impounded aircraft.'

I pretended to ponder his suggestion deeply, while Sputnik rocked back and forward on his chair in unashamed delight.

'Colonel', I said, 'perhaps you don't remember, but three weeks ago you arrested us for being mercenaries when scores of others were allowed to remain free. So, thinking about it, I cannot come up with any reason why I should help you obtain the release of one of your men.'

Egge's smile stayed frozen on his face as he bowed stiffly from the waist and then stalked from the room.

The full story of the aircraft's surprise arrival was later told to me by a Federal official. The pilot had apparently been instructed to do recce work over Jadotville in the commandeered Piper Cub, but he feared being shot down by the prowling Magain, so instead, he had headed for Ndola on some pretext or another.

Eventually the pilot was released and the light aircraft returned to the Katangese Air Force.

It appears the little Cub was destined to be the epicentre of a fair amount of tragedy in its short life. After damaging one Swedish Air Force officer's career, it several years later claimed the lives of two young Portuguese Air Force officers in Angola.

At that stage the Katangese Gendarmes had gone into exile in the Portuguese territory with their aircraft. Two pilots, based at Texeira de Sousa, decided to go for a joy ride. On landing approach the aircraft stalled, flipped a wing and crashed. Both pilots were killed.

Back in Ndola relations between the UN and myself degenerated further when I complained to the hotel manager about the UN troops coming into the dining room toting their submachineguns.

The manager — also no friend of the UN — ordered them all out.

When Sputnik and I eventually caught our South African Airways flight to Jan Smuts Airport in Johannesburg three days later, it was under the malevolent glares of a handful of the UN troops, and a barrage of catcalls. Sputnik and I bowed graciously and promised to see them back in Elisabethville — on the underside of a bomb sight.

It was the same old bustling Jan Smuts when we arrived back. We made contact with Fields' Air Services who were contracted to repair and maintain Katangese Air Force aircraft, presented our credentials and were told that the aircraft would be ready in a few days.

We were not the only strangers in town, Jimmy Hedges and Vosloo, two other Katanga hands picked up in *Operation Rumpunch* had been repatriated via Leopoldville, and teamed up with us.

Leisure time. While the mechanics tinkered away Sputnik and I spent several restful days at Springs with my mother and family.

Sputnik — with his strange name, Hungarian folk dances, broken English and developed sense of humour — proved a big success with my children.

As always the time was only too short and late on the evening of September 22, Fields' Air Services telephoned to say that the aircraft would be ready at first light the next day.

Early morning goodbyes over, Sputnik, Hedges, Vosloo and I were soon flying in formation astern over the Johannesburg mine dumps, the rolling savannah of Northern Transvaal and Southern Rhodesia, the bush of Northern Rhodesia and finally over the copper rich Kolwezi plateau.

We landed at Kolwezi — new base for air operations and free from UN presence — and taxied the aircraft to the camouflaged apron that had been prepared adjacent to the strip.

It was then that we became aware of a little group of people determinedly striding towards us. I immediately recognised the dapper little man leading the knot at once — it was Moise Tshombe.

Sputnik and I climbed out and were instantly greeted by the President. The rest of the entourage — Katangese officials, Air Force officers, Gendarmes — crowded around. And there, right on the airstrip with typical African spontaneity, we held an impromptu promotion parade.

Delin was made head of the Air Force in Kolwezi, Magain was given a rise in rank and I, with much praise and back slapping, became Chief of Operations of the Katangese Air Force. But even as the President was conferring the title on me I began to quickly run through our air strength in my mind — it was four aircraft . . . including the Doves we had just brought from Johannesburg.

In a few simple words the President thanked us for our dedication and paid special tribute to the indomitable Magain.

It was a spirit and loyalty that would be tested to the maximum in all of us in the months ahead.

9

Targets: Hits and Misses

The quartermaster's eyes opened wide in amazement. He swung his feet off the shiny desk top and leaned forward towards where I was comfortably ensconced.

'Let's get that straight Major. You want two fifty calibre machineguns at Kolwezi airport to put in your aircraft?'

'That's right, Captain. To position near the side hatches so they can fire out — strafing and that sort of thing you know', I replied coolly.

The grizzled old veteran took another look at me and saw that I was serious. 'Has it ever been done before?'

'I don't know but we're prepared to give it a bash'.

He resumed his seat and sighed resignedly

'Two fifty calibre Browning machineguns, pedestal mounted with spares, belts and trays coming up'.

I thanked him and left.

Of course it would work, I confidently told myself on the long drive back from the *Etat Major* in Elisabethville to Kolwezi. My pilots and I had gone into the mechanics of the operation to the last detail. The only problem was that we would have to be extremely careful not to shoot the port wing or port tail plane while the aircraft was in flight. Otherwise it was a sure-fire bit of offensive audacity that would stun the ANC ground forces.

I drove the jeep through the last of the UN checkpoints on the way to Kolwezi and opened up along the tarred road. Things were finally getting into gear and soon, very soon, I hoped to be in a position to be of real service to Tshombe and Katanga.

The jeep snaked through the last curves on the approaches to the pleasant tree-lined boulevards of Kolwezi. I took the airport road and travelled the last eight kilometers in record time; through the perimeter gate, past two listless Katangese behind a Bofors gun which was pointing a snout menacingly skywards and then towards the far end of the field.

There, backed up under some trees and covered with camouflage netting, stood the two de Havilland Doves which were to form the nucleus of the offensive wing of the Katangese Air Force.

The ground around the aircraft was littered with boxes, tools, workbenches and meters of flex.

I pulled the jeep to a halt nearby. Five black air mechanics, stripped to the waist and glistening from the stifling heat, crowded around.

'We got them. No problem at all. Two Brownings.'

A burst of applause and ivory white smiles.

'How are the racks?' I addressed Leonard, a slightly built Katangese sporting faded overalls and a grease smeared face. He was an airframe mechanic and senior NCO in charge of the Katangese Air Force ground crew.

He gave a thumbs up sign and beckoned me towards the interior of the Dove.

It was the same system we had rigged for the Upemba raids. Reflectively I joggled the release lever, images of those broken villages crowding into my mind. This time though it would be different. This time it was against a real enemy — the ANC.

'And the bombs?'

Again Leonard beckoned. We left the Dove and walked to a nearby tree where several large crates stood broken open. Leonard burrowed inside one and gingerly hauled out a squat, white painted sausage- shaped object rather as one would lift a slippery fish from a basket. He fingered the tail fin approvingly. The 12,5kg bombs were turned out by the Union Miniere workshops by the thousand. Each had a contact fuse in the tail section which unwound and armed the bomb when lobbed from the aircraft.

Simple and safe.

I took the bomb in my hands and ran my fingers lightly along its cool, smooth and deadly exterior.

'Bad news for somebody', I said quietly.

Leonard smiled and signalled his colleagues to return to work.

Within seconds the stifling air was heavy with the noise of hammering, drilling and tinkering.

Once again I was given cause to admire the spirit of determination and ingenuity among the black and white members of the Katangese Air Force. We were desperately short of spares. Unrecognized and unloved Katanga was forced to turn more and more to cannibalising other knocked out aircraft or to manufacturing spares in the Union Miniere workshops. Stripping, maintenance and repairs to our aircraft were done largely by Leonard and his black Katangese technicians who showed a perseverance and originality I had rarely seen in ten years service in two other national air forces.

In all our operations in Katanga we were never to lose a pilot through engine failure — a record due largely to the unparalleled devotion of our ground crews.

Throughout the stifling Congo heat we worked under the camouflage nets at Kolwezi to prepare the aircraft. Eventually the work was complete and we quietly waited to test our convictions and our expertise in the heat of battle. For battle we well knew, was on the way.

In Katanga the situation had degenerated into an ominous state of no war, no peace.

On October 13, the United Nations and Tshombe had signed a final ceasefire that everybody implicitly knew was simply a breathing space.

While the United Nations and Katangese troops edged warily around each other's strongpoints in Elisabethville and Jadotville, the huge American transporters kept flying in increasing amounts of material and troops in direct contravention of the agreements signed with Tshombe.

The president, meanwhile, cast around desperately for more weapons, more aircraft, more men, more time and more understanding.

In Baluba areas of Katanga, the policing activities of the Gendarmes were crippled by the actions of the United Nations and once again, scores of missionaries, teachers and pro-Tshombist tribesmen were at grave risk.

On the borders of Katanga the situation since mid-September had bubbled over into open war between the Gendarmes and attacking elements of the ANC Leopoldville and ANC Stanleyville.

Late October brought slight relief to the hard-pressed Katangese Air Force when six brand new twin engined Dorniers arrived straight from their German assembly lines. How Tshombe dodged UN strictures to get the aircraft, I never did find out. It was just one of those mysterious arms deals which kept Katanga supplied with aircraft during its short existence.

Our only problem was that the Dorniers had no spares and it was not long before a defective braking gear took its toll on the shiny new aircraft.

We lost one after the other in ground loops.

In October came the long awaited attack by the ANC on Katanga's northern border.

In late September two battalions of ANC troops were flown to Luluabourg from lower Congo. The troops began exploratory thrusts against the Katangese border from Kasai in early October but had little success.

Shortly afterwards Gizenga, in Stanleyville, ordered his troops into the attack along the Kivu-Katangese border.

The noose began to tighten.

Gizenga's troops captured Bendera about fifty kilometers north of Albertville on the Kivu-Katangese border after a sharp engagement with Katangese Gendarmes. Because of the presence of UN troops in Albertville it was impossible to bring mercenaries into the area to stiffen the Katangese Gendarmes.

As soon as the ANC troops had seized the town the UN started issuing placatory statements about the Stanleyville ANC not wishing to move further into Katanga.

The next attack, independent of the Stanleyville thrust, came at Kaniama on the Katangese-Kasai border in the north west of Katanga by the ANC from Leopoldville. I received a terse message from *Etat Major,* Elisabethville: prepare to move.

Early next morning we wheeled the Doves from under the camouflage nets and, to the accompanying cheers of our mechanics, taxied to the runway. Sputnik and I were in the one Dove while Bracco and Libert and Vosloo crewed the other.

Dependable pilots in dependable aircraft, I thought as our heavily laden Doves crawled into the still lightening sky.

We headed first for Kamina and the Area Commander's HQ. It was from here that the ground operations against the ANC were being directed. The briefing was short and sombre. A Belgian, Lamouline, who was Area Commander, pointed out the sector on a large scale map. Reflectively he arced his pointer across a wide swatch covering the Lubilash River.

'Here's where the action is, Major. The ANC have attacked in upwards of battalion strength and crossed the Lubilash River to establish a bridgehead. Major Baron is holding them as best he can with his Gendarmes and mercenary officers but with the UN cordon . . ?

The officer stopped and shrugged expressively. I knew what he meant; no reinforcements, no extra mercenaries, no ammunition.

'Your job will be twofold; tactical air strikes in support of the ground forces and strategic bombing of ANC concentrations and supply lines?

I couldn't help but suppress a smile. Christ, this officer was talking as if we had one squadron of jet fighters and another of bombers instead of two Doves with homemade bombs, racks and sights and two pedestal mounted Brownings.

I buried my nose in the steaming mug of coffee to stifle a guffaw.

Immediately after the briefing Bracco, Libert, Vosloo, Sputnik and I straggled out to the waiting Doves. The two Belgians jocularly referring to themselves as wing commanders and myself as air field marshall. Sputnik had to be content with the title of squadron commander.

Several mercenaries were lounging near the Doves. A slightly built, sandy-haired man advanced towards us and held out his hand. He told me that he and his comrades were on their way to help Baron and would gladly man our Brownings on the trip.

I missed his name in the hurried introductions as we made our hurried pre-flight checks. In later years though, I and indeed the world, would get to know him very well; he was Jean Schramme — later to become notorious as 'Black Jack' Schramme.

We clambered into the Doves and started engines.

Little groups of Gendarmes waved as the two Doves, machineguns impertinently jutting from their ribs, lumbered into the sky.

The cloud layer reared up threateningly before us shortly after we had left Kaminaville — bank upon bank of writhing vapour stalking proprietorially across a great swathe of the blue Congo sky.

Sputnik and I looked apprehensively at each other. The Hungarian gave a thumbs down sign.

I checked and saw the other Dove keeping loose formation several hundred meters astern of us on the port side.

The Dove hit the clouds; a sudden enveloping shroud of white- grey opaqueness; a silent insular world of aircraft and self.

We knew we were in trouble. All flying in the Congo at this time was very Heath Robinson — rule-of-thumb. It was very much a question of accurate map reading and direction by well-known landmarks. Met reports and wind velocities at the various levels and other important factors in navigation were not available to us when we were flying blind.

Sputnik and I had rough bearings for Kaniama, so we ploughed on through the voluminous, billowing clouds checking our instruments and desperately probing the clouds for signs of a break. By this time the Doves had become completely separated in the swirling void. Several times we descended dangerously low in a bid to break out of the encapsulating cloud banks. No luck. Time dragged on.

Thirty minutes later the Dove knifed through the last remaining vestiges of the cloud and we suddenly found ourselves blinking in the bright sunlight flying over totally unfamiliar terrain.

I made some quick calculations. Judging by our speed and the time we should have been several kilometers east of Kaniama but on which exact bearing we would find the front, we had no idea.

Desperately Sputnik and I began scanning the ground for some feature.

We began slowly swinging back and forth on a central bearing in the hope of picking up a landmark. Suddenly on the port wing, a rail line sprung up out of the surrounding dense bush. Hastily I consulted the map. The rail link ran right through Kaniama so, if we followed the line west, we were bound to hit our target.

Simple.

With new heart Sputnik and I set course.

And sure enough, minutes later, a small deserted overgrown air strip with a single prefab hut and a tattered wind sock loomed up. Sputnik and I exchanged quizzical glances.

The airfield was on a bearing which, according to our calculations, should have been Kaniama but it certainly looked deserted.

'Perhaps the Gendarmes are on the perimeters under cover,' Sputnik said as if reading my thoughts.

I nodded and gave a thumbs up sign.

We circled the airstrip several times before making our approach run. Below us we could already see a lone figure on a bicycle pedalling furiously towards the strip. Again Sputnik looked at me. Again I gave a thumbs up. The Dove dropped, landed bumpily and taxied towards the approaching figure. Where the hell were we?

Sputnik brought the Dove to a halt and we looked at each other.

'Are you going to find out where we are?' Sputnik asked politely.

I nodded, not entirely enthusiastically, clambered past the anxious faced mercenaries and their traversing Brownings, and dropped to the ground.

'Turn her round and keep the engines running,' I shouted and began loping towards the cyclist — now only a score of meters away.

The cyclist — who at close quarters turned out to be a chubby Baluba with an engaging smile — appeared singularly touched that an aircraft had deigned to put down at his long-neglected airfield. Slamming on creaky brakes he brought the bicycle to a slithering halt and gracefully dismounted.

'Good day, sir. I am the *Chef de Aerodrome*. May I be of assistance?' he said, his eyes shrewdly taking in my camouflage jacket, paratrooper boots and dangling pistol holster.

'Yes, please, where are we?'

'Sir, you are at Laputa airfield.'

'Where is Kaniama then?'

The *Chef de Aerodrome* pointed to the east.

Christ, we had overshot Kaniama and were now in Kasai — ANC territory.

I hardly had time to thank the cooperative official, or even reflect upon the extraordinary fact that our exchange had been in the most perfect English in the midst of French-speaking Congo, before I began tearing back to the aircraft and the waiting Sputnik.

Even as I sprinted towards the Dove I saw a plume of dust rising into the air from the scrubland on the western side of the airstrip. ANC trucks, I thought grimly to myself.

I brushed past the mercenaries at the hatch and scrambled into the aircraft, shouting at Sputnik to get moving. I was hardly through the entrance before Sputnik, now fully aware of the danger, had urged the lumbering Dove down the runway, propellers in fully-fine and throttles fully forward.

In the fuselage the mercenaries crouched grimly behind their Browning determined to give as good as they got.

The runway appeared absurdly short for the needs of our overloaded little plane. It didn't seem possible we could make it. Still gasping from the exertion, I stood in the cockpit behind Sputnik watching as the trees at the end of the runway loomed up with breathtaking rapidity.

We seemed desperately short of speed. Could we make it?

Sputnik momentarily relaxed his hand on the throttle.

Christ, was he thinking of aborting the take off?

From behind the pedestal and still standing, I brushed his hand away and pushed the throttles fully forwards.

Sputnik occupied himself with the stick while I worked the throttle.

Flaps down 12 degrees for greater lift.

The Dove bounced once or twice, shuddered then clawed her way into the air well into the overshoot area and only a few meters above the treetops.

We didn't even have time to congratulate ourselves before we were over the cause of the dust plume — three grimy olive green trucks packed with ANC troops.

For a moment aircrew and black troops stared at each other with something akin to surprise and then we were over them and scudding away to the east.

From behind came a forlorn crackle of gunfire.

Several rounds found their targets, a spent bullet lodged in the fuselage, but we had escaped.

In the aircraft the mercenaries grinned tightly while Sputnik and I, weak from tension, could only smile foolishly.

'That was fun. We really must do it again some time', Sputnik said dryly and then giggled hysterically.

None of us bothered to think about what would have happened if we had been caught by the ANC.

The faithful Dove droned on eastwards and within a short time the bridge at Kaniama loomed up below us.

A ragged cheer came from the tension-dried throats of the mercenaries.

As we crossed the Lubilash River a splutter of gunfire greeted us from below. The ANC had indeed established a bridgehead.

At Kaniama we landed at the airstrip and were delighted to find Libert and Bracco's Dove already there. Our arrival drew a crowd of Gendarmes, Major Baron and the nominal head of the Gendarmes, General Muke.

Muke was a former adjutant in the colonial Force Publics, a slow Swahili and Lingala speaking man who remained doggedly loyal to Katanga and Tshombe.

Like all black officers he was dominated by the vastly more experienced and educated Belgian advisors.

From Sergeant Major to General is a pretty big step for any man and I fear that Muke's expertise never quite achieved the same leap as his rank.

Major Baron — a taciturn French officer who had arrived with the ill-fated Tranquier mission a year previously — was directing operations in the area under the 'command' of General Muke.

Smiles and handshakes were the order of the day as we were ushered towards the ops room.

'You will bomb today, Major. Right now in fact', Muke promised expansively before we had even reached the door of the room. And bomb we did.

As a test of the air strength it was agreed that an operation would be laid on against the ANC troops entrenched only a few kilometers north of Kaniama.

Hastily we unloaded all our surplus bombs and kept only the twelve rack bombs aboard.

Manoeuvreability was the essence. From the briefing we had a fair idea of what we were looking for and where we would find it.

Finally, the two Doves bounced down the rough strip and rose steadily into the air.

Bracco, Libert, Sputnik and I flew our Doves in formation, Libert slightly behind me and in constant radio contact. We were all excited, both at the experimental nature of our mission and at the chance to strike back at the ANC, then crowding like hungry wolves around Katanga.

Within minutes we had quickly discerned the ANC trenches, stretching in ragged strands for about half a kilometer in from the river bank. As we flew low overhead we were greeted by a splutter of gunfire — all of which went wide.

Visibility excellent, wind minimum.

'Kilo Alpha Tango 129 . . . calling Kilo Alpha Tango 214 . . . making approach run . . . over.' I radioed Libert.

'Roger Kilo Alpha Tango', came the reply.

We ducked low over the ANC lines.

Crouched on my stomach above the bomb site I waited for the ground to resolve itself into a trench system. I saw the yawning gap, an impression of startled upturned black faces and a few crates.

I quickly raised one finger.

A crewman violently jerked the bomb release lever and we were away.

Exactly five seconds later, as arranged, Libert dropped his bombs.

Again and again we crisscrossed the ANC lines, skimming at one hundred and fifty meters up, twelve times in all, each dropping one bomb in each run, wheeling around and then zeroing in again on the target.

Eventually the area was dotted with tall plumes of smoke.

Many of the bombs fell precisely astride the trenches and in the confined space we could imagine the terror spawned among the ANC.

Never in their whole historical experience had they suffered aerial bombardment.

By the twelfth run the shattered emplacements were plain to see, fiercely burning scrubland, and in one place we noted a small section of troops desperately scrabbling out of their trenches and making for the cover of the bush.

We never even used the Brownings.

Our return to base was greeted with rapturous acclaim.

Baron and Muke had observed the whole action through field glasses and both were in high spirits that the ANC attack could be stopped in its tracks with a little more of the same pressure.

That night we hit the hay early — the five pilots crowded into a single room in the ramshackle building serving as HQ.

I lay in my sleeping bag on the concrete floor and above the snoring of my companions, listened to the sporadic angry muttering of gunfire and mortars only a few kilometers away. It was the nearest I had been to conventional warfare in the Congo and the immediacy of the danger facing Katanga came suddenly and forcefully home to me that night.

We were up the next day before dawn — checking bomb loads, stacking ammunition trays, checking the Brownings and getting last minute briefings.

Today's would be a combined ground and air strike.

The sun was hardly above the trees when we flew out of Kaniama and set course for the ANC lines, easily visible by the small smouldering heaps of rubble left by the previous day's attack. This time they were waiting for us.

A vicious hail of gunfire was audible long before we even reached their lines. The poor bastards were firing wild and firing scared.

It was a re-run of our preceding operation — only more successful. Again we crisscrossed the ANC emplacements laying stick after stick of bombs until the air was thick with acrid smoke and many of the ANC emplacements were reduced to rubble.

For the ANC troops, poorly trained at the best of times, the experience was too much. At first in ones and twos they scrambled out of the trenches and began to run for the bridge. Then came handfuls . . . then what seemed like the whole force in huge numbers.

Once our bombs were finished the Doves became infinitely more manoeuverable, so we gave the doggedly waiting mercenaries an opportunity to use their Brownings.

Time and again the Doves swept low over the ANC, blasting them with the machineguns, the little aircraft shaking with the effort, cartridge cases cascading from the exit hatches, and acrid cordite fumes wafting through the fuselage.

Below we could see the explosive bullets winking as they struck the ground.

The effect on the ANC was electrifying. The retreat became a rout . . . suddenly the ANC had become a terrified and undisciplined rabble intent only on reaching the bridge and safety.

Spiralling out of one of our many strafing runs, I looked back to where the Gendarmes' emplacements were. It was not unlike a volcano erupting as Gendarmes rushed forth to take advantage of the ANC's confusion.

Row upon row of Gendarmes advanced in skirmish order through the soft early morning light harrying the ANC rear.

The demoralization among the ANC caused by the air action was complete and, apart from a few minor firefights, the Gendarmes met no opposition.

By breakfast that day, although no one ate that meal, the last ANC soldier had been thrown off Katangese territory.

72

10

Border Wars and Domestic Developments

From the air the passage of the train was clearly visible from kilometers away; a steady column of black smoke rising above the emerald green jungle blanket. Heading east to Kaniama from Liputa and Mwene Ditu, the train was carrying ANC reinforcements from Luluabourg to the torn battalions at the front.

Sputnik and I saw the plume of smoke at the same time. I radioed Libert and Bracco.

'Kilo Alpha Tango 129 . . . calling Kilo Alpha Tango 214 . . . train on starboard wing . . . going in . . . over.'

'Roger, Kilo Alpha Tango 129 . . . we have him in sight . . . out.'

The Hungarian banked the Dove steeply and dropped in an arc to come in from the west behind the train.

From the fuselage we heard a flurry of activity as the Browning's crew made last minute checks on their weapons. Behind us and slightly to port I saw Libert's Dove follow us down.

We traced the rail line for several kilometers and until the black snake of the train appeared in front of us. I calculated its speed at about fifty kilometers per hour.

We roared in on its starboard side at an altitude of one hundred and fifty meters and a speed of one hundred and eighty kilometers an hour.

They didn't have a chance.

Tacked on to the rear of the train was a flat car with a mounted Bofors — rearward air defence.

The three khaki-clad gunners on the flat car didn't even wait for us to open fire; they simply bailed over the side, landed sprawled on the gravel alongside the track and before we were quite over, had managed to sprint for the jungle. The Bofors stood in magnificent and impotent isolation on the flatcar.

So much for rearward defence.

Then we were parallel to the last coach. The Dove shook violently as our Browning opened up on the defenceless rows of glinting windows and the thin skinned hulks of the nine railway coaches. Above the harsh clatter of the gun we imagined the hysterical hooting of the steam locomotive up ahead. Our own gun fell momentarily silent and, as if in echo, we heard a muted chattering from behind us - Libert's Dove.

Train windows shattered, neat lines of holes stitched themselves into the coach walls, a rifle barrel was imprudently thrust from one window and then immediately wrenched from unseen hands by the gunfire.

In the middle of the train we came across another flatcar, another Bofors, another three gunners. Two of them bolted over the side but the third foolishly tried to slew his gun to face us.

A hail of bullets rattled on the exposed steel of the flatcar and from the Bofors itself as our gunner concentrated on eliminating the danger.

The lonely khaki-clad figure bucked convulsively and slumped forward on to the pedestal holding the Bofors.

As we raced past I gained a momentary impression of the top of the man's head neatly and cleanly disintegrating.

By this time the driver of the locomotive had decided discretion was the better part of valour. The coaches swayed and rocked alarmingly as the crew slammed on brakes amid a shower of sparks and clouds of steam.

The Dove roared past the locomotive and the gunners poured a solid but ineffectual stream of fire against its iron-ribbed hulk. Inside the crew crouched low as the bullets zinged off the steel plate.

We pulled out above the trees and wheeled for a return run.

By this time the driver had managed to pull the train to a halt and reverse it. It was now chugging furiously away in the opposite direction — back to Libouta. Sluggishly at first, then increasingly faster as it tried to flee our attentions.

Sputnik raced the Dove along the other side of the train, our gunners spewing mayhem into the densely packed interiors of the thinly walled coaches. This time we saw knots of desperate troops clinging to open doorways, waiting for the opportunity to leap clear of the train and escape into the safety of the bush.

As we slid past the middle flatcar I saw the body of the heroic gunner grotesquely slumped in an almost erect stance against the Bofors and its pedestal . . . the blood-spattered corpse swaying in rhythm to the speeding train.

At the end of our final run we climbed back into the azure sky, Libert following closely behind.

Sputnik looked at me and silently held up one hand with all his fingers extended. He bunched the hand into a fist and then held up four fingers. I knew what he meant. We had sent ten trains in four days scuttling back towards Mwene Ditu because of our strafing runs.

The rail line was not the only target during those two weeks of operations in the north. Obvious military traffic also came in for a plastering by the Brownings so expertly wielded by our attached mercenary gunners. But as effective as the raids were on rail and road traffic, the challenge began to wear a little thin after the first few days.

The pilots began moaning about the length of time they were spending at the front, complained about sore backs from sleeping rough.

They never stopped talking about the delights of Elisabethville.

I decided it was time for a little action to get them right.

Muke was in the ops' room when I finally tracked him down.

'Mon General, it would appear to me that our daylight raids against the ANC positions are largely fruitless because they disperse as soon as they see us coming.'

Muke nodded in despondent agreement.

'With your permission *'mon'* General, I would like to fly night missions against them so as to catch them when they are grouped and unsuspecting.'

The general sat up and took note.

'Yes, yes, Major, but how? You don't have navigation aids, there are no landing lights at the field. How would you do it?'

I waved a placatory hand.

'Mon' General, this is how we do it . . .' He listened intently, nodding every now and then.

When I had finished he gave a roar of approval. We were in business.

That night Sputnik and I, Libert and Bracco, walked across the darkened airfield to my waiting Dove.

'What the hell have we got to do this for', carped Sputnik.

'Hell, if I'd known it would come to this I would never have complained about my sore back.'

We climbed into the aircraft.

'I only hope this works Jerry. If anybody falls asleep we're in for trouble', Sputnik chuntered as we guided the Dove to the end of the runway and scooted down the darkened runway.

We lifted off easily.

As Sputnik circled Kaniama I hauled out the maps on which Baron had painstakingly marked the ANC troop concentrations as revealed by ground recces. The majority of pinpoints fell within a fifteen kilometer radius of Kaniama airfield itself — an indication of how close to the front we were.

I gave Sputnik exact bearings and instructed him to keep a constant speed. Dead reckoning it is called and, if done properly, it's a piece of cake.

The heavily laden little Dove droned through the darkness, Sputnik, being the competent pilot he was, keeping constant direction and speed. I closely watched the luminous dial of my watch.

Three minutes . . . four minutes . . . five minutes.

'You should see the lights now', I said quietly and peered ahead.

As if on cue a cluster of pinprick lights hove to out of the dark directly ahead and several kilometers away.

There had to be camp fires at the ANC base.

I snapped my fingers and in the pale light cast by the instrument panel I saw Sputnik's face break into a half smile.

'Steady at two hundred meters until the last bomb and then sharp on the reciprocal course, okay?' I reminded the Hungarian.

Sputnik nodded.

I clambered to the rear of the aircraft and hunkered down over the bomb sight. Libert and Bracco were standing expectantly by the bomb racks.

Suddenly the camp fires were immediately below the bomb sights.

I raised one hand.

Libert jerked the lever furiously twelve times without a second's break.

The Dove droned on, banked sharply and then flew back over the target.

Inferno!

Huge flames leapt skywards illuminating a wide tract of the surrounding clearing and bush, only partially obscured by the billowing smoke.

Below us we could see desperate activity, diminutive figures running in all directions, matchbox size cars blazing furiously, an old building, probably a farm house, half demolished, tents on fire. I couldn't imagine the number of troops we must have caught in the sudden visitation of destruction.

Sputnik meanwhile had expertly picked up the reciprocal course and we were bearing back towards Kaniama.

Soon the holocaust was left behind us and we were swallowed by the inky darkness, a void in which land and sky were indistinguishable.

'Hope your organization's okay, Jerry,' Sputnik said mournfully.

'About now,' I said aloud, still scanning my watch. Seconds later a mortar flare fired from Kaniama exploded in the black sky ahead. A phosphorescent glow eerily lit the night as the flare gently drifted to earth.

Sputnik altered his course fractionally so as to bring him in line with the flare.

'Not bad,' he conceded grudgingly.

Three minutes later we were over Kaniama.

'Let there be light,' I said trustingly.

On cue the headlights of a truck below flickered on, then another, then two more, then half a dozen within seconds.

Sputnik whistled respectfully.

Below us, laid out in perfect lines, was an illuminated landing path for Kaniama airfield.

We landed in safety, equalled only by an international airport.

The night raid — which was repeated on more than one occasion during the next two weeks — caused demoralization among the ANC unequalled by anything they had suffered that far. We had hit them at their weakest point and time — militarily and psychologically.

The vast number of ANC troops were essentially illiterate peasants with very deeply ingrained fears and superstitions concerning the dark.

Because of this fear they kept their fires burning in the dark - militarily a crassly stupid thing to do — because of this fear they bunched at night and because of this fear they refused to fight once the sun had gone down.

The two weeks of operations we did at Kaniama were full of excitement and challenge. Even Sputnik forgot his sore back and threw himself enthusiastically into our efforts to contain the ANC advances.

The net result of our activities was to sow total confusion and despair among the ANC. From intelligence sources we heard that there were mutinies among the troops who refused to leave Luluabourg, brave the train trip and then face ground and air attacks at the front.

On November 1 matters came to a head when a number of ANC troops revolted in Luluabourg, raped a few women as solace for the rigours of war and were eventually flown back to Leopoldville.

The fighting around Kaniama slowly wound down and it became apparent that our services could be better used in other theatres.

As a parting shot we bombed the long suffering Kaniama bridge out of existence.

Virtually the entire senior command of the Gendarmes in the Kaniama sector arrived to say farewell as the battle-scarred Doves took off in the still African air.

After the Kaniama campaign we flew several more missions in the Kongolo area of Northern Katanga where Stanleyville troops from Kivu had launched a halfhearted attack. The Katangese under Major Kimwanga easily contained the thrust and it eventually petered out.

All told the fighting with both ANCs in the initial stages took no longer than two weeks.

As a possible recompense for their poor showing on the battlefield, the same Stanleyville ANC troops subsequently seized and partially ate the more delicate portions of thirteen hapless Italian civilian airmen then based with the UN contingent in Kindu.

From what we could see from experience, it didn't much enhance their fighting abilities.

For us though, it was a return to Kolwezi from which we again flew missions on an as and when required basis by the Gendarme ground forces in the various sectors.

It was on one of these follow-up missions that I scored one of the easiest and most spectacular successes in the whole bombing campaign. Late one afternoon, returning from a bombing mission in Kasai, we passed over a village previously occupied by the ANC. The village fell in a fiercely contested region in which the ANC were thrusting south towards the Lunda city of Kapanga near the Katangese Angolan border.

Several jeeps were parked alongside the huts, a few ANC troops scrambled for cover as we approached at one hundred meters.

'How many bombs left?' I asked Sputnik.

'Four.'

'Let them have it,' I replied perfunctorily, my mind more on getting back to Kolwezi before dark than on the target looming below us.

Sputnik shouted an instruction through to the crew in the fuselage and one of them pulled the bomb lever four times with as much enthusiasm as I had shown in ordering the drop.

Sputnik and I heard the clatter of the lever and with half an ear waited for the customary dull explosions aft of the aircraft as we flew on.

This time they were not dull.

A terrific roar jerked us from our daydreams. The Dove bucked in the disturbance caused by the explosion and Sputnik shouted a wild Hungarian curse.

We turned back for another look. What had been a hut was now a yawning crater with a few wisps of smoke still rising sluggishly.

By sheer fluke we had put a bomb right into a major ANC munitions depot. The hut was actually only a blind over a much larger subterranean storeroom.

With one bomb we blasted Lord knows how many kilograms of ammo to smithereens.

We heard later that one of the Katangese prisoners held by the ANC in the village had escaped into the bush and hot-footed it back to his lines . . . thus avoiding an end at the ANC hands that would certainly have been bloody and painful.

The incident was only one of the Biggles' type adventures we were to experience in the trackless Congo wilds during our border missions. It was a time of Huckleberry Finn navigation with only mapping skill, courage and a good deal of praying keeping the pilots of the Katangese Air Force out of serious trouble.

Just an example of our problems: In late November Hedges and I were on a bombing mission near Kongolo, a day-long affair that found us still in the air as evening approached.

We decided to make for Kaniama to the west because of fuel problems, and set a course we thought would bring us to our destination.

Kilometer after kilometer fell away under our wings and still no telltale reflections of zinc roofs and glass windows that bespoke a town.

In the soft evening light we decided to turn east and make for Kamina, our fuel gauge now alarmingly low.

On and on through the gathering darkness, into pitch black night. Although we never spoke to each other, uppermost in our minds was the thought that if we had to put down, we'd zero chance of escaping the tender attentions of the hostile Balubas who inhabited the land over which we were flying.

The minutes ticked away and the gauge fell lower and lower.

18h00 . . . 19h00 . . . 19h30.

The gauge was now on empty.

Suddenly below we saw the lights of Kaminaville winking in the dark. We managed a breathless cheer between the two of us. The airfield had no facility for night flying, of course, and so we had to frantically circle the airfield until the worthy citizenry of Kaminaville had time to park their cars along the runway with lights on to illuminate the landing path.

The Dove made it just to the end of its landing run before the engines cut.

We were bone dry.

God had been kind to us.

And while we were busy on our missions, in the halls of the UN matters were moving rapidly to end the Katangese secession.

On November 24 a number of resolutions appeared, one of which conferred on the Secretary General, U Thant, all necessary powers to expel the white mercenary advisors and paramilitary forces from Katanga.

I was told by a journalist acquaintance that in the debate my name was mentioned as an example of the type of recalcitrant adventurer who needed a firmer hand. If this is so I count it high praise for my efforts in the service of Katanga.

It was obvious to everybody that the UN was gearing itself for what it hoped to be the final showdown with Katanga. Vast amounts of extra material — bren gun carriers, jeeps, recoilless rifles, mortars - kept arriving and by the end of November there were many thousands of UN troops in Katanga.

U Thant was meanwhile playing both the USA and the USSR tunes — for a unified central Congo — although the two superpowers would obviously back different contenders for leadership of that Congo.

In Katanga O'Brien was still in office and putting obstacle after obstacle in the way of Tshombe as the president sought some compromise.

I well remember when I first heard the terms of the November 24 resolution. Late one night a number of us — air force and Gendarme officials — sat in the flyblown room which served as a mess in Kongolo. We were tired but confident.

My air group had been carrying out strikes against the Stanleyville ANC north of Kongolo to Kasango — halfway to Kindu — making life miserable for the ANC troops. Generally we were confident of our ability to halt the ANC attacks. The radio was tuned in to the United Nations station and while listening, we heard recordings of the speeches made at the debate on Katanga.

In silence we heard the ominous resolution calling on U Thant to employ 'vigorous action including the requisite amount of force if necessary for the detention and apprehension pending legal action and/or departure of all foreign military and paramilitary personnel and mercenaries not under the UN command'.

We looked at each other and immediately a veil of depression settled over our previously buoyant spirits. We had foolishly allowed ourselves to wax heady on our successes over the poorly trained and motivated ANC, thrusting to the back of our minds the real enemy of Katanga — the United Nations.

The next battle would not be with a few terrified peasant soldiers but with highly professional national armies. Then we would require every ounce of our ingenuity, courage and skill.

All accords signed by Tshombe with the UN were meanwhile being systematically broken as the UN continued ferrying in troops and support weapons.

While the tension grew the Katangese Air Force continued its various operations on the borders of Northern Katanga and the encircled Kongolo region.

At Kongolo the pro-Tshombe Bahemba tribesmen had been surrounded by the dissident Balubas and cut off by the UN cordon. A lack of road communications and freedom of movement meant hunger for the people and, as the weeks dragged on, it deepened into starvation.

Len Robinson, the tireless American missionary, stepped back into the picture and an air bridge was established to Kongolo.

During the next few months the Air Force's sole DC-4 began flying food to the starving villagers. Later the Doves and Dorniers were also pressganged into helping in this operation.

But the humanitarian aims of the airlift also had a tangentially beneficial effect on the war effort.

In between the loads of skimmed milk and protein rations being dispensed by Reverend Robinson, we flew in arms and ammunition to the Gendarmes then locked in skirmishes with the Stanleyville troops under General Lundula.

At this stage a new and important factor entered the Katanga equation. The UN forces received air support.

India supplied a bomber squadron of six Canberras, Ethiopia gave four Sabre jet fighters and Sweden kicked in with four Saabs.

It was a whole new ball game.

Whatever we chose to do now had to be done discreetly.

Gone was the old Magain panache.

My first contact with the UN jets came a very few days after they were first seen arcing in over the streets of the capital to land at Elisabethville's main airfield.

As luck would have it, I was with Sputnik and the indefatigable Len Robinson on a mercy mission of food to the Bahembas.

We were in the Dove travelling about seventy kilometers south of Kongolo when the Saab, with Swedish Air Force markings, first came streaking past several hundred meters off our starboard wing — a flash of graceful silver in the bright blue sky.

Sputnik made a rude noise with his tongue.

We watched the Saab swing wide in a loop and come back again on the starboard wing, dramatically reducing speed and for a few seconds flying parallel to us. The jet was close enough for us to clearly discern the pilot's silver helmet and white face staring at us from behind the canopy, then it shot forward and banked steeply across our beam.

'I guess he's trying to say something', Robinson said.

'He's trying to say we should go home but he's got two chances', I replied through gritted teeth.

'Bloody Commie', muttered Sputnik. 'Bloody Swedish shithouse!'

Again the Saab lunged behind us and came screaming in. This time he was closer, much closer.

'Hold your hats', Sputnik hissed and took a tight grip on the controls.

The Saab shot past on the starboard wing close enough to rock the heavily laden little Dove.

Robinson grunted angrily but it was only the beginning.

Another nail-bitingly close pass on the starboard wing, then on the port, a dive across our path so near that we could clearly see into the cockpit and the hands of the pilot through the canopy as the jet thundered in front of us.

The game little Dove rocked furiously from side to side in the slipstream.

'Doesn't he they frighten you?' Robinson demanded above the scream of the Saab's engine as I battled to keep the Dove on an even keel.

'I've had plenty of practise.'

'Where?'

'Berlin, 1948. Then it was the Russian Migs shooting up the Royal Air Force and American transports bringing food in during the airlift.

'See, I told you they were bloody commies', Sputnik shouted triumphantly as the Saab came in for another swoop.

'Well, we'll have to see about this', said Robinson in his most ominous tone. 'UN jets interrupting the flow of food to starving people. We'll have to put a stop to this.'

And put a stop to it he did.

He despatched a wad of vitriolic messages to every conceivable church or government authority likely to have any pull with the UN and within a few weeks the UN puerile attempts at intimidation faded away with an abruptness I could scarcely believe.

For us, jets or not, it was business as usual on the bombing front. The only difference was that when near UN areas, we took exceptional care not to get caught red-handed. One could always bluff one's way out in an innocuous eight seater aircraft in the air, but it would be a good deal harder to do if we had been seen with hatches open and bombs spilling out.

I am not sure what the UN jets would have done if they had caught us but, as the situation never arose, I was never enlightened.

Not that the UN contingent and I did not have our little encounters in those early days. During one raid against known ANC troop concentrations I received orders to bomb a small village in Kasai.

As we approached we saw several ANC vehicles drawn up alongside a shiny aluminium hangar-type structure and naturally assumed it to be our target. A single bomb deftly directed blew half the hangar away to reveal, naked and alone . . . a UN helicopter.

As we droned back to base I had cause to wonder if the chopper had not in fact been brought to the spot by our old Albertville Scandinavian friends and wondered in fact if those same drinking companions had not been there when we dropped our bomb.

And it was at this time of heightened activity and tension in Katanga that my thoughts were distracted from the purely military to more gentle and pleasing pastures.

Her name was Julia, she was the twenty two year old daughter of a Belgian colon living in Kolwezi, a University of Liege graduate and quite an exceptional woman. My first contact with the slight, tanned girl was at her father's electrical engineering firm a few doors from our Kolwezi hotel.

A few polite words in my appalling French, several courteous replies and that's how it began. When not on operations I spent as much time as possible with Julia and through her, learnt more background to the Congo tragedy.

Fluent in the various Katangese dialects, Julia had watched the ravages of her war-torn country and had decided implacably in favour of either an independent Katanga or a strongly federal Congo under Moise Tshombe.

Her commitment was not merely academic. When I first knew her she was manning *Radio Free Katanga,* the sovereign state's national radio service. It later became Elisabethville radio and was eventually put out by UN action.

Even more importantly, she doubled as a co-ordinator on the Gendarmes radio network, monitoring all incoming signals and broadcasting on the single side bands and VHF.

Julia's warm and steady voice was to guide me on many dangerous sorties during the Katanga border clashes.

'Control to Kilo Alpha Tango 129', was to become more than just a call sign in the months ahead — it would be a comfort, a refuge and a beacon.

11

The Second War and a Mission Aborted

Midday was traditionally the quietest time of the Congo day. By then the shops were nearly deserted, offices skeletally manned and crowds of sunstruck people lazing under the shady boulevard trees.

On December 5 1961 a few of the more observant wayside dozers in Elisabethville may have noted unusually intense activity at the UN strongpoints during the morning. Come 12h30 however, and all speculation ended. The UN in general, and Brigadier Rajah in particular, were on the unilateral warpath again.

All traffic in the vicinity of the UN HQ was stopped and, before the eyes of the battle-wise Elisabethville citizens, the blue helmeted troops came thundering out of their compounds yet again. This time the huge armoured personnel carriers swung north towards Elisabethville airfield. By 13h45 Gendarmes and the UN troops were locked in a bloody battle over the roadblock set up at the airport. The Second Battle of Katanga had begun.

Within hours it was a more intense, more unforgiving re-run of the September War. A myriad of furious firefights between small groups of Katangese and UN troops developed at key points throughout the deserted and barricaded capital's streets.

From the first the outcome was foreseeable. Out-gunned, out-flown and out-armoured, the Katangese could only hold on as best they could. Victory was impossible, the only hope was that by doggedly resisting, conceding only step-by-step, world opinion would have time to swing against this barbaric face of the world's peace-keeping organisation.

From their entrenched positions small knots of Katangese, sometimes, but not always, commanded by mercenaries, would exchange hours of gunfire with the cautiously advancing UN troops. Carefully sighted light and heavy machineguns would pour deadly streams of lead down the UN advance paths, skillfully directed mortar barrages would check and often rout the exploratory thrusts.

And when the ammunition ran low, the UN air pressure became too great or the armoured opposition overwhelming, the defenders would quietly pack up and steal away to another vantage point.

A key factor in the battle was the mobile fireforces — jeep mounted mercenary and Katangese elements armed with bazookas and recoilless rifles. The jeeps, sturdy little battle horses of the Congo, would scream from threatened point to wavering position to stiffen opposition.

The crews would stop only long enough to establish a fire base, empty several trays of ,30 cal machinegun bullets or a score of exquisitely directed rockets into the UN advance lines, check the UN had been halted and then roar off to the next contact.

Under constant air and armour pressure, the Katangese and mercenary groups fought with a persistence that drew the reluctant admiration of the world and the unbridled ferocity of the UN troops in Katanga towards civilian targets.

Unmotivated, tired of Congolese politicians and politics and the strange procedures of international power play that kept them confined in a steaming tropical country among a hostile people, the UN troops proved anything but doughty fighters.

Moving cautiously from cover to cover, stalling at every serious show of opposition, the UN infantrymen universally preferred to rely on their overwhelmingly superior air and armour support rather than expose themselves to danger. Understandably perhaps. It wasn't their country. They, too, were only mercenaries temporarily in the employ of the UN . . . and this is how history will probably view them.

The local population, not unnaturally, moved massively to support the Gendarmes. Housewives telephoned command centres with details of the UN troops digging strongpoints in their gardens, small children acted as couriers and old men demanded to be allowed to fight.

Everyone was united in their efforts against the UN — black and white.

And for their support the civilian population of Elisabethville paid dearly.

In a stunning disregard for the principles of its founding charter, the UN's own troops haphazardly lobbed mortar bombs into clearly civilian parts of towns, bombed hospitals, machinegunned ambulances and, in its moments of worst excesses, actually raped, murdered and looted in a way Elisabethville had not seen since the *Force Publics* had mutinied.

A fearless press corps in Katanga brought some of the atrocities before the eyes of the western world, leaving many people wondering what exactly was a 'UN peace-keeping' force.

Prince Leopold, Queen Elizabeth and Shinkolobwe hospitals were all at one time or another bombed without warning . . . and the UN forces knew their locations exactly.

In a number of cases civilian cars were machinegunned at roadblocks by UN troops.

Bodies were dumped in roadside ditches to hide proof of murder.

Worst offenders in this regard were the Ethiopians — scruffy and quite ruthless — they pillaged with a panache.

In one incident alone the UN troops in the Les Roches district of Elisabethville killed an advisory director of Union Miniere, machinegunned his eighty six year old mother and their servant — all in their own home.

Later, several members of the Elisabethville Bar were to try to recreate scenes of the worst atrocities. Caught by the Ethiopian troops in one of these endeavours they were all, including Etienne Falmage, the Senior Public Prosecutor, hustled off into detention.

The eminent men of the bar were later released but valuable evidence they had accumulated against the UN was never returned.

Notch up one for UN justice.

The war didn't catch us in the Air Force by surprise. Rumours began gathering strength just before December 5 and intelligence observations by the Gendarmes of UN dispositions convinced us that the worst was imminent.

I realised immediately that our airfield at Kolwezi would be one of the first targets, so we had surreptitiously moved out a number of aircraft and dispersed them at other bush strips and at a small strip in Kolwezi itself. Unavoidably we always had a few aircraft out on the runway for inspection and repairs. On the night of December 5 it was a DC3 and DC4, a Dove and several smaller aircraft.

All afternoon of December 5 we sat grouped around the radio room monitoring the incoming information on the fighting in the capital. The news was very grave.

'Gentlemen, I think we should do something to help', I said finally.

The little knot of pilots sprawled in the tatty armchairs around the mess-cum-ops room at Kolwezi looked at me warily.

'Like what?' asked Hedges, a slightly built South African who had been with the air force since the early days. He was a competent pilot for transport work in his beloved DC4, but had never shone in operational flying.

'Like bombing Elisabethville airport', I replied coolly.

There was a pregnant silence.

'In what?' asked Hedges.

'In the DC4. In your bloody DC4. We can load up with bombs and toss them out of the hatch. I'll strap myself in over the front hatch and give directions.

More silence.

'It's just got to work. The UN will never expect us to be crazy enough to come and bomb them in a crappy old DC4. Once we knock the airport out that's the end of reinforcements for a while.'

'Crazy is the word', agreed Hedges.

'Enough back chat, who's coming?'

I glared round at them.

Hedges, as chief pilot of the DC4, felt obliged to raise a hand. So did Fouke, a Belgian pilot also experienced with the aircraft. Several others did as well.

'Great', I shouted and reached for the telephone to give instructions for our ground crew to bomb up the DC4.

Our war began six hours after the UN and Katangese troops first clashed in Elisabethville.

Six of us eventually clambered into the heavily-laden DC4 that night. Lying in snuggling rows in the belly of the aircraft were nearly two tons of fifty kilogram bombs — a nice enough present for the UN.

As madcap bomb aimer for this makeshift bomber, I was securely strapped into position near the forward hatch so as not to fall out in case of any evasive action the DC4 might have to take. I suppressed a certain queasy feeling in my stomach as the straps were firmly tightened. What would happen if we had to bail out suddenly?

Three men positioned themselves near the stockpile of bombs in readiness to throw them out the main hatch to my signals, while our two experienced DC4 pilots were up front.

The aircraft trundled down the Kolwezi runway and sluggishly lifted her nose into the chilly night air. Strapped into my forward observation post, swaying with the motion of the aircraft, I looked down at the darkened Katanga landscape, pricked every now and then by a cluster of lights and occasionally by a reflective marsh or a silver strip of river.

I idly thought that I seemed to spend a good deal of my life on my stomach, waiting to bomb the yielding Congo earth.

I began to think of the havoc we could wreak on the UN by our surprise raid — perhaps even catch a transport on the deck disgorging its load. I checked my intercom with Hedges and then patiently waited.

The minutes ticked past.

Things started going wrong as we approached the Elisabethville skyline. The city was in darkness except for a few smouldering points of light — wreckage from the vicious fighting then going on in the city. It was strange to think that below us the macabre side-dances of death were being played out by thousands of faceless units. Then disaster.

Several streams of tracer bullets delicately picked paths in the dark ahead of the DC4. There was no doubt over enthusiastic machinegunners of one side or the other, caught in a furious firefight below, had shot into the air in anger or mistake. I'm still damned sure it wasn't aimed at us.

Hedges and Fouke, however, decided simultaneously that the best thing to do was to return to base.

'We're going back to base', Hedges voice came through the intercom headphones.

'You're what?' I screamed.

'Going back. We're being fired at.'

'You go back and I'll break both your fucking arms off', I shouted heaving at my restraining harness.

'If I go on I'll probably get them both shot off . . . so what's the difference', came back the reply.

The DC4 banked steeply to starboard. I tried pleading, threatening, bribing and taunting, but to no avail.

In the end there was nothing to do but accept it.

By this time the aircraft noise would have been heard, in any case.

Hedges refused to release the controls and I couldn't very well have dragged him away.

We were stuck.

Morosely I stared at the ground as we streamed back to Kolwezi and the inevitable ridicule.

Even then we had problems landing.

We couldn't jettison the bombs for fear of hitting an innocent village and we had a surfeit of fuel.

It would have been foolish to land heavily and so for three hours we circled Kolwezi airstrip until we had dropped the fuel level. Below us the good citizens of Kolwezi kept their vehicle lights on the whole while so as to illuminate the field, most probably scratching their heads at the bizarre behaviour on the part of their air force DC4.

Once we had landed I confronted a thoroughly crestfallen Hedges.

'Your action will not be forgotten,' I hissed angrily; 'let's get that quite straight. Tomorrow at first light you will take this DC4 off the airfield and to Texeira de Sousa in Angola. Understand? I don't care what happens to you but I want this DC4 out of the firing line.'

Hedges nodded despondently.

I returned to my office at Kolwezi and began trying to write a report that would delicately explain the night's abortion. It was the old dilemma of what discipline to apply to a mercenary. Hedges had disobeyed orders, sure, but what could I do to him that wouldn't have had the rest of the pilots up in arms against me?

I couldn't very well turn him over to the rough and ready justice of a Gendarme court martial.

No, the only thing was to employ the ultimate sanction — have him sent out of the Congo permanently. But — before he went — he had one last chore to perform; fly the DC4 to safety.

At Texeira de Sousa in neutral Portuguese Angola, the plane would be immune from whatever action the UN might take.

That the UN would seek to wipe us out on the ground I was in no doubt.

That they would come for us in the morning, I was prepared to wager my life.

With my feet up on the desk I looked at the ceiling and began mentally reviewing our defensive positions around the airfield.

12

The Agony and The Absurdity

It was just first light when I gunned my jeep through the deserted streets of Kolwezi towards the airfield after a few restless hours sleep in my hotel room.

My thought's revolved around what the dawn was likely to bring. At least the DC4 would be out of the way, I consoled myself.

I approached the boom-controlled entrance to the airfield. Two Katangese guards waved me through. The jeep swung wide along the apron towards the administration block. Then I saw it.

On the tarmac, exactly as we had left her the night before, was the DC4. She stood as an implacable monument to Hedges unreliability — naked and alone. I scrambled out of the jeep and began sprinting towards the administration block.

Bloody, bloody Hedges.

All we needed was a UN attack.

As if on cue I heard the low thunder of the Canberra's powerful jet engines. It swept in at treetop height over the southern end of the runway, Indian Air Force insignia clearly visible on its tail plane, fuselage faintly glinting in the first feeble rays of the morning light — ominous, deadly, determined.

I fell flat and began wriggling on my stomach towards the nearest emplacement. Snatching a glance upwards, I was just in time to see the bombers twin 20mm cannons erupt into smoke and seventy meters away, huge gaping tears appeared miraculously in the mid-section of the DC4.

The Canberra pilot had not even bothered to take preliminary runs. The earth-trembling roar faded.

Only the retreating tail fin of the Canberra was visible by the time the Katangese gunners on our defence perimeter had managed to slew their weapons around. There was a futile burst of machinegun fire and several rounds from the Bofors.

Then silence.

I had time to give thanks for having ordered the bombs unloaded from the DC4 the night before.

Heavy hearted I took up my position in a sandbagged gun emplacement alongside the airfield building and waited for the inevitable. The DC4 stood like a massive reproach in front of me — tattered, undercarriage shot off, lurched on to one wing, quite immovable. It would never fly again.

I rested my head against the cool breech of the ,50 cal machinegun in the pit.
Hedges!

The two Katangese gunners in the pit made sympathetic noises.

We waited impatiently as the sun's rays warmed the dew damp airfield.

An hour later the UN jets came back in force and the grim little game was really
on.

Two Canberras swept low over the trees again and made straight for our stranded
aircraft on the hard top strip. Several puffs from their rocket rails and a sharp tongue
of flame stood starkly against the tail section of the DC4. A blinding flash, a
thunderclap explosion and within seconds the old bird was a sea of writhing flames.

More Canberras and then a flight of Saabs, immaculately piloted by the Swedes,
more rocket bursts and then five planes were burning merrily. Above the scream
of the jet engines and the exploding fuel tanks rose the sustained and hysterical
chatter of the machineguns and the hoarse bark of the Bofors.

Dense, choking clouds of oily smoke rolled over the airfield. Time and again
the UN jets returned, diving through the twisting plumes of smoke, howling at
roof top level over the emplacements, flaunting their invulnerability at our puny
ground defences.

Red-eyed from the acrid smoke and deafened by the jets' engines, the Katangese
gunners still kept up vitriolic gunfire, their faces shiny with sweat, teeth gritted
as they hammered away at the flashes of wing, fuselage or tail plane that showed
through the smoke.

If the ANC had had people like that at Kaniama and Kongolo, I doubt I could
have lasted a day in the converted Doves.

Then the jets were winging their way east again.

I clambered stiffly out of the gun pit and checked my watch. Twenty-five minutes
air attack.

Five of our precious aircraft knocked out — two Dorniers, a DC3, a DC4 and
a Dove.

The DC4 was the victim of Hedges' stupidity and the other four aircraft had
proved easy targets as they stood awaiting repairs on the Kolwezi dispersal area.

I walked to the radio room and reported the attack to the *Etat Major*. Outside
the hut four soldiers were lifting a wounded comrade on a blood spattered stretcher
into an ambulance. Shrapnel. Not far away a squad of Gendarmes were furiously
repairing an emplacement that had taken a direct hit from a rocket. I sat at the
ops room table, head in hands. I heard the sound of the ambulance klaxon receding.
There was only the crackle of the burning aircraft on the runway.

A loud whistle and then a sharp burst of gunfire.

'Here they come', shouted somebody. I launched myself out of the ops' room,
raced to the gun pit and dived in head first just as the gunners opened up on the
first Saab sweeping across the field.

I suddenly realised that, whereas there had previously been only three of us in
the gun pit, there were now four. The newcomer was dexterously feeding the belt
into the machine gun. I recognised the scent before the face.

'Julia! What the hell are you doing here?' I demanded angrily.

88

'Have you had breakfast?' she shouted back over the fierce chatter of the gun.

'No.'

'Thought not. I've brought some sandwiches and coffee.'

The jets disappeared and the guns around the field fell momentarily silent.

Julia wiped her hands on her faded overalls and then opened a wicker hamper lying in the corner of the pit. She poured two mugs of coffee from a thermos flask. One mug she gave to the two Katangese to share and we shared the other. She passed around a cake tin of sandwiches.

'I'm very, very angry with you,' I said through mouthfuls of sandwich.

'Why?' She asked innocently.

'Well, dammit. There's a war on right now. What if your father found out you were down here, what would he think of me letting you stay in such danger?'

'Don't give me that rubbish,' she snapped back angrily. 'My father doesn't mind my being here for the same reason that you shouldn't. Katanga needs soldiers, of any sex. So save me your gallantry.'

I knew better than to argue.

'Enemy, major,' a Katangese shouted.

'Break open those boxes at the back and start loading the belts,' I shouted to Julia as the first jet swept in over the trees.

And so it went throughout the blistering heat of December 6. For several hours at a time it would be sheer pandemonium. A torture cell of noise and heat, and then the jets would disappear. Hastily we would check for additional damage, treat our casualties, reload, grab a snack and then wait silently among the crackle of flames for the next round.

By day's end — after six strikes — we had lost only one man. Several had been wounded. Five aircraft were now blackened heaps of ashes and charred ribs on the disperal area. A huge fuel dump had blown and there was some marginal damage to buildings.

The jets had mercifully not used bombs so that there was no damage to the runway.

The last attack came shortly before nightfall. It was the most vicious of all; an inferno of flying lead, screaming shells, explosions and billowing smoke. For the first time that day the Katangese gunners didn't even attempt to fire at the jets. We just kept our heads down and prayed. I poked my head out of the pit as the attack tailed off, just in time to see the last Swedish Saab arrogantly complete a victory roll over the tattered little airfield.

Victory over what?

Victory for what?

When they should have been fighting against Hitler . . . where were they then?

As the roar of the jets' engines faded away into the deepening gloom I bitterly turned to thoughts of revenge.

They had us by day, but, by God, we would have them by night.

I dragged weary feet to our ops room-cum-mess which had been miraculously saved from damage. Inside were gathered a number of the pilots. Others drifted in as the evening wore on. Most of them had made damn sure they were nowhere near the airfield during the daylight attack, but now, with the danger reduced, curiosity or a belated sense of duty brought them dribbling back.

Again I faced a grim-faced team.

'We're not taking this lying down.'

'What now, Jerry?' Sputnik sighed.

'A night attack on Elisabethville Airport.'

'You tried that last night'

'And tonight I'll really do it. Who's coming?'

Sputnik's hand shot up. So did Libert's and Bracco's.

'Sounds mad enough,' said Bracco approvingly.

Several others volunteered as well.

I nodded slowly, surprised and gratified at the response.

If ever the saga of David and Goliath had meaning, it had for me that night as we piloted our creaking little Dove — salvaged from a nearby airstrip — with its load of 12,5 kg bombs towards the capital of Katanga. All day we had been under attack by the most sophisticated jet fighters and bombers of the day and here we sallied out in response in a beat-up old eight seater transport turned bomber.

That night I felt closer to the mercenary pilots who were with me than ever before. Some of them were adventurers and scoundrels, sure, but men brave enough to reckon the odds and still volunteer.

The bombing run was actually a great success. We swept low over the darkened airfield at Elisabethville. Feverishly shovelling bombs like unwanted newspapers out of the hatch, crisscrossing the airfield, we were in and out like greased lightening. Strapped securely in the hatch as bomb aimer, I saw the bombs winking a thousand meters below on the runway. The defences were so astonished at our arrival that they never succeeded in putting a shot in the air while we were overhead.

There wasn't much that we could achieve against the airfield with our bombs but at least it would serve to boost morale of the Gendarmes on the ground.

On our return we stopped off at Kipushi airfield on the Northern Rhodesia border, about twenty five kilometers south of Elisabethville. It was UN-free and half in and half out of Katanga.

At the guest house I quickly fell into an exhausted sleep — the whine of the jet engines and the picture of burning aircraft still large in my mind.

Early next morning we were awake and plotting our next move. Kipushi itself was a hive of activity. Large numbers of refugees had flooded into the town to escape the fighting and some were crossing into Northern Rhodesia.

On the Rhodesian side of the border units of the Federal forces, armour and infantry, had taken up positions 'just in case'.

This later led to the assertion in the halls of the UN that Rhodesian Federation forces had actually entered the war incognito on our side and were fighting in the capital.

The claim patently stemmed from people who could not believe that the poorly armed Katangese could put up the bitter resistance they did.

Such people clearly overlooked the fact that a sense of burning injustice is its own good reason for spirited fighting.

Early next morning we decided to go into the battle-torn capital to receive further instructions and liaise with the ground forces. All the way to Elisabethville we passed the tragic flotsam of war trundling back to Kipushi — loaded cars and lorries, columns of walking Africans, stray goats and donkeys. As soon as we entered Elisabethville we were made painfully aware that it was no longer the happy capital it had once been.

Everywhere houses were barricaded or deserted, streets ghastly quiet, only a few lean dogs snuffling in the gutters.

We had approached from the Kipushi side, a part of the capital as yet untouched by the bitter fighting then raging in other suburbs.

From a distance however, we could see huge palls of smoke hanging over sectors of the gracious city, small arms fire was clearly audible on the still air — punctuated occasionally by the crump of exploding mortar bombs.

As we drove closer to the centre of town we began to notice the odd home with gaping holes in the roof — victims of a 10,75cm UN mortar bomb lobbed from a distance of up to seven kilometers away.

Once we passed a mobile fireforce, obviously pulled out into a quieter sector for a rest before rejoining the fray. Four jeeps, spaced in a row under some trees.

The crews were sprawled out on the grass verges in every sign of total exhaustion. Outflung arms and legs, faces sheltered by hat or hand, rifles close nearby, the dozen or so men slept as if eternity had begun. Sitting awake in the lead jeep, arms dangling loosely over a ,30 cal machinegun, was a white mercenary. I noticed his ashen face drawn severely into lines of weariness, red-rimmed eyes blearily studying the smoke curling from his cigarette, grey stubble painting the lower part of his face. His camouflage uniform was filthy and tattered, a yellow scarf pulled loosely around his neck and tucked into his jacket, bush hat low over his face. As we passed he looked up and gave us a slow and sardonic thumbs-up sign.

Slap in the centre of Elisabethville we managed to locate the command post of Colonel Roger Faulques, OC Elisabethville defences.

Faulques, ex-French Foreign Legion paratrooper, a veteran of Dien Bien Phu and Algeria, was one of the finest soldiers ever to serve Katanga.

We found the scarred legionaire ensconced in his sandbagged and camouflage netted redoubt plastered with large-scale maps of the capital. Around the room, suspended from beams, on chairs, standing on the ground, were a dozen walkie-talkie radios.

We were in the nerve centre of the battle against the UN.

Faulques stood in the middle of the chaos.

Grey with fatigue but still completely in charge of the situation, he would rush from radio to radio barking orders or gathering information. The radio sets, each on a different frequency, were his link with the key points and mobile fireforces scattered throughout the city.

As we came down the steps he cut short a series of exchanges over one of the radios and came limping towards us. We shook hands.

'Thank you for your effort last night at the airfield, Major . . . first class.'

'Thank you, we were wondering if . . .'

Before I could finish he had spun on his heel and was shouting orders into one of the radio headphones.

'Delta group to Rue de Vallier and Leopold. Enemy armour arriving from west. Over.'

'Delta . . . roger . . . out.'

He came back smiling wanly.

'Pardon the interruption.'

'We wondered if you would like more of the same.'

'Yes indeed, yes indeed, Major. Give them hell. Spreads good cheer among the troops.'

He ducked sideways towards another radio.

'Alpha here . . . send Lima.'

A crackle of static and then the strained voice of one of the sector commanders.

'Two companies Ethiopians with armour support on Route 126. We have no rockets left and two injured . . . heavy pressure . . . instructions . . . over.'

In the background we could hear sustained gunfire.

Faulques thought a moment. Then; 'Pull back Lima to the bakery and RV with Echo group . . . over.'

We didn't want to waste any more of Faulques' time. As we turned to leave I had time to note that in the midst of all the chaos and pressure and after three days without sleep, Faulques still remained clean shaven and impeccably dressed in neatly pressed, if faded, battledress.

He was the perfect soldier.

We had promised him air support and air support we gave him.

That night, and on consecutive nights thereafter, we pulled out all the stops. Using the Dove and two Dorniers we launched a series of provocative attacks on the airfield at Elisabethville. Always we drew light machinegun fire but nothing very serious.

At Kolwezi our landings would be late at night with all the town's patriots lining the runway with their cars so as to provide illumination.

For its part the United Nations carried out return raids against our field but never managed to locate the well dispersed aircraft. And so the absurdly uneven battle went on — jets for light aircraft, cannon and rocket for homemade lobbed bombs — day attacks against night attacks.

And it was in this frustrating and dangerous period of the war that we received a most welcome addition to the pilot strength of our air force. Twenty year old José, younger brother of my close friend, Julia, had only just passed his flying test and had come straight into the air force under my protective wing.

Like Julia, he was a dedicated Katangese patriot and, like her, he was committed to a stable multi-racial Katanga as envisaged by Tshombe.

A fearless pilot fighting for ideals rather than money, he was to become a valuable member of our team.

13

Sortie, Storm and Salvation

I could hardly believe my ears.

'Are you quite sure you want to come on a mission?' I asked incredulously.

Hedges looked selfconsciously at the floor and nodded.

'But why?'

He shrugged his shoulders.

Ever since he had turned back from his first Elisabethville operation, Hedges had been subjected to the merciless taunting of his colleagues and a persistent disdain from myself.

My earlier resolution to have Hedges sent out of the Congo had fallen by the way in the mad scramble following the renewal of hostilities. Between night raids on Elisabethville and day time defence actions at Kolwezi, I had little time to think of Hedges.

Then suddenly on a bright and sunny December morning, a few days after the UN's first attack, Hedges buttonholed me in my office and asked if he could come on a raid.

'Actually, we weren't intending to take a night off tonight but as you've kindly offered to assist I'm sure we could lay something on', I replied eventually.

Hedges nodded miserably and shambled off.

At 20h00 that night — amid intolerable summer heat — Hedges, José and I took off for Kolwezi in a heavily-laden Dornier. The plan was to pass over Elisabethville and drop our load of bombs, land at Kasumbalesa airstrip near the Katangese-Federation border, bomb-up and refuel, then pass over Elisabethville again on our way back to Kolwezi.

Glasspole — under strict instructions to be punctual — had been sent to Kasumbalesa to arrange landing illuminations and stores.

The Dornier ploughed through slightly turbulent air conditions towards the embattled capital. Inside the gently rocking cockpit I kept a watchful eye on Hedges. I wasn't risking a re-run of the first raid.

One hour later the darkened capital loomed up — a few isolated fires burning at key points below us. Hedges' face was set grim and determined. By the light of the instrument panel I could see sweat beading his forehead.

I have him an encouraging slap on the back and started to move back towards the fuselage where the bombs were neatly stacked.

'Almost there.' I shouted over the engine noise.

The Dornier droned on, dropping slowly, until it began its approach run to the Elisabethville airport.

I stood near the open side hatch and braced myself to start lobbing the bombs.

Then all hell broke loose.

A torrent of ground fire arced to meet us. Livid tracer streams intersected across the sky. Bofors shells, light and heavy machineguns.

'Christ', I shouted to the cockpit, 'They're certainly better jacked than on our last visit.'

Hedges piloted with the skill of a veteran.

Deftly he took the necessary avoiding action, resumed his course and then steadied as we furiously shovelled bombs out of the hatch on to the winking points of light below us.

I had just lobbed out the last bomb and stepped back from the hatch when we were hit by ground fire.

The Dornier jumped as if nudged by a heavenly hand, then banked sharply to starboard. I was thrown roughly to one side and fetched up in a heap against the wall of the fuselage.

Desperately I prayed Hedges would keep his head.

He did.

Gently the Dornier righted itself and we were thundering away from Elisabethville and on to Kasumbalesa.

I staggered forward to the cockpit.

'Bloody marvellous, Jimmy. Handled like a champ.'

Hedges flashed a wan smile and went back to checking instrument panels and controls to see where the Dornier had taken the fire.

We found out soon enough.

José pointed to the fuel gauge which was flickering with the intensity of a shy maiden's eyelashes.

We were losing fuel steadily.

'Don't worry', I comforted an apprehensive Hedges. 'We'll be over Kasumbalesa soon.'

Fifteen minutes later we were over the little town.

'Where are the lights?' Hedges asked tautly.

'I don't know', I said peering desperately down through the inky blackness at where the field should have been.

We made another pass and then another. Still no lights.

'What's happening down there?' Hedges demanded through gritted teeth.

On our fourth pass I accepted that Glasspole had left us in the lurch and we were not going to be able to land at Kasumbalesa.

'Only one thing for it and that is to push on to Kipushi', I said.

Hedges swore. 'Why the hell can't people do what they are told. That bastard Canadian's really dropped us now. No bloody sense of responsibility.'

I couldn't help but smile.

Through increasingly turbulent air conditions we pressed on south-west to Kipushi. Within the Dornier the atmosphere became tense - Hedges grim-faced, José unusually silent and myself trying desperately to appear unconcerned.

The fuel gauge began to drop steadily.

'Just my luck to go on a raid that becomes a bloody fiasco. Bet Kipushi isn't even lit up', grumbled Hedges.

Kipushi was indeed lit up.

The whole area was ablaze with arc and searchlights. Only problem was that a row of vehicles buttressed with empty oil drums had been strung across the runway. The Katangese, obviously afraid of a sneak UN troop airlift, had securely blockaded the runway.

With empty stomachs we circled the field once or twice, hoping that somebody would hear us and move the barricades.

No such luck.

'Turn north-west Jimmy. It's Kolwezi or nothing', I said eventually.

Three hundred kilometers on a nearly empty tank lay before us.

Hedges moaned: 'Why me, dear God. Why me?'

Our luck was definitely out that night. At the speed we were going and the rate of fuel loss we could probably have made Kolwezi. But bad luck comes in batches of three. Minutes later, over Elisabethville, we ran into our third and most disastrous stroke of ill fortune . . . an electrical storm.

I have flown many thousands of miles throughout the world in very bad conditions, but I swear that I have never experienced an electrical storm as intense as the one we encountered that night.

It was a tropical front — a maelstrom of buffeting winds, jagged lightning, and deafening thunder claps. Rain and hail drove continuously against the cockpit wind shield, jagged shards of lightning blinded us and sent our precious radio compass jigging wildly. A giant hand took the Dornier, shook her, tried to turn her on her side, on her head and on her tail. It lifted and dropped her and generally treat her in a most shamefully ungentlemanly way.

Hedges hung on grimly — his lips drawn into thin lines of concentration, his forehead creased by frowns.

The radio beacon at Kolwezi was too weak to receive, the one at Elisabethville had closed down because of the fighting. We were flying blind, lost and frightened. Miraculously the Dornier kept an even keel - a tribute to German engineering skill and Hedges' flying ability.

Then, just as it seemed impossible for Hedges to ride the bucking Dornier any longer we were through the cloud layer and sailing as peacefully as if on a millpond. I snatched a glance at my watch. Forty minutes in the storm. I looked at the fuel gauge. Fifteen minutes flying time left.

'Where are we?' Hedges asked plaintively.

'Don't have the faintest idea', I replied.

'Christ, I know I wanted action, but this is a little too much action.'

'Turn south. I think we have been blown north of our course. We should hit some airstrip to starboard.'

Without comment Hedges banked the Dornier.

The sky was still intermittently rent by the huge sheets of lightning. In the few seconds of illumination provided by each flash I could discern the taut expressions on the faces of José and Hedges.

When we spoke it was in short concise terms.

We did not have to inform each other of the danger we were in. It was clear enough that we would have to make a forced landing.

But where?

Below us the ground spread a uniform inky black, occasionally splashed by the eerie glow of the lightning.

Nine minutes flying time left.

Hedges turned an inquiring face towards me. I waved him on.

Six minutes.

Five minutes.

Hedges and José shifted uncomfortably.

Four minutes.

'There, that's what we need', I said and pointed to an area a few kilometers to port.

A marsh, apparently stretching for kilometers, lay luminous in the dark night. Soft landings.

Hedges did one circuit then flew a little lower with all landing lights on. Didn't look too bad. We checked our safety harnesses. Hedges and I exchanged glances and I gave a thumbs up sign.

We made our final run, Hedges throttled back fiercely, reduced air speed to a fraction over 50 kilometers per hour. The Dornier dropped several more meters and then the rushing marsh land seemed to be almost on top of us, almost growing from under the nose of our aircraft.

Down a few meters again.

We braced ourselves for impact on the shore of the marsh.

Suddenly looming out of the dark, rushing towards us in the probing beam of the landing lights at an apparently incredible rate, a clump of trees and scrub.

Hedges seemed momentarily mesmerised.

We continued ploughing towards the trees.

Perhaps Hedges would have acted in time but I never gave him the opportunity to prove it.

My feet jabbed instinctively forwards, both foot brakes locked and we were suddenly airborne upside down.

A roaring in my ears, blood pounding to my head, sharp pain from the constricting harness.

Ground loop.

Absolute silence.

The Dornier had flipped nose forward on to its back and Hedges, José and I were left suspended in our harnesses upside down — three bats in a dark little shelter out of stormy weather.

Gingerly I moved my limbs to check for pain — nothing.

I pressed my release button, grabbed the nearest projections and dropped lightly to the up ended ceiling of the Dornier.

José followed suit and then Hedges.

96

1. Enter Independence — Whites and blacks cheer King Baudauin of Belgium and Mr Kasavubu, first President of independent Congo, later Zaire, as they drive through Leopoldville during celebrations in July 1060. The happiness and high hopes dissolved into blood and anarchy only a few days later

2. Anti-white street-level violence after independence. This white woman was knocked off her scooter and severely beaten up

3. The country crumbles into chaos. Troops of Force Publics rescue a dying black — victim of inter-tribal fighting

4. Enter UN Forces — local commander, Colonel Janssens, greeted by Moise Tshombe, President of secessionist Katanga, on his arrival in Katanga with his troops — August 1960

5. Exit the Belgian ambassador — Baron Jean van der Bosch leaves his embassy in Leopoldville and the country under UN guard after the Central Government Premier, ex-post office clerk, Patrice Lumumba, broke diplomatic relations with Belgium on 10 August 1960

6. Exit Lumumba — the highly controversial but courageous, Patrice Lumumba, bound up and under guard shortly before being beaten to death by Mobutu's men — December 1960

8. Enter Government troops from Leopoldville into
asai province — they show no mercy and give no
uarter to civilian or soldier in their fight to quell the
ovincial rebellion led by Albert Kolonji. The
yoneted civilian's trilby hat is on the road in the
reground

Enter Jerry Puren, mercenary lieutenant and platoon
nmander with the Gendarmes — North Katanga,
rch 1961

10. Left — Katangese Gendarmes and mercenaries operating against Baluba rebels in early 1961

11. Centre — Jerry Puren in the cockpit of the lone mercenary-flown Fouga Magister of the Katanga Air Force. It challenged the might of the United Nations and won

12. Bottom left — Katangese Air Force mercenary pilots, (l to r) Peter Wicksteed, Jimmy Hedges, Jerry Puren, Commandant Jan von Resighem (the first commander) — 1961

13. Bottom right — Mercenary pilots Jerry Puren, Vosloo and Roger Bracco at a lonely air strip at M'bululu, North Katanga — 1961

14. Aftermath of an airstrike on Elisabethville by the UN 'Peacekeeping' Force — December 1961

15. Katangese troops fire gamely but futilely at United Nations' Indian-crewed Canberra jet bombers strafing the Elisabethville Post Office — 9th December 1961

16. President of Katanga, Moise Tshombe, and Minister Munongo, take time off from war to attend a family occasion

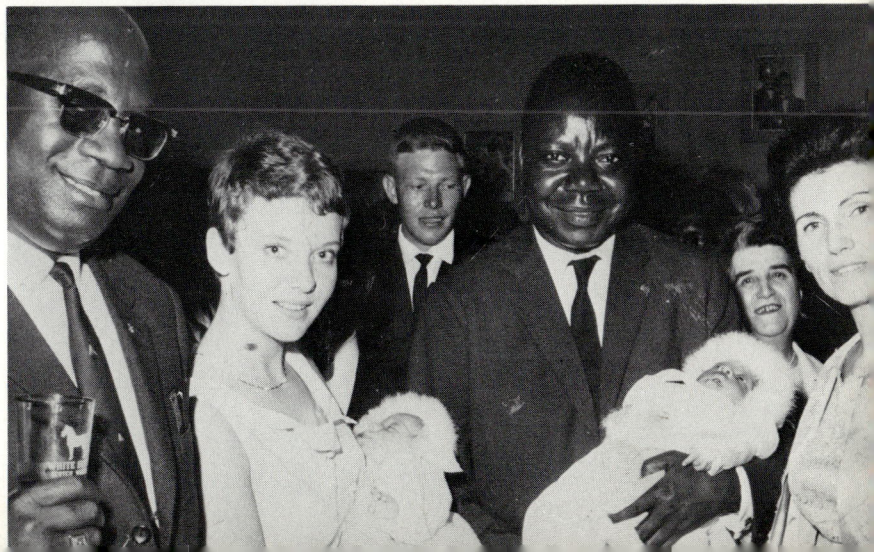

RHODESIA NYASALAND

Regulations section 18 (1).

IMMIGRATION ACT, 1954

Notice to Prohibited Immigrant

Jeriniah Cornelius PUREN

Busca Minima

Take notice that permission to enter the Federation of Rhodesia and Nyasaland or to remain therein is refused to you on the ground that you are a prohibited immigrant by reason of the operation of—

*(a) paragraph (g) of subsection (1) of section 5 of the Immigration Act, 1954;

*(b) subsection (2) of section 5 of the Immigration Act, 1954;

*(c) section 6 of the Immigration Act, 1954;

*(d) section 25 of the Immigration Act, 1954, in that you have *entered/remained in the Federation in contravention of:

....

....

*(e) subsection (3) of section 22 of the Immigration Act, 1954.

*Immigration officer to delete or complete as appropriate.

You are notified that, in terms of the Act, you may appeal to the nearest magistrate's

(a) on the grounds of identity, as provided in section 10 (1) of the Act, if you have been alleged to be a prohibited immigrant by reason of the operation of paragraph (a) or (h) of subsection (1), or of subsection (2), of section 5 of the Act; or

(b) to determine whether or not you are a prohibited immigrant if you have been alleged to be a prohibited immigrant by reason of the operation of any other provision of the Act.

Such appeal must be noted within three days after this notice has been given.

....

Immigration Officer.

[P.T.O.

21 DEC 1961
NDOLA

21. Notice declaring Jerry Puren a prohibited immigrant in the Rhodesian Federation after his aircraft had crashed there while on a bombing mission against UN forces

22. In exile with Moise Tshombe — Jerry Puren and another Tshombe official feeding the pigeons in Trafalgar Square — London, 1964

17. Left top opposite page — Julia Puren — the prettiest mercenary of them all — early days in Katanga

18. Right top opposite page — Julia Puren's brother, José, gunned down and killed by drunken Congolese Central Government troops in 1963

19. Left bottom opposite page — Bob Denard — Algerian policeman turned Katangese mercenary commander — 1961

20. Right bottom opposite page — General Muke 'commander' the Katanga Gendarmerie in late 1961 when the ANC invaded Katanga. All operations, however, were run by white advisors and mercenaries. Muke rose from sergeant major to general in less than a year

23. Putting V Commando together — Commander 'Mad Mike' Hoare and RSM Jack Carlton-Barber confer while another officer looks on. Mercenary recruits are in the background

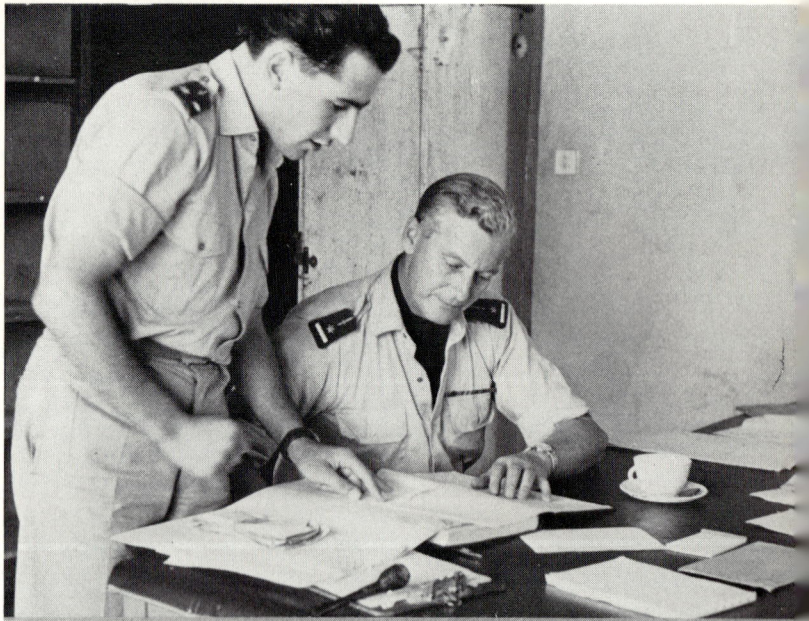

24. Seated — Alistair Wicks, Mike Hoare's V Commando 2 IC

25. Siegfried Meuller, wearing his Iron Cross (1st class), takes charge of the first recruits for V Commando arriving at Kamina air base

26. Violent death — the body of a rebel floats in the river near Bukavu

27. Mercenary and government troops free Bukavu of rebels in a quick thrust

28. Mercenaries see to their own — V Commando burial party after Bukavu

29. Front row (l to r) General Mulamba, General Mobutu, Major 'Mad Mike' Hoare, back row with forage cap, Cmmdt Tavernier and other unidentified mercenary officers — mid 1964

30. V Commando mercenary with typical weapons — 80mm mortar, ,30 calibre Browning, FN rifles

31. The ubiquitous warhorse of the Congo mercenaries — Jeep with thirty calibre Browning

The Push to Free Stanleyville — November 1964

32. V Commando — an informal officers' mess on the road

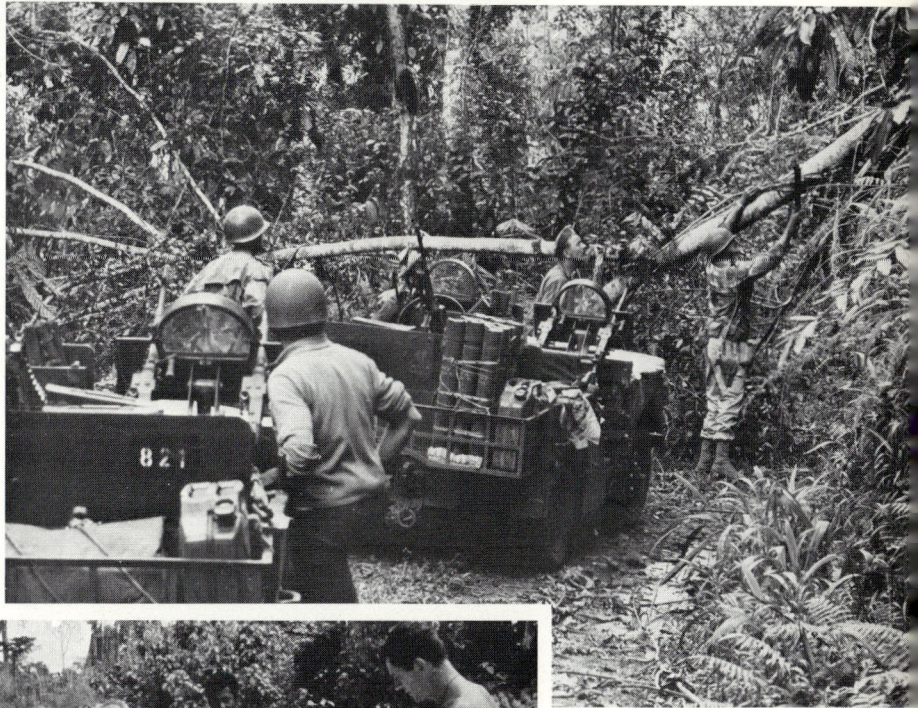

33. A delay as trees felled by Simba rebels are cleared

34. Another delay — sappers lift a mine

35. Top — a real skull and crossbones — a grisly adornment for a grim mission — mercenary jeep in the Stanleyville column

36. Centre — a heavily armed V Commando jeep halts for a moment in a friendly native village

37. Left — Colonel Vanderwalle, OC 5th Mechanised Group, stops on the road to speak to a white civilian rebel movements — November 1964

38. Above — a mortar and a bazooka used in support of the advance

39. Top right — Stanleyville's outskirts

40. Right — Final stages — a wounded and bandaged Mike Hoare O-groups with his men

41. Below — V Commando subdues a rebel Simba strongpoint en route to Stanleyville

42. The opposition — Colonel Olenga, (2 from l), brutal Simba rebel commander in Stanleyville. Picture taken from a captured rebel

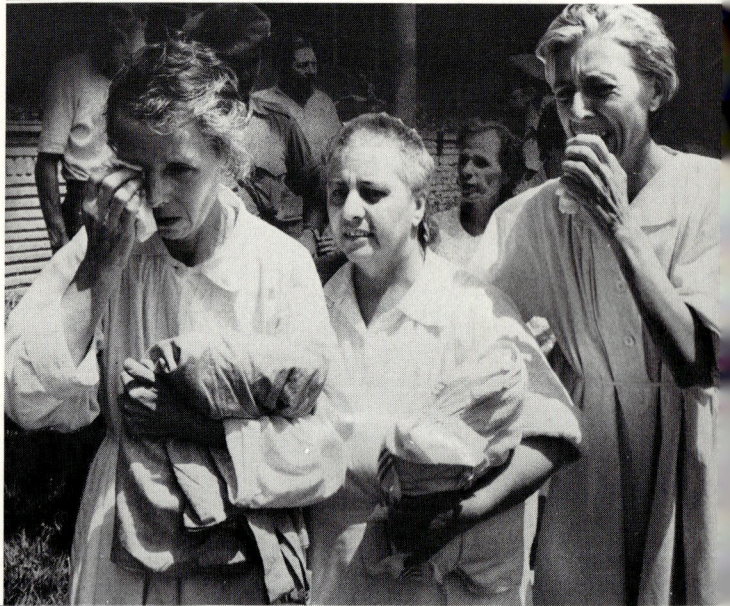

43. Horror and salvation: Belgian nuns whose lives were saved only by the timely arrival of the mercenaries

44. The less fortunate white missionaries who didn't get away. Corpses of white nuns and missionaries butchered by Olenga's Simba rebels being boated down the Congo River

45. A young boy made prisoner by Simba rebels — they chained him up for days because he refused to fight for them

46. Top right — a V Commando mercenary having helped to knock the gilt off the Simba gingerbread, takes tinsel as a souvenir from the bloody shrine to their hero, Patrice Lumumba, in Stanleyville

47. Right — Jerry Puren assists with the moving of a woman fatally wounded either by Simba rebels or by ANC troops — her infant son survived

48. Below — White mercenaries give a helping hand to young black refugees

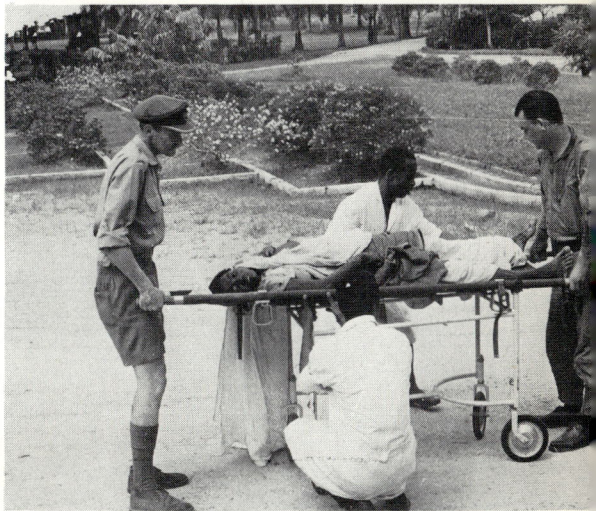

49. Jerry Puren and Mike Hoare discuss the current situation after Stanleyville's liberation

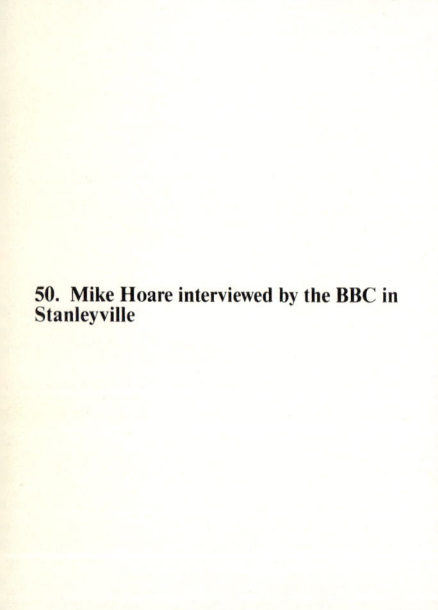

50. Mike Hoare interviewed by the BBC in Stanleyville

51. Officers examine a captured Soviet-made RPG-2 rocket launcher

For the first few moments we didn't bother to talk. We just checked our limbs and delicately prodded for bruises.

Mercifully we were all safe except for José who had some nasty bruises across the top of his thighs from a loose safety harness.

'Catch me volunteering for an operation again', was Hedges first woeful comment as we started moving cautiously in the pitch dark towards the exit hatch.

José and I giggled with relief.

We knew there was no danger of the aircraft exploding because she was bone dry.

After a few short tussles we managed to get the hatch off and then we all three scrambled out. A steady drizzle was descending. We stared morosely at the darkness, our up-ended aircraft and at each other.

'I vote we go back inside and wait in shelter until the morning', I said.

The others nodded and we crept back for a few hours restless slumber.

At the first sign of a flush in the cloud-laden sky we were outside waiting for sight of what was around, but, as the sun rose, our spirits dropped in inverse ratio.

If we had hoped for some landmark we were disappointed. On either side spread the marsh, isolated clumps of scrub sticking up in a completely featureless landscape. Our Dornier lay ungainly on her back in several inches of water. The steady drizzle of the night continued unabated.

Where the hell were we?

As we stood staring moodily into the wilds, we distinctly heard the muffled report of several explosions.

We cocked our heads.

'Mortars', said Hedges.

Several more explosions, a little to the east and far away.

I listened carefully.

Hedges could be right — arrival explosions of mortars.

'It could be the fighting in Elisabethville', José said eventually.

We listened again.

'I think it is. That means we are west of Elisabethville and if we want to reach Kolwezi, we must strike farther west. Right?' I asked.

The other two nodded.

'Second point, do we want to sit here and wait for rescue or do we walk?'

'Walk', José and Hedges both simultaneously agreed.

We gathered our weapons, pistols for Hedges and I and a submachinegun for José. We were all dressed in light tropical clothes - shorts and shirts. Just before leaving I unbolted the aircraft compass and stashed it in a canvas bag.

'Any food?' enquired Hedges.

José held up a bar of chocolate. It was all we had amongst three people.

Moments later we were splashing through the marsh, thankful to be alive and not unduly pessimistic about our future.

We made two miscalculations that day.

The first was that we would be better legging it to the west. As luck would have it, that very afternoon, a helicopter on prospecting work accidentally stumbled across the wreck. If we had been there it could have saved us the immense inconvenience that followed.

The second miscalculation was that we believed we were in Katanga. In fact our aircraft had put down in Northern Rhodesia and the explosions we had heard came from distant prospector blasting.

For four agonising, muscle-wrenching, skin-sopping, empty bellied days we ploughed relentlessly west through those God-forsaken marshes. We were fit and we were confident. Thoughts of death never crossed our minds, but when I think about those days now I am astonished at the tenacity we showed. We were never dry, not for a single second of the day.

The rain was there to greet us in the morning, it stayed with us during the day as constant companion and at night it was with us as we huddled to sleep.

There was no dry wood to give tinder for a fire.

Our half bar of chocolate lasted the first day and then it was finished. Thereafter we had absolutely nothing to eat.

Our pistols and José's submachinegun were useless in trying to shoot the wary guinea fowl we came across and we never had time to stop and set a trap.

Walking through the marsh soon became agony. Every step had to be wrenched from the cloying mud of the swamp. We were all wearing shorts and after the constant emersion of our stockinged calves in the water, we suffered agonies when hard branches or sprouts of grass brushed against the tender skin. Every grass blade became a potential instrument of torture. By the third day I had developed an infection that made walking even more difficult.

Day after day it was an endless vista of marsh land and leaden skies. Despite the desolation of the landscape, it never crossed our minds that we might not be in Katanga. It just seemed that we were taking a long time to reach a distinguishable landmark. Among ourselves we carefully avoided false notes of optimism or undue pessimism. We helped and encouraged each other where necessary, occasionally joked, never argued. Our energy was too precious to waste in stupid recriminations. Thoughts became fixed on simply reaching the next clump of bushes, on seeing over the skyline, on reaching the end of the day, on waking next day.

But, at least, we were never short of water.

On the fourth day came rescue. After nearly eighty kilometers of gruelling scrambling I was now hobbling badly. José was striding out ahead several hundred meters when I suddenly noticed him stop and stare intently ahead. He came hastening back through the scrub.

'Village ahead', he said.

Despite the pain I managed a little jig.

114

14

Detention

The 'village' turned out to be the home of a single man — a lean fine featured Chokwe tribesman. As we approached he was bent double carrying a huge log towards the uncompleted wall of a cattle boma.

José ran forward and gave a shout of greeting. I will never forget the look on that man's face as he spun round.

Stunned surprise.

In the middle of African marshland, with no roads, no transport, three bedraggled unshaven and armed white men had come hobbling into his shamba.

He dropped the log, raised a subconscious hand in respectful greeting . . . but he remained open mouthed.

It took only a few minutes of hand gesture and smiles to convince him that we were friendly and an approximately equal time for him to confirm our worst fears that we were not in Katanga but very much in Northern Rhodesia.

Hedges, José and I stared at each other in dismay. We had suspected it for some time because the river source we were following flowed south and we knew that southern Katanga was in fact a watershed and rivers should flow north.

'Well, I don't really care what they do to us as long as we get dry,' said Hedges with a shrug.

Our black host, meanwhile, was ushering us into his smoke filled hut and gestured that we should squat around the fire.

A calabash of sorgum beer was produced and passed among us. As beer trickled sourly down our throats we sighed in relief. Warmth and sustenance. Our host was bustling around giving last minute instructions to his wives and children curiously pressing around us. All done, he picked up an assegai and beckoned us to follow him.

Soon we were out in the rain once more, following in single file behind our host.

For the rest of the day we hobbled behind our guide, winding our way along the game paths he obviously knew so well. Light was fading when we eventually reached the little village. We had been walking for more than six hours and I had cause to wonder about the relative advantage of living completely isolated with one's women and children.

The village we were eventually brought to was poor but extremely hospitable. A few mud huts, a cattle boma and a patio affair before the main hut. Children and women hung in knots around us as a venerable grey-bearded old man indicated that our presence was a great but nevertheless welcome surprise.

Poverty precluded giving us food but we were nevertheless handed another calabash of sorgum beer and shown to a hut in which a fire was merrily crackling, the smoke mercifully keeping the mosquitoes at bay. There for many hours we slept the sleep of the just.

A few minutes after first light we were again on the road with our attentive mentor. This time it was a four hour trek to the nearest mission station.

I was having serious trouble walking and my painfully swollen feet could hardly bear me the last few agonising steps through the neat station gardens and up to the brick and zinc house that accommodated the missionary.

Our guide rapped on the back door and it was opened by a chubby little African maidservant. She took one look at our party, squeaked. and then slammed the door shut. Our guide began cajoling her to open up. Five minutes later the door opened a crack and the maid peeped out again. A ten minute diatribe from our guide and the door was thrown wide and we were graciously ushered in and through to the sitting room.

The missionary was out, we soon gathered, but was expected back soon.

We collapsed in the missionary's chairs and closed our eyes trying hard to ignore the painful rumblings of our stomachs.

Our guide melted quietly away and no doubt resumed the long trek home.

We never even had a chance to thank him for the help he had so willingly rendered.

As we lolled in the easy chairs the smell of roast chicken wafted in from the adjoining kitchen. We all three desperately fought the rising surge of nausea induced by desperate hunger; our stomachs doing headstands and somersaults at the tantalizing aroma.

Eventually, as if with one mind, we stumbled to our feet and made for the kitchen.

'Could we possibly have some of that chicken?' I asked as politely as I could in the circumstances — trying to stop short of actually licking my lips.

Hedges and José were meanwhile hovering around the stove like jackals at the kill.

'I make it for you master', the maid explained with an understanding nod. 'You eat just now.'

'If it's all the same to you we'd very much like to eat right now', I said.

Hedges and José deftly opened the coal oven door and hooked out the roasting dish with a towel.

The chicken, a scrawny farm bird, was half cooked and boiling hot.

No difficulties.

Using our hands we took the carcass to pieces and gulped down the red-fresh, half-cooked meat.

The maid smiled broadly and shook her head.

'Masters hungry?'

I felt our bulging cheeks and greasy fingers were a sufficient reply.

Perhaps two hours later the missionary arrived. He turned out to be a squat, iron grey-haired American with a skin beaten rough by the African sun and eyes seeming wise to both the frailties of man and vagaries of Africa.

'I've been expecting you,' were his first words.

'How come?' I asked surprised.

'Radio . . . soon after you went in Katanga put out an alert . . . so did the UN — they want you arrested on sight. A prospecting helicopter from Ndola found your aircraft some days ago.'

José, Hedges and I exchanged despairing looks. If only we had stayed where we were.

'Then, through the grapevine, I started hearing stories about three lost white men in the area. I knew it was only a question of time before you turned up here.'

'What do we do now?' I asked.

The missionary stared at us.

'Do now? Why, I radio Solwezi, the district capital, and tell them you're here.'

I nodded miserably. We knew what that would mean; arrest by the Rhodesian Federal authorities. Well, nothing for it.

A few minutes later the missionary returned.

'I've radioed the District Commissioner's office in Solwezi and they have asked me to bring you in immediately. Shall we go now?'

That same afternoon we jolted in the missionary's Land-Rover to Solwezi — a distance of about thirty kilometers from the mission station. By this time my feet were excruciatingly painful and I was having a great deal of trouble walking.

With a farewell wave of the hand that resembled a benediction, the missionary dropped us outside the DC's office. Now we were really in the hands of the authorities.

What we did not know at this stage was that our pathetic little trio had become something of an embarrassment to our Federal hosts. Sir Roy Welensky, Prime Minister of the Federation, was firmly behind Tshombe and, on his own, would certainly have turned a blind eye to our little territorial transgression. In this I am sure most of his civil servants were behind him. The only problem was that our disappearance had been widely publicised and it was impossible for us to just suddenly reappear in Katanga.

A complicating issue was the fact that Lord Alport, the British High Commissioner in the Federation, was towing the strictly UN line of no mercenaries in Katanga.

We were thus not only to be dealt with strictly according to the letter of the law, but we had to be seen to be dealt with that way as well. This schism between what had been ordered from on high and what the various administration officers presumably felt, was to account for much of the ambivalent treatment we were to receive at the hands of the Federal officials.

It started at Solwezi.

We were marched into the District Commissioner's office and lined up before his desk. My feet were killing me but I refused to show it.

The DC, a hard-faced, middle-aged man, stared at us intently for a few moments.

'Names?' he barked.

We replied, one by one.

I felt like punching his face.

The DC looked down at a sheet of paper in his hand and recited with feigned boredom the section of the immigration regulations under which we were being held 'pending repatriation'.

He finished and waved the guards to take us away.

That night we were confined to a rondavel under guard.

For Hedges, however, it was quite irrelevant what great power play was in the air. At last he had a bed to sleep in, had actually had a bath and was boasting a full stomach. The devil could take the rest.

Early next morning a police Land-Rover arrived in a cloud of dust to pick us up. Two Federal customs and excise officials — including a Mister Evans whom I had met before — and two rifle toting troopers accompanied the vehicle.

I noticed the magazines in the troopers' rifles and would have bet my bottom dollar that the weapons were cocked.

They were taking no chances.

The grim-faced troopers herded us into the back of the Land- Rover and clambered in with us.

Thus we began our four hundred and fifty kilometer ride to Ndola, a jolting, dust blown ride during which we neither ate nor drank nor were able to wrest a single word from the lips of our escort.

Things were beginning to look pretty bad.

At Ndola we were given a thorough grilling by Evans (anybody would have thought we wanted to overfly) and then thrown in the clink as illegal immigrants. And there we sat without comfort of medical treatment, frustrated and depressed.

The only people who appreciated our presence were the other common criminals in the cage with us. As soon as they found that we were Congo mercenary airmen who had spent five days trekking through the wilds away from the scene of an air crash we became lionized as heroes.

Food was brought to us, our shoes cleaned, our clothes washed and expectant knots of prisoners gathered to hear our slightest word, even if it was only a gripe about the food.

It was while we were crushed in the stifling conditions of the communal cell that I received a most unusual visitor. A prison warder came to the grille late the second day and beckoned me to the gate. The gate was opened and I followed the warder through several corridors and finally to a small room, bare except for a table and two chairs.

I immediately recognised the figure lounging in one of the chairs — Glasspole. He leapt to his feet and rushed forward with hands outstretched. The warder took up a position in the corner of the room.

'What the hell are you doing here?' I demanded in amazement.

'Just passing through,' Glasspole said with another of those conspiratorial winks. Another mystery deal I thought to myself.

'How did you know I was here?'

'Everybody knows you're here.'

We sat in silence. I leaned forward over the table and whispered discreetly. 'Any messages for me?'

'No, no. None at all,' replied Glasspole loudly, as if surprised.

Silence.

'Any idea of what's going to happen to us?' I asked.

'No, no. None at all.'

Again silence.

'Do you want to ask me something?'

'No, not really.'

I sat nonplussed for a moment.

'Look, Max, can you help? I believe that if we can raise twenty five pounds each as deposit we can be released. Could you make out a cheque for all three of us?'

'Sure, Jerry', Max said without hesitation and scribbled out an amount of seventy-five pounds. He handed the cheque to me and we again sat in silence.

The warder approached us.

'Time's up.'

Glasspole rose with alacrity, shook hands quickly and then scuttled out of the door.

I shook my head in puzzlement.

What was the reason for his visit?

Was I going mad or was he?

It was only when I was back in my cell that the most likely motive struck me; remorse. In that Glasspole had failed to illuminate Kasumbalesa he was very largely to blame for our unfortunate predicament. He had probably come to see me in an attempt to expatiate the guilt.

Much later I was to find out that the delights of Elisabethville had overcome Glasspole's never very developed sense of duty and he had wound up stupefyingly drunk in a bar on that crucial night.

Later that day I asked for permission to see the warden. I presented him with Glasspole's cheque and asked for our release. He held the cheque between two fingers and then neatly tore it in half.

'You appear to have been misinformed about the requirements under the immigration regulations.'

I hobbled back to the cell.

Very soon we heard via the grapevine what was in store for us. Under UN pressure we were all to be sent home to our countries of origin — José to Belgium and Hedges and myself to South Africa. Two days later Hedges and I were put on an internal flight to Salisbury and José was led in handcuffs to board a Belgian box car military aircraft. As he was taken away he turned and gave me a wink.

'See you again', he shouted in French.

The tone was both humorous and challenging.

I grinned.

At Salisbury our life improved slightly. Although still kept in the prison we found ourselves honoured by being entertained to meals by the prison warden — in his own home. I'll never forget the exquisite taste of home cooked food after our days of hunger and prison fare.

The warden was a kindly man with a deep-seated sympathy for Katanga and we spent several enjoyable hours discussing politics, the war in Katanga and our life as mercenary pilots.

It was also at this stage that we received a visit from an official in the Federal security services — a fresh-faced man who tendered apologies for the treatment we had received at Ndola.

'The problem is that there are spies around and we knew that our treatment of you was being watched. We couldn't afford to embarrass the Federal Government by showing undue favour to you. You know how it is', he said and gave me a playful punch on the shoulder.

Soon afterwards a doctor arrived, examined my feet and hastily prescribed some drugs. Hedges and I began to feel a little more relieved.

Several days later it was another snap move — this time to Bulawayo for a night. Again dinner and conviviality with the warden. Early next day, without fanfare and with only two plain clothes men as escorts, we were put on a flight to Jan Smuts airport.

Somebody had done their homework and when we landed at Johannesburg, destitute, without passports or health certificates, we were simply waved through immigration control.

An even greater surprise awaited us in the airport lounge — my mother and all my children.

A welcome end to Hedges' first 'quick' operational sortie.

15

Return and Promotion

It seemed so strange to be back home in my own bed in my own home. I stared reflectively at the ceiling and tried to ignore the pain in my feet. The family doctor had prescribed some drugs which seemed to be helping. All day friends and family had drifted in for chats about myself, about Katanga, about the crash. But now I was alone again with the burning question.

How to get back to Katanga?

I began reading the latest reports on the position in the embattled country.

As was to be expected, we had lost the military confrontation. Bled white by the fighting, the Gendarmes had been forced to retire and the UN had seized the centre of Elisabethville on December 15. The Gendarme forces had pulled out to Kipushi for regrouping, though, and Katanga forces still held Jadotville and Kolwezi.

The wily Tshombe, seeing the writing on the wall, had decided to play for time. A meeting between him and Addoula, Prime Minister of the Congo, was called at Kitona and they both attended on December 21. After hours of wrangling Tshombe — his mauled armies still valiantly battling the UN — signed an agreement that amounted to a virtual end of the Katangese secession. Tired and dispirited he flew back to Elisabethville and almost immediately the agreement became a dead duck.

The Katangese simply ignored the terms.

In the quarterless world of politics, Tshombe had seen his opening and taken it, neither more nor less principled than the men he had to deal with.

Meanwhile an uneasy ceasefire came into being in Katanga.

My thoughts turned to José's mischievous and challenging wink on our parting. He didn't really need to challenge me. There was no question but that I would return to Katanga. The country needed me and I needed Julia. It was that simple.

I dashed off a note to Julia asking her to send my passport and asking for news. Within a week the document came back express, with a note from Julia saying Tshombe himself was asking after me and wanting me back. The letter strengthened my resolve to return — UN or not. But how? I knew the UN would be watching Elisabethville airfield for me so it was impossible to take a regular flight. I also knew I couldn't very well pass openly through the Federal border posts, having just been deported from that country.

It suddenly struck me. I 'phoned Field Air Services at Germiston near Johannesburg, told them who I was, and asked if there was anybody going Katanga way.

'Well, you're certainly in luck,' the receptionist replied.

'We've got a Commanche in for repairs and it's due to return in a few days. Perhaps you can ride with that.'

'Who's taking her back?' I asked eagerly.

There was a shuffle of papers on the other end as the receptionist obviously looked through a file.

'Some people called Demoulin and de Wolf.'

I pursed my lips with surprise. I knew both of them from Elisabethville days when they had been in the Katangese Civil Air section. Dicey types.

'Thanks,' I said and put down the 'phone.

I managed to hobble down to the airfield later that day and had little difficulty finding Demoulin examining the Commanche.

'Have you had any instructions about me,' I asked after greetings were over.

'None at all,' Demoulin said with a bland smile.

Strange, I thought.

'Look, Tshombe wants me back. Please keep in touch with me at this number and I'll go back with you.'

Demoulin nodded absent-mindedly and went back to examining the aircraft.

I left with serious misgivings.

Two days later I still had not heard from them. I rang Field Aircraft Services and spoke to the same helpful official.

'What's happened to KAT 231,' I asked.

'Hell, that left the day before yesterday. Those two froggies took it the day after we last spoke. Back to Katanga I believe.'

'Thanks again,' was all I could manage before putting the 'phone down, shaking with rage.

Those bastards had deliberately left me for God knew what reason. I made a routine check at Defence Headquarters on the two pilots but drew a blank. Then I 'phoned Julia in Kolwezi and spilt my tale of woe.

She listened quietly and then said: 'Don't worry, we'll work out things from this side.'

The days dragged by and I became increasingly desperate about how to return to Katanga. Then very early one morning I received a 'phone call. It was Pierre Retief from South African Defence HQ.

'Been having fun, Jerry?'

'If you can call it that.'

Retief dropped his jocular tone and came straight to the point.

'We've received a message from your uncle. He's very keen that you return to the farm right away.'

I was momentarily stunned. Tshombe had actually contacted the South African Government to help get me back to Katanga? Astonishment and pride battled for upper place.

'There's just one problem, Pierre. I don't have any transport.'

'Contact Hedges and stand by at that number. You will be hearing from us', was all he said.

The 'phone went dead.

I shook my head in admiration at Tshombe's ability to pull the right strings. He really must need me.

Two days later another 'phone call and a message.

'We have the go, Jerry. Pick up Hedges and report to this address tonight before 20h00'. Retief read out a street address in Pretoria. 'Be prepared for travelling'.

It was a flurry of goodbyes and then we left for Pretoria.

The address turned out to be a tiny flat perched above a grocery store in Pretoria's northern suburbs. We knocked on the door and Retief opened it. He ushered us inside. A stocky, short haired man advanced to greet us with outstretched hand.

'Major, military intelligence', Retief tersely introduced his companion.

'He's going to be your guide for the first leg'.

The major nodded agreeably.

'You will be driving with the major to Messina tonight. Once there you will be met by a Security Police agent and escorted across the border. Federal contacts on the other side have arranged the rest of the trip. Good luck'.

We knew better than to ask too many questions.

'By the way, if you get caught, we don't know you from a bar of soap', Retief said coolly.

That night we drove hour after hour through the inky darkness, both Hedges and myself lost in thought. The major chain smoked all the way but was apparently relaxed behind the wheel of the powerful sedan.

Early next morning we grabbed a hasty breakfast at Messina. Three kilometers short of Beit bridge, the main link between South Africa and what was then Rhodesia, the major gently pulled the car on to the shoulder of the road behind a huge American saloon car.

Standing by it was a youngish looking man dressed in a crumpled grey suit.

'Piet, security', was all our guide said by way of introduction.

Still smiling, the young man opened the cavernous boot of the saloon car and gestured towards the yawning cavity.

'Not exactly first class but guaranteed draught free'.

Nothing loathe, Hedges and I clambered in, snuggled together and within seconds we were locked tightly in the enveloping dark. We hadn't even had a chance to say goodbye to our guide major.

The engine coughed into life and soon we were rocking gently with the motion of the car as we bore down on the border post.

Minutes later the car eased to a halt, we heard muffled voices, a burst of laughter and the slam of a door. Then the car slid forward a short while and stopped again.

Rhodesian customs.

More voices, laughter, a door slammed again.

An agony of delay while we waited in the confines of the boot, now unbearably cramped. Then there was a final shout and we were on our way out again.

Release from tension took over and Hedges and I writhed in paroxysms of laughter in the boot.

'It's called being booted out,' roared Hedges, and I held my sides.

We were still deafened by our laughter, red faced and eyes streaming with tears of mirth when our car again eased to halt and the boot was opened.

'What have you guys got in there with you — tear gas?' our guide asked.

We clambered, coughing out of the boot.

On the road in front of us was a small, battered VW. A lanky blonde man detached himself from some trees nearby and came over to us. More introductions. The new face was actually a member of the Federal Government security services.

I suddenly began to realise exactly how carefully orchestrated this whole operation was; obviously organised right from the top. Here was a member of the Federal Government actually assisting in the transport of two illegal immigrants across the country; the same two *illegals* who had been kicked out only fourteen days before.

The mind boggled.

Our new guide proved to be a friendly and entertaining young man and the rest of the journey to Salisbury was accomplished in high good humour.

That night we stayed over in Salisbury and then it was on to Lusaka.

At Lusaka we were put up by a Mister Bennet, employed by a large South African firm, and arrangements were made for a private air charter to fly us back. Early in the morning of December 27, Mr Bennet drove us to Kitwe and dropped us near the air strip. The last leg of the journey was about to begin.

Hedges and I strolled on to the airfield and towards a heavy jowled man working on a light aircraft. We knew our instructions and went right up to him.

'We're here,' I said simply.

He glanced at us, jerked a thumb in the direction of a nearby aircraft and told us he would be back. Ten minutes later the Cessna was airborne and we were heading north towards Katanga.

The pilot was a taciturn man who maintained almost complete silence for the entire journey. Only once did he give any sign of interest and that was when he dropped the aircraft low over some marshland near the border and pointed wordlessly to our port side.

Below us was the Dornier in which we had crashed three weeks before. She still lay on her back, undercarriage clawing at the sky, but stripped of virtually everything else.

As we looked down I thought incredulously of the scores of top level Federal officials, policemen, security policemen and politicians involved in getting us from the wreck to South Africa in maximum exposure and then from South Africa back to Katanga with maximum secrecy. And if we had just remained at that damn spot we might have been picked up by a helicopter and dropped back on the Katanga border.

We reached Kolwezi at mid morning and our small aircraft circled the field twice. Below I could see an official Katangese car bumping its way towards the landing strip. Even before the aircraft had taxied to a halt, the car was beside us. The door burst open and out jumped Julia. I was out of the Cessna's hatch in seconds and into her arms.

'*Bonjour, mon Commandant,*' she said teasingly. 'The new head of the Katangese Air Force will have to ensure that he completes his assignments more timeously in future. Twenty one days for one bombing mission to Elisabethville . . . Really!' She shook her head in mock seriousness.

Then we were hugging, kissing and laughing.

16

Pilots and Problems

The reason for Tshombe's determination to see me back in Katanga was for me to take over as Chief of the Air Force.

I was both pleased and apprehensive.

Julia and I walked arm-in-arm across the airfield to the administration building. I savoured the familiar scent and her warm proximity. Twenty five days had seemed an eternity.

'Are you sure about the promotion?' I asked.

'Quite sure. Tshombe personally ordered it and everybody here has known about it for some time. Delin is only too happy to hand over.'

Demoulin and de Wolf suddenly flashed into my mind. So that was why they were so keen to keep me out of Katanga. It wouldn't do to have a non-Belgian take over as Chief of the Air Force. I smiled inwardly.

As we approached the ops' office a harassed looking Delin rushed out and grabbed me by the hand.

'Glad to see you back, Jerry. Damn glad to see you back. You've heard about your promotion?'

'Well, not officially.'

'No problems, no problems. Believe me it's official and I'm damn glad. You can have my job with pleasure. All I want is a cushy job flying commercial aircraft in Belgium.'

'Why are you so keen to leave?'

'Three reasons: The UN has told me to go and go I will; half the bloody Katangese Air Force pilots and mechanics have stationed themselves at Kipushi with all the aircraft and won't come back, and finally, I'm just bloody tired of all this chaos.'

He waved a hand around the rocket-pocked airfield, the scrap aircraft, the idling guards and the litter of spare parts. Christ, the place certainly had gone down. I began to have doubts about my new appointment.

'Anyway,' Delin said, probably sensing he had gone too far. 'I wish you the best of luck.'

He turned and disappeared at a brisk pace towards where his car was parked.

Delin had been a pleasant enough man but with little sense of rapport with the black Katangese under his command. A South African Air Force trained pilot, Delin had been station commander of the Katangese Air Force in Kolwezi at the time of Magain - Dag Hammerskjöld crash period and had attended the UN inquiry into the death of the Secretary General. Shortly afterwards the UN had recommended to Tshombe that Delin be sent out.

I had never found Delin very effective as chief of the Air Force, but had always thrown my weight behind him.

I took a long look at the airfield and scratched my head. What it amounted to was that I was in charge of a run-down air base with all the aircraft held by a rebel faction three hundred kilometers away. I sighed deeply. Suddenly Julia's hand was in mine.

'Go for it, Jerry.' It was all the encouragement I needed.

The first step then was to establish my credentials with the hierarchy.

That very afternoon Julia and I drove all the way to Elisabethville, cleared the Gurkha checkpoints and won an audience with Tshombe himself. Quietly he listened to my problems and then gave a wave of the hand.

'Do exactly what you want, Commandant. I have confidence, and trust you will take all the steps necessary to get the air force functioning again.'

I bowed my thanks and clutching my official letter of appointment we hurried back to Kolwezi.

Second step was to establish a proper base for my air force. Mindful of technicalities, I had the air force HQ officially transferred from Elisabethville to Kolwezi, something nobody had thought of doing although we had not been operating from the capital for five months.

Then there was the whole atmosphere of the base at Kolwezi. It needed sharpening up.

I ordered all Katangese ground crews and base staff to parade and I set out exactly what was required. Within the day, work crews were pulling out the stores, neatly repacking them, repairing and repainting the more visible signs of the UN rocket damage. The old crocked aircraft were dragged away and dumped. I drew up proper duty rosters and ordered a general smartening up in uniformed personnel. Deadwood was ruthlessly chopped — Demoulin and de Wolf headed the list. By the end of the week I had reason to feel satisfied at the changes that had been wrought.

Now all we needed were the aircraft.

At that stage the rebel Air Force consisted of Peter Wicksteed, von Resighem, my old OC, and Verloo. With the entire air strength of three Commanches, they were undertaking the occasional night raid against the UN positions in Elisabethville but without very great success.

Verloo meanwhile was carrying on his passionate love affair with his Elisabethville resident mistress.

All three pilots obviously preferred proximity to the Katangese capital rather than the quieter Kolwezi life style.

I decided on a straight approach initially. My radio operator fired off a curt order instructing them to return to Kolwezi immediately. I signed it as Chief of the Air Force. Two days later we still had not had a reply. Right, I thought, time for a discreet show of force.

I drew up another message:

Chief of Air Force to all pilots Kipushi Base — Stop — Supply airbridge to

M'bulula imperative by presidential order — Stop — Further to this all repeat all Katangese air strength to report to Kolwezi at 06h00 January 14 — Stop — Acknowledge receipt — Message ends.

I gave one copy to the radio operator and the other I adorned with as many official stamps as I could find and sent it off post haste by despatch rider for personal delivery to the recalcitrant pilots.

Later that afternoon the radio operator handed me a message:

Air Base Kipushi to Puren — Stop — Message received — Stop — Affirmative RV Kolwezi 06h00 January 14 — Message ends.

I smiled to myself. As expected the pilots could hardly refuse to fly a bona fide mission, especially at the orders of the President. I picked up the 'phone and got through to the black Gendarme adjutant in charge of airfield defence.

Shortly before 06h00 the following day the three Commanches appeared from the south-east, circled the field once and then landed one after the other. They jolted to the parking bays and disgorged their pilots — the rebel three. As soon as they had alighted and started walking towards the administration block a detail of submachinegun-toting Gendarmes casually took up positions around the aircraft.

The adjutant, with a section of soldiers, stood expectantly at my door as the three were ushered into my office one by one. Wicksteed was the first.

'Hello, Jerry. Congratulations on your promotion', he said casually and dropped into an easy chair. I nodded affably and then came straight to the point.

Delin was telling me that there were some problems getting you guys to come back here', I said.

Wicksteed shrugged.

'We just feel that it's better to be out at Kipushi. Closer to the action'.

'And I think it's better that you operate from here — farther from the UN ground forces. I'd like you to move your operations back to Kolwezi from today'.

Wicksteed started to protest but I raised a warning hand.

'Look Peter, I'm not trying to pull rank but as far as I can see only one person can run this show at a time and at this present moment that person is me. Do we understand each other?'

Wicksteed started muttering darkly.

'If you don't like the arrangement that's fine by me. I can arrange to have you taken back to Kipushi by military transport and sent across the border'.

The ex-RAF pilot rose to his feet and walked over to the window. He looked out at the soldiers surrounding the aircraft, swung and scowled at the broad back of the adjutant planted in my doorway and then turned to me.

He held up his hands in mock surrender and sighed.

'You win, Jerry'.

Von Resighem eventually was the only one of the trio who preferred to remain in Elisabethville. My ploy had worked and I breathed more easily. I knew full well that I could not have afforded the loss of three top-class pilots.

It was the beginning of a long and difficult road as I battled to tame my wild bunch of pilots and form them into a relatively cohesive unit. The next few months I walked a tightrope between regular military authoritarianism and natural mercenary comradeship, balancing the legitimate demands and interests of the

Katangese Air Force against the pilots' natural disinclination to be anything but high flying individualists. I knew the minefield I was in; too strict and the pilots would, at the very least, refuse to fly and at the very worst, seek to put me out of business — permanently; renounce all leadership and the air force would fall apart as it had under Delin.

Eventually it was by dint of personal example and the pilots' fear of losing out on a lucrative means of employment that kept them in step — but only just.

As in all volunteer forces the real problem lay in the element of unreliability among the force. The pilots reserved the right to weigh the odds and pull out summarily if they didn't like them. Hedges had done that before, so had Glasspole.

But a pilot could only do it for so long and then he became a liability to his comrades and a target for his superiors. The worst that could happen was that he would be 'sent out'. Very few pilots actually suffered that fate and there were a few who came perilously close to being unceremoniously kicked out.

In overview though, when I think back on the type of operations that we did and the planes we had, I think we gave a very fair account of ourselves. When it was necessary to do bombing runs, dangerous as they might be, I never usually found it difficult to find somebody to crew with me.

Salaries were high — very rarely below a thousand US dollars a month — and the pilots were able to live fast and dangerously on that salary in the high spots of Elisabethville and later Leopoldville. Some of the people I worked with in Katanga were to remain in close touch with me during the ensuing years. Like old friends returning for a reunion they would jet back into the Congo in times of war or revolt . . . they were Tshombe's soldier children.

I tried religiously to restrict myself only to considerations of the pilot's work and his competency and ignore his outside life. But this was easier said than done.

Some of my brood of adventurers and carpetbaggers had the wit and charm of professional diplomats; wittily they conned each other and charmingly they stole from outsiders. In general, the greatest losers were the Katangese people and in particular, the Katangese Government.

All the pilots, with rare exceptions, had some 'deal' or racket working for them; some with government funds, some with taking bribes from traders for extra air space freightage, some discreet and gentlemanly, some crude and violent.

One incident comes particularly to mind. It was in mid-1964 and we were then in Leopoldville, as always in Tshombe's service, but this time in different circumstances. A number of mercenary pilots were then in town, deep into the usual Congo racketeering and double dealing. Late one stinking hot night, I received an urgent 'phone call from a Surete official to say that one of my pilots had been shot at an address in Leopoldville.

I eventually located the place, Tavern Sentimentale, a tatty bar in the combat quarter of town. Pushing through the jostling crowd I found one of my Belgian pilots sitting bolt upright in a chair in an anteroom to the main saloon. He had the touch of death in his ashen face, sweat beading his marble forehead, lips trembling but unable to speak. The front of his pale blue shirt was covered with a huge and startling rosette of blood. Around him hovered two of my most trusted pilot comrades.

'What happened?' I asked wearily.

'Shot himself', replied one pilot without flinching. 'Something about a girl.'

I busied myself trying to staunch the flow of blood. Seconds later an ambulance arrived and the pilot, by now wracked with tearing gasps, was loaded into the vehicle and raced through the streets of the Congolese capital. I followed to the hospital where an emergency team began resuscitation there and then in the hospital corridor. It was too late and the young pilot died minutes later.

The secret of what had happened that night died of course with the pilot. As did the secret of what happened to the enormous filched diamond and several million stolen francs the pilot was known to have had in his possession right up to the time he went drinking that night with my two pilot colleagues; as did the secret of how a man can shoot himself in the chest with a heavy calibre pistol and not leave scorch marks on his clothes.

Back to Kolwezi. While in the town all pilots were accommodated at the Bon Auberge Hotel opposite Delin's old flat which I had by then requisitioned. It was an old colonial hotel with a good bar and dancing every Saturday night. An even greater attraction was the owner who proved himself possessed of superhuman patience. Month after month he would religiously try and collect his bills from the pilots and month after month he would be deftly evaded.

In Katanga, one friend was continuously in trouble. He showed a propensity for operating other people's bank accounts which badly backfired one day when he started blithely drawing from a fellow pilot's account under the mistaken impression that the pilot was not returning to the Congo. The pilot did in fact return and discovered the fraud. Instead of wreaking personal and probable violent revenge, the pilot took the most uncharcteristic step of reporting it to the Katangese *Surete*. My poor friend was dragged off to court, convicted and thrown into a stinking Katangese jail until the combined pressure of increased UN raids and my pleadings managed to bail him out to come and fly a new consignment of aircraft. And so he went.

The attitude of the black Katangese to all this crookery was, of course, one of anger and suspicion of all white personnel. The black members of the Air Force were quite aware of the penchant for dishonesty among the mercenary pilots and strongly resented it. Unfortunately they had neither the flying skills nor the expertise for running the air force, a fact pragmatically accepted by Tshombe. The antagonism of the black Katangese, however, was never better demonstrated than the day Glasspole returned to Katanga.

The Katanga veteran had actually returned at my bidding. As soon as I took over I had set about finding where Glasspole had got to because, at that stage I still had a very high regard for his administrative and flying skills. Tracked down to Northern Rhodesia, he was cordially invited to return.

Within days he was back, irrepressible as ever but this time (did I imagine it) slightly apprehensive.

The day he arrived I received a message to see Tshombe in Elisabethville. I decided to make a round trip to Kipushi to speak to the ground crews there who, only the day before, had been deprived of their three Commanches by my tactical action against the rebel pilots. I decided to take Glasspole along.

The New Zealander-Canadian and I clambered into a Piper Tri- pacer and set course for Kipushi. Minutes after take off Glasspole fell uncharacteristically silent.

'What's up?' I asked as we landed.

'Nothing at all,' he replied, apprehensively eyeing the crowd of Katangese ground crew and Air Force personnel coming out to meet us.

I recognised the leader of the black Katangese delegation, Lieutenant Tumba Joseph, an air frame mechanic and in nominal charge of the ground staff at Kipushi. I guessed that they would be unhappy about the sudden relocation of the aircraft to Kolwezi and I was not to be disappointed.

'What's happened to our aircraft, Commandant?' Tumba demanded with a mixture of plaintiveness and arrogance.

It was time for diplomacy and I started out by praising the ground crews at Kipushi for the fine work they had done on the Commanches and begging them to come to Kolwezi. It seemed to work. The murmurs of dissatisfaction died down.

Then suddenly Tumba pointed to Glasspole, who was standing quietly beside me, and burst into a stream of quite unintelligible French. The others joined in the outburst. All of it apparently aimed at Glasspole.

'What are they saying?' I asked, my French unequal to the torrent of words.

Glasspole meanwhile had gone deadly white and was desperately casting around for a means of escape.

'What's worrying them?' I asked again.

'They don't like me,' Glasspole blurted out.

'That's obvious, but why?'

Glasspole shrugged.

'Something about money,' he muttered.

A section of the crowd seemed about to lay hands on Glasspole.

It was time to assert myself.

'This man's coming with me to see the President today,' I announced grandly. 'We'll see what he has to say about this display.'

'Well, we're coming too,' the burly Lieutenant Tumba shouted, uncowed and stepped smartly forward. Mwanke Gregoire, another mechanic, joined him.

Nothing for it, I decided, and Glasspole, myself and the two black Katangese officers climbed into a car. In tense silence we gingerly negotiated the road blocks all the way to Elisabethville. Several times I tried to pump Glasspole as to the reasons for the Katangese hostility but always he shrugged it off.

At the presidential palace we were granted an audience with Tshombe and General Muke. As Glasspole and I strode into the august presence of the President we were uncomfortably aware that, hard on our heels came the determined and indignant Tumba and colleague. We all four came to a halt before the President's desk. Tshombe seemed a little disconcerted about the size of the deputation but, nevertheless, began giving Glasspole and I our orders.

The mere mention of Glasspole's name was enough to bring forth another torrent of denunciation from Tumba about Glasspole, the State Treasury, individuals' bank accounts and the mess funds. Tshombe cut the man short with a wave of the hand and repeated emphatically that Glasspole was to remain on the Air Force strength. The little pilot breathed easier while I tried to make head or tail of Tumba's accusations.

130

Then suddenly the spotlight was on me. Tumba launched into a diatribe against the appointment of a white man to head the Air Force when better black officers were available.

Again Tshombe cut him short and patiently explained that as President, he was not in the habit of reversing his orders. The constant interruptions from Tumba were just too much for the quick-tempered General Muke who climbed into Tumba and forced him from the room in a torrent of swear words and some resounding whacks with his baton. All rather unfortunate I felt.

In retrospect the little scene with the black Katangese officers in Tshombe's office was cathartic. After that Tumba and I became close associates and we worked extremely well together. I like to believe that the black Katangese realised that my intentions were not exploitative and that I identified with the political aspirations of the Katangese. I too felt fury at the white mercenaries who selfishly built personal empires while Katanga was struggling for its life.

The fact that I willingly flew dangerous missions and was never implicated in a racket also counted for a lot. And then there was the simple question of human relations. I never pushed anybody around, black or white, never ordered anybody on a mission that would be dangerous.

I just made sure that I volunteered first and then let it be known that all comers were welcome. The method never failed.

17

Palace Revolt

And so we began from scratch to build an Air Force. We had three Commanches, a Dove and one remaining serviceable Dornier; a start at least.

Then one hot midday the dauntless Magain, pickled as usual, claimed the Dornier for a mission. Misjudging the runway, he aborted the take off, flipped the aircraft and wiped out our surviving Dornier. The little Belgian emerged from the wreckage with a sheepish grin on his face. Then there were only three Commanches and a Dove.

A few weeks later we were able to supplement our strength with two aircraft. I appealed to Tshombe to make his personal DC4 available to us. At the time it was being flown by the Rhodesian Jack Malloch, civil airline owner, in Salisbury. The Abbe Fulbert Youlou of Congo Brazzaville, a staunch ally of Tshombe, had meanwhile also declared he would donate his private Heron.

Things began to look up.

On the borders of Katanga, meanwhile, the situation had deteriorated dramatically. Under the protective shield of the UN the ANC troops had moved in and engaged Tshombe's Gendarmerie.

With supply lines cut by the United Nations and their mercenary advisors constantly harassed, the Gendarmes were at an obvious disadvantage.

By January that year the ANC had reached Kongolo, where they celebrated the victory by butchering twenty three missionaries, and were menacing M'Bulula, Manono and Nyemba.

The United Nations must have applauded.

The situation was critical, and we were convinced of the urgent need for an air bridge to the beleaguered troops in the north.

Supply efforts were redoubled and week after week we flew in quantities of desperately needed ammunition, weapons, food and medical supplies to the bush strip at M'Bulula. On the return runs we would bring back casualties — bandaged, bleeding victims of the treacherous bush warfare, stretcher-ridden soldiers whose distinguishing feature was an incredible stoicism despite the most fearsome wounds and the often rudimentary bush medication.

On the international front Tshombe had refused a UN demand that it be allowed to occupy Jadotville or Kolwezi.

The ANC would be right behind, Tshombe had soundly argued.

Shortly afterwards, however, Tshombe agreed to visit Addoula in Leopoldville — an indication if ever of the Katangese leader's determination to seek a peaceful solution.

On March 15 Tshombe arrived in Leopoldville with the UN and British guarantees of safety and began negotiations with Addoula, always under close and restricting UN supervision. After several breakdowns Tshombe offered an option that would allow an allocation of Katangese financial resources to the central government but would leave the Gendarmerie intact.

In an effort to hasten negotiations Addoula suddenly went on a tour of Equateur Province leaving Tshombe with a set of unacceptable proposals.

Tshombe left for home on April 19, astutely ducking the implicit ultimatum.

Again the treacherous ANC tried to bar his exit but the UN, for once, honoured its undertaking and Tshombe was given free egress.

On his return to Leopoldville Addoula accused Tshombe of bad faith and threatened he would seek military aid from the Afro-Asian bloc.

Back in Katanga I was busy re-equipping the Gendarmes in M'Bulula, staging area for the proposed counter thrust into Kongolo. Both Muke and Tshombe had impressed upon us the urgent necessity to recapture Kongolo — for strategic and prestigious reasons.

Then early one March Sunday the Katangese Gendarmes under Colonel Kimwanga and the Belgian mercenary, Christian Tavernier, struck in battalion strength at the ANC in Kongolo.

It was a rout.

Still dazed from the traditional Saturday night debauchery the ANC broke from their positions and stumbled off into the bush with hardly a struggle.

So hastily did the staff officers desert their HQ that the Congolese flag fell intact into Colonel Kimwanga's hands.

Minutes after the last erratically firing ANC troops had been driven from the centre of the town I landed on the airstrip in the Dove with more equipment and instructions. At the ANC HQ I found Kimwanga holding the blue and gold starred flag draped over his arm. Around him the Katangese Gendarmes were rooting through the building looking for documents and prisoners. An ANC officer lay sprawled dead across the entrance to the room and all visitors stepped nonchalantly over his inert form.

Sporadic firing could still be heard from the northern sector of the town.

'Take this back to the President to prove our victory,' said a beaming Kimwanga, reverently handing me the flag.

I grinned and returned to the Dove.

The flag was later to feature prominently at a Press conference called by President Tshombe to announce the capture of Kongolo.

Shortly after this, and completely unknown to me, Tshombe left for Europe for medical treatment and for some hush-hush negotiations not entirely unconnected with the future of the Katangese Air Force.

It was at this crucial juncture, with Tshombe away, that palace politics among the white civilian advisors in Elisabethville intruded disastrously into the supply work carried out by the Katangese Air Force. One day I was suddenly summoned to the presidential palace for a round table.

At the palace we were ushered into a hall packed with white civilian advisors — some of them former members of the Civil Aviation branch of the *Travaux Publics,* people like Bertier and Andrieux, and a number of black Katangese officials. Presiding over the meeting was the Prime Minister, Evariste, Kimba and General Muke. Julia, the ubiquitous Glasspole and I slipped into vacant seats at the back of the room.

Kimba came straight to the point and explained that the military functions of the Katangese Air Force were to be taken over by the *Travaux Publics* and all our aircraft were to function strictly according to civil aviation standards.

I was stunned.

Not a word had been mentioned about this before and already I could see in my mind's eye the possible disastrous consequences. Although I had no authority to oppose the decision I felt I could not stand idly by; I had to say something for the record.

'Mister Prime Minister, might I ask the reason for this rather sudden decision?' I asked, rising to my feet.

'Commandant Puren, It is of no concern of yours', was the curt rejoinder.

I ploughed on regardless.

'Mister Prime Minister, I feel it my duty to bring to your attention the possible terrible consequences of this action. Spares are in critically short supply. We could not possibly operate our aircraft to strict civil aviation standards. Whatever problems we have now will be magnified a thousand fold if we allow . . ?

I had hardly begun to talk before one of the *Travaux Publics* officials was on his feet interrupting. Ever the gentleman, I resumed my seat and was forced to listen to twenty minutes of justifications, denials, boasts and assertions by the official. Not only would the aircraft be better maintained than hitherto but they would provide an even better service. When the official finished I rose again and addressed Kimba above the hubbub.

'Mister Prime Minister, might I request the *Travaux Publics* to explain what is to happen to the troops we are presently supplying in the North. Are they still to have recce services?'

A sudden silence fell on the room. The Belgian advisor struggled to his feet and told Kimba that that was still a matter for discussion between the *Travaux Publics* and General Muke.

I turned to Kimba again.

'Mister Prime Minister, I would respectfully like to suggest that I cannot be held responsible for any of the misunderstandings that may arise between the air wing and the army because of this arrangement.'

I sat down. There was nothing further to say. Kimba assured me that I would still be in charge of flying operations.

The administration of the air wing was, however, to be sited in Elisabethville and a few *Travaux Publics* officials would be based in Kolwezi. And that was that.

As far as the takeover went, Tshombe and his advisors believed there were sound political reasons for the move. The President obviously felt that the United Nations pressure was near breaking point and it was held advisable to halt the military air operations as a placatory gesture and put the whole air force under completely civil administration. For my part I could not quite shake off the suspicion that the Belgians, active in both Elisabethville and Leopoldville, had stuck their oar in somewhere.

The scheme was greeted by the Katangese Belgian advisors with delight on two counts. Firstly, they got their hands on the thirty million franc air force budget to balance their own books and secondly, they believed they had usurped my position.

The last ambition came as no surprise to me. The overwhelming majority of Belgian advisors believed they should have a monopoly of positions of influence and authority in Katanga.

Because of their former colonial status in the Congo they felt they had first pick of the administrative positions in independent Katanga or the Congo.

All other nationalities were thus regarded with suspicion and often downright hostility. In my case it was regarded as incomprehensible that a foreigner, and a South African at that, should be in such a position of authority. The invective that had been directed at me personally by the Belgians at our meeting with Kimba only served to convince me of the depth of the hostility.

I shrugged figurative shoulders and watched the little air wing go exactly the way I had predicted it would go — downwards.

Travaux Publics's first step was to ground all the aircraft for a week to inspect if they were up to civil aviation standards.

The response from the embattled troops in Kongolo was immediate and vociferous.

Desperate messages flooded in from the front for the life line of food and ammunition to be re-established.

But, no.

With Katanga struggling for its life the *Travaux Publics* insisted that the aircraft be maintained at international aviation standards.

It would have been a comedy if it were not so tragic.

Eventually we managed to get one aircraft to Kongolo with supplies. Its return brought a very disgruntled Colonel Kimwanga, area commander in Kongolo. The tall, well-spoken Katangese came straight to the point when he saw me at Kolwezi.

'What the hell's going on, Jerry? We don't have food, ammo or evacuation facilities for the wounded.' he said.

'Easy, Colonel. I'm not in charge of the Air Force any more and the people who are don't think it is essential to supply the front.'

Kimwanga grimaced angrily and swung on his heel. He stalked off to find Muke.

Although distressed at the problems faced by Kimwanga and his men I could not suppress a little feeling of vindictive pleasure that the takeover had indeed been as disastrous as I warned.

General Muke apparently promised some sort of compromise but things continued deteriorating. From flying twelve tons of supplies a day to Kongolo we were now down to three or four tons. Even a fool could see that the army was being slowly strangled. Aircraft that had previously been available at a moment's notice for operations from the front were now grounded, and critically injured Gendarmes were needlessly dying at the makeshift casualty clearing stations waiting for the arrival of non-existent aircraft. Worse still, an element of the pilots under my command took advantage of the new civilian guise of the air wing and refused to fly military supplies, recces or lift out the wounded.

To their eternal credit Bracco, Libert, Wicksteed and Vosloo were not part of this element.

Large scale corruption, never far below the surface in any part of the Congo, came to the air wing in a big way. In an effort to stimulate commerce in Northern Katanga it had been decided to allow traders from the southern regions limited transport facilities on the aircraft for their goods.

Between carrying vital military equipment and missionary Len Robinson's US AID stores, the amount of room left to the traders was necessarily curtailed. Inevitably corruption reared its ugly head as the traders bought extra space on the aircraft from people such as Glasspole. It was difficult to pinpoint or to prove but it was there — a constant albatross to the air wing's genuine relief and supply operations to the north.

For my part, I took my Commanche on many surreptitious missions to the front on recce operations for the army. As I was the only pilot doing this type of work my little snooping Commanche became a familiar sight to the ANC ground forces who always showed a high regard for the work I was doing by letting fly at my aircraft with everything except the mess cat.

The mismanagement of the aircraft and flying time by the *Travaux Publics* was meanwhile wreaking havoc on ground forces' morale. Always plentiful supplies of food and ammunition were now severely rationed, proper intelligence by air recce was limited and the reassuring knowledge that the wounded could be airlifted out was now gone. The mutters of disapproval became a roar and inevitably reached the ears of Muke and Tshombe on the latter's return from Europe.

On one of the recce missions to the north that April of 1962 I happened to come across somebody who was later to become a powerful and loyal friend — Godefroid Munongo, Minister of the Interior.

I had just landed my Commanche at Kaminaville airfield and alighted when an airfield official rushed over.

'Where are you going?' he asked breathlessly.

'Recce up towards Kongolo.'

'Forget it. The Balubas have cut the rail link to Lubudi and the Minister of the Interior is stranded here. We called for an aircraft from Kolwezi but . . .' he shrugged shoulders expressively. I knew what he meant — *Travaux Publics* inefficiency. 'The minister desperately needs to get to Lubudi. Can you take him?'

'Sure,' I answered and signalled to the ground crew to refuel the Commanche.

It was not the first time I met the minister but it was the first time I had actually had a chance to have a decent conversation with him.

He arrived at the aircraft; tall, fine featured — and — as befitted Bayeke royalty — slightly arrogant. Politely he bowed his thanks and then clambered into the Commanche. We jolted across the runway and then lifted into the sky.

Munongo was a relaxed passenger and an easy conversationalist. Inevitably the Katangese situation came up for discussion; the travails of the infant country. Imperceptibly the conversation moved to the mercenaries and the takeover of the Air Force. I seized my opportunity.

'Mr Minister, you might be aware the Air Force was recently taken over by the *Travaux Publics*. I wonder if I might discuss the merits of that move with you.'

Munongo nodded his acquiescence. I launched into a background to the takeover, the immediate results of it and the possible future effects. It was a sombre picture and I spared no effort in painting it as accurately as I saw it. The minister nodded several times as I spoke and once posed a question. Behind those perennial dark glasses I could imagine his eyes brooding over what I had just told him.

When I had finished he nodded his head once.

'Commandant, thank you for your opinion. I will certainly carry this information back to the correct quarters.'

We went back to discussing general topics.

Shortly after this trip the rangy Rhodesian, Jack Malloch, brought the DC4 from Salisbury and we were able to marginally boost our supplies to the north.

The disastrous *Travaux Publics* takeover ended as suddenly as it had begun.

Tshombe, on one of his many meet-the-people trips was taking a train ride to his home town of Sandoa and passing through Kolwezi. At the station, accordingly, a huge crowd of Katangese had gathered and on the platform was a little knot of the *Travaux Publics* officials.

Although they had known beforehand about the arrival of Tshombe they had not bothered to tell me and it was only because Julia and I were picked up personallly by Kimwanga, then in Kolwezi, that we arrived at the station at all.

As soon as we reached the platform I marched up to the most senior Belgian adviser and demanded to know why I had not been informed.

'I didn't know Tshombe wanted to see you', was his evasive reply.

'Neither do I, but at least for protocol's sake you should have told me', I replied heatedly.

The man shrugged and I stamped off to stand a little way apart from the officials. Julia was with me and soon a few senior Gendarme officers, including Kimwanga, joined us. It was clear where their sympathies were.

The train arrived amid great excitement. Tshombe alighted, addressed and greeted the waiting group of civic dignitaries, walked right past the knot of gawping *Travaux Publics* officials and with an affectionate grin, greeted Julia, myself and the officers.

Tshombe beckoned the *Travaux Publics* officials over and there and then on the platform we had a round table discussion.

The President had obviously been briefed about the state of the air wing but nevertheless he asked my opinion. I held back no punches and in front of the silent *Travaux Publics* officials catalogued the list of omissions, errors and inadequacies that had accompanied their administration.

None of them even attempted to contest my charges.

'Commandant Puren will now take charge of the air force again and the *Travaux Publics* will have one aircraft for their purposes', Tshombe said definitively and moved off.

Unfortunately, he never said anything about the budget.

The *Travaux Publics* eventually handed over all the aircraft except for the one Dove which, it is interesting to note, crashed a bare two months later killing Fouke and his Italian air mechanic at the controls. While taking off, the heavily laden

Dove had developed engine trouble and spun in. During the entire time I ran the Katangese Air Force on a shoestring and gum basis, we never lost a single pilot. In a few months the *Travaux Publics*, flying according to international civil aviation standards, managed to claim the lives of two men.

Both Muke and Kimba were later to apologise to me for the takeover.

The little interlude with the *Travaux Publics* proved at least one thing. That in the most trying conditions, dedication and ingenuity can overcome those problems which bureaucracy and convention only amplify.

By the beginning of August 1962 our air lift was functioning better than ever and the Katangese Gendarmes were holding the ANC on a wide front.

In August also I had the dubious honour of ferrying my former captors, the United Nations representatives, on an inspection tour of Northern Katanga. It happened like this: the ANC had been making thrusts into Northern Katanga for some time, all of which were stoutly denied by Leopoldville and the United Nations. To prove his point Tshombe decided to challenge the United Nations representatives remaining in Katanga to undertake a tour of the area by air to see the ANC dispositions for themselves.

Accordingly, at 09h00 a neatly dressed Malloch and Puren landed the Katangese DC3 at Elisabethville airfield and taxied to the airport building. I noted with quiet satisfaction the considerable damage to the installations our earlier impudent bombing raids had wreaked. I also saw with real regret the fourteen Katangese aircraft seized in the first war, still wired off and mouldering under UN guard.

A mixed bag of six military and civilian personnel clambered aboard and we took off into the steadily warming air.

Prime Minister Kimba was the guide; I was tour manager.

At that stage I was the only pilot who had been flying recce missions so I knew exactly where the ANC were; Lord knew they had shot at me often enough.

For four hours we wheeled over the densely wooded north Katanga landscape, diving low over the known ANC dispositions circling many of the disputed areas. In a number of these areas the Central Government flag could quite clearly be seen fluttering and, on more than one occasion, a rattle of gunfire greeted our arrival.

After two such receptions, the last particularly warm, the UN representatives decided they had seen enough and would be happy to return to base.

Point proved.

18

New Arrivals and
One Near Permanent Departure

I twice rubbed my eyes hard. Then once more. The apparitions still did not disappear. Squatting proprietorially on the Kolwezi runway below was a Vampire jet fighter. In the circuit above the airfield with me were three stubby nosed T6 fighter trainers, unmarked and gleaming burnished silver in the clear September sunlight. What the hell was going on? United Nations aircraft at Kolwezi? Impossible. They would have had the insignia of the country of origin. Central Government? Our airfield defences would have shot them up.

Only other alternative was that they were ours.

Impatiently I called up the tower and sent my little Commanche dipping into its approach run. Once on the deck I raced it towards where a knot of people, including a number of new faces, were gathered around the jet. The Katangese ground crew made way for me as I pushed through the crowd to find myself facing a stocky, middle-aged man leaning nonchalantly against the jet.

He thrust his hand out and took mine in a finger pulping grip.

'Wojik, sir. Stefan Wojik with the first consignment of T6s for the President. Mr Browne will be arriving later to take charge.'

Two surprises for me. I didn't know the President had ordered any new aircraft and who the hell was Mr Browne anyway?

The mystery was soon solved. On his last trip to Europe, Tshombe had contacted an international arms dealer in Paris, Pierre Laureys by name, and bought a consignment of ten T6's and two Vampire jets for an undisclosed sum. Part of the package deal involved the hire of the necessary pilots. Lorez had contacted swashbuckling adventurer-cum-smuggler, Jean Zumbach, then running a restaurant in Paris, and asked him to take care of the details. Zumbach, alias Mr Browne, was an expatriate Pole who found little difficulty in raising his mercenary pilot strength from fellow Polish refugees of the same hardy and competent east European stock that bred such people as Sputnik Gurkitz.

The actual purchase of the aircraft and the hire of the pilots was done in the greatest secrecy because of the UN surveillance and Tshombe's earlier assurances that he was not recruiting mercenaries. Zumbach, formerly RAF, became plain Mr Browne and the aircraft were to be classified as purely civilian.

Introductions over, I decided to take a closer look at Tshombe's acquisitions. My first flush of enthusiasm cooled rather rapidly.

A cursory examination of the Vampire showed that although it had made it to Katanga, there was no certainty it would ever be able to take off again. The whole engine needed an overhaul and the nearest place for that was Johannesburg. We could cross that Vampire off our list.

The T6s were a little more promising. Although completely unarmed, I was sure we could rig electronic circuits for bomb racks. Rocket pods were out of the question and a brush of camouflage paint was urgently required.

As I stood surveying the decrepit Vampire and the toothless T6s I shook my head sadly. Tshombe had been taken for a ride with this lot. What we could have rather done with was several B26 bombers, which I later learned had also been available, and Tri-Pacers fitted with machineguns and rockets. It would have been enough to have blasted the UN troops from their smug complacency and machinegunned them out of the cities. Anyhow, I sighed, we had to make do with what we had.

I walked to my office and put a call through to the President's residence in Elisabethville.

'The first consignment of aircraft has arrived from Europe, Mister President', I informed Tshombe.

'I am pleased to hear it, Commandant. Have you had a chance of examining them?'

'Yes I have, Mister President.'

'What is your opinion?'

He noticed my hesitation.

'Your honest opinion, Commandant.'

'Mister President, the jet will never be serviceable for operations unless it goes to South Africa. The other aircraft needs a lot of work. They have no machineguns or rocket rails. At present they are no more use than the Commanches.'

There was a pause.

'Commandant, I would be grateful if you take the necessary steps to see that they are rigged sufficiently to be used for offensive action.'

'Thank you, Mister President.'

I hesitated a second and then decided to pop the question.

'There is one thing that concerns me, Mr President. I understand a Mr Browne is coming soon to take over the new consignment of aircraft. I would ask what my position in the Air Force is to be?'

Tshombe sighed deeply.

'I made certain agreements in Europe with the arms dealers . . .'. He tailed off for a moment. As if hesitating to tell me more. 'But please let's leave that question until Mr Browne arrives.'

'As you wish, sir.'

'One last point, Commandant.'

'Yes Mister President.'

'Please see that the pilots who have arrived are accommodated in Kolwezi as discreetly as possible. I am sure you will appreciate the delicate state of our relations with the UN. At this stage they must have no hint of our arrangements, certainly not before the rest of the consignment is here safely.'

140

'Of course, Mister President.'

The 'phone went dead.

I smiled to myself. Keep secret the arrival in Kolwezi of a Vampire Jet, three T6s and four wild-eyed mercenary airmen? Fat chance.

Several days later the mysterious Mr Browne, alias Jean Zumbach, arrived with the other seven T6s. At first sight I was impressed by him. Powerfully built, intelligent eyes, he had that authoritative, competent air so essential for commanding mercenary forces.

As soon as he had landed he was surrounded by his fellow pilots, all firing questions at him which, I gathered centred largely on the question of pay. Zumbach deftly parried the questions, broke through the importuning pilots and came striding over to where I was standing aside.

'Commandant Puren,' I said.

'Mr Browne,' he said with a wink.

We walked together towards my office chatting about the flight over and the T6s performances. In my office Zumbach asked me to contact the President. I put the call through to Elisabethville and handed the receiver to him. It was apparent that he and Tshombe were old friends.

'Mr Brown here, Mr President. Your loyal servant has landed in your beautiful country with the consignment as requested.'

I began to have my first doubts about Zumbach.

'No, no problems at all . . . perfect trip. All safe . . . No, the restaurant is doing fine, thank you . . . Yes. Who? Oh, Commandant Puren, yes, we've met . . . Both of us? Immediately, Mister President.' He replaced the receiver. 'The old man wants to see us both in Elisabethville, now.'

I borrowed Julia's father's Mercedes and soon the pair of us were speeding east through the Gurkha checkpoints to the presidential palace. On the way Zumbach regaled me with details of his rather checkered past and the restaurant he owned in Paris.

Once in Elisabethville we went into conference with the President. Secrecy was of the utmost importance, said Tshombe, because the UN were spoiling for another excuse to fight. I remained discreetly sceptical of our chances of keeping the secret longer than a few days. Then the President got down to the nitty gritty.

'Mr Browne, you will take over as head of the air force.'

As if to forestall any objections from me (I actually didn't have any) Tshombe nodded towards me and said : 'Commandant, because of your long and valuable experience you are to remain operational chief of the Air Force. Because of your increased responsibility you will of course be paid commensurately.'

I bowed my thanks.

Actually my designation and de-designation as head of the Katangese Air Force meant very little to me. My work remained essentially the same, my pay never decreased and my responsibilities stayed static. I had no objection to Zumbach's takeover provided he could do the work required of him. We both returned to Kolwezi on good terms.

The very next day Browne disappeared back to Europe via Angola. It was the first of many away trips that were to give him great scarcity value as far as combat action in Katanga went. It became quite clear to me that my sphere of operations was to remain virtually unchanged despite a nominal new head of the Air Force.

I turned my attention to the ten brand new T6s squatting on the apron under camouflage netting. The first and most obvious task was to set up electronic circuits for the bomb racks. I didn't have far to look for an electrical contractor. Julia's father owned one of the biggest electrical engineering firms in Kolwezi and was delighted to accept the job. The very next day, Victor and his two sons, Raymond and Michel, pitched up with their equipment and from then on for the next two weeks they worked ceaselessly on the expectant row of T6s. I couldn't resist an inward smile. Julia in radio control, José a pilot, Victor the electrical contractor and his two sons assisting. It was indeed a family affair.

Day after day the trio toiled through the summer's heat over the aircraft. Twelve year old Michel threaded the flex through the more inaccessible parts of the aircraft. One by one the trainers changed coats from gleaming silver to drab camouflage olive green, yellow and khaki patches. It was all completed in two weeks. The ten T6s stood in a silent row, menacing in their war paint, threatening with the bomb racks under their wings.

Fully loaded they could carry one hundred kilograms of bombs, one fifty kilogram bomb under each wing. On the tailplane and wings of each aircraft proudly glinted the triple copper cross of the Katangese Air Force insignia.

I rang Tshombe and told him that we had the aircraft ready and armed, the pilots waiting and a target earmarked. The only thing missing was the Chief of the Air Force.

'Go right ahead on your own, Commandant. Good luck and well done.'

That evening I called all the pilots together — Browne's collection of mid-European refugees and my rag tag brood of adventurers. As I surveyed the dozen faces I knew there was bad news for the ANC on the way. We crowded into the ops' room while I unfurled a number of large scale maps of northern and north eastern Katanga.

'Gentlemen, tomorrow we go operational for the first time in squadron strength. It is to be a show of strength along the front and also an effective demonstration of our offensive capability. We can't afford to waste the impact of our first appearance so we must hit hard and accurately. The sight of those ten aircraft tomorrow is going to scare the hell out of the ANC and put a little heart into our own people.'

I tapped the map with my indicator.

'We lift off at first light and fly north north west along the Kaniama front in a show of force. Then it's on to Katea and Kipombe, here, west of Kongolo on the road to Sentery. These towns are important staging areas for the transport of the ANC; put these out of action and we interrupt their supplies for months.'

I looked at the expectant faces. There was little doubt Katea and Kipombe were in for a shock.

It was with a special sort of pride that I led the ten dappled T6s out of the Kolwezi circuit in the dawn light next day and headed them north in loose box formation. At that stage, apart from the UN, there was no Air Force in the Congo to compete with our flight of armed and expertly piloted trainers.

A thousand meters below I could see the upturned faces and pointing arms of groups of civilians and villagers as we droned towards our target. Near Kaniama we passed directly over the no-man's land between the ANC and the Katangese. I would dearly have loved to have launched a little dive bombing along the ANC emplacements, but I felt it important that we should not blunt the effect of our entry into the theatre with isolated tactical strikes against dispersed ground troops. I smiled wryly as we passed unmolested over the ANC lines, the soldiers obviously so astonished at our appearance as to wonder who we really were. The Gendarmes knew; we could see them waving from their trenches as the shadows of our aircraft fled across the ground below.

Then forty minutes later we were approaching Katea. I couldn't repress a tightening of my stomach muscles at the exhilarating prospect of a squadron force raid. The radio was buzzing with chatter between the pilots. I called for silence and we roared closer and closer towards the unsuspecting Katea.

Suddenly the town was below us, several blocks of central shops and businesses, some dusty streets, then sprawling residential slums on the outskirts. On the western side of the town nestled our target, a radio transmitter, extensive stores and transport area.

Once past the town we swung wide to port and circled back. With the squadron due east of Katea again I spoke evenly over the radio.

'Kinghorn to flight. Beginning bombing run now. Out.'

The T6 banked steeply to port, the drone of her engine rising to a high pitched nasal whine as we dropped like a falcon towards our target. At a thousand meters we levelled off. I checked our rear. One after the other the T6s were peeling off and following us in.

I hadn't seen anything like it for more than ten years.

Suddenly we were shooting over the target area. I depressed the button on the bomb release control and felt the aircraft perceptively lift with the release of weight. I looked below. The two black specks curved gracefully down and down until both miraculously became transposed into a billowing mushroom of smoke and fire. One bomb struck a shed and the other the edge of a vehicle park. I just had a chance to see a jeep speeding away west. Then we were over the target and climbing steeply.

Minutes later the squadron had reformed and we were flying a final run over the town.

What an unholy mess!

The explosions had torn loose iron sheeting leaving crooked, twisted pieces of metal pointing skywards, virtually all the sheds had been blown flat, the transmitter station was horribly scarred and vehicles lay scattered and broken across the yard. Three or four wooden structures burning furiously.

I guessed it would take the ANC a month to get the depots working again.

It actually took two months.

'Kinghorn to squadron. Nice work. Out.'

It was only the first of a number of such raids that I was to lead in the absence of Browne. The new show of force was of course regarded with the utmost alarm by the UN who put the screws even more firmly on the unabashed Tshombe. Negotiations and counter-negotiations continued with the sinister influence of the US's State Department Advisory Council on African Affairs never far absent.

At no stage was there any doubt as to their determination to crush the secession and establish a United Congo headed by the puppet, Addoula.

Tshombe had already given one and a half million dollars to the central treasury but this had not seemed to lessen the antagonism of Addoula — bolstered as he was by US money. More negotiations towards the end of June had collapsed when Addoula accused Tshombe of bad faith and called again for Afro-Asian military aid. For the UN's part, they were feeling the economic squeeze of their costly Congo involvement more than ever before and U Thant had warned that a solution would have to be found and very soon.

Even more troops were drafted in and the UN jets suddenly boasted heavy duty rockets for strikes against installations, a compromise on the UN demand for 500kg blockbuster bombs which had been turned down by the western member nations.

It was at this period, November 1962, that I foolishly sent one of my least trusted pilots on a mission more or less into the firing line. It was a mistake that was very nearly to cost the hapless man his life. The pilot is still alive and so, to save him embarrassment, I will only call him *Badger*.

Basically, there was little risk attached if *Badger* had followed orders. Early one morning we had loaded the Dove with vital supplies for the troops at Kongolo — then under heavy attack by the ANC. No other pilots were available so I reluctantly asked *Badger* to take the Dove on the mission. *Badger* even more reluctantly, accepted. Once in Kongolo *Badger,* apparently so distraught at the very audible rumble of the guns from the nearby front, forgot to unload the Dove completely before starting for home. The whole freight compartment remained untouched. Now this in itself was not such a serious error but what followed was sheer catastrophe.

Minutes before *Badger* was about to take off from the dusty bush strip, Kimwanga, his chief of staff, and two leathery mercenary advisors, came striding over to the cockpit of the aircraft.

'Where are you going?' one mercenary demanded.

'Kolwezi, very urgently.' *Badger* managed to shout.

The four officers piled into the Dove before *Badger* could say a word and slammed the hatch shut.

'We've got news for you,' said one of the mercenaries hovering over *Badger* threateningly. 'The Gendarmes are pulling back to M'Bulula for regrouping and we have to get there. It looks as if another attack is building up in that sector. Take us there.'

Badger started muttering something about an appointment in Kolwezi before the mercenary pulled out a wicked looking bush knife and made a threatening gesture.

'It's just down the road Mister Pilot. Won't take you a minute and then you can be off back to Kolwezi and beddy-byes with your girl friend.'

Badger miserably agreed to fly them to M'Bulula.

'Thanks,' said the mercenary and clumped back to the fuselage. *Badger* snatched a glance behind and found the four officers, including Kimwanga, sprawled on the floor of the fuselage, passed out with weariness. What entered poor *Badger's* mind I don't know but instead of flying the short hop to M'Bulula 'as requested', he set course for Kolwezi two hours flying time and four hundred kilometers to the south. No hero, he obviously decided that a heavy ANC thrust towards M'Bulula was bad news.

144

Exactly two hours later the Dove did its first circuit at Kolwezi. I came out of my office and stared perplexedly upwards. *Badger* back so soon? The Dove landed and taxied towards the hangars. I began walking casually in the direction of the aircraft. The shouting and swearing from inside the Dove was audible twenty paces away. I broke into a trot. *Badger* brought company, I thought. Just as I reached the aircraft's open hatch a grey-faced *Badger* was propelled forcefully out. We almost collided. Springing out behind the luckless pilot came Kimwanga, his face suffused with rage I had rarely seen before, the chief of staff and the two mercenaries. The mercenaries were both Belgians, ruddy brown faces a deeper hue with anger.

'What's going on?' I managed to say before the outraged Kimwanga and his three colleagues took over.

'This, this, this . . . pig!' screamed Kimwanga pointing at *Badger.*

'We asked him to fly us to M'Bulula and when we wake up we find ourselves at Kolwezi. Kolwezi . . . four hundred kilometers from the front, from my troops. Is this man mad or just a coward?'

I was about to point out to the enraged officer that I strongly suspected *Badger* to be both but decided it was not the time for such a comment.

'I really am sorry, Colonel. I assure you I will take immediate steps to see you are returned to the front . . .'

'That's not good enough, Jerry. This fool must be punished. It's disobeying an order. That's what it is. Insubordination — cowardice in the face of the enemy . . .'

'Now, now, Colonel, I'm sure there's been a mistake somewhere.'

'Mistake, mistake. You're damn right there's been a mistake. It's a mistake to let this coward live any longer. That's the mistake.'

The colonel's comment was obviously taken to heart by the two mercenaries because there was the sudden ominous clash of two Uzi submachine guns being cocked simultaneously. Poor *Badger* by this stage, had gone quite pale. Not completely able to understand what was going on he had decided to remain silent. But rather than look sullen or apprehensive he had chosen to wear a bland grin. It was the most incredible scene; four enraged battle-saturated army officers were about to summarily execute the benignly grinning *Badger* on the runway.

One of the mercenaries grabbed *Badger* roughly by the arm and began pushing him backwards towards a nearby tree trunk. The other mercenary followed a few paces in front of the pilot with his Uzi cradled in his arm and the safety catch off. *Badger,* by now insensate with fear, merely grinned more broadly and then, to cap it all, winked impishly at his would-be executioner as if it was all rather a good joke. I despaired of saving him.

'Colonel, please let's talk this over. You can't just shoot this man like this.'
'Why not?'
'Dammit, he hasn't paid his hotel bill.'

It was a weak joke but it did the trick. Kimwanga, who had a developed sense of humour, burst into laughter. The two mercenaries stopped in their tracks. *Badger's* stupid grin disappeared for a second.

'Okay, Jerry, perhaps we're being a little hasty. It's just that I don't think a person like this should be loose in Katanga.'

'Believe me, Colonel, I will take all steps necessary to see that this man is punished for his behaviour and I promise you I personally will fly you back up to the front.'

Kimwanga turned to the two mercenaries.

'Let him go.'

Reluctantly they released *Badger* and snapped their safety catches back on. Still glowering at the pilot, they followed us to the administration building.

Later that same day it was arranged that Kimwanga would take the opportunity of going to Elisabethville while I arranged to return the chief of staff to M'Bulula. Better still, I thought on the spur of the moment, a little bit of stiffening of the Gendarmes was needed and who better to do it than myself. It was a decision that nearly terminated my Congo adventure and indeed my life.

19

Near Escape

Having once made up my mind to return to the field there was nothing that could stop me. One or two problems had to be surmounted, though first I needed an excuse to return to the north. Simple; I wanted to recce the area and check the bridge at Kongolo had been properly blown by the retreating Gendarmes. Secondly, I wanted somebody to take me up. Bracco and Vosloo were reliable and available as usual and after a few disbelieving glances agreed to drop me at the bush strip in M'Bulula. Thirdly, I needed somebody to accompany me into the field. I found José cleaning his submachinegun in an empty hangar.

'Want to come into the bush?' I asked.

He hastily began reassembling his Uzi.

'Wait until I've finished.'

Early next morning, before the airport had really begun to stir, we left in the Dove — myself, José and Kimwanga's chief of staff, a lithe Bahemba given to wearing sporty sunglasses. I was dressed in my peaked flying cap, my tatty camouflage jacket and a pair of shorts. Lying close beside me was the FN rifle I had carried almost uninterruptedly since my arrival in the Congo. I was so pleased to be escaping from the administrative problems of Kolwezi that I couldn't help but feel that I was heading for some sort of holiday rather than the grim and deadly business of bush warfare.

José was in equally high spirits and Bracco and Vosloo were continually left to shake their heads in wonder at our antics as we bore north towards M'Bulula and combat.

Dutifully we flew over the bridge just outside Kongolo, saw the centre span was down and the structure was drunkenly lurching into the river; then we turned for M'Bulula.

The aircraft had hardly touched down and taxied to a halt at the grassy M'Bulula strip when we were surrounded by a crowd of very worried Bahemba tribesmen. Leading the field was Chief Kitengetenge, principal chief of the area. In good French, accompanied by numerous gestures, he made it clear that he and his people were desperately worried at the sudden disappearance of Colonel Kimwanga and the white mercenaries from the north. The ANC had taken Kongolo and would soon be crossing the river.

Kimwanga's chief of staff, himself a Bahemba, launched into an extremely plausible sounding harangue that seemed to quell all fears fairly rapidly. When he turned and pointed to José and myself, explaining that we had come to help achieve victory, there was a ragged cheer from the crowd. José and I put on our meanest looks and hefted our rifles into the air. More cheers from the crowd.

Within minutes the crates of food and ammo in the aircraft had been unloaded by many willing hands.

Chief Kitengetenge paraded the eighty or so tribal militia who had just pulled back from Kongolo and three trucks miraculously appeared from nowhere. The militia were dressed in khaki uniforms and appeared well equipped. I was unsure of their training but was confident that their spirit would carry them through. It was, after all, their own tribal lands they were defending, a powerful factor for any troop morale in black armies.

Half an hour later our mini convoy pulled out of M'Bulula and headed west towards Kongolo thirty two kilometers away, ragged crowds of Bahembas braving the billowing dust to cheer us on our way. José and I sat in the lead truck with the chief of staff while the other trucks followed bristling with rifle barrels. The convoy slowly wound its way along the dirt roads hemmed in by kilometer after kilometer of scrub and jungle. Densely forested, inhospitable terrain; good for ambushes.

Tensely José and I kept a sharp eye for likely ambush positions along the road. For the first time I began to have my doubts about coming back into the quarterless world of bush warfare. I thought of Julia. Where the hell were the Gendarme lines?

Our truck swung around a sharp bend in the road and almost ran full tilt into two dusty olive green trucks coming in the opposite direction. For a mad moment I thought they were ANC. There was a desperate scrabbling for my rifle.

With the trucks still slithering to a halt I recognised the red berets and camouflage uniforms of the crack parachute battalion of the Katangese Gendarmes. The next obvious question was why they were leaving the Kongolo front.

José and I scrambled from our truck and walked over to the paras vehicles — now slewn into the grass verge on the side of the road.

The paras spilt out of the trucks and gathered in a knot. I noticed their crumpled and torn uniforms, stubbly jowls and red rimmed eyes.

With growing apprehension I noted the sullen and disorderly way they gathered behind an enormous shaven headed man, who although wearing no insignia of rank, carried an air of authority that would put a general to shame.

'What's going on here?' I asked menacingly in my best French.

'1st Parachute Battalion from Kongolo. We are retiring.' The man's voice was deep and even.

'Retiring to where?'

'Retiring home. We've had enough.'

I must admit I was nonplussed as to the next step. Secretly I fully sympathised with the paras. They were Chokwes and others from the south, not Bahembas, it was not their tribal land, their white advisors and OC had mysteriously disappeared, possibly deserted, and this element had in fact been stranded on the opposite side of the Lualaba River for some time after the general withdrawal of the Gendarmes.

'You are surely aware that it is against orders to leave the front like this.'

An angry muttering.

'What do you have to say?'

The big paratrooper spoke up again.

'It's all very well for you. You've just arrived. Try spending some time out there without supplies or support.'

'That's precisely why I'm here. To give support. Are you not coming back?'

There was a vigorous shaking of heads.

'Do you realise that by leaving the front you are throwing open the whole of Northern Katanga to the ANC. Throwing open the door for them to come and take what they want — your lives, your homes, your women.'

A murmur of dissent from the group.

'Let somebody else come and fight. We've had enough,' somebody shouted from the back.

Then I made a cardinal error.

'Why, are you too cowardly to fight them yourselves? You and your leader here.'

There was a sudden rattle as a score of the paras cocked their rifles and Shaven Head jerked his submachinegun up, pulled the cocking lever and deftly flicked off the safety catch.

An absolute silence descended and for me all the world shrank into a tiny capsule containing myself, the para and his steadily tensing trigger finger. I knew I wouldn't have time to swing my own FN up, let alone cock it. It was not the first time I had faced imminent death. I was completely detached. But it did still seem a hell of a stupid way to die; over a few ill chosen words.

After what seemed an eternity I heard the Chief of Staff's angry voice bellowing from beside me.

'Have you all gone quite mad? What do you think you are doing? Fools! Look around you. If one person moves then you all die, everyone of you.'

The staff waved his hand to the sides. I tore my eyes from the menacing trigger finger and cast a quick look around. Sure enough, unknown to me, the militia had silently encircled the knot of paras and were now standing with their weapons trained on our tense little group.

The paras resistance crumbled immediately. Rifles were hastily lowered, sheepish smiles appeared on faces, an embarrassed scuffling of feet. I breathed a little more easily.

'Okay, okay. Let's talk about this sensibly. Why don't you want to come?'

The shaven headed leader began cataloguing the travails of the group, their fear at the apparent desertion of their white mercenary advisors, the lack of support. I could see that the men were irredeemably dispirited. There was nothing that could be done with them. A demoralised soldier was worse than no soldier at all.

'Okay. Carry on to the rear. It's no point your coming with us.'

A ragged cheer arose from the paras. Hastily they piled back into the trucks and within seconds we were left with our group of militia, highly indignant at the treachery of the paras.

I waved an authoritative hand.

'Let's go and clean up the ANC. When we are finished we'll invite the paras to come and see how soldiers fight.'

Amid cheering and laughter the militia clambered back into the trucks and our mini convoy was on the road again.

Another hour brought us to the banks of the Lualaba River and the crazily lurching bridge. Through the field glasses I scoured the town on the opposite side and found it deserted; only a few prowling dogs and chickens. Occasionally we heard the departure report of a mortar and the dull crump of an explosion. Several plumes of smoke drifted lazily over the town. It was clear the ANC had not occupied the town yet.

Reflexively my thoughts turned to the fate that would befall any of the luckless Kongolo residents captured by the advancing ANC. *Rattisage* — revenge, a French word with ineluctable Congolese connotations in my mind. *Rattisage* appeared in many guises in its long and bloody path through Congolese history. It could be almost casual; a few rapes, perhaps a murder or two, a bit of looting. It could be more organised; one man in every ten shot, their women raped, a sector of the town plundered. In its worst excesses it could amount to genocide; the eradication of an entire village, machinegun firing squads, razed homes, piles of stolen possessions. The justification behind it was simple; if you lived in a village held by the enemy for any length of time it was assumed you were one of them. Otherwise, the argument ran, one would have attempted to flee or been identified as an enemy and killed. The real motives of course were a lot less contorted; greed and lust, qualities which no victorious army in the world has ever been entirely free of but the ANC had elevated it to the status of fundamental military truth.

It was now obvious that the ANC were still some distance from Kongolo, merely contenting themselves with some haphazard mortaring. It was also quite apparent that we would be unable to ford the river to engage them and so we made the best of a bad job and dispersed the troops along the river front.

For four days José and I lived with our contingent of militia on the banks of the Lualaba, tensely waiting for ANC exploratory thrusts.

They never came.

We shared food and blankets with the men, endured snap equatorial rain showers and searing midday heat, suffered mosquitoes and the flies. Then on the fourth day, satisfied our troops were properly deployed José and I returned, grimy and aromatic, to M'Bulula. We radioed through intelligence reports to the *Etat Major* in Elisabethville and waited for a reply.

Back came the message:

Alpha to M'Bululu Sector — Stop — Message Read — Stop — Remain M'Bulula until new OC arrives — stop — Well done and thank you. Message ends.

José and I shrugged shoulders. Back to Kolwezi it seemed. In M'Bulula we also came across the tattered para group who we had met four days earlier. Very downcast, they lounged around the streets of the tiny hamlet, desperately hoping for some sort of airlift out back home. It was not to be. Before long their OC arrived, no nonsense, Colonel Mbayo. They were drawn up in ranks alongside the airfield by a swearing Gendarme officer. The Dove dropped from the sky with Bracco and Vosloo at the controls. The first aircraft in five days. Extra equipment was unloaded and Colonel Mbayo climbed out stiff legged.

He thanked us for our help and then strode off to where the shamefaced paras were drawn up. I felt sorry for them the way Mbayo mercilessly tongue lashed them for their cowardice. They were presented with the options of returning to fight the ANC or staying in M'Bulula and being picked off by the Bahemba tribesmen. They all, not unnaturally, chose to fight the ANC.

On the trip back to Kolwezi Bracco laughingly told us of an incident at the town in our absence that once and for all sealed my dislike and mistrust of Glasspole. Apparently Tshombe and Muke had arrived on a surprise inspection at Kolwezi airfield and stumped into the administration office. Glasspole had dutifully leapt to his feet and come to attention.

'Where's Puren?' Muke demanded.

'He has deserted, *Mon General*' Glasspole had replied without a second's hesitation although he knew full well where I was and what I was doing.

Unfortunately for Glasspole both Tshombe and Muke had also known I was risking my neck at Kongolo with the ground forces. There had been a silence.

'And where has he deserted to?' Muke had asked ominously.

Glasspole, sensing a rat had been forced to mutter, 'To Kongolo, *Mon General*'.

According to Bracco, Tshombe had exploded at this and shouted: 'If more of you would desert to the front we might get something done.'

Glasspole's motives in the incident were, as usual, obscure. I believe he may have been attempting to discredit me because I knew too much about and opposed his excessive commercial use of the DC4. Perhaps he was hoping to gain a higher post in the air force with me out of the way. I really don't know.

It was in fact one of the last incidents involving the New Zealand Canadian in the Congo. Very shortly afterwards his dealing and racketeering were to become too much even for the easy going Katangese. Glasspole's cardinal sin was to get caught red handed, using my office telephone, giving his UN cronies in Elisabethville exact details of our air strength at Kolwezi. His second crime was to be found out operating some sort of racket with the Greek traders with whom he seemed to keep excessive company. Canny as a jungle cat he managed to jump the border into Northern Rhodesia one step ahead of a firing squad.

Glasspole was one of those peculiar creatures cast up in troubled times; the professional adventurer, self-serving and unscrupulous. He had divided allegiances to various masters and owed real loyalty only to himself and, as with many of his ilk, Lady Luck seemed to take pleasure in accompanying his adventurous soul.

When Glasspole finally left Katanga he reputedly took with him a foreign bank account that ran into the tens of thousands of dollars.

One of the questionable characters who did not unfortunately take Glasspole's example and leave was one 'Remy' Martin, a former group captain in the Royal Air Force. This individual arrived at the same time as Browne and held down a vaguely defined administrative job that kept him poring over the Air Force balance sheets all day. He was a firm friend of Glasspole.

20

The Final Stages

We flew back into a sullen and tense Kolwezi. Across the whole of southern Katanga, in the main cities, along major communication routes and in villages, the country could be seen gearing itself for imminent battle with the UN. Any country entering a violent twilight of existence is not a happy place. Katanga was no exception.

My first visit in Kolwezi was to Major Yav, a taciturn black Katangese and *Commandant de District*. Sombrely I told him about the critical situation in the north and the need for the air force to take precautionary steps to disperse aircraft in case the UN caught us with our defences down. I also suggested it was about time Zumbach returned from his interminable absences and shouldered his responsibilities. Yav listened thoughtfully, nodded and walked away. Next day he came back with instructions from Tshombe that I was to do what I could to disperse the aircraft.

I needed no second bidding.

The Lodestar was with Zumbach and thus out of danger, the Doves, Commanches, Heron and Tri-pacers were brought to a smaller air strip in town and we took steps to protect whatever aircraft remained at Kolwezi airfield.

Revetments were dug for the disabled Vampires and machinegun emplacements strengthened. All this did not go unnoticed however as the United Nations jets arrived with clockwork regularity two or three times a week to photograph our positions. Zumbach, meanwhile, remained scarce.

It was at this stage that I came down with my first attack of malaria — an unpleasant legacy of my field excursion to Kongolo. Huddled in bed, between alternating shifts of shivers and sweating.

Major Yav solicitously visited me and kept me posted of developments on Katanga's borders (serious) and in Elisabethville (even more serious).

The ANC had seized Kongolo and were taking the offensive at Kansimba while in Elisabethville the UN troops' presence had greatly increased. War was a matter of days away.

I went to see Julia.

'I need your help.'

'Of course.'

'We have to get information out to South African Military Intelligence about what is happening. I feel honour bound to keep them posted. Will you help?'

'Jerry, you know I can't leave Katanga now.'

'Please, it's urgent.'

Julia studied me for a few seconds. I put my arms around her shoulders and squeezed.

'It'll only take a few days. You can stay at my home in Springs and meet my family at the same time.'

For a few seconds she remained silent.

'Okay, I'll do it but if fighting breaks out here I'm coming straight back.'

I gave her shoulders another squeeze.

Immediately I began work on a long letter to Pierre Retief detailing the balance of forces, the state of the secession, the morale of the people and a projection for the future. I gave the secession no more than a few weeks longer.

Clutching the dossier I managed to coax a reluctant Julia on to an aircraft. The loneliness overwhelmed me almost before the aircraft had lifted off.

On December 23 there were a few isolated clashes between the United Nations and the Gendarmerie. December 28 and the UN armoured cars and personnel carriers were again roaring through the streets of Elisabethville, seizing key points, easily overcoming opposition and within a few hours the city was under their control.

The Third War had begun.

Colonel Faulques had left Katanga several months earlier and the Gendarmes were immeasurably the poorer for the lack of the wily street tactician.

Elsewhere in Katanga determined but sporadic opposition flowered momentarily before the irresistibly superior forces and eventually crumbled. And as the fighting spread to the other key points we knew the air force was next on the list.

Late on the night of December 28 I received information that the UN were to attack our airfield at dawn the next day.

Christ, we still had six T6s on the runway apart from a number of unserviceable aircraft.

Urgent 'phone calls to various parts of Kolwezi and by 04h00 next day I had assembled all the pilots in the ops room.

We gathered around, bundled up against the dawn chill, haggard faces drawn in the weak light from the naked light bulb, subdued murmurings lapping the walls. I came straight to the point.

'Gentlemen, we have received information that the airfield is to be bombed at dawn. That gives us exactly . . .' here I studied my watch . . . . 'one hour forty minutes to clear the decks.'

There was a scramble for the door. Outside the ground crews were already refueling and arming the T6s in anticipation of the dawn. At first light we were ready and waiting. A heavy mist lay across the field, mercifully covering our installations. The six T6s stood in a neat row with propeller blades slicing the cool air, the morning loud with the throaty roar of their warming engines. I checked my watch: 05h20. One by one the T6s taxied off to their hold positions at the end of the runway; 05h25.

The first T6 skittered along the runway, bounced into the air and clawed for the mist layer. Then the second and third. I noted the mist beginning to break from the east, lift slightly, the early morning sun thrusting rays through; 05h30. Number four and five were airborne. I heaved a sigh as Wojik's T6 began its run. Almost clear. With a whine of straining engines Wojik's T6 had just lifted off the runway when our first gate crasher arrived. Bursting through the dispersing mist layer at the eastern end of the field a Saab jet fighter dropped smoothly from the sky and screamed across the runway right on Wojik's tail. Two short bursts from the Saab's cannon and I saw Wojik's aircraft shake furiously then correct itself a split second before scrabbling away into the sheltering wreaths of mist. The Saab shot past and disappeared into the murk.

I dived for the nearest gun pit. Two more Saabs slipped from the sky like avenging angels and the deadly and so familiar game was on the go again. From our gun emplacements we saw their rockets riddle the remaining T6s, the Vampires and the DC3 on the ground. Within a matter of minutes they were blazing wrecks.

As the mist lifted under the sun's rays the Saabs came back again — this time with their heavy duty rockets. Above the continuous chatter of the machineguns we heard the whoosh of the rockets and the reverberating explosions as buildings, hangars and installations came in for relentless attention.

Far better equipped than our last little duel, the jets soon left large parts of the airfield smouldering heaps of rubbish and twisted metal. Clouds of masonry dust and smoke hung over the field and we fired off futile belts of ammunition at the occasional flashes of jet fuselage. Perspiration, cordite, grease, frustration, noise and stifling heat; the old story.

Shortly after noon a sweating Gendarme dived into my trench with a message from HQ, by then in Jadotville, to report to them immediately. Waiting for a lull I scrambled to my feet, dashed to the airport boundary to a waiting car and roared off east to Jadotville.

The trip was as harrowing as only a ride through a war torn country can be. Streams of refugees' cars, buses, trucks and even bicycles trundled west towards Kolwezi, away from the advancing UN troops.

Again the pathetic piles of personal possessions, the wide-eyed children, the scrawny dogs chained atop heaps of household goods on the back of trucks, the frightened people.

I shook my head angrily at the suffering caused by a 'peace keeping' force attached to a world organisation ostensibly dedicated to international peace. Once or twice we passed small convoys of military vehicles also hastening towards Jadotville; jeeps and trucks packed with weary camouflage clad troops, one or two white mercenaries usually slouched in the lead vehicles.

Once two Saabs swept low over the column of refugees. Vehicles were slewn on to the verges of the road, people scrambled out and ran mindlessly for cover in the savannah scrub lining the road, children screaming and holding their ears in an attempt to blot out the deafening howl of the jets as they swooped at treetop level. The UN had not, however, quite stooped to strafing refugee columns.

Jadotville itself was a town in mortal fear. Homes had been hastily deserted, doors left gaping open, shops unprotected, dogs abandoned in the streets. The fear was not entirely for the UN troops, (although they were later to kill several civilians in taking the town), it was for the ANC brigands the population knew were hard on the heels of the blue helmeted UN soldiers.

I found Muke in the temporary HQ of the Gendarmes. He was pacing anxiously up and down and raging.

'Where's your Air Force. Why isn't it flying?' He angrily rounded on me.

I couldn't resist the retort.

'But, *Mon General,* the Air Force is under Zumbach's command.'

Muke nodded miserably and asked me in a more subdued manner why we had not made our air presence felt.

I explained as gently as I could that it was not possible for T6 trainers with bomb racks to take on Saab jet fighters in aerial combat.

Muke nodded even more despondently and then, obviously trying to make the best of a bad job, laid a reassuring hand on my shoulder and whispered: 'You are now in full command of the Air Force again.'

I wasn't sure if I should laugh or cry.

The tragic truth was that Tshombe had been ill advised as to the arms purchase by Pierre Laureys. Zumbach had seriously misled the president and Muke.

Although the T6s were effective as bombers they had no other armaments. The Gendarme ground forces had special Matra rockets which they fired with deadly effect from bazooka tubes but we had nothing comparable to fit to our aircraft.

As I was leaving the temporary HQ a message was thrust into my hand. Julia was on her way back from South Africa and was due in Jadotville. I smiled to myself. Instinctively I had known that the news of the fighting in Katanga would bring her back as music calls a dancer. José and I did our best to find her in the swirl of terrified refugees passing through Jadotville but to no avail.

Leaving José in the town I hastened back to Kolwezi.

Only a few hours back in Kolwezi and I had an unexpected visitor. A light aircraft from the same charter firm that flew Hedges and I in from the Federation, suddenly appeared in the circuit. The aircraft landed and trundled to a halt before the airport building. Out clambered none other than the President of Katanga. Moise Tshombe had cut short a European tour to hurry back to his war-torn country.

He was depressed and immensely tired.

'Can you arrange transport to my Kolwezi residence?' he asked as we greeted each other.

Within minutes I had arranged a car and we were speeding through the streets of the town.

'What is the position, Commandant?' he asked.

'Critical, Mister President. The UN are completely in control at Elisabethville and are advancing on Jadotville. It is only a question of time.'

Tshombe sighed deeply.

'Anything to do at this stage?'

'Bring Schramme and his battalion in from Kansimba to fall back on Jadotville. He can reinforce the other forces there.'

Tshombe nodded.

A few minutes later we were at his residence. I dropped him and turned a car towards my flat in the town, sunk deep in thought at the problems with which we were faced. Still in reverie I walked into my flat.

Julia rose from the sofa.

'Hello Confucius', she said jokingly.

I felt almost painfully happy at having her back — radiant, energetic and daring as ever. She told me of the lines of refugees streaming into Kitwe in Northern Rhodesia, the horror stories, the shock when she said she was trying to get back into Katanga when everybody else was trying to get out.

We found it in us to laugh at some of the exaggerations the refugees had managed to spin about the conditions in Katanga.

Less amusing though was the fate that had befallen a good friend of ours and our principal contact in Ndola. On her return to Katanga Julia had routinely stopped by to say hello to our Mr Andre, to gather news and messages. Instead of the warm welcome she was expecting, she found a slightly bored Federation policeman standing outside the man's securely locked house.

'Is Mr Andre here?' she asked the ebony policeman in her fluent English.

'He has been taken up', replied the policeman with a sonorous voice.

'Taken up where? By the Police?'

'No ma'am, by the Good Lord. He was shot last night.'

Bit by bit the story came. Old Andre had been found that same morning with a single gunshot wound in the back of his head. The job had been done efficiently and quietly. Professionally is the word. Julia and I puzzled over the motives for the killing. All we could think of was that he had been killed by an anti-Tshombist agent or that, possibly, he had been found double-crossing the Katangese and neatly despatched.

We never were to find the reason; it was just one of those mysterious murders with which the Congo's history was littered.

Julia and I turned to other things.

'The secession is nearly over', I said.

Julia accepted the bald statement without demur.

'What do we do?' she asked.

'We go with Tshombe. He's not just going to fade away; he'll be back for sure and we must be with him when he does come back, even if it means going into the bush and mounting a guerrilla war.'

Julia nodded. I moved close to her.

'I have this idea. Why don't we go at this together, you know, as a team', I felt myself stammering.

'What do you mean, Jerry?' she asked with a faint smile playing on her lips.

'I mean will you marry me.'

She broke into laughter. 'That's somehow what I thought you were trying to say. Sounds pretty good to me. When?'

'Soon, within the next few days. Let's rather get married in an independent Katanga.'

For a while the war was forgotten as we lost ourselves in discussing preparations for the wedding and our future.

21

Secession Ends

I glared angrily at the man in front of me in the crowded little Kolwezi ops room. He stared back insolently.

'Where the hell have you been, Zumbach?'

'Arranging supplies', he replied coolly.

'What supplies?'

'Come and look at the Lodestar. I've brought four cannon for the Vampires and . . .'

I exploded.

'Cannon for the Vampires! Cannon for the Vampires! You know damn well that the only way we will get the Vampires into the air is to throw them'.

Zumbach glared at me. He had just returned from one of his interminable trips to Europe via Angola. The only consolation was that this time he had brought back a consignment of Sterling submachineguns.

By this stage I, and indeed his own pilots, had completely lost faith in Zumbach.

'I've got a great idea. You and I will go on a mission tonight to Elisabethville. A bombing mission. How does that suit you?'

Zumbach nodded angrily and stumped off.

Fortunately for him the raid never materialized. I received a message instructing me to report to Tshombe's Kolwezi residence — urgently.

I drove through the teeming streets of Kolwezi, now swollen with refugees, to the spacious residence on the outskirts of the town. Around us the Katangese secession was collapsing in a series of bitter little rear guard actions, streams of refugees, piles of rubble and the abiding hatred of the Katangese civilians for the United Nations and their proteges, the Central Congolese Government.

The mercenaries and Gendarmes had been steadily retreating in the face of the UN advances, their last act of defiance had been to blow the bridge on the road from Jadotville by the simple expedient of packing a truck with explosives, parking it on the bridge, and then detonating the whole bang shoot in a deafening blast and massive plumes of smoke, flame and dust. It succeeded in delaying the UN for only one day.

On January 3 1963 Jadotville fell and on January 13 they were in Shinkolobwe. The end was very near. The next major town in their path was Kolwezi.

I found all Tshombe's senior military advisors gathered at the residence. Schramme, clean shaven and spruce, Denard, tough and taut and a number of black officers.

At that stage the Gendarmes were strung out in a defensive perimeter some eighty kilometers east of Kolwezi.

Tshombe looked haggard and anxious. He spoke quietly and unemotionally but we could all see the tremendous strain he was under, the occasional falter in his speech, the hand passed frequently over his face.

The Katangese secession was nearly at an end, he said flatly, and soon, very soon, he would have to sign a capitulation.

'But gentlemen this is only a phase. I shall return when the time is ripe. It is essential now that all steps be taken to get everything of military value out to neutral Angola — this has already been arranged with the Portuguese. We must take out our vehicles, our aircraft, our soldiers, our weapons. Gentlemen, the Gendarmes must become an army in exile. Katanga and the Congo will need them again very soon.'

Grim faced the mercenaries and Gendarme officers listened as Tshombe gave detailed instructions for the withdrawal; Denard to pull back to Kolwezi first then move on to Dilolo, farther west and very near the Angola border.

Schramme, with four thousand Gendarmes and approximately fifty mercenaries, would later stage at Dilolo before retiring across the border into Angola. He would remain in charge of the army in exile which would be housed in special camps.

The rest of the mercenaries would be disbanded.

Tshombe turned to me.

'What would you have to air lift out?'

I thought for a few seconds.

'We have to take out our T6s, one Commanche, some Pipers, and a DC3. The unserviceable aircraft will have to be destroyed where they stand. We will also need about one thousand drums of aviation fuel and then perhaps twenty tons of spares. We've also got four helicopter jet engines. They will have to be sent out. But we can do that by rail.'

Tshombe nodded.

'Any weapons?'

'QM at Kolwezi tells me they have one hundred Sterling machineguns, one hundred machinepistols and probably thirty extra tons of assorted weapons and ammunition.'

The President turned to Schramme: 'How many days at maximum can we hold?'

'No more than ten, Mister President.'

Back to me again.

'Can you move that load in ten days?'

'Undoubtedly, Mister President.'

Denard whistled between his teeth and shook his head.

'If you can shift that I'll buy the first beer in Texeira de Sousa.'

'One other thing, Commandant,' Tshombe interrupted.

'Yes, Mister President.'

'Can you fly the treasury out?'

'Of course.'

Just before the meeting broke up Denard held up a hand.

'Mister President, we can't just be thrown out of Katanga without showing our real displeasure. We must do something dramatic.'

'Like?'

'Like blowing up the hydro electric installations at Nzilo.'

I shuddered inwardly as I thought of the multi-billion franc investment disappearing in a cloud of smoke at the hands of Denard's expert sappers. I thought of the havoc, the dislocation, the fury of Mobutu the Belgian mining houses and possibly the Katangese themselves.

Tshombe thought deeply for a second and then shook his head.

'That would be criminally irresponsible.'

The meeting broke up in a depressed mood.

I remember those dying days of the secession as a kaleidoscopic vision of furious work and towering resolve. We worked around the clock shuttling tons of spares and ammunition out to Texeira de Sousa in Angola.

Every available pilot was dragged in to help.

A constant stream of aircraft shuttled between Kolwezi and Texeira de Sousa. On the Katangese side perspiring Gendarmes, stripped to the waist, levered up the chunks of machinery, the crates, the drums into railway trucks and aircraft.

On the Angolan side Portuguese troops and navvies unloaded and stored the goods in anticipation of our arrival. The one thousand drums went, so did the helicopter engines and the weapons.

Surviving on four hours sleep a day we cleared that town of everything with the slightest military value in just nine days. It was back-breaking, exhausting work.

Finally we packed the Katangese treasury. Several closed vans arrived at the airfield under heavy guard. Senior officials supervised the loading of the innocent looking wooden crates in which was packed an estimated five million pounds in notes. The DC3 climbed into the sky and set course for Angola. The money was to become the stockpile with which Tshombe paid his Gendarmes in exile and many years later helped him bankroll an attempted coup against Mobutu.

Meanwhile the long columns of Gendarme trucks packed with dispirited troops, were rolling west to Dilolo, while closer and closer to Kolwezi came the dull thump of the mortars and the rattle of the machineguns.

Then the UN troops stopped on the Lualaba River and politely waited for us to evacuate.

Kolwezi itself was packed with mercenaries and Gendarmes and inevitably law and order became slightly stretched — especially when Denard's column hit the town on their way through. Late one night I was dozing in my first floor flat when I heard some suspicious noises from the street below my bedroom window. Glancing out I saw two vague shapes hunched over the ignition system of the military jeep that I had used as my personal transport for months. I shook with rage. My jeep!

'Hey you.! Whacha-think-you're-doing?' I screamed through the window.

The two figures dropped everything and bolted up the street. Just not good enough, I thought, grabbing a towel to cover my nakedness and haring down the stairs. The would-be car thieves had little chance. It was heavy combat boots against my near nudity and sprinting skills. I caught them at the first corner under a dull street lamp. Instantly I recognised them as Denard's mercenaries.

'What are you up to?'

'Order to collect vehicles', one sullenly muttered.

'Bullshit. Let's go see Denard about this.'

The response from the one mercenary was instantaneous. Deftly he bent down and drew a wicked looking knife from a scuffed and well travelled combat boot.

Curtains for me, I managed to think before I heard an angry shout from behind. We all spun round. Trundling up the road came Vosloo, my old loyal Vosloo. This time determinedly clutching a submachinegun. He had heard the ruckus from his flat on the opposite side of the street and was now coming to my assistance.

'Touch him and you're both dead, but really dead', he puffed as he reached us.

The mercenary shrugged and returned the knife to his boot sheath.

We frog-marched them off to Denard's temporary HQ, myself still clutching a towel around my middle.

Typically the burly Frenchman gave a wide grin as I told him of our difficulties and then slapped me playfully on my bare back.

'Come on Jerry. Nothing personal. We just needed transport.'

I stumped off with Vosloo hard on my heels. Fortunately Denard's group pulled out that night and early next day Schramme's followed through.

Also the next day Julia and I were married in a pretty white walled Kolwezi church. Our minister was an American Methodist who stammered sweetly over the words of the service. He was very young and it was his first nuptial ceremony. Julia's family and a few friends of ours attended. The bride was, of course, beautiful.

The last blessing over and we all walked out of the church into the silent streets of Kolwezi. The rear guard Gendarme force had passed that morning.

The UN troops were expected next day and the good people of Kolwezi were keeping prudently in doors. As we stood in the tranquil night time heat accepting the congratulations of our friends, I thought of what two years war in this central African country had cost me — and gained me.

That night friends held a going away-cum-wedding celebration for us at the Bon Auberge Hotel. Above the gaiety and indescribable happiness, though, hung the constant awareness that an epoch in Katangese and African history was drawing to an end while we rejoiced in our personal happiness.

An attempt at multiracial society in black Africa had been opposed, thwarted and eventually destroyed.

Super power involvement had turned a Third World success in stable Government into a wasteland of burning antagonism.

For me personally it had been a three year journey through good times and bad, through adventure and danger, and finally from rank self interest to a commitment to Katangese pride and to a loyalty to its leaders. Even if I had to return to the bush as a guerrilla fighter I was determined not to ignore the desperate calling of my adopted homeland.

Dawn next day, January 23 1963 and my young bride and I sat in the Tri-pacer at the little airstrip in the centre of Kolwezi. The engine was warming and inside the aircraft we had packed all our personal possessions. We looked for the last time at the familiar surroundings.

A United Nations ferret armoured car, blue pennant whipping on the end of its antenna, came nosing along the road that ran parallel to the airfield. Several armoured personnel carriers followed and then a truck.

I pushed the throttle forward and the Tri-pacer started down the runway, bounced and climbed into the clear sky. We turned towards Dilolo and the long road into exile.

Several hours later Tshombe was to sign a declaration ending the secession. Katanga reverted to its status as a province and Tshombe remained Governor. It had temporarily ceased to be a sovereign state, but neither Julia nor I were by any means finished with Katanga, the Congo or with Tshombe.

22

Retreat and Relocation

Dilolo, a small and dusty town at the best of times, was now packed to the gunwales with an army in transit. Columns of trucks were parked under the trees on the approaches to the town, squadrons of jeeps stood haphazardly on pavements and squares, mounted machinegun barrels pointing vacuously skyward. And everywhere soldiers; in knots, masses, individually, the Gendarmes spread out and took over every available scrap of space.

Officers were crowded into the single Dilolo hotel, spending the hot and tense days drinking, arguing and occasionally sallying out to quell the more violent forms of confrontation between members of their equally insecure troops.

Julia, myself and the pilots kept very much to ourselves.

Amongst other things it was a time for recriminations, post mortems and speculation.

We were going to Angola.

We were disbanding.

The UN were coming.

Anxiously we waited word from Tshombe.

The two week stay in Dilolo was one of uncertainty and confusion. Tshombe, although no longer President of an independent Katanga, was now Governor of Katanga Province under strict UN supervision. Because of this new dispensation it was extremely difficult to communicate freely with him.

Meanwhile the UN troops came closer and closer.

Eventually the uncertainty became overpowering and I resolved that we would have to get explicit instructions from the former President. But who to send? Julia sensed my quandary immediately.

'I'll go', she said.

I shook my head.

'It's too dangerous. There are a hell of a lot of the UN and ANC troops and officials between here and Tshombe'.

'That's precisely why I should go. Who's going to suspect a woman?' Her logic was infallible.

Early one Friday morning, Julia, dressed casually and carrying a number of anthropology books for disguise, boarded a train at Dilolo. Two of my most trusted black air force colleagues, dressed in shabby workmen's clothes, got on with her. They remained constant, if surreptitious, shadows on her journey.

On the interminable trip from Dilolo to Kolwezi, Julia was the only white face among the mass of blacks returning to their homes after flight.

Innumerable times the train had to stop on the route because of sabotaged signals or tracks. At places it seemed the train would have to turn back.

In one village UN troops boarded and began a person-by-person search. When the Indian sergeant eventually reached Julia's compartment he found a young Belgian woman student poring over her anthropology books. A bow of apology and he hastened his detail on. The train resumed its painfully slow progress.

At Kolwezi Julia jumped out, borrowed a car and drove the rest of the distance to Elisabethville. The area was firmly in the hands of the UN with troop convoys a regular sight. In Elisabethville it was a round trip to the Governor's residence, a dexterous back entrance and a hurried word with a delighted Tshombe.

At this stage the former President was in an extremely delicate situation. He had theoretically accepted the termination of the secession and the disbandment of the Gendarmes. The former President was now no more than a provincial governor and, by definition, very much subservient to the Central Government of Cyrille Addoula.

The truth was slightly different.

Far from disbanding the Gendarmes or integrating them into the ANC, Tshombe was actually preparing to move them, lock, stock and barrel into Angolan exile.

At this point the intentions of the former president were not known by the Central Government or the UN and it would have been fatal for Tshombe to have been seen liaising with this body of armed and loyal men from a supposedly defunct organisation. In his own palace Tshombe was surrounded by spies and hence the conspiratorial meeting with Julia.

Several days later she arrived back at Dilolo with a message from Tshombe that the Gendarmerie were to stand firm in Dilolo until he arrived.

He was as good as his word and seventy two hours later a private light aircraft dropped smoothly on to the Dilolo airfield. Tshombe bounced out, plunged among his beloved Gendarmes and spread light and encouragement.

That night he held a round table of his senior officers and mercenary advisors. Our final instructions were confirmed in greater detail. The whole column was to go to bush camps in Angola with Schramme taking command. The other mercenaries would be paid off, the air force spares would go to Luanda in Angola for storage and the air strength would also be demobbed.

Tshombe emphasised that hard times were ahead for the Gendarmes but patience and faith would be the watchwords. Soon, perhaps sooner than expected, the Gendarmes would be needed again.

We drank a final toast and the officers began filing out.

Tshombe detained me by the arm as I was about to leave. We were alone in the little room. 'Jerry, what are your plans?'

It was the first time he had used my Christian name and I was touched. I shrugged my shoulders.

'Both my wife and I have been honoured to serve you for the last two years, Mister President, and we hope to continue, in whatever capacity we can.'

Tshombe's tired face split into a grin.

'I thank you both. Certainly I shall need you in the future. I shall be in touch.'

He slapped me on the back and I left relieved and excited.

Before the sun had risen next morning the whole of the Katangese Gendarmerie were on the road west to Angola. By sunup the thin line of olive green stretched over kilometers of road, billows of dust marking the progress of the army of a now legally defunct country.

At the border several platoons of black and white Portuguese soldiers stood by watching silently as our heavily armed column moved into the colony. The commissioner for the area, a sturdy little man with great charm, met the first elements of the column. Among them was Tshombe, secreted in the back of a panel van.

It was clear that this tactical withdrawal into Angola had been planned as an eventuality many months ago and had been sanctioned from the highest Portuguese authority. Nobody challenged us and there, in the Angolan bush, Tshombe and the Portuguese officials made the final arrangements that were to keep the Katangese Gendarmes alive and fighting as a unified force for many more years.

The Gendarmes were to remain restricted to their camps near the border where they could retain their weapons. Tshombe would have to pay for their maintenance out of his treasury. Arrangements were made through the Portuguese for the Katangese treasury to be transferred to a Swiss bank account.

It was a temporary parting of the ways.

Tshombe went back to the intrigues of his role as Governor, Schramme disappeared into the bush with his dust streaked vehicles and loyal troops, and I, together with the air element, moved on to nearby Villa Luso.

The Portuguese attitude to Tshombe perhaps needs some explanation here. Basically, in their foreign policy, the Portuguese had always been strongly pro-Tshombe and in favour of an independent Katanga. The reasons were obvious. Tshombe was a conservative and pragmatic leader who desired stable and profitable relations with his white run southern neighbours; South Africa, the Rhodesian Federation and the Portuguese territories of Angola and Mozambique.

While Katanga had been independent the Gendarmes had kept a tight control on the border with Angola, effectively blocking the Angolan nationalist guerrilla forces, then fighting the Portuguese, from using the Congo for sanctuary. Once Tshombe was deposed from the presidency of an independent Katanga the policing fell to the ANC and their leader Joseph Mobutu, who was very favourably disposed towards the FNLA guerillas under Holden Roberto, Mobutu's brother-in-law.

For the Portuguese then, the sheltering of the exiled Gendarmes promised two possible advantages; one, they could form the nucleus at some time in the future, for an attempt to reinstate Tshombe by force of arms, and, two, their mere presence in northern Angola would act as a deterrent to the guerillas.

In Villa Luso's small but comfortable hotel the remainder of the air contingent, Julia and I temporarily established ourselves. The first few days were idyllic after the uncertainty of our last days in Katanga; lazy days in the hot Angolan sun, evenings drinking cold Portuguese beer and eating prawns peri peri.

Then, as always, the intrigue began to sour our existence. Two Belgian civil servants, Andrieux and the other, a former *Travaux Publics* man and no friend of mine, were in charge of administering Katangese funds in Angola.

It was not long before I began to notice that my allowances were shrinking rapidly. I ignored it on the grounds that I was amply provided for already. Then stories began circulating that the couple were running a currency exchange racket. Interesting!

The final straw came when a contact in the Portuguese Intelligence Agency, PIDE, in Angola, tipped us off that our mail was being interfered with by the Belgians.

Things had come to a head and I decided that somebody would have to go to see Tshombe to establish clearly what was to happen to us. The choice was not unnaturally, Julia.

The Portuguese, surprisingly, objected as soon as they heard Julia intended returning to Katanga. After a few sharp words in which I pointed out that my wife was a Belgian citizen and could thus go wherever and when ever she liked, they backed down.

Julia once again caught the train, crossed the border and jumped off at Kolwezi. From there she ploughed the three hundred kilometers to Elisabethville by Volkswagen through the UN held countryside and again made it to Tshombe.

Meanwhile, I was busy supervising the discharge of the last of the Air Force pilots with whom I had become so closely associated during the last few dangerous years; Bracco, Libert, Vosloo, Hedges, Wicksteed and the Belgians. In many cases it was a sad parting.

Bracco, Libert and I got nostalgically drunk together on Portuguese beer and promised to keep in touch, no matter what.

Two months later they left with that other arch adventurer, Denard, for the Yemen where they had heard vaguely that there was a war in progress. It was, however, by no means the last I was to see of the terrible twins.

Before Hedges and Wicksteed left for South Africa I made a special arrangement with them. I knew instinctively that Tshombe was going to need mercenary pilots in the near future and I made them promise to keep in close touch with me in South Africa so that I could recruit them immediately. In fact, I was later to put them up at my own home in Springs and later in a nearby hotel in anticipation of Tshombe's call.

Eventually all the old crew had gone and I was alone with the Belgian civil servants.

A rich and adventurous saga in rough and tumble aerial warfare had drawn to an end. The brave men who had accompanied me on those outrageously impudent attacks were dispersing across the globe, some going home, some moving on to other adventures. I felt the poorer for the loss of their irrepressible and daredevil company.

Julia's message from Tshombe was quite simple.

We were to return to South Africa post haste and then make our way back to Elisabethville after a short holiday. Tshombe wanted us near him.

We still had several days left in Villa Luso. It was while there that the submerged antagonism between the different nationalities and between officers themselves emerged.

Away from the immediacy of war, in the strange limbo that was awaiting the demobbed mercenaries, tempers flared often and bloodily in the little Portuguese town.

It was there that de Clary, French liaison officer and an original Trinquier man, came in for brutal and special attention from his colleagues. I was never to know what it was exactly that the man had done that resulted in such approbrium.

First explosions were in a tawdry little Villa Luso pub where a few of the French mercenaries, mostly Foreign Legion veterans, took fists and boots to the hapless de Clary in a way that could possibly have killed him.

I happened to be passing at the time when I heard de Clary's screams and the sickening thud of fists and boots on human flesh. Inside the smoke wreathed pub, a wide circle of civilians and Portuguese troopies stood watching as three of Denard's mercenaries demolished de Clary. I pushed my way through the crowd and confronted the three battle scarred mercenaries, then standing aggressively over the bleeding and moaning de Clary.

'Leave that man alone', I ordered.

The mercenaries glared at me but fortunately bowed to my senior rank. They allowed the battered de Clary to hump his form out of the pub and away to bed.

I left the pub still marvelling at the fact that, despite the near anarchy among the demobbed mercenaries, I was still able to pull some rank. The incident was my second brush with Denard's mercenaries and did not go down too well when it reached the ears of the band's mercurial leader.

Similar such violent outbursts of ire between the mercenaries in Villa Luso were quite common during this time and I will always admire the tolerance of the Portuguese who accepted the furores with Iberian smiles until the last of the mercenaries swaggered abroad to their next encounter.

Julia and I eventually caught a flight out of Luanda to Jan Smuts airport in Johannesburg, South Africa. Our arrival did not go unnoticed and, at the gate, we were met by two taciturn gentlemen who revealed themselves to be from military intelligence. An hour after touching down and without even seeing our family, we were in Pierre Retief's office at DHQ, Pretoria.

'What are Tshombe's plans?' was his first question.

I shrugged my shoulders.

'General elections throughout the Congo are looming. Perhaps he will stay and work towards them with his Conakat party. Perhaps pressures will be too great in Katanga against him and he will prefer to go into exile. At this stage we don't know.'

'What are his chances in an election for the central government?'

Julia answered the question.

'Good. Amongst the people of Katanga he is regarded as a demigod. He is personally descended from Lunda nobility and is married to a daughter of the *Mwata Yamvo*, the Emperor of the Lunda. That in itself carries a lot of influence. I believe he has good grass roots support in the rest of the Congo as well because of his intelligent approach to administration in Katanga during the secession.'

Retief was listening intently.

'The whole question now is whether he will be allowed to campaign properly for that election. At the moment he is a virtual prisoner in Elisabethville, surrounded by UN and ANC spies.'

166

I felt it was a good moment to push the point home.

'Look Pierre, this is the only chance the Congo has. Tshombe talks in terms of a federal government, he's got charisma, he's sincere, he can talk to any nation in the world as an equal. Added to that he's very good news for the whole of southern Africa. He hasn't gone overboard with impractical rhetorics as have the other black leaders. He's pragmatic. Work with the white southern states and it will be to everybody's advantage. Basically what he's talking about is a vast bloc of southern African states with incredible economic potential, strategically vital, firmly in the western camp. Christ, he's giving it to us on a plate. If he doesn't make it to power in the Congo, all hell will break loose. The bunch of clowns in the central government cannot hold that country together, even with every US dollar in the world. And when it really splits, as it's bound to do, Russia and China aren't going to take back seats. Look, Pierre, we've got to . . .'

Retief held up his hand to stop the flow of words.

'Jerry, Jerry. You don't have to convince me of all this. It's them up there.' And here he jerked a thumb in the general direction of Union Buildings, executive heart of South Africa.

'I just want to know now what you two intend doing.'

It was a difficult question to answer.

'Tshombe has asked us to remain in his service. What he expects us to do, I can't really say. We don't even know if he is going to pay us.'

Retief shook his head and stared at the pencil in his hands.

'I think you should pull out, Jerry. Settle down again. You're backing the wrong horse. The party's finished.'

That expression again.

'I'll prove you wrong, Pierre — and quite soon.'

He smiled and shrugged his shoulders. The interview was over.

Later that day a government car dropped us off at my Springs' home; the first time Julia and I had been together with my family at our house. Also joining us in the haven of domesticity and peace was Julia's family. Only days after the secession had ended the whole family had pulled out of Kolwezi in a mini convoy; my father-in-law driving his precious Mercedes, Raymond piloting a big truck, José in his pickup and eleven year old Michel expertly handling the family VW Beetle. Running the ANC gauntlet the family had passed through the Federation and made their way into South Africa with refugee status.

We hadn't been in South Africa a few days when Julia and I were called upon to render services to Tshombe. Immediately after fleeing Katanga in the closing days of the secession, Zumbach had arrived in Johannesburg and proceeded to pick the meat off the Katangese bones.

Convinced Tshombe owed him money, Zumbach brought a civil action through the South African Supreme Court laying claim to two of Tshombe's aircraft then in South Africa for repairs.

Tshombe's instructions to us, backed with the money, were to hire the best South African legal men and defend the action. It was a long and costly exercise that eventually retained us our aircraft, and achieved their return to Tshombe when he became Prime Minister of the Congo.

23

Double Murder

Two weeks after arriving in South Africa we received the expected summons to return to the Congo. Tshombe wanted to give us instructions and documents for the case then pending against Zumbach.

The decision to acquiesce was not taken entirely lightly. Julia and I discussed it at length; the probable dangers we were riding into, the intrigue, the suspicions and the anxiety. We looked at it from all sides and eventually came back to the decision we both subconsciously knew we would take anyway — to return.

Father-in-law, Victor, and José decided to come with us as they had uncompleted business in Kolwezi. It was in the Mercedes and José's little pickup truck that the four of us left early one morning.

Driving shifts we pressed on through the Transvaal, through the border post (the Federal officials were reluctant to let a former deportee through, but eventually after a 'phone call to Salisbury, gave in), through the Federation and eventually to Kipushi, twenty two hours after leaving Springs. The small Katangese Federation town was quite devoid of UN or ANC troops, it being generally felt that the proximity of these forces to the Federal troops might lead to incidents.

Victor and José pushed on to Kolwezi while Julia 'phoned the Governor's residence in Elisabethville from Kipushi and, without giving names but still identifying ourselves, told the secretary we had arrived. A pause and then the man, a devoutly loyal Tshombist, instructed us to go to the Governor's residence in Kipushi and await word.

We hadn't been in the spacious and elegant residence longer than ten minutes when one of Tshombe's *Surete* agents arrived, a lithe, intelligent man we had both known for some time.

'The Governor extends his welcome and hopes to see you soon. Meanwhile you are to make yourselves quite at home.'

The man poured three stiff drinks and we idly chatted.

'You're not the first people to use this route,' the agent mentioned conversationally at one stage.

'Only yesterday that Belgian chap, Andrieux, was here. He left this morning to see the Governor in Elisabethville.'

Andrieux to see Tshombe? I wondered casually if it was to do with his handling of funds in Angola.

Very early next day a large car, driven by two plain clothes men, arrived and we were shepherded into the plush interior. Minutes later we were spinning out of Kipushi along the twenty five kilometer tarred road to Elisabethville. Twice we passed through UN checkpoints with no more than a wave from the guards.

Into Elisabethville, now quieter, palpably more abandoned, along the near deserted streets and finally through the gates of the Governor's residence. An ANC guard saluted us and we drove past a small knot of bored looking UN soldiers. I smiled to myself. Two months ago I was bombing the daylights out of them and now they were saluting us. Half an hour and much furtive scurrying later, we were standing in Tshombe's office.

He greeted us with a wan smile and seemed genuinely pleased to see us. Julia was hugged, my hand pumped, and a series of solicitous questions fired at us.

Julia asked how the change in status had affected him. The former president spread his hands.

'The status does not concern me. It is the loss of free action. My every move here is watched by ANC and UN spies. My telephone is tapped, my mail read. All my close aides have been forced to resign under pressure. Only my private secretary remains. I am also under constant subtle threat.'

He turned to me.

'Jerry, I understand there were problems in the administration of funds in Angola. I have looked into this and Andrieux is to see me today. I hope you were not affected.'

'Not seriously, Mr President.'

Nothing more was said about it and Tshombe stood for a moment staring reflectively out of the window.

'You will be my guests here at the residence for a while, but I must warn you not to leave your rooms. Be prepared to move at any time. If you are caught it will be serious for you and reflect heavily on me. There are spies everywhere.'

Julia and I nodded. He didn't have to spell it out for me. I was a well known senior mercenary and if captured by the ANC, there was every likelihood the Congolese Central Government would do what the UN had been trying to do for two years, get rid of me permanently. At their hands a firing squad would have been the greatest mercy to expect.

Julia and I were led by one of Tshombe's loyal aides to a comfortable flatlet in one of the residence's visitors' wings — a pleasant little enclave in the hostile winds of Congo politics then raging around Tshombe.

We spent a restless day and night waiting for further instructions, every footstep outside the door was a possible threat, the bland face of the black servant who regularly wheeled in the laden meal trolley could be an enemy. It struck us painfully that in the residence we were as much prisoners as Tshombe was a prisoner of the Congolese political situation.

The next day we heard a scrabble rather than a knock, at the door. Julia stood quite still and I moved rapidly to open the door. On the threshold, looking slightly dishevelled but cheerful as ever, stood my old faithful, former comrade at arms, Vosloo.

'What the hell are you doing here, Vossie?' I demanded.

'I was told I'd find you here,' he said and deftly side-stepped me into the lounge.

Vosloo came straight to the point. Glasspole had suggested that he come and see Tshombe, pledging his undying support and present the Governor with a foolproof scheme to once again liberate Katanga. It was a typical Glasspole intrigue and even more typical tactics — the vacuous Vosloo sent out as bait.

'Listen, Vossie, it may not be perfectly clear to you but the secession is over. Mercenaries are not exactly welcomed around here, especially if they have harebrained schemes like yours. Take my advice and forget about it before the ANC jump you.'

Fortunately he took my advice and left Elisabethville the very next day.

That night Julia and I went to bed early, worn out with the strain of waiting in constant fear of discovery and betrayal. It seemed I had hardly closed my eyes when the jangling telephone alongside our bed pulled me upright. My hands instinctively reached for the pistol under my pillow. I orientated myself and snatched the receiver from the hook. The voice on the other end was authoritative and familiar — the *Surete* man who had met us in Kipushi.

'The Governor's orders are that you be ready to leave the residence in five minutes. Somebody will come and pick you up.'

The 'phone went dead. I checked the bedside clock; 23h00. Julia was already awake. In desperate haste we pulled on our clothes, gathered our belongings and waited anxiously by the front door. What now!

Five minutes later there was a knock. We opened up and found one of the men who had driven us up from Kipushi standing outside, casting furtive glances up and down the corridor.

'Come,' was all he said and began leading us at a brisk lope down the passageway, along the stairs, through a doorway, into a courtyard, through another doorway and finally into a dark underground garage.

'Wait here,' he hissed and disappeared.

Julia and I followed his progress through the pitch dark by the slight scuffle of his feet, the creak of his leather holster and eventually the slam of a car door.

The brittle silence was broken by the roar of a car engine, there was a flash of light and suddenly the dark form of a large American car was beside us. Dutifully we climbed in.

The *Surete* agent drove quickly and deftly. The car shot out of the garage, cruised down the drive, stopped momentarily at the gate of the residence and then rocketed into the dimly lit road.

'Keep your heads down,' he snarled as I vainly tried to see what was going on.

Then we were on the open road and purring smoothly and rapidly towards Kipushi. The agent was unbending about our sudden departure.

'I know nothing. Just following orders,' was all he could manage.

Thirty minutes later we stopped at the Kipushi residence and climbed out. Everything was laid on. Servants appeared and noiselessly spirited our luggage away. Minutes after entering the residence the telephone rang. I picked it up and waited. Again the familiar voice on the other end — our *Surete* mentor.

'Are you there safely?'

'Yes, we're fine,' I replied.

'Good.'

170

The 'phone went dead.

It was only the next day that we found out the reason for our hasty departure from the residence.

The ANC must have been tipped off about our presence and decided to conduct a raid on the Governor's residence. Fortunately for us espionage works both ways and somebody tipped off Tshombe about the raid, no doubt the result of a bit of judicious palm greasing. Rumour had it that Tshombe had a UN Ethiopian army captain in his pay.

Only minutes later, after we had left the Elisabethville residence the ANC had arrived in a convoy of trucks, sealed off the streets surrounding the residence and conducted a room to room search. They found precisely nothing.

Next day our faithful *Surete* friend came to see us. He poured himself a stiff drink and collapsed in an easy chair.

'Heard about Andrieux?'

We shook our heads.

'His body was found early today in an Elisabethville street; stabbed, mutilated, partly burnt. Very messy.'

The officer appeared neither regretful nor even surprised at the turn of events.

'When was he murdered?' I asked.

'Sometime last night. He was staying at the Governor's residence and then disappeared. He must have been there the same time as you were.'

'We never saw him,' said Julia puzzled.

'Of course not. You were in one part of the residence and he in another. All of you in hiding.'

'Who do you think would do a thing like that?'

The agent shrugged.

'Who knows. Andrieux was a man of many parts, most of them crooked. He had many enemies.'

We turned to other topics.

When he had gone Julia and I fell to discussing the incident. There were two possibilities. One, the ANC had wreaked a typical revenge on a known pro-Tshombist, or two, the full extent of Andrieux's fiddles had become known to the Katangese and appropriate punishment meted out. Whether Tshombe knew or sanctioned his demise I was never to find out. Although no friend of mine, it was a terrible end for anybody. Andrieux's former accomplices in crime, another Belgian were later to make a quick escape from all connections with the Katangese in exile or indeed the Congo. Altogether I estimated that the unholy alliance made off with more than twenty million francs of Tshombe's money during their time in Angola.

The news of Andrieux's death meanwhile served only to increase our anxiety as we sheltered in the Kipushi residence and waited for our next instructions in the bizarre game of high stakes hide and seek.

We didn't know if the Kipushi residence was likely to suffer the same fate as the Elisabethville residence, and so every day Julia and I packed a picnic hamper and walked to the airfield, half in and half out of Katanga, and spent otherwise lazy hours in the grassland right on the border. If the ANC came we were ready to cross firmly into the Federation. In those long and tense hours, sprawled under the trees, we often discussed the future of Katanga and Tshombe. Not once do I remember us ever contemplating the possibility of throwing in the towel and high tailing it back to South Africa and safety.

Two days later Tshombe slipped into Kipushi and came straight to see us. He stood breathless and aged before us.

'I have decided to leave Katanga temporarily. To go into voluntary exile. All visitors leaving my residence are being searched and arrested. The pressures are intolerable.'

'Will you fight in the elections, Mister President?' Julia asked.

'I will run my campaign from exile. There is little chance of doing it while I continue living in the country. I have not left the country for good, it will be just a short while.'

'And us, Mister President?'

'I want you to go back to South Africa. I will call you when I need you. It will be soon.'

A few short words about the course of action we were to take to counter Zumbach's attachment order on the aircraft and with that he was gone.

Next day José arrived in Kipushi and after a round of hugs from Julia and sisterly admonitions he told us that his father had already left for South Africa. The situation in Kolwezi had become intolerably strained since the ANC had taken over from the Gendarmes, he warned us sombrely. Rank-and-file Katangese civil servants had been replaced by Leopoldville appointees, the soldiers were intimidating the people, there were summary arrests and mysterious disappearances — *Rattisage*.

'I think it's about time that we all went to South Africa. Right now,' Julia said firmly.

José shook his head.

'There are still some things I have to sort out at Kolwezi, then I'll be back. I'll drop you and Jerry at the station in Ndola though.'

Julia grabbed her brother's hair and gave it a shake with mock severity.

'Imbecile. Go back to Kolwezi, now? What can possibly be so important as to risk your life?'

The boy was as obstinate as his sister. He had things to do, he would go back. Julia eventually acceded but the argument raged the whole journey back to Ndola in José's little pickup truck.

Driving through the rest of that day we made it to Ndola in time to catch the Johannesburg bound train. José stood and waved farewell. As the train jerked out of the station he shouted:

'Tell Mama I will be back on the 11th for my birthday for a big fiesta.'

Julia smiled wanly and waved as the train gathered speed and José became a rapidly diminishing figure on the platform. She turned to me and I could see the concern clouding her eyes.

'Don't worry, he's tough and wise enough to look after himself,' I told her with an assurance I did not feel.

She bit her lower lip and turned away.

Three days later the train pulled into Johannesburg central station. On the platform to greet us was another of Retief's ubiquitous, serious faced men. Without a word he shoved a telegram into my hands that had been sent to Retief by a mutual acquaintance in Katanga.

Request inform Jerry and Mdme Puren of death by shooting of José. Details following by letter.

I read it twice and, with misty eyes, handed it to my wife. Julia scanned it then turned to me.

'Told you so', she said in a barely audible whisper.

Together we began walking towards the exit and ran into Victor. He had already heard the news. Julia and her father clung tightly and silently to each other and then we were all driving in a shocked silence back to Springs. As we arrived home the one o'clock news on Radio South Africa announced the death.

Two days after dropping us at Ndola, José had been driving his truck through the Kolwezi streets towards the riding club. It was late in the evening and few people were about. He swung round a corner and almost hit the boom slung across the road. A knot of ANC soldiers, some teetering dangerously on their feet, were manning the roadblock. A witness later told us they were drunk. Perhaps they were drugged, it's impossible to know.

In any event they forced the little truck to a halt and ordered José to climb out. He did and stood quietly while the soldiers rummaged through his truck for valuables.

He did not even object when they took his watch and made him turn out his pockets. Then one of them told José to put his hands in the air, turn around and march back the way he had come. He walked away, slowly, unhurriedly, head held high. Ten paces later the bullets thudded into his defenceless back and he collapsed on the road he had traversed so many times before.

A military truck was brought, José's lifeless form dumped in the back, the boom was hauled away and the soldiers hastily dispersed. It was late and the road was deserted. They probably thought nobody had seen the incident. But somebody had and many months later we were to learn the whole story.

Next day, family friends found José's body lying half in and half out of a ditch near the ANC camp. The same friends took over and arranged the funeral. It was said to have been one of the biggest ever held in Kolwezi. Victor had been a Belgian colon since the 1950s, his children had been brought up and had gone to school there, they were all well known and respected members of the town.

Hundreds of mourners, black and white, followed the hearse on foot. Through the empty streets of the town the silent and bitter procession wound with only the tolling church bells background to the shuffling feet. Not an ANC soldier was in sight.

José was a student who had been dragged into the deadly business of war because of his loyalty to an adopted homeland and in defence of his family's property. He escaped death then, only to lose his life later in a random, senseless outburst of ANC violence; cut down on that fine Kolwezi night a few days short of his twenty first birthday.

And I admit there was never a death in the Congo's bloody history that affected me as much as the loss of my young brother-in-law.

24

One Year

I showed the telegram to Julia as soon as it arrived at my Springs home.

'Am safely in Barcelona and awaiting your arrival Stop Regards to Julia Stop.'

It was from Tshombe and a Barcelona address was appended.

Neither Julia nor I were surprised at its arrival. Only two weeks previously Tshombe had finally fled Katanga and the constrictions of Addoula and UN politics.

'Are you going?' asked Julia.

'Of course.'

'How? We have no money.'

I shrugged my shoulders.

'Leave it to me.'

I actually had no idea in what capacity Tshombe wanted me, what services I could render or even how to get to him.

It was a leap into the unknown.

A careful review of the finances proved Julia correct; I was not going to be able to afford the air fare to Spain. Alternative steps were called for. I telephoned Jack Malloch in Salisbury and asked if he knew of any cheap flights.

'No problem, Jerry', came the reassuring drawl. 'I'm going to Europe in a week's time with the DC4 and you can come with me. It will cost you though.'

'How much?' I asked with sinking heart.

'Five rand for food', he replied with a chuckle.

Hasty last minute preparations. I left as much money as I could with Julia, said goodbye to the family and headed off for Salisbury on my big new adventure. Two days later I was in the United Kingdom; it pays to have contacts. From Gatwick I caught an airbus to sunny Barcelona where Tshombe was based and, feverish with anticipation, presented myself at his hotel.

Speedily I was ushered into the former President's suite.

'My loyal Chief of the air force has flown five thousand miles to see me', he laughed. 'I'm very, very happy to have you.'

We chattered inconsequentially. He appeared far more relaxed than in the dark days of post-secession. I chose my moment and then asked him delicately what my duties were to be.

He looked at me intently for a second time and then winked.

'Let's say you are an aide to the president of Katanga in exile.'

I had to be content with that.

An extremely comfortable room had been reserved for me at the hotel in company with the rest of the small staff then serving Tshombe in his private suite.

My first evening in Barcelona began inauspiciously. After a short rest, bath and shave I left my room that evening to dine downstairs with Tshombe.

Relaxed and refreshed I shut my bedroom door and began walking down the corridor. I recognised the youngish, blonde woman coming out of her hotel room at the same time she recognised me: Andrieux's widow. I had not seen her since Katanga days and my first instinct was to hasten over and express my sympathy at the loss of her husband.

'Madame, I am truly sorry at the unfortunate death of your husband,' I said taking her hand and bowing.

I may not have liked the man personally but I had every sympathy for his widow after the foul way in which he had been done in.

Madame Andrieux meanwhile, had not stopped gaping since setting eyes on me. She widened her eyes in horror, jerked her hand away and with a petrified squeak, hastened down the corridor. I never saw her again. Very strange.

At dinner that night with Tshombe I was lost in thought over the bizarre encounter with the Belgian widow. Tshombe noticed my silence.

'What's wrong, Jerry?'

'I just met Madame Andrieux in the passageway . . .'

Tshombe interrupted: 'Yes, she has come to see me about some financial matters. She is staying in the hotel for a few days.'

'She seemed very strange just now when I met her.'

The Congolese statesman cocked an eyebrow quizzically.

'Strange?'

'Yes, she acted as if she was terrified of me.'

Tshombe gave a little snigger.

'And you don't know why?'

'Not at all.'

'Then I'll tell you. The rumour is circulating among the colleagues of the late Andrieux that you ordered his death. That's why she was terrified. She imagined she had come face-to-face with her husband's murderer.'

I was appalled at Tshombe's revelation. Simply because I had disliked the man for his fiddling there was no reason to believe that I could or would order his death. The story was absurd but in a situation like the Congo, intrigue and rumour fed upon itself until it became entrenched as well attested fact. I still remember, with sorrow though, the horrified look in the little woman's eyes when we met in the dimly-lit hotel corridor.

Tshombe's information also suddenly brought other hitherto unexplained incidents into focus; incidents like that involving 'Remy' in Villa Luso. 'Remy', Zumbach's alcoholic associate, chose to come into Angolan exile with us for, I strongly suspect, another attempt to fiddle the books.

As soon as I saw him in Villa Luso I asked him to report to me to discuss 'certain matters' — routine inquiries about pay, as it happened. I remembered 'Remy' nodding and then hastily shambling away. I never saw him again. He left Angola the same day and never again associated himself with the Congo.

With hindsight I realised that the poor man believed that I was going to visit some terrible retribution on him for cooking the books in Katanga. Even before Andrieux's death then, I was carrying this label of chief executioner.

Back in Barcelona, Madame Andrieux left the hotel that same night without even sleeping in her bed. A note was delivered to Tshombe expressing her regret at not seeing him, but saying she had to return urgently to Brussels. Did she perhaps think she was my next target?

The incident was the beginning of an extraordinary twelve month period of my life during which I was at times bodyguard, at times confidant, at times emissary and at times general dogsbody. It was an easygoing, convivial, undemanding lifestyle. Sometimes I was busy, often not, sometimes I was in South Africa, sometimes in Spain. Julia was with me for long periods and at other times not.

And if I were asked now what my job was and what I did, it would be difficult to answer. My generic title was 'aide to the former president of Katanga' but the designation covered a score of functions and duties.

In Barcelona, Tshombe had a small staff, including a white secretary, Christine, a former black aide Naweji and several other loyal Katangese aides. For them most of the time was spent planning for the approaching Congolese elections, a never ending procession of visitors and importuners, memoranda, reports and messages. I had little to do with the mechanics of the campaign. Tshombe frequently flew on trips to various points around Europe and Britain and I was honoured to often find myself in the entourage as aide and trouble shooter.

Within a few weeks of my arrival in Spain, however, an important role emerged for me; one which I enthusiastically accepted and into which I poured body and soul. It was suggested circumspectly by Tshombe, expanded by me and developed into a regular process of shuffle diplomacy.

I became Tshombe's link man with the South African Government.

Tshombe was fighting an election and needed assistance; Tshombe was good news for South Africa and indeed the whole of the sub-continent; therefore South Africa should assist the former Katangese president.

Defining and extracting that assistance from the South African Government became my central and frustratingly elusive objective during the next twelve months.

Altogether I made a dozen trips to South Africa on various missions for Tshombe. Originally my key linkman was my old friend Pierre Retief at Defence HQ. Patiently he listened to all my expositions about the importance to South Africa of aiding Tshombe. Delicately I probed the possibility of some form of tangible assistance from Tshombe, vehicles with PA systems for electioneering in the Congolese towns and villages, funds, expressions of moral support. Inevitably Retief would promise to pass the requests on to higher authorities, inevitably he would smile cooperatively and equally inevitably he would tell me he thought I was mad to tie my tails to Tshombe's star.

Unknown to me at this stage Retief was having problems of his own. The sphere of operations of Military Intelligence were being drastically curtailed; gone were the free and easy days of covert operations such as Retief had laid on for us when we were smuggled back to Katanga at Tshombe's behest in 1962. Now the emphasis of power was slowly but surely devolving on the security section of the South African Police. At that precise moment a vicious internecine power struggle was going on between the military and civil security with military intelligence losing ground step by step. It was a struggle that was only to be properly resolved some years later with the formation of the autonomous and embracing BOSS — Bureau for State Security.

And month after month I went to an increasingly haggard Retief and pleaded, urged, cajoled, bullied, quite unaware that my mentor's sphere of operation was decreasing proportionately to my increasing stridency.

After several months of frustration I decided on a new tack; an approach straight to cabinet level. On one of my trips I twisted the arm of my Springs Member of Parliament, Len Taurog, sufficiently to gain an audience with the then Minister of Police, Mr Balthazar John Vorster, soon to be Prime Minister of South Africa.

Our meeting was incongruously at the official opening of a police station in Kwa Thema, Springs and I was able to snatch a few moments with the minister. All my pent up frustrations and carefully thought out defences for Tshombe came to the fore and in a short time I had available to me I argued forcefully and fluently in my mother tongue, Afrikaans, for increased South African support for Tshombe.

In all his public statements Tshombe had expressed pro-South African statements. A Congo under such a man would be a powerful ally to South Africa and would help stabilize the situation among the other southern African countries. The links of common financial interests in the subcontinent could not be overlooked. It was owed to the Congo, to Southern Africa and to the West.

Mr Vorster took it all in, serious eyes fixed on my face, nodding occasionally. When I had finished he replied carefully, considering every word.

'You understand, *Meneer,* that we are not unaware of the advantages that will accrue from Mr Tshombe's success in the elections. However, you must also be aware that, because of the nature of independent African politics, we have to be extremely circumspect. It is not the policy of this Government to interfere in the internal affairs of other black nations. You have presented your case cogently and I will certainly consider it. I thank you.'

He bowed as if to end the interview. I turned to leave.

'One minute, *Meneer* Puren. Perhaps I can assist by providing you with an introduction to somebody who might be in a better position to consider your proposals; Colonel Johann Buys, in Pretoria — tell him everything.'

Buys turned out to be an intelligent, competent man; a well built, police officer versed in Africa and its politics; revolutionary and evolutionary. He proved to have an insatiable interest in whatever I had to say about the Congo. Better still, he seemed genuinely interested in Tshombe's fortunes; unusual at the time because of the almost universal tendency to dismiss Tshombe as an also ran.

My view that Tshombe's interest and South Africa's were synonymous was something I propounded endlessly in the corridors of power in Pretoria . . . but always to a diminishing audience.

Buys, however, stood firm in his optimism for Tshombe's future, and as the civil security service was taking an increasing role, I began from this point to see less and less of Retief in connection with the Congo and Tshombe.

My attempts to interest South African political leaders in Tshombe did not end with Mr Vorster. In mid 1964, I was able to wangle a meeting with Sir De Villiers Graaf, leader of the official opposition, at which I discussed my hopes very generally. Unfortunately he was surrounded at that point with other people and I could not speak as freely as I had wanted.

During all this time Julia remained a constant competent help to Tshombe. Based sometimes in South Africa and sometimes in Spain with me, she ably represented Tshombe's interests in my absence and frequently was host to high ranking Katangese and Congolese government officials while they were on surreptitious visits to South Africa.

Usually the VIPs would stay at my Springs home with Julia and the local gossip this caused can only be imagined.

Springs is basically a small and conservative town and 1963 was the height of Verwoerdian separatist dogma. Yet, here was this white woman often host to these coal black men. What the neighbours, let alone the precinct constabulary, thought, I often wonder. Julia of course sailed through it all with her typical devil-may-care charm.

One incident in particular says much for the people and the politics of my disturbed country. Two very senior former Katangese officials had come to South Africa at my suggestion to see a cabinet official and they had been accommodated, as usual, at my Springs home. Also as usual, two ranking security officers arrived in an official car next day to pick up the VIPs and Julia to take them to their meeting in Union Buildings. Once at Union Buildings the five clambered out and marched up the stairs to the lobby and towards the lifts, the two officers leading, followed by Julia and the two VIPs.

Firmly planted in front of the lifts (which were marked 'Whites Only') was a dumpy middle-aged, empty-headed white lift operator of the professional sheltered employment type that the South African civil service is so competent at attracting.

This fine representative of white susceptibilities took one look at the two black Katangese, shot out his finger and hissed very loudly in Afrikaans: 'Those two Kaffirs are not using this lift.'

The tone, more than the racially abhorrent appellation, brought the two security agents and Julia up short, wide-eyed. One just did not talk to VIPs like that. Not unnaturally the two guests didn't understand the insult and merely turned quizzically to Julia.

'Nothing to worry about; the gentleman says the lift is out of order,' Julia lied.

Shrewdly she had realised that it was better climbing the flights of stairs rather than risking a nasty scene with the overbearing little Napoleon of the lift shafts. The two officers nodded, glared furiously at the triumphant little man and led the way up the stairs.

Back in Spain our social life was full. While still in Barcelona, Tshombe was invited to many functions, all of which I was too poor to attend. When he dined at home though, I invariably found myself sitting with the president.

On one of these occasions I found myself interpreter at a bit of high level politicking involving Harry N'kumbula of Northern Rhodesia. By this time the Federation had dissolved and N'kumbula was fighting an election against Kaunda. For an election one needs money and N'kumbula unerringly made for the money bags, Tshombe, former president of the land to the north of the foundling Zambia, commander of a still sizeable army in exile and possessor of a national treasury.

Tshombe spoke good French but little English, while N'kumbula spoke good English but no French. Jerry Puren, whose mother tongue was Afrikaans, was called in as interpreter. Despite my worst fears the evening progressed famously with witty repartee from both sides being liberally translated by myself.

I still wonder if the bursts of laughter from Tshombe were at N'kumbula's witticisms or my translations.

N'kumbula, however, did not broach the delicate issue of funds at that meeting and the conversation was fortunately largely uncomplicated.

Also soon to visit Tshombe was Mathews Phiri, who led an abortive opposition against Hastings Banda for the premiership in Malawi, the former Nyasaland.

A few days later Tshombe and the entourage moved to Madrid where the former President brought himself a town flat and began to collect an assortment of free loaders and adventurers. As usual, the presence of money and the possibility of excitement attracted various adventurers and con-artists from all over the globe, many of them old Katanga hands, all of them with some bright idea for getting Tshombe back. Throughout his political life Tshombe was destined to be surrounded by knots of importuning wheeler-dealers, invariably white.

Election campaigning moved into top gear with plans and 'fool-proof' strategies as bountiful as the cool Mediterranean breezes. For my part I kept strictly to myself conferring occasionally with Tshombe when he wanted me.

In Madrid at that stage there were a wide variety of exiles, has-beens and optimistic would-bes. Among the colourful characters with their place in the Spanish sun were Skorzeny, the SS officer who daringly rescued Mussolini from his mountain top prison during World War-2; Argentine's Peron and the Cuba's ex-dictator, Batiste.

Almost the entire Roumanian Government in exile had taken up residence in Spain and from these Iron Guard members I was to draw two particularly close friends, Oanca and Calistrat. Both were later to serve in the Congolese mercenary forces.

It was a strange time of my life. Unlike the others I did not draw a regular salary but lived from week to week on what Tshombe gave me, a system that threatened me with dire poverty one day and promised great wealth the next. At all times though my family in South Africa was provided for and, on balance, I would say that Tshombe erred more on the side of generosity than meanness in his dealing with me.

Times were hard though sometimes. I remember once arriving very late in Paris from South Africa, this time accompanied by Julia. We had just enough money to take a taxi to the centre of town and book into a cheap pensione for the night. Next day we were due to meet Tshombe but at that moment we did not have a franc to split between us. Dispirited and hungry we walked along a Paris street trying hard to ignore the wafting and tantalising aroma coming from the street side café's. Despairingly we looked at each other.

Suddenly Julia stopped, stooped, and in a single smooth movement, plunged her hand into a puddle of water alongside the pavement and drew up sixteen or seventeen francs in coins; somebody's loss, our gain. We burst out laughing at our fortune and hastened over to a street café where we bought bread, sausages, cheese and wine. Next day Tshombe arrived in Paris and we had a couple of thousand dollars in our pockets. Rags to riches.

Then the return to Madrid. The coterie of hangers-on had swollen, the schemes were woollier, Tshombe seemed drifting and I began to despair of the campaign ever getting off the ground.

For a moment my confidence in Tshombe began to falter. I began to question our hopes of returning to the Congo; our reasons for being in Spain at all. Home, my children, regular employment beckoned. And then, quite suddenly, the dice of history rolled in Tshombe's favour.

25

A Promise

The eastern regions of the Congo are a desolate insular area, ideal stamping ground for a particular brand of Congolese obduracy and brutality. In these unpoliced areas the Leopoldville Government had never been accepted as national leaders, their writ ran only as far as the nearest ANC detachment and the image of the martyred Lumumba still played an important rallying role there.

Under Christopher Gbenye, Gaston Soumialot and Pierre Mulele, the wild eastern tribesmen found natural leaders and within months the ragged, feathered Bafulera spearmen and archers from the forest were fomenting rebellion in the Kivu and Kwilu provinces and in north eastern Katanga. Invariably drugged, heavily doctored with witch doctor's potions that were supposed to make them immune to bullets, the *Mulele Mi* or water of Mulele, the tribesmen confronted and defeated the terrified and undisciplined ANC forces facing them.

The ANC troops fled, throwing their sophisticated weapons away or simply joining the rebels. Others scrabbled for places on the hastily retreating army trucks.

Rebellion, originally sparked in Katanga's Albertville, spread rapidly to Kindu and then towards Stanleyville. In Leopoldville, Addoula and Mobutu watched impotently as their armies fell apart and the rebellion flourished with a barbarism hitherto unseen in an already turbulent Congolese past.

Prime targets were western orientated people, educated people, missionaries and later all whites. It was, as somebody has since observed, decolonialism in its purest and most irrational form. Albertville fell followed soon by Uvira.

What had first been considered by the UN and the US's CIA as a minor disturbance soon turned into a ravening tide that threatened the Addoula Government. Chinese support for the rebels, mainly by way of Burundi and Tanzania, quickly turned the hapless Congo into another playground for superpower involvement.

In Madrid we carefully monitored the course of the revolt and its effect on the Congo. All parties instinctively realised that the key to the success or the failure of the revolt was Katanga, and the key to Katanga was Tshombe. We awaited developments.

Before long Albert Kalonji of Kasai put in an appearance to 'discuss developments' with Tshombe (read ask for a seat in any future coalition government Tshombe might set up) and two rebels from north Katanga Province also arrived.

They told us arrogantly that they would soon topple Addoula and Mobutu. The writing was on the wall. Tactfully they sounded out whether Tshombe would support them. The master tactician remained masterly taciturn.

One evening it fell to me to entertain the two rebel delegates and Kalonji at dinner, a dinner dominated by the rebels' dire warnings against the Addoula regime. Over sweets, eyes fixed on the two vociferous guests, I had time to reflect that all the major Congolese liberation movements stemmed from Katanga; even this rebel outburst had started at Albertville and later spread to Kindu.

Another visitor was Thomas Kanza, an intellectual Bakongo who was later to change his support to the rebel movement. He came from a family with a long history of opposition to Kasavubu.

Even Mobutu deigned to visit Europe and a meeting was set up between him and Tshombe on the borders of France and Spain. The comings and goings sparked intense debate among Tshombe's entourage and stayed whatever moves I might have been considering about leaving Tshombe. Still the former Katangese president remained silent.

Meanwhile trouble had been brewing among the exiled Katangese forces in Angola. Living in difficult and often appalling conditions in the bush camps, listlessly waiting for action, it was natural that disaffection should set in among the by now six thousand troops.

A lot of it was directed towards Schramme, the white martinet OC, who struck many of the black troops as too autocratic. A delegation of senior black Katangese officers, led by Kaniki, a former air force armourer, came to see Tshombe with an impressive list of grievances. After lengthy and sometimes heated discussions with Tshombe it was agreed that the dissident troops could split and set up their own camp. Eventually four thousand did elect to join the new camp under the command of the likeable and competent Kaniki. Under the circumstances Tshombe's decision was the wisest one and despite the split, no antagonisms emerged between the two camps and at no time was their over riding loyalty to Tshombe in question.

In Spain rumours began wildly circulating. It was obvious that the communist backed rebels were in imminent danger of toppling the West leaning CIA-propped central government. Western nations had accepted that although Addoula and Mobutu were good front men, it was essential that somebody who could operate from a strong power base should take over the reigns and rally the opposition, somebody for example with an army in exile.

To compound the urgency of the situation, Secretary General U Thant of the UN had meanwhile warned that the last UN troops would have to be pulled out by June 30 1964, four years after independence, and the whole expensive UN operation wound down.

In May 1964 I was suddenly asked by Tshombe to accompany a delegation to London. Again my role was ambivalent but I gathered our purpose was to visit top British officials and parliamentarians to drum up support for Tshombe's return to the Congo. There was intense speculation that Tshombe's return was inevitable. The former Katangese president quartered at the Savoy Hotel while I was accommodated at the Strand Palace, the hotel I had used during and after the war whenever I stayed in London.

182

I spent the days of that week renewing old acquaintances and taking nostalgic walks along the streets while Tshombe rushed from one meeting to the next; MacMillan, Churchill and several prominent Tories on the list. One of the old associates I made contact with was Stefan Wojik, formerly Zumbach's 2 ic and a man whose courage and ability I had always admired. We met in an English pub on a fine spring evening.

'Doing anything special in the near future?' I asked casually over a frothy head of Watney's Red.

'What have you got for me?' he replied with a grin.

'Possibly some more Congo flying. And this time not against the UN.'

'When do I start?'

'Not quite now but be on standby. Very soon, I hope. Very soon.'

We spent the rest of the evening in nostalgic discussions on the Katanga days.

Back in Madrid activity reached a frenetic pitch and it became common knowledge that Tshombe was about to return to the government of the Congo — by invitation. I judged the moment right and one night tackled him when we were alone in his office.

'I understand you are to return to the Congo soon?'

Tshombe shrugged.

'Perhaps. I do not wish to say anything at this stage.'

'Assuming you return might I ask how you intend to halt the rebel movement?'

'By negotiation of course, Jerry. By talking and reason.'

'And if that fails, sir?'

'By force.'

I came straight to the point.

'If it's necessary to use force will you recruit mercenaries?'

Tshombe appeared lost in thought for a few seconds.

'Jerry, I believe you knew the answer before asking the question. The ANC are useless, that is no secret. They desert at the first sight of the rebels. If I have to fight the rebels, I have only two possible weapons, the Gendarmes and . . .'

'And mercenaries,' I finished for him.

He nodded.

'Sad but true. It will be the only way we will halt the scourge if negotiations fail, which pray God, they will not.'

'Mister President, I wish to make a special request. If it unfortunately becomes necessary to hire mercenaries, may I be in charge of the operations, Julia and I? Might I request that we recruit only from South Africa and Rhodesia?'

Tshombe stared at me surprised.

'Why only South Africa and Rhodesia?'

'Because we need a cohesive unit if it is to be of any effect. We saw the problems in Katanga from having too many nationalities in separate commands; the jealousy, the rivalries, the distrust. In South Africa and Rhodesia I can recruit two hundred men for you in a week and have infinitely more thereafter. They will be easy to get to the Congo and I know just the man to command them.'

He seemed hesitant. I pushed on.

'I promise you that with the force I have in mind we can turn the rebels in a matter of days. As for the air wing, I have for some months past taken the liberty of having certain of the old Katanga pilots in South Africa on standby. I can have them available in a day's notice.'

Tshombe made up his mind.

'Agreed then, Jerry. If it's necessary to raise mercenaries, you will arrange it and they will be recruited from Rhodesia and South Africa.'

I was elated beyond all bounds. The likelihood of Tshombe returning was excellent, the use of mercenary forces in quelling the rebellion almost certain. I had the assurance that only Rhodesians and South Africans were to be recruited and I knew the man I wanted to head them.

Tshombe's decision that night was to lead to the creation of a mercenary force soon to become legendary and was to place the achievement of a real South African involvement in the destiny of the Congo, tantalizingly within grasp.

That night I telephoned Julia in South Africa and told her to inform my standby pilots, Hedges, Wicksteed, and a young South African called Errol, to be ready to move soon.

The three had originally been quartered at my house in Springs but when their rumbustious activities had become too overwhelming, they had later been moved out to a local hotel. The long suffering hotelier endured two inconveniences — the one of having the hell raisers and the other of having to wait up to four months at a time for his bills to be paid. Fortunately he knew me well enough and was quite prepared to wait patiently until I had wheedled enough money out of Tshombe to pay the bill.

I went to bed satisfied that the future was promising and my long wait with Tshombe was worth every second.

As soon as it became apparent that things were really moving, Julia came winging her way into Spain, never one to miss the action. The expected news was broken early one morning by a delighted Tshombe aide.

Addoula, with US agreement, had invited Tshombe to return to the Congo as Prime Minister under the presidency of Kasavubu. It was to be an emergency government to last as long as the rebel threat endured.

Immediately a flood of instructions emanated from Tshombe's office. Julia and I were packed off back to South Africa to await instructions.

Commandant Wautier, a Belgian advisor, one of the Madrid coterie and an agent for the Belgian Secret Service, was despatched to Angola. His instructions were clear: prepare the Gendarmes for action.

Tshombe was keeping his promise to return.

26

Return and New Blood

First telephone call when I returned to South Africa was to the man I had in mind for the command of the mercenary force, Mike Hoare.

'Are you interested in another post in the Congo?' I asked the Katanga veteran after the first round of convivial chat.

'What type, Jerry?'

'Command of a mercenary group to spearhead the turning of the rebel movement.'

There was an instant's pause.

'Sounds promising, but on whose authority are you offering the job?'

'Nobody's yet, but I know the post is going to be opened soon and I want to have my man there and that's you.'

Another silence.

'Of course I'll come. When do we move?'

I chuckled loudly.

'That's my man. Wait until you hear from me again. It won't be long at all, I promise.'

'Just one question Jerry.'

'Yes?'

'What are *you* doing?'

That was more difficult to answer.

'I don't know exactly at this stage. I'll definitely be heading the air element and initially arranging recruitment for the mercenaries. Apart from that I don't know.'

A few more questions and answers and we rang off.

Hoare had been in the Congo before as leader of a mobile group but was still largely unknown to Tshombe. I had been tremendously impressed by the discipline and the effective force he had engineered from the disparate southern African adventurers in those early days of the Katanga secession.

Since leaving the Congo he had settled into a comfortable accountancy job near Durban, bought himself a yacht and showed every sign of permanence. Obviously, though, the spirit of adventure ran deep in his Irish blood.

Tshombe eventually arrived in Leopoldville at 05h00 on June 30 1964 to take up his post as Prime Minister under Kasavubu's presidency. Only a few days earlier

Tshombe's enemy of old, Jason Sendwe, had been hacked to pieces by the rebels in Albertville. By this stage the rebels held virtually half the Congo unchallenged and were then moving on Luluabourg in Kasai. The situation was critical.

South African newspapers were full of the recall. Intense speculation continued that even Tshombe would not be able to hold the westward thrust of the rebels.

Two days later I received the telegram from Tshombe. It was concise and to the point. Addressed to Colonel Puren it simply stated that my services were urgently required in Leopoldville. Although there had been no confirmation that Hoare would be put in charge of the mercenary ground force I knew the Congo ways well enough and realised that it was essential to have my man on the spot right from the beginning.

I telephoned Mike Hoare in Durban and that same afternoon he, Julia and I were flying out of Jan Smuts airport on our way to Leopoldville, in all of us apprehension was outweighed by excitement. With us were Jimmy Hedges and Errol.

On arrival at Leopoldville we were met by Congolese officials in an impressive looking Limousine and hustled off to an executive suite in the Memling Hotel, best in the capital.

And there the great wait began.

Tshombe, besieged now by a host of pressure from all sides, internal and external, was desperately working for a conciliation within the Congo. Bravely he decided on a tour to the interior, Bakavu and Stanleyville, in an attempt at rapprochement with Gbenye and Kanza.

Tshombe, always a man for talk and reason, was taking the olive branch.

Hoare and myself represented the big sticks in reserve.

It was impossible at this stage to see Tshombe personally and Munongo, Minister of the Interior, became my main link man.

The days passed while Tshombe continued his peace making trip to the interior.

Mike began to express impatience, suggested he should return home. I placated him, told him that patience paid dividends, especially in Africa. We waited.

Eventually Tshombe returned from the abortive peace mission. The rebels had demanded that Mobutu be replaced by General Lundula and that Kasuvabu be sacked. Tshombe had naturally and loyally refused.

It was apparent that the talking was over; now it was war.

The rebels had taken Baudouinville, Coquillatville, Albertville and Stanleyville; they were now swarming across Kasai. Conditions in the ANC were chaotic and it didn't seem possible to muster a single platoon of loyal ANC troops to stand against the rebels.

At this point things started moving internationally and domestically. On the international front the Americans belatedly realised how much they had underestimated the strength of followers of the rebels and pulled out all the stops. Four huge C-31 transports of the USAAF lumbered on to the tarmac at Ndjili airport near Leopoldville; the first of a flood of American military aid that was intended to help halt the rebel tide and 'save the Congo for the West'.

Sure we were happy to have the gum chewing crewmen in their sunglasses and flag emblazoned overalls, even happier to have their transports.

A shuttle began between the Angolan Gendarme bases and points deep in the

186

Congo. Having been instrumental in driving the Gendarmes into the bases a year previously, the Americans were now busy ferrying them back out.

On the domestic front we had a number of T6s given to the Congo by the Americans. The powerful little fighter trainers were the same as we had used in Katanga but far more effectively and lethally armed; rocket rails, two ,30 Browning machineguns and rocket pods.

It was a nucleus for the air element against the rebels. My mouth watered just seeing them standing on the apron.

Very soon afterwards I got my chance. Early in the morning I received a 'phone call at the Memling from the ANC *Etat Major;* a brief instruction to take three T6s and head for Luluabourg which was to be used as the staging area for a counter thrust against the rebels. I was out of the hotel in five minutes.

Apart from Hedges and Errol, a Frenchman called Davrinche, and several other pilots had already arrived in the Congo on my instructions and within the hour I had them down at the airfield checking over the T6s.

Soon we were winging across the rolling jungles of Kasai and Luluabourg. It had been more than a year since I had flown across the verdant green carpet and mighty rivers of the Congo. I smiled wryly. Last time I had been a loner, an outsider, an outlaw from the international community, an antagonist of the US and the public enemy No 1 for Mobutu and the ANC. And here I was head of the only operational squadron of the Congolese Air Force, in the vanguard of the West's defence of the Congo against the rebels and a key element in ANC strategy.

Circumstances had changed but not my loyalties. I was still a Tshombe man.

On the long haul to Luluabourg I had time to reflect upon the strange marriage of convenience between Tshombe and his former antagonists. I laid no bets on which party would be the first to sue for divorce.

At Luluabourg, Errol, who was piloting the aircraft I was in, badly misjudged the airfield and overshot. The boy obviously had a bit to learn about Congo style flying. We careered into the overshoot area, jammed on brakes and wiped our undercarriage out. So much for our grand entry to war. Ruefully the pilots gathered around the wrecked T6. Errol seemed overcome with embarassment.

'Don't worry about it, lad. Part of the game. Only problem now is that we won't all be able to take part in this operation.'

I noticed a telltale flicker of light in Hedges' eye.

'I suppose you want out Hedges?'

'Well I won't say I'd be disappointed', he replied accurately. 'I'll go back and fly the DC3.'

'Okay. You can get a ride on one of the Yank transports and we'll carry on with the op in the remaining two T6s.'

Hedges nodded eagerly and we all sauntered off to the administration offices and area HQ. Around us the airfield was bustling with activity.

The USAAF C-31s were rumbling in throughout the day discharging platoon after platoon of fit, disciplined and eager Gendarmes, Kaniki's men. More than six hundred of them had already arrived and more were pouring in every hour.

The town was packed with the familiar camouflage clad troops and it wasn't long before I was running into well known faces. Invariably our greetings were enthusiastic and rowdy. After more than a year in the privations of the bush the Gendarmes were itching to get back into action.

My little group of pilots watched a platoon disembarking and forming up on the tarmac to the shouted instructions of their NCOs. The uniforms were neat and well pressed, webbing new, rifles still over oily from the armoury. The men had the lean and rapid movements of well trained troops. Davrinche nodded his head approvingly.

'We can't go very much wrong with those boys.'

I nodded my head in silent agreement.

They were not the only Gendarmes arriving back in the Congo. Others, this time Schramme's men, were landing at Elisabethville and Kamina for the Albertville thrust; the same class of eager and professional soldiers. Tshombe's soldier children had come home to be with their father.

That same day I managed to wrangle Hedges a lift back to Leopoldville on a USAF transport. He showed no reluctance to go and as he left with the spare, sandy haired captain of the transport, I reflected how unwise I had been to bring him back with me.

The only reason I had in fact kept Hedges on the payroll in South Africa was because I needed a pool of readily available pilots for Tshombe's return. It would have been impossible to raise a contingent in South Africa at short notice without creating a stir and possibly attracting press attention. Still, I should have learnt my lesson with Hedges in Katanga.

Eventually he was to be sent out of the Congo by my successor, Stefan Wojik, a man a good deal less tolerant of failings in his pilots.

At dawn next day we took the two T6s on a recce north east of Luluabourg towards Lusambo and Lubefu, areas of known rebel concentrations. We didn't have much trouble finding them.

I was co-pilot with Errol and we were about thirty kilometers east of Lusambo when the T6 banked and dropped suddenly towards the dusty road. I peered out the perspex canopy and on our portside had my first glimpse of this invincible horde, this victorious army which the ANC were unable to check.

A column of about three hundred meters long, perhaps a thousand rebels in all, formed up in ranks, marching obviously towards the ferry. I had a flash glance of ragged warriors, monkey skins, furs, feathers, a palisade of spears, one or two automatic rifles, and then we were past.

Errol wheeled and we came back for a second look. This time I noticed the distinguishable remnants of ANC uniforms, tunics and trousers, obviously on deserters or stripped from dead bodies. Rows upon rows of bare feet, one or two pairs of boots. I stared carefully at their weapons. By far the majority wielded thin spears and bows. The firearms were irregularly spaced; mostly FNs, a few communist RPG rocket launchers, one or two LMGs. I fancied I saw one AK-47 in the crush of people.

On the third run the column wavered and ran for cover. The invincible tide was about to be sharply turned, I thought to myself as Errol pulled the T6 out and we recced farther east.

More poignantly we flew low over several missions and saw the huddled, anxious white faces of the nuns and missionaries looking up at us. A few waved. Later they were all to be rounded up by the rebels and sent to Stanleyville as hostages, there to suffer unspeakable indignities and tortures.

We dipped our wings solicitously and headed back to Luluabourg with our intelligence.

Next day, fully armed, we took to the air and retraced our path to Lusambo. Sure enough we again came across the *Jeunesse* columns marching in the road. This time it was the real thing. We roared over the fast dissolving column at treetop level with our Brownings hammering, traversing the length of the road with thousands of rounds. We pulled out, wheeled and came in again. This time the road was empty except for maybe two score inert forms. For the rest the *Jeunesse* had disappeared into the bush. It was an inconclusive and unsatisfactory encounter. We returned again to base.

Two days later we saw that the rebels had crossed the river and were heading west from Lusambo. The O group was tense and excited in the dawn light, the young Katangese officers eager to let their Gendarmes off the leash. By this time they seemed prepared to run on foot all the way to Lusambo to fight the rebels.

Kaniki and General Marsiala pointed out the estimated positions of the rebel column on a large scale map and soberly gave orders to their officers. Then Marsiala turned to me.

'And now for the essential ingredient, Colonel; air support. If you would oblige with some close support until the Gendarmes . . . I mean until the ANC . . . clash with the rebel column?'

I nodded and the O group broke up and walked out into the still grey morning light.

Without fuss the troops boarded their trucks and jeeps with their ubiquitous pedestal mounted machineguns, formed into columns and motored rapidly through the streets to the cheers of the town's people.

The Gendarmes met the rebels about fifty kilometers west of Lusambo on the Luluabourg road. It was a massacre.

From the air we harried the Simba column as requested until they actually clashed with Kaniki's Gendarmes-turned-ANC forces.

From three hundred and fifty meters above we took grandstand seats of the battle unfolding below us. The rebels, by now many strong, moved on foot and by truck. Densely packed, they surged down the road towards the approaching Gendarme column, a long snakelike movement of people, weapons and vehicles.

The lead jeep of the Gendarme column didn't even reduce speed as it approached. I held my breath as the two forces drew closer. The thin line of olive green vehicles were partially obscured by billows of dust; the black mass of Simba infantrymen equally obscured. It looked as if the lead Gendarme jeep was only meters away from the first ranks of rebels when the gunner began blasting furiously, almost at point blank range, at the surge of faces.

Battle hardened as I was, I felt sickened at the slaughter that followed. The lead jeeps clove a path through the chanting, swaying spearmen and, at almost arms length, mowed them down in swathes. I could imagine the drugged, sweating rebels desperately holding out their ampoules of *dawa,* the medicine that was to turn the ANC bullets to water.

The outcome was inevitable. Rebels scattered for cover, clawing each other to get away from the merciless hail of bullets. The rebels disappeared off the road and, over a long stretch of track the Gendarmes jeeps moved slowly forward, sometimes over heaped bodies, as the sweating gunners raked the bush with belt after belt of ,30 and ,50 calibre bullets.

From the air bodies could be seen scattered astride the road and on either side right up to the bush wall as carelessly as shed clothing. The *Jeunesse* and rebels were never to threaten Luluabourg again. A turning point had been reached.

On the way back to the Kasai capital I had time to marvel at the infinite variety of nations, empires and tribes that constituted the Congo. So this was the reality of this ravening and unstoppable force that was supposed to topple the central government; ignorant and untrained peasants armed with spears, bows and a few firearms. Yet the ANC had been quite incapable of administering as simple and as salutary a hiding as had the Gendarmes done that day. In terms of discipline and courage the Katangese were streets ahead of the rest of the herd.

On balance, as well, I had reason to be proud of the activities of the fledgling air force. Although I had not come to the Congo to be a liaison officer but rather as an aide to the Prime Minister, the critical situation made it necessary for me to adopt *de facto* control of the air force. Some of the pilots I had under my command had never been in any type of operation before and had never even fired rockets or machineguns. Not a bad showing for a first try.

27

The Wild Geese Come Home To Roost

It was four very worried men who interviewed Mike Hoare the same evening that I left for Luluabourg with the T6s. Prime Minister Moise Tshombe was there, as was my friend Godefroid Munongo, Minister of the Interior, the slightly sinister Victor Nendaka, Minister of Security, and of course, the Commander in Chief, General Joseph Mobutu.

Julia presented Hoare and did the interpretations in what turned out to be a surprisingly short exchange.

Tshombe told Hoare that it had been agreed to recruit white mercenaries and no objections had been received from either Belgium or the US State Department, provided the mercenaries were not Americans.

The Commander in Chief then gave Hoare written instructions to recruit two hundred men immediately and another eight hundred in two further phases.

Both Julia and Hoare were staggered at the numbers ordered by Mobutu but willingly accepted the task. Tshombe had indeed kept his word.

Delighted, Hoare caught the next flight back to South Africa followed shortly afterwards by Julia who deposited forty thousand dollars in a South African bank. Now came the impossible task; to recruit a thousand mercenaries without any publicity.

Advertisements appeared in all South African and Rhodesian newspapers calling for fit young men 'looking for employment with a difference'.

The response was overwhelming.

From all corners they came tramping into our two recruiting offices in Johannesburg and Salisbury; former servicemen, adventurers, romantics, students, derelicts, idealists, criminals and cheated lovers. And inevitably the press seized upon it as the story of the year.

Within days the cover was blown and the world knew that Tshombe was recruiting mercenaries from racist South Africa (what a horror) and Rhodesia (what a scandal).

Then came the inevitable howl of condemnation from the second and third world powers who, up until that point, had remained strangely silent on the well documented atrocities being committed by the rebels in the Congo. The recruiting went ahead and bit by bit the ANC's famed V Commando took shape, the rough ready and lethal contingent of mercenaries that Hoare would call the Wild Geese.

In the Congo by this stage there was a desperate need to take emergency tactical counter strikes against local targets and then a long range counter offensive against the rebel heartland, one spearheaded by an effective mercenary force.

In South Africa Hoare's initial recruiting drive was necessarily hasty and the general quality of the first men he attracted was not overwhelmingly high. All told thirty mercenaries returned with him to the chaos that was Leopoldville. They were sent out to Kamina base, by now a derelict ghost camp.

Bungalows had to be prepared, uniforms and weapons drawn, food supplies ordered and the first steps taken to build a disciplined force.

Hoare overcame the logistical problems one by one.

Literally within days of his return Hoare was given orders to lead a waterborne assault on the rebel held airfield of Albertville, in a bid to establish a bridgehead for the ANC forces then threatening the town.

A series of misadventures and sheer bad luck dogged Hoare's operation and it failed with the loss of two German mercenaries.

Back in Leopoldville the reaction to the abortive raid was instantaneous and vocal. One good result though was that the Belgian Colonel Vanderwalle, in charge of Fifth Mechanised Group which included V Commando, agreed that better training facilities should be established and the mercenaries given longer instruction periods . . . a total of three weeks.

Unfortunately, the Congolese now decided to shop around Europe for additional mercenary troops; a move I had opposed from the beginning. The troops were, however, to be attached to the ANC units themselves and never formed a composite command as did V Commando.

Albertville was a bad start for Hoare, but he soon showed his mettle and, within weeks the South African and Rhodesian mercenaries were pouring into Kamina, receiving longer and better training periods and going into the field better equipped. They embarked on the first of a series of whirlwind successes.

V Commando was divided up into eight smaller sections ranging from Commando 51 through to Commando 58.

The South African and Rhodesian mercenary force in the Congo operated under trying and frustrating conditions, and certainly not all the flak was from the rebels.

The Belgian technical advisors, four hundred of them and still playing an important role in Congolese affairs, strongly resented the influx of southern African mercenaries and put every obstacle in the way. The old Congo intrigues and antagonisms began.

And not surprisingly, Julia and I found ourselves slap in the middle of it. Since returning from South Africa after depositing the money for recruitment, Julia had been commissioned a lieutenant in the ANC and, based at *Etat Major,* Leopoldville and was in charge of inducting, equipping and despatching the mercenaries. It was a hard job involving unremitting, petty quarrels with uncooperative Belgian officials.

Already the original figure of one thousand mercenaries had been whittled to three hundred by the Belgians.

Matters came to a head when a platoon of mercenaries, the raw material for the proposed Commando 51 under Gary Wilson, arrived in Leopoldville one evening before being sent to Lisala from where they were to be deployed against the rebels.

The Belgians refused point blank to help.

We were kept in the dark about their arrival, and valuable time was wasted while the bewildered mercenaries were shunted from pillar to post.

I was away on a mission at the time but Julia located them and fell to using all her wiles in an effort to find them equipment. No avail. 'Phone messages were left unanswered, senior G-4 (Supply) officers unavailable.

In desperation she drafted a note to Vanderwalle and asked him to sign a declaration that he was aware of the mercenaries' arrival but refused to equip them. The ploy worked. In short order Vanderwalle had Commando 51 equipped and sent out to Lisala.

This continual obstruction from the Belgians came as no surprise (I had been two years in Katanga), but it still angered me how petty jealousies could intrude into matters of desperate urgency.

Eventually V Commando took Lisala, Mobutu's birth place, under Lieutenant Gary Wilson, a Sandhurst graduate. In approved mercenary style the forty white commandos roared into the town in their jeeps under a furious barrage of machinegun fire and drove the Simba rebels out.

More than one hundred and fifty dead rebels were left.

Again the *dawa* hadn't helped.

The victory at Lisala, however, brought to light one of the more tricky aspects of mercenary officering. Gary Wilson, with some justification, believed he had achieved an important victory in the counter offensive against the rebels. Not so understandable were his expectations, indeed his demands, for some type of immediate promotion.

Among all young mercenary officers there was a general ruthless striving to win promotion and superiority. In strictly disciplined and hierarchical national armies these ambitions can generally be directed through clearly established and time honoured channels and procedures, but in a mercenary force with less rigid traditions and hierarchies, unchecked ambition among subordinates can be divisive and fatal. Hoare was obliged to act quickly and authoritatively to re-establish his command. Hoare was himself not against a little palace politicking — particularly when it was directed against Vanderwalle.

The incident was not the first of its kind. In the vast reaches of the Congo it often happened that the individual commandos would be out of touch for weeks at a time. Maintaining discipline was just that much more difficult. Under the circumstances Hoare did a highly effective job of holding together and keeping motivated V Commando. It's achievements were a tribute to Hoare's determination and skill.

Within weeks the commandos were deployed on a wide front against the Simbas; heated, bloody and fast moving engagements against an implacable foe.

During this time Hoare's basic intention was to build a unit of highly disciplined mercenaries fighting according to conventional battle ethics, an attempt to return an air of dignity to mercenary soldiering that had tended to be lost in the wild and woolly days of the Katangese *Les Affreux*.

In terms of tactics, the defects in the use of the available mercenary forces became apparent and Hoare urged that they be formed into a cohesive strike force rather than in small groups dispersed in limited engagements on a wide front.

The point was well taken and soon the ANC began mustering two strike forces for an attack directly at Stanleyville.

Lima 1 was under the command of Colonel Liegeois and Lima II under Colonel Lamoulin.

Hoare, then a major, fell under Lamoulin and commanded the V Commando element of the Stanleyville column, the spearhead of the entire two hundred vehicle column.

And while this was taking place I was concentrating on the task which I had originally set myself; building and training a credible Congolese Air Strength. Immediately after my return from the raids at Luluabourg I was asked to report to Mobutu.

I found the bespectacled, sturdily built man standing behind his desk, impeccably uniformed as always. He waved to the ubiquitous bottle of chilled French champagne in its silver bucket and an aide poured us each a glass. We toasted the success of the Luluabourg operation.

'Colonel Puren, I want to say how much I appreciated your operations at Luluabourg, just the sort of thing we need for ground force morale.'

I inclined my head. I already knew that General Marsiala, Sector Commandant of Luluabourg, had wanted me permanently based in Luluabourg.

'Now about the future,' he said firmly and I looked at him with raised eyebrows. He shuffled the papers on his desk in apparent embarrassment.

'Colonel, you must understand that I can't appoint you as my air advisor, as much as I would like that. As you know we have arrangements with certain foreign powers, political arrangements, about technical advisors. The Israelis instruct our paratroopers and the Belgians our army and air force. I have at the moment an air advisor, Colonel Bouzin . . .'

Mobutu tailed off and glanced at me.

'General, with respect, I have not returned to the Congo to be any sort of liaison officer for anybody. I came to do a job of work which, I respectfully submit, is to build up the Congolese Air Force. I want to do that job as a member of the air force, as a Congolese, not as a mere advisor.'

Mobutu nodded.

'We understand each other then, Colonel. I would value your services in that capacity. You understand that the air force will have to be under the nominal command of one of my officers, a colonel from *Etat Major,* but this will not interfere with your work. You will of course continue recruiting foreign pilots to assist until such time as alternative arrangements can be made.'

'Of course, *Mon* General.'

We drank to it.

I wasted no time in getting stuck into my appointed task. Telegrams were despatched throughout Europe and the faithful came trundling in again. One of the first back was Wojik from London, then Jackie Demoulin, a competent Belgian pilot not to be confused with the Demoulin of the Katangese *Travaux Publics* who took such great steps to keep me out of the secessionist state.

Also the terrible twins, Bracco and Libert; both back from fighting as ground troops in the Yemen against Nasser's Egyptian troops. It was like old times again as we gathered at the Memling Hotel and drank to the past and the exciting future.

A few days later I met the black Colonel appointed 'commander' of the air force. He proved to be a dumpy little man who lived with a perpetually bemused look on his face.

Several times I saw him hesitantly inspecting the T6s on the airfield, poking at control dials and running fingers along the smooth wing surfaces. Apart from that he spent most of his time in his office poring over T6 manuals and keeping as much out of the way as possible.

On the two occasions thereafter that I actually had to confer with him I treated him with the full deference his status deserved and he seemed relieved to let me take the decisions and run the show as I thought best.

Meanwhile the 'alternative arrangements' mentioned by Mobutu at our little conference were becoming rapidly apparent. As part of their drive to contain the rebels the CIA had decided to go one step farther and support the ANC by establishing covertly an operational air wing to be staffed by their own mercenaries.

The Americans clearly thought that overt aid in the way of air transport work was acceptable, but that tactical and strategic air support for the ANC ground forces was beyond the pale for their public's consumption. Hence the CIA mounted *Operation Wigmo,* a multi-million dollar project operating out of Lichtenstein in Europe which provided exiled Cuban pilots to fly the T28s (more powerful versions of the T6s), the B26 bombers and DC3 transports.

The aircraft were brand new and the pilots competent if grossly overpaid.

This new force in the Congo was formed fairly rapidly and it gradually took over most of the functions of my tiny air wing. Eventually the majority of my pilots, Bracco, Libert, Wicksteed, Demoulin, Bell, and Klootwyk were to join *Wigmo* and serve with them for the duration of the Simba revolt. But that was all still well in the future.

I had every reason to feel satisfied with the way things were going for Tshombe and for me. South African and Rhodesian mercenary forces had become the key factor in ANC counter attack strategy and I, also South African, had *de facto* control of the air element and still retained very powerful contacts with the office of the Prime Minister.

The time was ripe for a greater and more overt expression of the South African Government's interests in the future of the Congo. Ceaselessly I pressed the theme in letters and reports I sent to senior security and military intelligence officers in South Africa.

Tshombe's interests were South Africa's interests, I hammered home.

The weeks dragged by and I feared I was pouring water on to barren soil.

Then quite suddenly I received a telephone call at the *Etat Major* from Tshombe himself.

'Jerry, I want you to go down to the Ndjili airfield immediately and take all steps to see that journalists are kept away. We have a surprise for you.'

'Yes, Mister President,' was all I managed before the telephone went dead.

Hastily I called an official car and raced through the streets to the airport. As I reached the tarmac I saw the two huge C-130 transports standing self assuredly on the far side of the field. Instantly I recognised the Cape of Good Hope Castle insignia on the tail planes; the South African Air Force was in the Congo.

28

Plans and a Victory

The SAAF aircraft were carrying precious cargo indeed on that day — official and unofficial. The official component entailed several tons of desperately needed medical supplies. During the continuing actions and dislocations in the interior, the wounded and diseased increased dramatically in numbers and Tshombe appealed for world assistance. South Africa had responded by sending the two loads of medical supplies.

The unofficial cargo was in the form of a dapper, sophisticated man who walked with a military bearing and spoke French fluently; Brigadier Robbie Robertse, former South African military attaché in Brussels and Paris, a career soldier and shortly before his arrival in the Congo, OC Natal Command in South Africa. A highly professional and exceptionally clear headed man, Robbie had arrived in the Congo unofficially as observer and discreet advisor.

I found him standing besides one of the C-130s and hastily spirited him away through customs and passport control to accommodation in Leopoldville.

Before we could clear the airport, however, I had an unpleasant task at hand. Tshombe had told me to keep the press away and as we left I encountered a group of pressmen standing in animated conversation on the apron. Reluctantly I ordered the airport troops to clear the area — one of those so moved turned out to be Anthony Mockler, then correspondent for a British newspaper and later author of several books on mercenaries.

He was to be unfailingly critical of me in his writings — an approach perhaps not entirely unconnected with our earlier encounter.

Immediately I warmed to Robbie's enthusiasm and intelligent appraisal of the situation.

'Why have you come to the Congo?' I asked him pointedly when we were in the safety of his hotel room.

'To observe, to see as many people as I can, to advise where necessary and to keep as low a profile as possible.'

'Whom do you want to see then?'

'I suppose the best thing would be to start with General Mobutu. Can you arrange it?'

I nodded.

Two days later I accompanied Robbie to the General's office and waited outside while he went into conference. It was an hour long discussion and Robbie emerged smiling and obviously pleased.

'How did it go?' I asked on the way back to the hotel.

'Very well indeed. The General seemed genuinely pleased to see us and we had some pretty meaty discussions about this and that. I think we are going to get along fine.'

'Did you mention the mercenaries?'

'Yes we did. I explained my government's position on that. The General said he appreciated it . . .' Robbie tailed off and I knew better than to press him for more information.

'There's just one thing, Robbie.'

'Yes?'

'Mobutu is a CIA man firstly and a Belgium — Spaak [Prime Minister of Belgium] man secondly. The Americans and the Belgians guard him like solid gold. They are going to be very, very unhappy if they find out he's seeing a senior South African army officer. Christ, they're hypersensitive enough already about South African mercenaries and my position.'

Robbie chuckled.

'Don't worry Jerry. I'm quite alive to the problems and I have no intention of standing on anybody's toes. General Mobutu gave me the same spiel this morning.'

It was a promising beginning to Robbie's stay. Personally I was delighted at the arrival of a representative of the South African government, covert or not. I saw it as the first step in a greater involvement of South Africa in the Congo's affairs in general and Tshombe's position in particular. The small beginnings for what I hoped would eventually become a far greater South African presence.

Over the next few weeks I began bit by bit spelling out to Robbie what I had in mind. A plan that had been slowly maturing in my mind during our exile in Spain and now was increasingly within grasp; a plot to strengthen Tshombe's shaky position in the coalition government in order to bring the Congo firmly into a southern African bloc of nations. As I unfolded the scheme to Robbie, I was delighted at the orchestration of ideas between the two of us on the subject. Robbie and I were definitely on the same wave length.

We discussed the plan in its entirety late one night in the privacy of my hotel suite.

'The key to the entire Congo is the ANC, Robbie, Whoever holds that sways this country in whatever direction they want. At the moment the CIA and the Belgians have the key through Mobutu. What do we have in our favour?

'One, a Prime Minister who is pro-South African, two a developing mercenary force that is largely South African and Rhodesian and that as a unit could take on the entire ANC with impunity, three, a South African in charge of the air element and in close contact with the PM's office.'

Robbie sipped his drink and nodded encouragingly.

'The plan is quite simple,' I went on. Phase one: extend our control of the mercenary elements in the Congo, build up the South African component, specifically the officer cadre, boost the air element under my command. Once the rebels have been defeated, which they will certainly be, we begin to move.

'Phase two: use our entrenched military clout, either overtly or covertly against the Belgian advisors, the CIA and Mobutu. Either Mobutu comes over to us or we throw him out.

'Phase three: the ANC swings unequivocally to Tshombe who now holds military and political power.

'Phase four: with Tshombe's permission we import South African civilian technical advisors to reconstruct the Congo; economically, agriculturally and industrially. Meanwhile we restructure the ANC with an officer cadre of Katangese or loyalists, introduce official military technicians from the South African permanent force and then gradually phase out the mercenaries. Strengthen the ties between the Congo and the southern states and we have a power bloc underpinned in the north by a stable and prosperous Congo and in the south by the industrial and technical might of South Africa.'

Robbie held his hand up.

'Two questions, Jerry. Firstly, after the rebels have been quashed the Congo are to have general elections for a new assembly and a new president with greatly increased powers under the new constitution. Will Tshombe win such an election and if so why don't we just wait for that without bothering about all the conspiracy?'

'Good point, Robbie. If an election were to be held after the rebel defeat I would bet my bottom franc that Tshombe would win hands down but if I read my Congo right, which I have always done up to now, there will be no elections. Once the rebels have been cleaned up by Tshombe's Gendarmes and mercenaries he will get the sack by Kasavubu who will then strike a deal with Mobutu that no elections be held, or maybe he'll be kicked out by Mobutu as well. Even if conceivably an election is held and Tshombe wins, you must remember that this is black Africa and invariably the man who holds the political power is the man who holds personal military power. Tshombe might have political power but Mobutu will still have military power. Back to square one.'

'Fair answer,' said Robbie. 'Second question. Where does Hoare fit into the scheme and why did you choose him originally?'

I sighed.

'Hoare unfortunately doesn't fit our scheme at all. He's a soldier, not a king-maker or politician. Besides his loyalties are more likely to be towards British interests than South African. The reason I chose him at the outset was because I knew him to be competent, because he is a fine soldier and because he was easily available. He was just the man the Congo needed to set the Commando up and I'll still say he's the best man to defeat the rebels.

'But Robbie, his contract ends soon and once he's done the job he was set, relieve Stanleyville, I'm sure he will retire. Then we can move in with our own man as commander of V Commando; our own men for the officer cadre.'

'Where from?'

'From South Africa; senior permanent force officers seconded by the South African Government.'

Robbie whistled.

'That's a long, long shot Jerry. I can't possibly say the South African Government are going to go even part of the way with your plans. I can say I think its great

198

but those guys down south may not like it. What you're proposing is to take on the whole of the CIA. It's ambitious, but . . .' he shook his head.

'And it'll work', I said confidently. 'You just keep contacts with Mobutu, I'll keep contacts with Tshombe and work on the air force and V Commando. We've got to work fast, though. Once the rebels are smashed it may be too late.'

I doubled my efforts to create an effective air wing to support the ground forces now preparing for the thrust on Stanleyville. New T6s were expected and we were recruiting pilots. Lady Luck was smiling on us.

Then inevitably, she frowned and we were sharply reminded that death walked closely with our profession and, in the Congo, treachery even more closely. In more than three years flying operations in unbelievably trying conditions in the Congo and Katanga, I had never lost a pilot in my command. I had been outrageously lucky.

Early one morning Jackie Demoulin was preparing to take a T6 on a test circuit above Ndolo military air base near Leopoldville. He was approached by a new arrival in the Congo, a young Israeli flying instructor called Eschel. The fresh faced youngster was keen on joining our air force and asked if he could go with Demoulin on the flight. Julia was nearby and warned Hedges, then temporarily in charge of the air force, that the Israeli was not yet entered in the roll of our air strength and it would be unwise for him to fly.

I was away on a mission, Julia left to attend other business, and Hedges, Demoulin and Eschel were alone. They looked at each other, shrugged shoulders, and Eschel and Demoulin clambered into the aircraft.

Eye witnesses said the T6 roared down the runway, lifted into the air at one hundred and thirty kilometers per hour, rose smoothly to fifty meters, banked sharply to starboard, and then dropped like a stone. Surprisingly the aircraft did not burst into flames but it was difficult enough extracting the two bodies from the mangled wreckage.

I arrived back the next day to find the whole air section plunged into the deepest gloom while civil aviation inspectors poked amid the roped off wreckage of the T6. What a blow!

Later that day I was sitting in my office, desperately trying to compose a letter to Demoulin's fiancee, when the senior aviation inspector knocked on on my door.

'May I come in, Colonel?'

'Of course', I said and waved him to a chair.

'I'm afraid I have some rather startling news for you.'

'What is it?'

'The T6 that crashed yesterday. We've discovered that the aileron wires and pulleys in the tail section were hopelessly jammed. That T6 was an uncontrollable flying coffin as it took off.'

I let it slowly sink in.

'You mean the aircraft was damaged while on the ground?'

The inspector nodded.

'That means it was . . .' I tailed off.

'Sabotage', the inspector calmly finished.

I went quite cold then reached for the telephone. This called for an *Etat Major* investigation, immediately.

Within hours the investigation was underway. All my pilots and myself were grilled by the military police staff. Depositions were taken, work logs confiscated, reports required. Exactly two days later I walked into my office building early in the morning to find our self-effacing black chief of the air force being marched out between two burly MPs. He had the grey look of utter terror.

I rang the officer in charge of the investigation and asked why my immediate superior had been taken away.

'Well, we've got our man', he said with a chuckle.

'Christ, you mean the colonel?'

'Correct. He's actually a rebel sympathiser. We have letters and other proof.'

'You mean he sabotaged the aircraft that he was supposed to be commanding?'

'Correct, Colonel. You sound surprised. Remember this is the Congo.'

'What is going to happen to him?'

'Don't worry about that. He's not likely to be around again.'

And in truth he wasn't. We never saw him again nor heard anything further of the investigation or the evidence. It really was the Congo.

As we buried our colleagues we had ample cause to ponder the intractable forces enmeshing us and the fatal intrigue that was the Congo in 1964. We were burying Demoulin and Eschel but it could have been Libert or Bracco or Hedges — or myself.

Outwardly we shrugged shoulders and went about our businesses but inwardly the memory of those two mangled bodies remained always a warning of how fragile our existence really was in those tense circumstances.

The death of Demoulin and Eschel was the first tragedy in a series that were to stalk our air wing over the coming months.

Towards the end of 1965 my old Katangese friend Wojik, then in charge of the air force, was also killed.

In one of the brand new T6s he had gone on a practise run with napalm bombs, a donation from our generous CIA mentors. On the range he had swooped low over the target zone and dropped his load, climbed, banked steeply and then swept back over the scorched and smouldering target zone.

In mock salute at the success of the run he gave a victory roll at twenty meters. Perhaps he was tired or hot, or perhaps at fifty three years of age, his reflexes had slowed. Whatever the reason he ignored the cardinal rule in a roll and failed to keep the nose of his aircraft above the horizon. It dipped slightly. The T6 slipped suddenly into a nose dive and ploughed into the embracing Congo earth. He died instantly.

Six months later tragedy was to strike again when Wicksteed and a co-pilot were out on a sortie in the eastern part of the Congo. The T6 ploughed inexplicably into a marsh and sank almost immediately. The two pilots are probably still there, strapped to their seats in the murky depths of the marsh. Wicksteed was a good man and a competent pilot. T6s did not traditionally give trouble of their own accord. I detected the hand of treachery.

But then, amidst the death of close friends and thousands of Congolese, there was ironically new life; the birth of my second son by Julia. With all the stress and problems I admit I had been a less than attentive husband. First news of an increase in my family had filled me with delirious happiness, but in the months that followed I was unable to devote myself as much as I should have to my gently ballooning wife.

On the evening of October 22, Julia and I had an invitation to attend a dinner party given by Tshombe at his residence. At 6.30pm I arrived back at our suite in the Memling Hotel and found Julia still undressed for our 19h00 dinner date.

'What's happening? Why aren't you dressed?' I asked frantically.

Julia was perfectly calm about it.

'I really don't think it would be wise to increase Tshombe's dinner party by one uninvited guest', she said and for the first time, winced slightly from pain.

I arranged a taxi and we drove through the streets of Leopoldville to the hospital at a speed unequalled since my dash to Ndjili airport to greet the South African C-130s.

Hugs and kisses and I left Julia to the tender ministrations of the doctor and sisters, rushed to Tshombe's residence and arrived apologising profusely for arriving late for the dinner party. Tshombe smiled broadly when he heard the reason for my lack of punctuality. That night I don't believe I was very convivial company.

Shortly after 20h00 a servant arrived with a message for Tshombe. The prime minister excused himself and went to take a telephone call. Seconds later the servant was back with a request from Tshombe for me to go and see him in his study.

Tshombe stood behind his desk with the telephone receiver in one hand and a broad grin on his face.

'Congratulations, it's a boy', was all he said. I grabbed the receiver and heard Julia's slightly weak but excited voice on the other end. It had been an easy birth. We had little trouble deciding on a name for our new arrival. Several days later he was christened Jose-Yves.

Hoare had always ribbed me about the super efficient Julia arranging to have the baby during the dinner hour. In the event he turned out partly correct.

Meanwhile back in the unrelenting war of attrition with the rebels, the ANC Fifth Motorised Brigade, under Colonel Vanderwalle, a composite group of French, Belgian and Spanish mercenaries in VI Commando and the more homogeneous and disciplined V Commando under Hoare, were preparing for the thrust on Stanleyville, heart of the rebel movement. From Kongolo the columns Lima I and Lima II were to push from Kindu through to Stanleyville.

During the previous two months the composition of the mercenary elements in the Congo had considerably changed.

Far from there being only South African and Rhodesian mercenaries that I had hoped for, as were indeed essential for my plan, a number of French and Belgian mercenaries had drifted back into the Congo. Fortunately, as said before, they had been split up among the various ANC battalions and not formed into a single unit like V Commando. Still, the advent of this new factor in the power equation caused me some sleepless nights.

One of the first foreign mercenaries to arrive back had been the old Katanga hand, Bob Denard. I met him quite unexpectedly in Mobutu's secretary's office one day. The burly Frenchman was standing impatiently in front of the secretary's desk and harrying him for an appointment to see the General. He spun around when I walked in and burst into a shout of glee.

'Puren; of course you're here. Faithful Puren. I never did have that chance to buy you a beer at Texeira da Sousa?'

I indicated that it was unimportant and we shook hands.

Denard told me that he had just come back from Yemen where he and the old warrior Faulques had been fighting for the Iman Badr against the Republicans who were aided by up to fifty thousand of Nasser's troops. Denard leaned confidentially towards me: 'Ungrateful bunch that. Take my word Puren and never fight for them.'

I was only later to find out that Denard had left the Yemen under a cloud of suspicion by both the Iman and Denard's own troops about the whereabouts of a big sum of money, including the men's pay. Same old Denard. He was reputed to be the only man to succeed in lifting money from the wiley Bracco. He swung towards the secretary.

'Tell that man,' he said while pointing at Mobutu's closed door, 'that if he doesn't see me now, he won't find me here this afternoon.'

Denard got to see Mobutu and got the job for which he had come.

By November 1964 the noose was tightening irrevocably around the rebel capital and Lima I and Lima II were ploughing rapidly through the hostile Bakusu and Batatela tribal territories. The Simba's had meanwhile gathered in white missionaries as hostages and concentrated them in Stanleyville, subjecting them to the most hideous indignities and tortures devisible.

By November 20 it became clear that the rebels were preparing to massacre the one thousand, seven hundred hostages in a bid to halt the steam-roller ANC forces spearheaded by the mercenaries. The Western Governments representing the white hostages held in Stanleyville sat up and took note. Preparations were made for any eventuality; including a para drop.

On November 23 Colonel Vanderwalle ordered Hoare to move through the last one hundred and eighty kilometers of hostile territory to be in Stanleyville at 06h00 on November 24. Belgian paras began arriving at Ascension Island. The Simbas started assembling the hostages. Tensely the world watched the unfolding drama.

Late on the afternoon of November 23, Hoare, forced to disregard his own first principle of never travelling in column at night, ordered his group into the attack.

The long line of trucks, jeeps, ferret scout cars, armoured cars and armoured personnel carriers began their perilous advance along the dusty road from Lubutu. Darkness fell and the column ground on through the pitch black night. Then it started.

At every village the column came under intense and often well directed mortar, rocket and machinegun fire from the rebels. Sudden winking flashes of light in the dark, an abrupt end to the brooding silence of the night, shouts, curses as the mercenaries went through their ambush drill, deployed and brought a hail of fire to bear at the elusive shadows that were the enemy. During that nerve wracking night Hoare and his men suffered numerous casualties and were hopelessly delayed in their advance. It was clear they would never make their deadline.

At 06h00 on November 24, the Belgian paras dropped on Stanleyville airfield and engaged the Simbas in a series of vicious firefights.

Hastily the rebels in the centre of Stanleyville began rounding up the hostages and driving them towards Lumumba Square. The hundreds of white civilians, men, women and children, waited in the cool Congo morning air for rescue or death.

A few minutes past 07h00 and the advance section of the Belgian paras were seen weaving from cover to cover up the avenue from the airfield.

The Simba deaf mute dwarf, Major Kasango, gave his panicky troops orders to fire on the praying hostages.

A blistering volley and twenty two people lay dead and another forty wounded. The rest scattered screaming for cover. The paras charged and, amid scores of firefights the Simbas retreated, split into small pockets and began withdrawing out of the city.

Two hours later V Commando finally punched its way into Stanleyville from the south east and roared in blazing fury into the Simba capital.

I had seen the whole bloody episode. Since early morning I had been circling the Stanleyville airport in a Congolese Air Force transport with some senior ANC officers. We had seen the paras drop, long lines of black dots eventually mushrooming into white parasols that drifted slowly earthwards from the lumbering silver transports.

We watched the first paras hit the ground and spray out, engaging the airfield defence troops, extending their perimeter and eventually spilling out into the avenues and making for the city centre.

Rapidly Stanleyville adopted the air of a city at war; plumes of smoke, deathly still streets, small concentrations of action at strategic points.

We waited only long enough for the paras to seize the airfield and clear the perimeter before touching down. We commandeered a vehicle and set off to inspect the city of blood.

Deliberately we avoided the Simba memorial where the massacre had taken place, preferring to push towards the east where we met the first units of V Commando, a lumbering Scania Vabis APC that had been bequeathed to the Congo by the departing UN Swedish component months previously. The bulky vehicle, this one with the name *Lizette* coyly painted on its snout, trundled down one of the main boulevards with helmeted V Commando troops scowling at the surroundings.

A few minutes later Hoare arrived on the scene and we snatched a few moments for conversation. The mercenary leader was very tired after the night's push and obviously tense.

'Do me a favour, Jerry, and see if you can get us an armoured car from Lamouline. We're going to need it for some of the tougher rebel nuts.'

I nodded and Hoare was off again, barking orders, speaking on a dozen radios seemingly at once, swearing at one volunteer who was walking around without headgear and comforting another whose arm had been splintered by rocket shrapnel.

I arranged the armoured car for Hoare but it came home forcibly to me just how touchy things were between V Commando and the Belgians if Hoare could not even ask for the car himself.

At this point I teamed up with a South African journalist, Jan van Vreden, later to become editor of a South African newspaper, and we toured the agonised city, he searching for stories and I just looking. It was eerie and sometimes frightening.

It was not the first time I had been in a city at war, but in this one the aura of violence and fear hung heavily. The usual lazy eddies of smoke, occasional rubble, empty streets, twisted and bloated bodies and litter, litter, litter.

And there was the Lumumba shrine before which we knew countless litres of Congo's finest and most educated blood had been spilt by the Simba's in horrifying ritual and cannibalistic tortures.

We drove unchallenged to Christopher Gbenye's palace, former residence of the Governor, a startlingly magnificent piece of colonial architecture. ANC troops had obviously been through before us. Paintings torn down, silverware scattered around, furniture overturned. Our footfalls echoed hollowly as we walked down the empty corridors and deserted rooms. I held my FN rifle comfortingly close.

But the fighting was not yet over. That same afternoon we moved into what we thought was a quiet sector of the town. In a street of bungalow type houses, we came across a number of white civilians busily loading their vehicles with everything valuable; trunks, suitcases, treasured pieces of furniture, pets in cages, all the bric- a-brac that refugees traditionally carry from modern war fronts.

They moved slowly and unhurriedly, seemingly dazed by their escape, unable to fully realise that they were safe and could leave the hell hole that had been prison for many of them for three days. It was an immensely poignant sight. We stopped and Jan van Vreden moved over to talk to them. I climbed out of the car and leant against the bonnet. Silence after the drama of the central city area.

Then all hell broke loose. From a line of trees, perhaps a hundred meters to our left, the sudden insane chatter of automatic rifle fire; a rear guard Simba detail. I heard the familiar crack of passing bullets at precisely the moment I dived for cover behind the car. Quickly I sized up the situation. The Simbas were too far away for accurate fire, they couldn't cross the open stretch of ground to get closer.

Just keep your head down, Puren, and wait. I cocked my rifle and peered out from behind the car in the direction of the rifle fire.

The effect on the civilians, though, were devastating. It was as if a thousand finely tuned nerves had been broken simultaneously. People scrabbled for place under cars, ran heedlessly in all directions, tripped, fell, pleaded, babbled and screamed. I was aghast.

Within minutes, however, four jeeps of VI Commando mercenaries raced up the road, slithered to a halt and poured a fusillade of machinegun fire into the swaying bushes that marked the presence of the Simbas. Instantly the rebel guns fell silent. Several mercenaries bowed theatrically at the ashen faced civilians and then they were speeding off again to the next firefight.

Dead-panned, the refugees resumed piling their belongings.

Over the next few days the ANC troops, undisciplined as ever, came straggling into Stanleyville on the heels of the mercenary force. No matter that there had been an ostensible change in Congolese political leadership, the ANC troops remained as brutal and dissipated as ever. Again it was *Rattisage,* this time I was unhappily on the side of the perpetrators.

Under the direction of Nendaka, Minister of Security, and a strongly pro-Mobutu man, the ANC began a systematic campaign of terror and intimidation that, by the end of their occupation, had notched up infinitely more fatalities than had ever been achieved by the Simbas.

Suspect Simba sympathisers were rounded up before popular tribunals, given open air hearings, judged by show of hands and summarily executed in the streets and soccer stadium. It was a sad and violent period in the ever turbulent history of the Congo.

Nendaka had always been scrupulously fair and even magnanimous in his dealings with me. He was a powerful figure in Mobutu's clique and quite ruthless in support of his beliefs. Two days after Stanleyville was taken, Nendaka was guest of honour at the officers' mess of V Commando.

The rebels had not been entirely cleared from the area and throughout dinner we heard the chatter of guns and the occasional mutter of the mortars from across the Congo River. Every now and then the explosions would be jarringly close to the brightly lit house in which the neatly attired officers were sitting to a four course meal with two wines, all served on spotless white table cloths.

Hoare kept a tight mess etiquette even in the middle of a war and Nendaka was incomparably impressed at the decorum in the midst of chaos.

But in the unfortunate city of Stanleyville the violence continued unabated. Next day Jan van Vreden and I again cruised the streets, now firmly in the ANC's hands. Evidence of their brutal excesses were everywhere apparent.

One incident sticks hauntingly in my memory. It began as we drove past a street front store in one of the poorer quarters of Stanleyville. Van Vreden pointed to the body of a man sprawled in deathly sentinel duty across the threshold of an ajar door. We slowed down and stopped. Van Vreden and I crossed the road to the building. Even before reaching the entrance I sensed the presence of death. Rifle at the ready, I kicked the door fully open and stepped over the body.

We found the precious stocks so diffidently guarded by the dead sentry. A twisted heap of bodies, tangled limbs, gawping mouths, dilated eyes and everywhere the dark russet brown patches of dried blood. Dead at least twelve hours. Men, women, children, young and old, the fine ebony skins now ashen in death. Already the bodies were swelling in the heat. *Rattisage.*

Van Vreden snapped some shots, the camera shutter sounding irreverently loud in the silence. I turned to the door, light and air. The faintest scrabble from under the pile of bodies arrested me. I bent down to look. The slight movement of a black hand; follow the russet blotched arm through the tangle of limbs to a shoulder; discern the shoulder supporting the head; a finely featured African head with darkly beautiful eyes. Through the shadows and the stench the huge eyes slowly closed, opened, looked faintly quizzical and then closed again.

'Give us a hand, Jan,' I said.

We began tugging the forms covering the wounded girl. In seconds she was free. Jan and I gently lifted her towards the door. She moaned and rolled her eyes in the direction of where she had been lying. Among the tangle of limbs I spotted what looked like a bundle of clothes; a tiny form huddled on the floor, exactly where the girl had been sprawled. A child, no more than three years, raised its head and stared uncomprehendingly at us. He had obviously been protected by his mother's body when the hail of bullets had scythed the people jam packed into the store. I lifted the child up and set him down besides his mother. Seconds later the young woman died.

'And thus the people play' — *en so speel die mense,'* the shocked Van Vreden whispered.

We hurried the child from the scene. Several days later I took the boy to Leopoldville and managed to have him admitted to the orphanage. It was a small personal triumph in the face of the overwhelming tragedy that was Stanleyville.

29

A Personal Defeat

The battle at Stanleyville heralded two things of import to the Congo; the first was the beginning of the end for the rebels; the second was the long slow fall from grace of the Prime Minister, Moise Tshombe.

On the first score the Simbas retreated in small pockets of defiant resistance, harried by the mercenaries all the way to the Rwanda border and north towards Bunia, Watsa and Paulis, north as far as the Sudanese border.

On the way the mercenaries rescued scores of hostages from the rebels. For many, however, the flying columns of mercenaries arrived too late.

On the second count the destruction of the rebel's power ironically also signalled the beginning of the end for Tshombe as Prime Minister. By invitation he had brought his skills, courage and determination to serve the cause of a unified Congo; the same determination he had once used in pursuit of an independent Katanga. Once he had employed his immense popular support and his army-in-exile to defeat the rebels, his use was at an end and his powerful mentors turned against him.

Everything was done to dispossess him of the position of power and prestige he now held and was consolidating in the Congo.

Towards the end of 1964 the Congo was working towards a general election. Tshombe and his Conakat party engaged considerable and increasing support and there was little doubt that the former Katangese president was very likely to become a popularly elected president of the whole Congo; a president with increased executive powers under the new constitution.

The thought, however, was anathema to the forces that had brought Tshombe back, set him to defeating the Simba's and were now working against him.

Key man in the anti-Tshombe faction was of course the enigmatic Mobutu, leader of a clique of Congolese politicians who were generally known as the Binza group because the majority lived in the Binza suburb of Leopoldville. Among this group were people like Bomboko, Minister of Justice, Nendaka, Minister of Security, and President Kasavubu.

And behind the Binza group spread the mysterious intangible presence of the real arbiters of Congolese fortunes; the US Government and its CIA.

Very soon after our arrival in the Congo, picked Mobutu men had formed themselves into an almost impenetrable screen of 'advisors' around Tshombe, successfully cutting his access to older and loyal aides and supporters.

The helpless Prime Minister had become by late 1964 a prisoner in his own palace, hemmed in by the pervasive forces of covert foreign manipulation. It was exactly like the dark days immediately after the collapse of the Katanga secession.

And with the onslaught on Tshombe came a corresponding disintegration of my carefully nurtured plans for the Congo. I was defeated by the power of the western foreign involvement, by the caution of the South African Government and finally by the speedy march of events. It was a disturbing process that began several weeks before Stanleyville.

Robbie had consistently maintained a low profile as promised but the mere fact of his presence rapidly became known and caused a stir in the CIA and Belgian dovecotes.

Puren and this Brigadier Robertse?

The South Africans up to something?

Conspiracy?

The invisible forces of western foreign interest began to show their manifestations.

After three lengthy and very cordial meetings with Mobutu, Robbie suddenly found it impossible to get to see the commander in chief. The General was 'unavailable' the first time. Robbie made another appointment and it was broken. I tried to arrange an interview. No luck. The whisper went around that Mobutu had been pressurised by his guardian angels not to see the South African.

Robbie was plunged into the deepest depression when I found him after his latest rebuff.

'Is there much point in staying?' he asked.

'Of course there is', I replied. 'Look, Mobutu is the disposable element in the scheme. If he won't assist us that's his problem. When we're ready to move he'll be the first one out. The thing now is just to cement ties with Tshombe and Munongo.

'What effective power do they have?'

'At the moment very little but if we move fast we can change all that. The split between the Mobutu Binza group and Tshombe is growing wider all the time. When it comes to breaking point, which will theoretically be when the rebels are completely defeated, we must be in a position to take the ANC over to Tshombe.'

Robbie looked doubtful.

'Jerry, you know the South African Government hasn't been over enthusiastic. We've had no positive feed back about the scheme at all. You don't know if they will release permanent force men to fill V Commando senior ranks.'

I shrugged. Robbie was actually quite right. Despite a number of appeals to senior security and military officials in South Africa there had been no response at all. And time was marching on. Hastily I arranged a series of meeting between Munongo and Robbie and later a few surreptitious get togethers between Tshombe and the South African. Robbie was impressed by the two Katangese ministers but quickly realised their caution about the rival Binza group.

Then suddenly another visitor appeared in Leopoldville, setting off another round of speculation. This time it was Colonel Buys, my South African security police contact. He was on a flying visit with the intention of meeting the South African black exiles then living in Leopoldville including none other than Mr Sam Nujomo, present leader of the SWAPO — South West African People's organisation.

Buys apparently saw his man and, after several discussions, returned home but not before confiding in me that my grand design for the Congo was being greeted with some scepticism at home. I decided to push on with the scheme nevertheless.

Constantly I maintained contacts with senior security officers in South Africa and through them was able to tentatively earmark the man Robbie felt was ideal for succession to head of V Commando. Commandant Louw was OC of South Africa's First Parachute Battalion, an iron hard man who had built up the crack South African unit to a standard comparable to the best in the world. I gathered that he was interested in the idea of coming to the Congo. Tentatively I broached the subject of recruiting South African permanent force officers with Tshombe and Munongo. They were guardedly approving in principle.

The matter was then taken up with Mobutu and I was told that he had also given a tentative okay; 'but it depends.'

I knew on what it depended; the CIA and the Belgians. The scheme entered its most delicate stage. Then disaster struck.

I visited Robbie's room early one morning and found him busy packing.

'Where are you going?'

'Home.'

'Why?'

'Orders. I have been recalled. No reasons.' He said it without rancour.

'I know what's happened,' I said and flung myself into a chair. 'Those bastards in the other agencies have got wind of the plan and through their governments put the pressure on the South African Government to recall you. It's clear as daylight. You now, then hopefully me tomorrow.'

Robbie was too much of a soldier to debate orders.

'They can force you out through the South African Government,' I continued, 'but they can't do it to me. I'm a free agent. It just means that my position has been weakened because now it's apparent the South Africans are pulling out.'

We shook hands and I left Robbie's room feeling sad at the loss of a good friend and terribly depressed at the blow to my plan.

From that point on things moved rapidly to a head. Mobutu, by now thoroughly intimidated, stopped seeing me altogether and developed an overtly hostile attitude. In the *Etat Major* my position became increasingly tenuous.

The functions of the minuscule air force that I had helped develop were largely being supplanted by the much larger *Wigmo* operation, a project over which I had no control and which eventually wound up recruiting all my pilots and undertaking all ops.

I became the victim of a systematic and very effective campaign to narrow my field of competency and operation; to prune my influence. And it worked. Pressures against Julia and I in the *Etat Major* increased daily and after the recall of Robertse we were virtually alone against a hostile body of colleagues and superiors.

The senior ANC officers were all hand picked Mobutu men while, ironically, the crack black ANC troops in the field were still the ex-Katangese Gendarmes fiercely loyal to Tshombe.

The white mercenaries and officers were, at this stage, largely loyal to Mobutu or at least sympathetic.

First loyalty of course was always to the paymaster.

Particularly hostile to Julia and I were the Belgian technical advisors who regarded us with undisguised suspicion. They were very hard times.

The climax came shortly after the Stanleyville operation; a make or break opportunity to put my grand scheme into effect or lose out altogether.

I was away on a mission at the time and Julia (we were regarded as an indivisible team) was summonsed early one morning to see Mobutu. She walked into his office to find his face suffused with rage.

'How many mercenaries left Johannesburg for Leopoldville yesterday?' he demanded.

Julia stared in amazement.

I don't know, I'm not responsible for recruiting in South Africa.'

'All you have to do to find out is tune into the BBC world service', he roared. 'Your idiot mercenary officers are holding press conferences at the airport before the mercenaries leave.'

Julia began protesting but Mobutu cut her short.

'This better not happen again', he snorted and pointed an angry finger at her. 'When those mercenary officers return they will be stripped of every decoration and insignia. Do you understand?'

The cause for Mobutu's ire was a press conference given by Alistair Wicks, Hoare's 2 IC, at Jan Smuts Airport, a singularly stupid bid at gratuitous publicity.

I instantly saw Mobutu's outburst as having two implications. Firstly, it could mean a last ditch opportunity for me to get my man in as commander of V Commando and secondly, it was obviously the final straw in the rapidly deteriorating relations between the general, myself and Julia.

Time was of the essence. Back to Munongo and Tshombe and after some impassioned pleading they agreed to press for recruitment of my choice as Hoare's replacement.

Then more negotiations with my South African contacts and a tentative promise that Louw would be made available.

A surprise message from Munongo that Mobutu had reluctantly acceded to my request; I could only assume that Tshombe had used every string he had and Mobutu, rather than risk a premature break up of the emergency Government, had given in to the Prime Minister's request.

More exciting news in that Hoare, by now weary after six months gruelling soldiering in the Congo, was quite prepared to submit his resignation voluntarily.

Julia, who had been involved closely in the Mobutu/Hoare row, reported that Hoare's resignation had actually arrived at the *Etat Major* . . . and his return ticket already booked.

Mobutu was still eager that Hoare should go. It looked as if it was all in the bag.

I sent a request to South Africa that Louw be seconded immediately.

Then the whole scheme crumbled in the space of a morning.

Hoare's resignation was on Mobutu's desk and the tough V Commando leader and his 2 IC, Alistair Wicks, were coming to see the General for their discharge at midday on a busy weekday.

Early in the morning the United States and Belgian ambassadors and the British military attaché suddenly arrived at the *Etat Major* and were granted instant access to Mobutu.

The group remained closeted for forty minutes and then came out with dead-panned expressions.

Hoare and wicks, by this time at the *Etat Major* and waiting for their appointment, went into Mobutu's office and emerged ten minutes later with smiles and promotions. Hoare's resignation was neatly forgotten.

The Western group had got wind of the plan and in a last minute effort had persuaded Mobutu to reappoint Hoare and keep out any South African involvement. It was the last straw for me. Stripped very largely of control of the air contingent, effectively isolated from Tshombe, thwarted in a bid to appoint a South African officer to head V Commando, deserted by the South African government, outflanked by the western agencies, under incredible pressure from ANC colleagues, Belgian technical advisors, especially air advisor Bouzin, detested by Mobutu, tired, dispirited and bitter, I decided to cut my losses and start on a new tack.

I went to see my old friend Munongo and outlined my difficulties.

'Mister Minister, it is impossible for me to continue in the ANC under these pressures. It is less than useless. I intend to submit my resignation, but I do not intend to desert the Prime Minister. Is there any other way I can help?'

Munongo stared at me for what seemed like an eternity and then spoke in his deep and resonant voice.

'You are aware of the danger the PM is in?'

'Yes, Mister Minister.'

'You are aware from which direction the danger comes?'

'Yes, sir, from the Binza group and the various western intelligence agencies supporting General Mobutu, primarily the CIA.'

Munongo nodded his head.

'For some time I have been toying with the idea of setting up a covert section attached to my Department of the Interior; an intelligence gathering section with the sole function of reporting, identifying, detecting and relaying specific threats to the Prime Minister. Threats from whatever source, inside the Central Government or from the outside. Are you interested?'

'Of course, Mister Minister.'

'You are aware of the dangers. We are entering a very dangerous period before the elections, dangerous for the Prime Minister, dangerous for the country and dangerous for everybody associated with the Prime Minister. I know you were regarded a threat in the ANC by certain foreign and local authorities. If it is found that you are engaged in such an operation as I propose to set up, then you will be regarded as an infinitely greater threat. Will you take the risk?'

'I'll take the post, Mister Minister.'

On January 14 1965 I resigned from the ANC. Julia followed suit and although begged by Mobutu to stay she refused. We were both to enter a challenging and frightening period of our Congo experience.

30

Another Kill

The man sitting before me was obviously terrified. His youngish face had aged visibly in the short space of time I had known him, huge pouches supported red rimmed eyes, his speech was jerky and fumbling and as I leaned forward to light his cigarette, I could see his hands shaking from fear and fatigue.

'What's the problem, Gabriel?'

'Same problem, Jerry. They are trying to kill me,' he said with a weak attempt at a grin.

'What are latest developments?'

'Last night four men, plainclothes, followed me back from the office. I drove all the way in the main thoroughfares and then just before reaching home I rang friends from a call box. They came with me the rest of the way. My followers did not dare seize me then.'

'Know who they were?'

Gabriel nodded.

'They are attached to the military intelligence section of the Parachute Regiment. I have seen them all before.'

I drew deeply on the cigar and watched the smoke curl lazily to the ceiling. The man was telling the truth of course. Nobody could fake that sort of terrified mien. Besides, why should he lie? Gabriel was an educated and intelligent man. He held a high post in *Sabena,* the Belgian national airline, and in fact ran their Leopoldville office. The man's fatal error, however, was that he was a Tshombist, an office bearer in the Conakat party and by definition, opposed to Mobutu. In the early part of 1965 that was a dangerous attitude to adopt.

Tshombists had disappeared before, completely and mysteriously. Gabriel had grounds for fear.

'What further can I do for you? I've spoken to the Minister of the Interior,' I said.

'Please get hold of Godefroid Munongo again. Tell him I am being followed — it is only a question of time. Can't you arrange something for me; an escort, something, anything?'

I held up my hand reassuringly.

'Gabriel, I will speak to him again. I promise. I will do what I can. Come tomorrow.'

Gabriel nodded and then rose. We shook hands and he surreptitiously slipped from the little two bedroomed flat in the Leopoldville side street that served as my office and home. I watched his departing back with compassion and concern. He was a close personal friend.

Please, Lord, may we be able to arrange something for tomorrow.

Gabriel was not by any means the first anxious Congolese to have come to our office. Over the several months of our operations we had received visits and messages from numbers of Tshombists in and around Leopoldville: officials, businessmen, intellectuals and soldiers. All were terrified for their lives. Among the clandestine pockets of Tshombist in the town it had generally become known that we had access still to Munongo and through him to Tshombe.

For by then the flower of the Tshombist cadres had been lopped off in the subterranean world of national politics.

The Binza group were pulling out all the stops in their bid to cripple Tshombe's swelling popular support; death, violence, intimidation, kidnapping and extortion were all part of the bloody campaign.

My job was quite simply to collate all information affecting Tshombe's position in the Congo and channel it through Munongo to the Prime Minister. I had been given carte blanche to get my information from whatever source I liked and by whatever means. After nearly four years contact with the Congo and its personalities I had a select number of people I could rely on for information; and I now began to cultivate their confidence as never before.

My staff had initially consisted of myself, Julia and the two Rumanians exiled from Madrid days who had become spies for Tshombe; Oanca and Calistrat. Later we were joined by two agents from the Portuguese secret police, PIDE.

In early 1965 there was no doubt in my mind that Tshombe stood in danger of both his life and his position, the danger increasing as the date for the scheduled elections drew nearer.

The Binza group were very powerful, devious and determined. Behind them stood the shadow of the CIA personified in its Congo operative; Laurence Devlin.

In that shadow the puppets danced to the grim tune of their foreign masters.

It had begun shortly after the Stanleyville victory. Leopoldville had been treated to an astonishing display of apparently spontaneous anti-Tshombe sentiment. Stadia full of youngsters at mass rallies with professionally painted signs gathered and chanted anti-Tshombe slogans. Speech makers had catalogued long lists of supposed Tshombe crimes. Carefully orchestrated demonstrations had been held with maximum effect for Western media consumption. At almost a day's notice surprisingly large numbers of protesters had been rallied and efficiently transported to given venues. The whole thing stank.

Soon enough whispers began drifting into our office. Details of huge bank accounts operated by key speechmakers at these rallies, large numbers of cars and buses hired for the protests.

Certain names had begun cropping up again and again and always, ultimately, that of the CIA.

It was a beginning of the campaign to destroy Tshombe. In Parliament the Minister of Justice, Justin Bomboko, proved himself in the forefront of the battle against Tshombe.

Then, as the weeks progressed, there had been a number of strange disappearances in Leopoldville, known Tshombists seized by plainclothes men and bundled away, a few cases involving uniformed ANC troops and jeeps. Always the incidents had been faithfully reported to Sapwe Pius, loyal Katangese, Tshombist and head of the Congolese police.

Always investigations by the police had led to the *Etat Major* and to a blank wall.

What troops?

When?

The police were forced to stand by while the army at Mobutu's behest formed a Praetorian Guard responsible to no constitutional authority, responsible only to their Commander in Chief.

I picked up the telephone and got through to Munongo. Using the code words I set up a meeting that night. We met in a safe house and I told him of Gabriel's forebodings. It was the second time I had mentioned the plight of the young executive to Munongo.

He shook his head in distress.

'Possibly the man is hysterical? asked Munongo.

'I don't think so. He is being followed for certain.'

'What do you suggest?'

'Perhaps you can get him a police escort.'

Munongo thought about this. As Minister of the Interior he had the portfolio of police but Munongo, like all Tshombe's colleagues, was under frightening pressure from the Binza group at cabinet level. He had to step warily.

'It is possible. Tell him to come and see me tomorrow.'

We parted after I had given him the latest intelligence reaching us on Tshombe's standing among the Leopoldville urban electorate.

* * *

As I drove back through the deserted streets of the city, I flicked through in my mind what we had experienced in the past few months.

Since people had started disappearing, the days had dragged uneasily by. Tshombe's opponents had moved to more radical tactics. One of Tshombe's young women secretaries had drunk a cup of coffee intended for the Prime Minister. She had collapsed and died several hours later. It was not the first attempt on his life.

For our part Julia and I watched anxiously from the side lines as a massive dossier built up to suggest that, at best, Tshombe was soon to be deposed and, at worst, assassinated. I passed every morsel of information to Munongo who, when he found the opportunity, passed it to Tshombe.

Always the same reply came back; do not worry about me. I know what is happening.

I had continued my contacts with the South African Government begging for assistance at elections. Again I wanted cars with PA systems, funds, campaign advisors. Having lost out in the Congo military stakes the South African Government showed even greater reluctance to become involved in the political stakes. Although sympathetic, they remained discreet and unforthcoming.

The Portuguese though, were a very different story. One of the most frequent visitors had been Rochas, a lean, hawk faced Portuguese PIDE agent in northern Angola and an acquaintance from exile days. He had regularly come to pass information on to us and ask for the details of the latest political events.

Like myself and the South African agents, the Portuguese had been suspiciously regarded by Tshombe's enemies; the CIA and their Congo surrogates.

Communications with Tshombe had been virtually broken by these forces and the Portuguese found themselves obliged to deal largely through me.

On his visits Rochas would never fail to assure me that the Portuguese Government were desperately keen to ensure that assistance in the case of a coup would be forthcoming if Tshombe failed to win the elections because of unfair actions by his opponents.

The Portuguese had their eyes squarely on the disastrous results if Tshombe should be deposed. With Tshombe's defeat would surely come the FNLA guerrillas back in their Congo sanctuaries from where they could deploy against the Portuguese troops.

Since Katanga secession days the Portuguese had assisted Tshombe by keeping the vital Benguela rail link open and carrying copper out and vital supplies in from Lobito. Inside Katanga itself the Greek and Portuguese communications had done sterling work in keeping the economic life of the war torn country alive.

With this background of cooperation then it was hardly surprising that the Portuguese were effusive in their support for Tshombe. Rochas and I had drawn up an elaborate contingency plan for the rescue of Tshombe in the event of a coup; a plan involving a helicopter on constant standby in Maquella da Somba near the Congo border, three selected landing sites in Leopoldville and even, at a punch, a commando raid for a snatch job.

Amid the growing signs of opposition I had always ensured that at least one of my agents was always at Tshombe's side on any trips, as bodyguard and observer. We were in real fear of his life.

Then again I had turned my attentions to the mercenary leaders in the Congo, well aware that the action of the mercenary forces would be of pivotal importance in any power play between the Congolese leaders.

The first thing I had learnt was that nearly all the mercenaries were agents in varying degrees for the Government's of their respective countries of origin. Although loyalty to the paymaster was the first precept there was still a surprising residual patriotism for their homelands, no doubt earned during their service in the national armies of their home countries.

Thus I had become fairly convinced that Hoare was an agent for MI 6in that he maintained links with them. Bob Denard's contacts with the SDECE, the French Secret service, were incontrovertible and Schramme, the former Belgian planter and now commander of the forces in the Maniema was, I firmly believed, an agent for the Belgian Surete.

As far as I was able to establish, the mercenaries were largely unawares of the tremendous power play then raging in Congolese politics. On the whole I know they were probably Mobutu men and because I was known as a Tshombist there were sometimes difficulties.

Another attempt on Tshombe's life. This time it involved a blonde and a secret assignment. But Tshombe was too fly for the age old ruse.

And then of course my role in Munongo's secret intelligence section had become common knowledge, both among the Binza group and the foreign agencies. Rumours of a Binza black list had been circulating for some time; the proof provided by the scores of grieving families of Tshombists who had mysteriously disappeared.

Early one day I had received a telephone call from the *Etat Major*.

'Have you heard of the black list?'

'Yes.'

'Well, you're pretty near the top.'

'No surprise to me.'

A chuckle and then more seriously: 'As a friend, Jerry, I suggest you make a move.'

I had ignored the advice.

I arrived home that night from my meeting with Munongo and found Julia preparing a late night snack in the kitchenette. The children were asleep. We sat down to salami sandwiches and coffee.

'What did Munongo say?'

'He'll see what he can do.'

'I hope its not too late.'

We looked at each other despairingly.

Next day Julia was at her office in town. With typical aplomb she had landed herself a job in the Leopoldville office of the Bell Telephone Company as a blind for her intelligence gathering activities. Julia never went in for half measures and after a few weeks she found herself in charge of thirty telecom operators. Her personal telephone rang shortly after 10h00 that day. It was the neighbour of our friend Gabriel.

'There are two army jeeps outside Gabriel's house. A section of soldiers have just forced their way inside. Please help.'

The 'phone went dead.

Julia immediately dialled Gabriel's number. Engaged. She swore. Again she dialled. Engaged. A third time and the telephone rang. After what seemed like an eternity it was answered. Through the sobs she recognised the voice of Gabriel's young wife.

'What's happened?'

'Army . . . they have taken him away . . . soldiers. God, they beat him terribly.'

It was all she needed. Seconds later she was through to Munongo. She was bitter, frustrated and anxious. My wife does not mince words and her message was short and curt.

'Mobutu's troops have kidnapped Gabriel. Now will you perhaps do something?'

Munongo was silent for a moment.

'This has gone far enough. I must take a stand against Mobutu and Bomboko or what is the point.'

Throughout the rest of the day Leopoldville knew something was afoot. Officials in the Government and foreign observers had an inkling.

Dawn next day and Sapwe Pius's police responded. Scores of heavily armed policemen fanned out throughout the city and began a series of house to house searches, dawn raids on the homes of known anti-Tshombists and spot street checks.

For several days Leopoldville crawled with police, road blocks blossomed at street corners, downtown bars were raided and clientele searched. Even senior Government officials were visited and questioned.

Leopoldville had never seen anything like it before, this impressive demonstration of the forces of constitutional law and order.

Mobutu regarded the operation with the greatest alarm. His crack paratroop unit at Camp Kokolo near Leopoldville went on full alert and several days were spent in tense anticipation of a clash between police and troops.

Then Mobutu backed down and his troops reverted to their old obstructionists tactics.

The police investigations turned up forty unofficial 'prisons' in Leopoldville where Congolese politicians incarcerated their personal rivals and enemies; dark and dank little rooms or cellars scattered throughout the city and the sprawling slums around Leopoldville. Scores of prisoners, those who were lucky enough to escape death, were released, numerous arrests were made and Pius began compiling dossiers that would have incriminated a number of political leaders, many in the Binza group.

But no sign of Gabriel.

Then Munongo received information from a man who had been at Camp Kokolo the day after Gabriel's arrest. The informant told of passing the military police barracks in the camp and seeing a hobbling figure being roughly pushed towards a waiting jeep by four paras. According to the witness the man had fallen on his way out. A hail of blows and kicks had rained on him. He had jerked himself to his feet and, streaming blood, been shoved towards the jeep. According to the witness the wounded man had screamed his name and said that he was being taken away to be killed. The name he screamed was Gabriel.

Seven days later Gabriel's body was found floating down the Congo River. He had been riddled with machinegun bullets and been dead approximately a week.

The disappearance of Gabriel and Munongo's reaction precipitated a show down. Mobutu was determined that never again would the arbitrary and terroristic writ of his Praetorian Guard be challenged by the forces of constitutional law.

Incredible pressures were brought to bear on Munongo to resign his post. He held on grimly.

Frustrated at his failure Mobutu sent his angels of death on a systematic program against any of Munongo's or Tshombe's supporters. Then, inevitably, my name came to the top of the list.

At four on a muggy afternoon, the day after Gabriel's body was hauled from the Congo River. I received a 'phone call from the Prime Minister's office. The voice was tired, strained and hurried but it was unmistakable; Tshombe's.

'Jerry, you must leave your flat at once and go into hiding. Mobutu has sent his paras to look for you with a death warrant. Take care.'

That was all.

31

Flight

Going 'underground' had always had romantic connotations for me; code signs and secret lofts, mysterious couriers, adventure. In reality it is none of these things. It is agonies of uncertainty and fear, it is overwhelming loneliness suffused with anxiety for one's family, it is restless nights, snap moves in darkness and always the dread fear of that final knock on the door. It is hell.

Instantly after receiving Tshombe's message I summoned Julia from her office and broke the news as gently as I could. Both of us had accepted this as almost inevitable.

'You must leave the Congo immediately, Jerry. I'll follow', she said.

'No.'

'Are you quite mad?'

'Nobody is going to force me out. I haven't stayed four years with Tshombe just to be scared out by a single telephone call.'

'What do you suggest?'

'We both go into hiding in Leopoldville and just keep feeling our way. We can still function in intelligence gathering. If things get too bad I am sure with Munongo's help we can get back to Katanga. I am not leaving the Congo now.'

Julia shook her head.

'That's quite impossible, Jerry. We can't both go into hiding with two small children. It's better if you go by yourself and I stay home with the boys. It'll also help us deflect suspicion.'

'I'm not leaving you alone with Mobutu's men on the warpath.'

My wife sighed, exasperated.

'Jerry, there's absolutely nothing to worry about. Even Mobutu wouldn't dare touch a white Belgian woman with two small children. Remember that his mentors are the Western powers and they wouldn't want their susceptibilities offended by such an action. Hell, why do you think you have lived so long? Because you're white and Mobutu doesn't want to offend his guardians.'

Reluctantly I had to admit there was truth in what she said.

There was no time for further discussion. I hastily packed a small suitcase of belongings. Before I had finished there was a knock at the door. Julia slipped into the front room and peeped through the curtains. It was one of Tshombe's men, Victor, who had been in close touch with us during the preceding weeks. Julia unlocked the door and he entered.

'Please come quickly, we have arranged a safe house.'

I quickly kissed Julia and the boys and was out the door and into a waiting car. We spun away from the curb, circled the suburbs for over an hour and then, twisting and turning along a side road, we came back to the same street in which I had been living. We stopped outside a tiny flat not fifty meters from my old two bedroomed flat, Victor's flat.

'They'll never suspect it', Victor said in answer to my surprised look. He was right. For several days I was to live *en famille* with Victor.

Meanwhile Julia had had her own problems since my departure. Barely an hour after I had left, two jeeps packed with ANC troops had screeched to a halt in front of the flat. The khaki clad submachinegun toting mob had stormed up the steps leading to the entrance and had begun pounding on the door with fists and pistol butts. Wisely Julia resolved that she would not open the door to the officerless mob of drunken soldiers. She had flattened herself against a wall in the lounge and had prayed desperately that they would leave. More pounding, kicking and curses. The door frame had creaked ominously. Julia had prayed harder.

And then miraculously, the troops had given up. Perhaps they had received a radio message over the field sets in their jeeps, perhaps they had decided to return for orders. We will never know. With a few parting kicks they had straggled back down the steps to the jeep, climbed in and roared away.

It was only the beginning of Julia's nightmare. Day after day she lived in constant fear of the knock at the door, the final undignified car ride, the inevitable bloody end.

Fear had become her living companion wherever she was and whatever she was doing. Years later the terror of those days still cause her to start from the deepest sleep at any sudden noises.

For myself those several weeks in hiding were terrifying and frustrating. Although theoretically out of circulation, the contacts I made still provided me with information which I deemed essential to pass on to Munongo. By dint of late night call box routines and secret meetings in safe houses I was able to keep the Minister of Interior fed about developments.

I picked up a rumour concerning another poison attempt on Tshombe and passed it on. Several weeks later a cook at the Prime Minister's residence was arrested for trying to lace a spicy fish dish with arsenic.

But it was all but impossible to fulfil my proper role. Virtually every night I was forced to move from house to house, contacts had disappeared, Munongo became increasingly difficult to reach and the loyal police agents that had assisted me came under mounting pressure.

Then, again, the reports I furnished at the real risk of life and limb never seemed to achieve anything. The Prime Minister, completely surrounded by sycophantic advisors, dismissed our sentiments and called us pessimists. I began to have doubts about risking my life and those of my family in Leopoldville when our advice was being recklessly ignored.

Was it worth it?

Was it time to leave?

My mind was made up for me by developments in the cabinet.

Pressures against Munongo grew to the point where he finally decided it was better to resign. As a sop he was offered Governorship of Katanga and he accepted. My position in Leopoldville was now obviously untenable and I made preparations to get myself and my family away.

The day before he resigned I had managed to meet him in Leopoldville.

'What happens to us now?' I asked wearily.

'There is no way that I am going to desert you.' Munongo said flatly. 'I have a cover job for you in Katanga where you will be quite safe. Arrange to get yourself to Elisabethville, I will look after Julia and the children.'

The meeting broke up when one of Munongo's security aides came rushing into the house to tell us that the paras were on the way.

Munongo left Leopoldville shortly afterwards and immediately the Binza conspirators renewed their efforts at routing out Tshombe's supporters. I knew it was only a question of time before they caught me. It was urgent I should get out.

Nendaka, an old acquaintance with the Binza group, now unwittingly became the instrument of our escape. The special security passes he had given us months previously had long since expired but Julia, with long experience of Congo intrigues, quickly corrected that and we were once again in possession of the most authoritative passes obtainable in the Congo at a time when the ordinary villager needed a permit to travel from one town to the next.

Next day I was dropped at Leopoldville airport and collected a ticket that had been booked by Munongo's department.

A bumptious luggage official asked for my papers and I flashed the green pass. He retreated.

A police adjutant strolled over and demanded papers. Again I showed the green pass and gave him a dressing down for having his top button undone. He retreated just as quickly.

Then I was on the aircraft and praying they would not catch on. Spot on time the aircraft trundled down the runway and lifted into the air. Katanga, here I come. Instantly my thoughts turned to Julia and the boys.

With my departure and that of Munongo, a heavy burden fell on Julia's shoulders. She was now the sole remaining white Tshombist in Leopoldville with even marginal contact with Tshombe.

The Prime Minister had just survived another assassination attempt and, as always in situations of stress, his heart and liver began to give trouble. Confined to his bed in the residence, Tshombe was treated daily by his Hungarian physicist.The Prime Minister asked to see Julia. How was she going to get past the solid phalanx of Binza conspirators and Mobutu's aides that encircled the prisoner Prime Minister?

Simple.

After every day of bedside negotiations, the bent little doctor would come stalking into Tshombe's chambers clutching his black bag and accompanied by his white clad nurse. The Prime Minister's aides- cum-spies would respectfully make way for the couple. The doctor would unpack his instruments and busy himself with the patient while the nurse would hover anxiously at the Prime Minister's side.

Casual observers might have been surprised at the stream of instructions and replies which flowed between patient and nurse. And the same observer might have been surprised at the nurse's failure to so much as open a thermometer case.

By such means did Julia keep the the communications open between the ailing Prime Minister and his loyalists scattered throughout Leopoldville. Had she been discovered there is no knowing what would have befallen her and the gentle doctor. The charade continued for two weeks and then Julia too received information she was on the black list.

Time to leave.

Loyal police agents booked a flight to Elisabethville for her and the boys. At the last moment the agents rushed her to Ndjili airport and through the formalities. One inquisitive official was flashed the Nendaka pass and retreated abashed. Then Julia was on the aircraft with Jose and Pierre. The wait began.

Take off was scheduled for 11h00. By 11h15 the aircraft was still standing. 11h30 and the passengers were getting restless.

Julia remained quite calm while inside agonies of impatience raged. Had she been discovered? Fearfully she peered out of the portholes expecting to see the ANC jeeps come streaming across the tarmac.

Then the inexplicable delay was over.

The aircraft lumbered to its hold position, opened throttles and roared into the sky. Julia sighed a shuddering gasp of relief and sank back into her seat.

32

Near Squeaks and the Last Flight Out

The inevitable occurred on October 13 1965. President Kasavubu declared Prime Minister Tshombe's task at an end and, as he was constitutionally entitled to do, dismissed him.

The new Prime Minister was announced as Mr Evariste Kimba, former Katangese Prime Minister, but now a loyal Kasavubu man.

Tshombe accepted his sacking with traditional good grace and turned his attention to the coming elections. All indications were that Tshombe's Conakat party would sweep the board in virtually every province.

For Julia and I in Katanga, however, the developments in Leopoldville had the air of some distant drama, its echoes unfelt in the quiet rusticity into which we had gratefully fallen after our harrowing experiences in Leopoldville.

True to his word, Munongo had organised a 'job' for me in Jadotville, the pleasant little plateau mining town north west of Elisabethville. I was to be in charge of the Katanga office of tourism.

I had a gruelling first day at work. Keen as mustard I arrived early at the red brick single story building which serves as the office. I was still there when the caretaker arrived at 10h00 with a huge bunch of keys and a monstrous hangover.

'You must be our new chief', he enquired pleasantly.

'That's right. Jerry du Plessis is my name.'

Munongo had decided it best that I adopt a false name and I had chosen my mother's surname, a good French Huguenot name.

'Bit early, sir', he said while valiantly trying to open the front door with the wrong key.

'Well the sign says the office opens at 08h00', I said defensively.

'*Non,* nobody believes that.'

Eventually I couldn't stand it any longer and grabbed his keys. I gave the handle a sharp twist and the door swung open. It had not even been locked.

Inside was a largish reception area with a few tatty chairs, a reading stand, several occasional tables, piles of tourist magazines (from foreign countries) and a large sign which said 'Katanga is fun'.

The caretaker led me to my office which contained a desk, two chairs and a defunct water cooler. The desk was covered in a thick layer of dust. Shortly afterwards the rest of the staff arrived; a smiling young Congolese called Pierre and two women secretaries. Introductions all round and everybody got down to their appointed tasks.

Pierre began reading a newspaper, the one secretary got on the telephone to a friend and the other disappeared altogether. I was left at my desk staring at the layer of dust and the dehydrated corpse of a cockroach. By lunch time I had managed to clear the desk but had not got around to anything else.

Shortly after lunch Pierre stuck his head through the open doorway.

'Do you want to sign anything?'

'Please God, yes. Anything.'

He reappeared with several pieces of paper. I signed a requisition form for more ball point pens and another for a subscription to the Belgian magazine *Pourquoi Pas*. And that was that.

At 05h00 Pierre came to tell me that the staff were knocking off for the day. He looked at me solicitously.

'Monsieur, may I make a suggestion? It is pointless your sitting here the whole day. We do not have enough work to warrant it. Why don't you come in only once a week to sign the papers?'

An excellent idea which I readily adopted. It was plain to me that some foreign tourists inadvertently walking into our office would create major consternation for the staff. There were no tourists, and in truth, there should not have been a tourist office.

From then on I turned my attention to the homestead which went with my post; a lovely rambling old house set on five hectares of land about seven kilometers from Jadotville. Within a few months our plot was yielding bountiful crops of tomatoes, egg fruit and lettuce. All lovingly tendered by Julia and myself.

'Du Plessis' Special Green Beans' flooded the Jadotville market and Munongo jokingly threatened to find me a real job in the province's agricultural services. I submerged myself in the simple pleasure and satisfaction of turning a barren plot of ground into something productive.

On the national political scene there were again dramatic developments. November 25 1965 and Mobutu, backed by the CIA, deposed Kasavubu and Evariste Kimba in a coup startlingly similar to the 1960 one. The General appointed Leonard Mulamba, a former ANC man and competent soldier, to the post of Prime Minister.

Full circle . . . Mobutu was again in power.

Tshombe, realising that constitutional and democratic methods of acceding to power were completely thwarted and that his very life was in danger, decided to go into exile. He made a fleeting visit to Elisabethville on his way to Brussels, conferred with Munongo, and sent a message to us that we must await his call. We had not been forgotten.

Shortly after this, Mulamba himself came to see Munongo in the capital of Katanga. Taking the bull by the horns, Munongo told him we were in hiding in Jadotville.

Mulamba, who had gained a high regard for my air services during the rebellion, magnanimously shrugged his shoulders and said he had no objection to our staying so long as I stuck to beans and stayed out of politics.

By this time I was so engrossed in my agricultural pursuits that I readily agreed. The vegetables grew more bountifully, Jose and Pierre grew bigger, Julia and I more mellow and the world seemed truly in its place. We lived extremely insular lives,

222

only occasionally, journeying into Jadotville. Once there, we made a point of visiting the Burgomaster of the town, one of the most handsome men I have ever met. We had known him from the Katangese secession days and regarded him as a loyal friend.

Momentary excitement visited us when an old face from the past pitched up. Michel De Clary, former mercenary, came to sell a scheme to overthrow Mobutu, reinstall Tshombe and win great riches all round. We turned him down flat.

But the inveterate conspirator was not to be put off. Munongo was next on his visiting list and Julia and I were therefore not surprised when we received a call from the recently appointed Governor next day to say that De Clary wanted an interview and perhaps we should come along to give our opinions.

When we arrived the ever conspiratorial Munongo ushered us into an anteroom of his reception room and when De Clary arrived we were able to overhear every word De Clary said — including his ringing denunciations of myself as a devious character who could not be trusted.

De Clary's idea was that Munongo should declare the secession of Katanga. Words tumbled out one after the other. De Clary promised he had financial backing for the coup and could deliver trusted French mercenaries to Munongo's side. It was sheer lunacy and Munongo wisely kept his own counsel.

Later we were to learn that De Clary was political advisor to Colonel John Peters, Hoare's successor to the post of OC V Commando. It was a particularly empty headed plan and an example of the short term adventuring which was rife in the Congo at the time.

After this little interlude Julia and I returned to our haven of tranquillity. As peaceful day followed peaceful day I began to wonder if this type of life was really what I had always been searching for in my restless past.

Then, for once, excitement came to us instead of us towards it. Events far away were moving, new plans being hatched for a coup, Mobutu more concerned than ever about his position.

Midday on a sweltering summers day we received an urgent telephone call from our friend the Burgomaster.

'Jerry, get packed and ready to move out with your family as soon as possible.'

'What now?'

'General Mobutu has given orders for you and your entire family to be arrested and flown to Leopoldville. He knows you are in Jadotville and a detachment of ANC troops are on their way from Elisabethville. I will try and delay them while you get away. I am sending a car now.'

It was a mad scramble but by the time the car arrived we were ready. We all bundled inside and took of at breakneck speed to a safe house on the outskirts of Jadotville.

And while we were in panic stricken flight a comedy of Gilbertian proportions was being played out in the town. True to his word the Burgomaster had intercepted the ANC detachment, inveigled the officer into the pub and was playing cat and mouse with him.

Every time the officer demanded to know where Puren was, the Mayor would make a great show of summoning people to ask them if they knew where to find me. All, of course, claimed they did not have the slightest idea.

By the fifth inquiry and the seventh pint of beer the officer had lost both interest and equilibrium.

Thus we sped away.

Julia and I settled into our new 'safe' house. Several days later Munongo arranged for us to be moved to a Government guest house near Elisabethville. A police car drove us all the way at break neck speed. Again a narrow escape awaited us.

While in the house a former Katangese finance minister, now a staunch Mobutu man, came for a spur of the moment visit, presumably to size it up for his own use. Only by a frantic scramble did we manage to hide ourselves away, knowing that discovery would have meant instant arrest.

In the tense days of our refuge we speculated about what had happened to make Mobutu launch such a sudden offensive to arrest us. Little did we know that new forces were moving in Brussels and elsewhere, new conflicts looming and that we were only part of a much larger sweep against anti-Mobutu forces.

It was now even too dangerous for us to live near the towns. Munongo again arranged for us to be moved, this time to a derelict hotel some twelve kilometers from Elisabethville. The hotel had been acquired by Munongo for his retainers and here we were billeted for two weeks. We lived with the black families, sharing their food, making do with cold water, no electricity and the ever constant fear of discovery.

At night I lay awake on the frayed canvas stretcher that was bed and tried to put the pieces together; what had been and what was likely to be. Was it worth it or should we leave the intrigue forever? Our return in 1964, so full of hope and confidence, the ideals we set ourselves, the plans we had made; all to end like this, fugitives in a rat infested hidey hole, isolated and powerless.

Then exactly fourteen days later we were rescued. An official car from Katanga Province swept up to the hotel and the ubiquitous agents climbed out. Together with our few possessions we were raced through the Katanga countryside towards Elisabethville. It was clear the agents were taking no chances.

At the various points along the road, at certain houses, stores, café's, the driver would pull the car on to the shoulder of the road and climb out with a reassuring smile. He would disappear into the building and come out after a few minutes. Obviously 'phoning ahead to see if there were any ANC roadblocks.

Eventually we arrived in the city and slipped through back streets to the capital's Luano airport. We were rushed through the crush to a private room in the airport building. Inside we found *Madame* Tshombe and five of her children. We greeted each other warmly for we had not seen each other for months.

Tensely we waited for several hours and then it was a quick whisk past customs officials and into a waiting Boeing destined for Brussels.

It was the last scheduled flight to leave directly from Elisabethville to Europe.

Thereafter all flights had to arrive and depart from Ndjili airport at Leopoldville, in the heart of Mobutu country.

Munongo had not failed in his promise to look after us.

The Boeing rumbled down the runway and lifted smoothly into the clear blue Congo sky. From the porthole I watched the familiar Congo jungle sprout from beneath the wing.

It was to be Brussels and the second exile.

33

Clowns and a Congo Revolt

Tshombe was in Brussels and Tshombe was in trouble.

As soon as Julia and I arrived in the capital and made ourselves known to the deposed Prime Minister, we discovered conspiracy abounding.

Gathered around Tshombe in his tiny Brussels flat were a number of Katanga hands and long time intriguers. Mario Spandre was there, a Belgian lawyer from Katanga days, as was Professor René Clemens, sociology lecturer at Liege University, creator of the original Congolese constitution, a committed Tshombe supporter but completely impractical in the field of military strategy.

Great plans were afoot, I was confidentially told; Tshombe would be returned to the Congo, the country would be saved. I took a closer look at the 'plans' — grandiosely named the *Kyrellis plan* - and decided immediately that Tshombe had a problem. I had never before seen such ill conceived notions committed to paper.

After our period in Leopoldville and our months in hiding, Julia and I were at that point having serious doubts as to whether we should continue our services to Tshombe or rather return to a peaceful and stable life in South Africa.

On our arrival back in Brussels, Tshombe's first question to us had been: 'Why did you leave your posts?'

It took perhaps ten minutes of straight talking to convince the former Prime Minister that we had left one step ahead of a firing squad and that the whole of the Congo was rife with rumours of a coup attempt.

Immediately Tshombe relented and asked us to stay on and assist in a personal capacity. I knew, however, that I could never work with the conspirators then around Tshombe. Was it worth staying? Would it lead anywhere?

The machinations of those conspirators decided us.

'We can't leave now Julia. I'm convinced we can get Tshombe back into power but certainly not through the idiotic plans of his present advisors. It is our duty to stay and warn him of the dangers.'

Julia agreed and we immediately rented a small flat in Brussels near Tshombe's. Ironically ours faced directly on to the flat of the former air advisor to the Mobutu regime, Bouzin. I rolled up figurative sleeves and got down to work.

The conspirators plot would fail on two counts. On the first count it was too complicated. Complicated plans for revolt must be avoided because the more things expected to go right, the more things there are likely to go wrong. In essence it involved simultaneous attacks by Katangese troops and internal and external mercenary forces on Stanleyville, Elisabethville, Bukavu and Albertville. It involved air drops and ground attacks, mercenaries and Katangese, split second timing and everything . . . except the US 82nd Airborne Division.

On the second count it would fail because too many people knew about it.

As part of the scheme the conspirators had hired a number of mercenary pilots to be on standby. Accordingly, a group of Congo vets, including the 'Terrible Twins', Bracco and Libert, had been hauled in from all points of the compass and billeted in one of the most expensive hotels in Lisbon. At the time the twins had been flying for Wigmo and their sudden departure for grasses greener could hardly have gone unnoticed.

The tortuous plot unravelled. The pilots remained in a state of high spending indolence and Tshombe's reserves diminished. Apart from that, there is nothing like a bunch of hell raising mercenaries sitting around drinking beer on a mystery expense account to set the rumours circulating.

A further folly; the plan counted on the support of V Commando, now under the command of John Peters, a ferocious soldier but fanatically pro-Mobutu. Spandre had accordingly begun jetting around South Africa and Rhodesia sounding out all V Commando leaders, past and present.

Spandre had seen Peters who was on holiday in Rhodesia while I was still in Katanga and had given him details of the plot. Peters and V Commando were to take and neutralise Albertville and seize the airfield. Simultaneously Alistair Wicks, former 2 IC of V Commando and by then in retirement, would recruit one hundred mercenaries in South Africa, take off from Henrique de Carvalho in Angola and seize Elisabethville.

What Spandre did not mention to Peters was that Wicks was to be in charge of the operation; a preposterous suggestion if one knew Peter's immense egotism.

In the final analysis it did not matter because Peters had done exactly what I would have expected him to do . . . he turned it down flat.

The intrepid conspirators then approached Wicks with the plan (failing to mention that Peters had turned down the scheme) and won a tentative approval.

Wicks telephoned Hoare who warned him that nobody would follow him 'in a month of Sundays'.

At that stage Wicks, most wisely, withdrew.

Thus collapsed any hope of a V Commando involvement.

At that precise point any sane person would have dropped the whole project. I could hardly credit the stupidity of the conspirators in approaching the people they had; confirmed Mobutu men. Peters had meanwhile acted according to expectations and taken news of the plot right back to Mobutu. The General had flown into a rage, ordered the rounding up of all pro-Tshombist groups, and succeeded in driving the Purens out of the Congo.

I went to see Tshombe.

'Sir, the plan won't work. It has not been thought through and for too many people are in the know. I beg you to drop it now, before it is too late.'

Tshombe gave a hunted look and shook his head.

'Jerry, I have been assured by these people that the plan can work. It is urgent that I return to the Congo, that elections be held. I am afraid to wait too long.'

He paused and stared at me.

'Do you feel there is no potential for a revolt?'

'No, sir, there is a vast reservoir of bitterness among the Katangese troops and the people of Katanga that could be utilised to spark a revolt, but timing is of the essence. A hasty move will needlessly and bloodily waste that valuable pool of support. I beg you to wait.'

'Wait for what?'

'Wait for the ruckus to die down and for Mobutu to drop his guard. But most important, wait until V Commando leaves the Congo. It is to be wound up soon, I know that. With V Commando there under Peters there is no chance of success. They will oppose the revolt.'

'Thank you, I will consider it', said Tshombe.

But I knew it was a losing struggle. The conspirators had the bit between their teeth and Tshombe, under who knows what pressure, had acceded. The plot moved towards its tragic climax. My opposition was strongly rejected by Tshombe's clique and I felt overwhelmed by frustration at the stupidity of people who approached the task of usurping a foreign, sovereign and dictatorial Government of sixteen million people as casually as they would prepare for a minor league football match.

Next stage in the plot came when the conspirators approached Commandant Wauthier, a Belgian officer, member of that country's secret service and commander of XI Commando, and Wilhelm of XIV Commando. Both these commandos were deployed along the rugged northern Oriental Province border with Sudan. The two mercenaries expressed themselves willing to join the revolt. The conspirators were elated.

During this entire period I had no contact at all with Spandre, architect of the plot. Several of the young Katangese on his staff, however, had kept me fully posted of developments. Among them, too, there was a feeling that the plan was faulty and the timing bad.

Kabeya, Tshombe's son in law and one of Spandre's men, came to tell me of the agreement with Wauthier and Wilhelm.

'How many men do they muster?' I demanded scathingly.

'About one thousand, two hundred Katangese and thirty mercenaries.'

'What strength does V Commando have alone?'

'About two hundred mercenaries.'

'Where does Schramme fit in? His Commando controls the whole of the Maniema after all.'

'He doesn't fit in.'

'Where are the aircraft that are needed?'

'We're working on that.'

'Who is going to bring in the foreign mercenaries for the air drop on Elisabethville and who is going to take Albertville?'

'Those operations will come about later. They have been dropped from the original phase.'

'Who else are you inviting to join?'

227

'Denard?'

That was the last straw. If Denard was included the conspirators might as well forget the whole thing. He had proved himself untrustworthy in the Yemen as well as in Katanga.

D-Day approached and the squabbling increased. I could see the plan was ineffectual. Disaster loomed. Again I went to see Tshombe. This time, sensing my mission, he said he was not available.

I left a message with Kabeya; 'I'm not staying around to watch this idiocy unfolding. I am going for a long walk in the country.'

Next day I took Julia and the children to their uncle's home in St Hubert. For the next ten cathartic days I rambled through the Belgian summer countryside, down to Luxembourg and back. Haversack over my shoulder, staff in hand, I buried myself completely in the beauty of the lush green countryside and the hospitable country inns.

Africa, revolutions and war, became a distant memory.

It was while I was lost in this rustic simplicity that the ill-fated first Katangese revolt began.

On July 23 1966 the Katangese troops in Stanleyville revolted. As expected, the conspirators plans had found a responsive chord in the frustrations of the Katangese troops who, for months, had been subjected to discrimination in terms of promotion and conditions of service because of Mobutu's life long distrust of them.

The plotters had kindled a fury of resentment which, if properly handled, would have burnt Mobutu and his dictatorial regime out of existence. It wasn't properly handled and the initial sparks of dissension were brutally doused.

The first step by the three thousand Katangese in Stanleyville was to kill the hated Colonel Tshatsi, in charge of Mobutu's paratroopers in the capital of Orientale Province, and to seize the radio station. An attempt to catch all the remaining ANC officers at a party failed and they rapidly disappeared.

Denard, with his commando, acted quickly and perfectly predictably. He seized the post office and the banks and 'phoned Mobutu to tell him there was a mutiny on the go, demanded that Prime Minister Mulamba come and negotiate, and then waited to see what the market would stand.

Being in command of the sole means of communications out of Stanleyville, he was in the pound seats.

The conspirators' key man in the revolt, Wauthier, exited bloodily and permanently from the scene a few days after the revolt in Stanleyville. The Belgian attempted to persuade some of Denard's officers to join the coup, a heated argument followed and Wauthier eventually ended up with a bullet in the head, fired by a French officer and, according to rumours, on Denard's orders.

The official version put about was that the French mercenary, Boucher, was talking to Wauthier while the Belgian cleaned his submachinegun.

It accidentally discharged — curtains for Wauthier.

Wauthier's body was flown to Leopoldville as a show of loyalty to Mobutu accompanied by some of the loyalist mercenaries. Their touching display of fidelity was not entirely appreciated there and the 'honour guard' to the corpse consequently spent some time in the slammer.

Wilhelm, the German mercenary commanding XIV Commando, had an initial success when his commando of twenty two whites and six hundred Katangese descended on Paulis in a whirlwind of death and destruction and routed the ANC within minutes.

Strengthened by the victory, Wilhelm led his commando on the next leg of their thrust towards Stanleyville and ran straight into one of those strange quirks of fate that dog the best (or worst) laid plans.

Several kilometers from Paulis the column came under blistering attack by a Simba group using mortars and rockets.

Within minutes the column was a smouldering line of burnt out vehicles, sixty Katangese dead and Wilhelm fatally injured.

In Stanleyville the situation dragged on in hopeless limbo for two further months with Denard holding the communications and the Katangese the airport.

Mulamba and Munongo tried unsuccessfully to negotiate a ceasefire; the rebels remained obstinate.

Then Denard suddenly attacked. By now, quite sure the revolt would collapse, he opportunistically threw in his lot with Mobutu and launched the surprise raid that quickly broke the Katangese ranks.

The terrified troops made a break for the Maniema where Schramme was based in the hope they would find protection.

To get there they had to pass through V Commando and VI Commando territory.

An untold number of the Katangese were slaughtered on Denard's orders and a lesser number made it to Punia and into Schramme's neutral command.

Many of the officers were flown to Leopoldville in chains to meet gory deaths at Camp Kokolo. A number never even made it that far.

Young Miji Athanase a former officer in the Katangese Air Force and well known to me, was thrown from an aircraft at three thousand meters above the jungle.

He was not the only one to go the same way.

And thus ended an irresponsible attempt to reinstate Tshombe.

It was badly planned, uncoordinated and completely premature. Lives had been wasted, future opportunities prejudiced and the Katangese scarred by the response of the white mercenaries under Denard to their grievances.

I returned from Luxembourg to watch from afar the collapse of the hair brained scheme. Abstaining from 'I told you so' recriminations I waited the inevitable summons from Tshombe.

It came several days after Denard's attack on the Katanga forces.

Tshombe was sitting behind his desk in the study, cradling his head in his hands. He seemed to have aged immeasurably in the last few months.

'Will you organise a revolt that will return me to my country?' he asked directly and simply.

I placed both my hands on his desk.

'I will do it on one condition, sir; that is that only you and I are involved in the planning. Only you and I.'

Tshombe looked up wearily and nodded his agreement.

34

Strides and Disappearances

And so I began plotting the downfall of a dictatorial regime holding sway over more than sixteen million people, bolstered by an army of fifty thousand men and supported by a Super Power.

Against this force I could muster the charisma of Tshombe, my own knowledge of the country, the abiding hatred of the Katangese for Mobutu and at most two thousand Katangese troops and two hundred white mercenaries.

The odds seemed good that we could win.

Already I had in mind the long term programme necessary to get a revolt of that magnitude defined, propagated and effective.

1 Identify the key dependable figures and groups within the Congo available for the revolt;

2 Choose the people necessary from outside the Congo for the planning and operation and then discreetly inform them;

3 Present the broad plan of action to the leaders within the Congo and allow them to develop the finer points;

4 Decide on the exact time for the revolt.

The first point then. Who was to lead the revolt in the Congo?

I didn't even look at the V Commando leaders. By the time our plan was ready V Commando would be disbanded and out of the Congo. All intelligence tended towards that and indeed, in February 1967, Colonel Peters resigned his commission and twenty four year old George Schroeder took over for a caretaker period of three months.

The last months of V Commando had not been happy. Under the martinet Peters, the 'elan' achieved by V Commando by Mike Hoare had become extremely tarnished, culminating in the mysterious death on 13 May 1966 of Hugh van Oppen, next in line of succession after Peters.

Van Oppen, 'died while cleaning his submachinegun'.

Suspicion, however, rested heavily on another mercenary, Ross-Johnstone, a close Peters' confidant.

The suspicion was hardly allayed when Ross-Johnstone took to parading around with the slug that killed Van Oppen slung around his neck.

Peters never called an inquiry despite the rumours so the truth will never be known. Suffice to say V Commando had slid a long way since those halcyon days when it was thundering down on Stanleyville.

With V Commando still loyal and operational in the Congo I knew that there could be no coup. Once out of the way there was a more than even chance.

Who was left? I realised that my man would have to be;

(a) Daring and imaginative;

(b) Stand to gain substantially by the deposing of Mobutu or by the installation of Tshombe or preferably, by both;

(c) Assured of the support of the Katangese troops;

(d) Fully acquainted with the eastern Congo; and

(e) Have a strong power base from which to operate.

The candidate stood out like a sore thumb; Jean Schramme.

The Belgian settler had remained loyal to Tshombe throughout the tumultuous seven years. While Denard and Peters had attacked and buried the dissident Katangese Gendarmes in September of the previous year, Schramme had remained silent, quietly absorbing the runaways into his command. The gratitude of the fugitives and the loyalty of his original *Leopard Group* troops that he had stuck by through exile and war, could not be overlooked.

Schramme's base too was a powerful starting block for any coup. At Punia in the vast Maniema, indeed at exactly the estate he was forced to flee in 1961, Schramme had succeeded in carving himself a feudal state buttressed by virtually a private army.

On his own initiative he had reconstructed roads, bridges and schools in the area, brought back planters and miners, begun crop production, worked the mines and resumed his old pre-independence life style in his rambling colonial mansion.

In early 1967 the omnipresent Schramme straddled the entire eastern Congo like a colossus. But would he risk all that in a coup?

The answer was simple . . . it was already at risk.

Mobutu, paranoiac, perhaps justifiably, about the Katangese, was threatening to disarm Schramme's X Commando.

With his troops gone, Schramme realised, his power would also go. Then would come the ANC, and the end of his African empire. But in the first months of 1967 Schramme was powerful, solidly based . . . and afraid.

He was the perfect man for our ends.

I considered the other mercenary leaders.

Denard?

I dismissed him from the plan almost as I thought of him. His actions in the first revolt were evidence enough of his treachery. As far as I was concerned he and his eighty French mercenaries could stay in Orientale Province. It was a pity because they were good fighters, but it was no point having suspect allies.

Noel and Michel, Schramme's officers, Bob Noddyn, and the other Belgian mercenary leaders would follow Schramme's lead I was sure. So much for the mercenary officers.

What of the Katangese troops?

From our intelligence reports it was abundantly clear that there was a strong impetus for revolt, undiminished (perhaps enhanced) by the bloody Stan coup. Mobutu's rampant corruption and brutality was now common knowledge in the blighted country.

I was convinced that not only the Katangese troops, but indeed the whole of Katanga and very likely large parts of the rest of the Congo would follow suit if the mercenaries came out in revolt.

Without popular support, I was the first to admit, the coup would never be a success. I was prepared to stake my life and those of the mercenaries that once the revolt got underway there would be no stopping it.

Second part of the programme; who did we need for co-ordination and assistance? Close to home I accepted automatically that Julia would be brought in. Her main task would be co-ordination work in South Africa. Then there were Tshombe's faithful aides, Leonard Monga, thirty two year old former ANC lieutenant and a graduate of the Belgian military academy, Marc Kalibiona and Naweji, both close personal friends.

Then the key issue . . . a link man to Schramme.

This could be a problem. We were not entirely sure Schramme would support us and the initial approach would have to come from somebody not easily identifiable as a Tshombist, somebody known to Schramme and able to judge the mercenary's reactions. I would have to work on that one.

Air strength?

Bracco and Libert were still circulating in Portugal and together with Jack Malloch, I reckoned we would have sufficient pilots. I would alert them to be on standby but would not reveal details, or even the country, until the last moment.

Extra foreign mercenaries for ground operations?

I could recruit those, again at the last moment, from any major city in South Africa or Rhodesia. I thought wryly of those scores of Congo veterans living together still on their memories and itching for a chance to get back to the excitement and the money.

Finally, I accepted that we would have to inform the Portuguese and South African security agencies of the plot. We would have to work from their territories and they would be bound to pick it up at some stage. I decided, however, to keep it secret until as late as possible.

At this point I went to see Tshombe. He listened attentively to my suggestions and nodded. We discussed Schramme.

'Do you think he is to be trusted?'

'There are always uncertainties in something like this. We won't know until he says 'yes' and even then we won't really know until he delivers the goods. Of all the mercenary leaders he is the best at the moment.'

'What other interests does he have?'

I shrugged: 'It is generally known that he is a man of many parts. One part possibly works for the Belgian secret service and the other part for the big mining houses. Perhaps it's the same part working for both. I don't know if loyalty to these two bodies conflicts with his loyalty to you.'

'We will use him all the same,' said Tshombe.

We turned to the subject of the best person to contact Schramme. I told him

I didn't have anybody in mind and that it would have to be somebody neutral and not identifiably pro-Tshombe.

As I was leaving Tshombe grabbed me by the arm.

'Just one point, Jerry. I do not want Denard in on this under any circumstances.' I strongly agreed.

Then it was back to Point Three on the programme; an overall plan using the forces at our disposal.

Hours on end I locked myself away pouring over maps, scanning intelligence reports, considering logistics and always praying that I was not missing anything important. After several weeks of careful thought I came to the conclusion that simplicity and directness were our best plan. Based on the assumption that Schramme would come in with us and that V Commando would, by that stage, be off the scene, the plan looked as follows:-

Phase One:

Schramme mobilises at Punia and sends two columns out; one column to strike four hundred kilometers east and seize Bakavu on Lake Kivu and the other to take Kindu two hundred and eighty kilometers south of Punia. A force of former Katangese Gendarmes supported by loyal Bahemba tribesmen would stage near Kongolo west of Albertville.

Simultaneously, five hundred ex-Gendarmes led by a small element of South African and Rhodesian mercenaries, flown in a few days earlier, would stage at Baudounville on Lake Tanganyika.

Phase Two:

Bob Noddyn and Colonel Kaniki with their IX Commando, brought in from Uvira in the south and Goma in the north, would stage at Bakavu and await the arrival of Schramme's X Commando element. The whole group, now sufficiently strengthened to meet any ANC threat, would then make for Kindu.

Phase Three:

X Commando elements with IX Commando would RV with the rest of Schramme's X Commando at Kindu and then the whole group would push for Katanga.

Simultaneously, the Baudouinville mercenary/Gendarme force would strike in a feint towards Elisabethville.

Phase Four:

IX Commando and X Commando RV with the militia/Gendarme/ Bahemba group near Kongola and the combined force, now at least three thousand Katangese with one hundred and forty mercenaries, would push hard for Elisabethville to reinforce the five hundred man task force.

Phase Five:

An immediate dash into Katanga proper, popular revolt, recruitment of militia and the investing of the whole province.

Phase Six:

Ultimatum to Mobutu or an attack on Leopoldville with a vastly swollen Gendarme force.

I had little doubt that the column could punch its way through any ANC resistance at any stage and into the welcoming arms of the Katangese population.

The plan was presented to Tshombe. I explained to him in detail, answering questions as we went along. The last question was the hardest of all: 'Will it work?'

'With surprise and speed it has got to work. If we lose either one or the other element we are in trouble.'

'Speed and surprise,' Tshombe said meditatively. 'Now for the final point in your programme. When?'

'Certainly not before V Commando leaves.'

'And how are we doing with our link man?'

'I'm still working at it, sir.'

Then it was back to the drawing board, working out more details, routes, relative strengths, logistical support and timing. I agonised over many of the points realising that one miscalculation could mean the difference between success or failure and failure in this case would be counted in terms of lives, many lives.

At times I felt obliged to stop and simply consider the enormity of what was unfolding under my maps and blue prints; not simply a novel type rescue of some imprisoned African president, or the seizure of a mine, but in fact the usurpation of a sovereign African state and the formation of a power bloc that would affect the course of African history.

It was time for a comic interlude. A former mercenary and adventurer, Gino Tozzi, appears on the scene with his own highly secretive scheme for the salvation of the Congo. He flies to South Africa and asks Mike Hoare if we would be interested in meeting Tshombe. Hoare thinks Tshombe has something up his sleeve and agrees. Tozzi then goes to Tshombe and tells him Hoare wants to see him. Tshombe, likewise, thinks Hoare has something up his sleeve. Hoare jets to Madrid and meets Tshombe. Neither knows what the other wants and Tozzi has disappeared. Hoare jets back to South Africa and that is the end of that.

Finally, I was satisfied with my plan. Time to bring more people in. Julia was carefully briefed as was Kalibiona, Monga and Naweji. They had all had some inkling of developments but this was the first unveiling of the master plan. Then it was the question of the link man.

I found him quite by chance in a busy Brussels street; Maurice Quintin, the building contractor whom I had first met in Elisabethville in 1961.

He shouted with pleasure at seeing me and furiously pumped my hand.

Over beers in the nearest pub Quintin spilled out his life story since leaving Katanga after the secession. He was battling to make a living in Belgium after being hounded out of the Maniema by the rebels and out of Katanga by the UN and the ANC. I could see he was no particular friend of Mobutu. The wheels began turning in my head.

We started reminiscing about the Katanga days. Schramme's name cropped up.

'I hear he's settled back at Punia,' said Quintin. 'I wouldn't mind seeing him again actually. We knew each other in the old days.'

We finished our drinks and I made arrangements to see him again. Twice more we met and then I went to see Tshombe.

'I think we have our link man.'

'Who?'

'Maurice Quintin. He's itching to get back at Mobutu and even more so into a stable Congo. Also we know that he and Schramme were once acquaintances and that Quintin is not immediately identifiable as a Tshombist.'

Tshombe nodded.

'Do you trust him?'

'Again we won't know until the time, but he's the best we have.'

I got the go ahead.

At our next meeting I broached the topic directly; would he act as our link man in getting the coup off the ground. The little Belgian agreed instantly.

The very next Monday Quintin began his dangerous shuttle between Madrid and Congo. The first visit he flew from Madrid to Kigali in Rwanda and then motored to Punia. He was away a nail biting week. On Tuesday an excited Quintin was back with good news; Schramme would come in with us.

The Belgian mercenary had received confirmed reports that Mobutu was about to disarm his mercenaries and disband the Katangese forces.

Schramme was indeed afraid.

At the beginning of March 1967 the pace quickened. Quintin returned to the Congo on a second mission to Schramme. We were taking the plot further. Another week's delay and then we received a letter from Quintin posted in Rwanda. He gave more details of Schramme's strength and reaffirmed the leaders support for the coup. Quintin suggested a meeting be set up between himself and Schramme or preferably Schramme and another emissary at a later stage to finalise details of the coup.

At this point a cloud crept into our otherwise sunny skies. Quintin said sombrely he believed Schramme was firmly in the hands of the Belgian mining houses: 'To think the miners have a veritable army at their service, paid by the Government. Their security and their police at the cost of several thousand francs deposited in Belgium for *The Friend*.'

In another part of the letter Quintin questioned whether the revolt would not clash with the interests of the mining houses. For his part, he said, he would rather not have anything further to do with Schramme. This was indeed a blow.

It was a few days after receiving this letter, at dawn on a week day morning, that Julia heard a knock at our flat door in Brussels. Consciously reminding herself that this was not Leopoldville, she opened the door and found four duffel coated men on the threshold.

'Bonjour Madame, Surete,' said the senior officer and flashed both his identity card and a search warrant. The men filed in and proceeded to turn the spick-and-span flat upside down. The international nexus, thought Julia, as she watched them rooting through drawers of personal letters. It was obvious that Mobutu or the Belgians themselves had got wind of the plan.

Hence the raid and hence, possibly, the end of all our dreams. Julia's mind leapt suddenly to the plans in the bottom drawer; reports, maps, drawings and Quintin's letter.

Too late. The policemen had found the trove and were stacking it all on the carpet. They began sifting through it, kneeling on the floor.

Two year old Jose appeared on the scene and made a dive for the papers. The Law sternly warned him off. Back to poring over my maps on which I had drawn a host of lines, routes of march, key towns and air distances.

'What is this, Madame?'

'Plans my husband is using for a book on the Simba rebellion.'

'And this?' he held up my notebook with my observations on ANC troop strengths.

'Also for the book.'

The officer took the maps and the notebook and set it on one side of the other documents. Jose dived at them, grabbed the pile and disappeared. After a hectic chase the police managed to recover some of the documents from the giggling child. The rest lay scattered and unobserved by the police.

Then they found Quintin's letter. All four crowded around and pored over the colon's appalling scribble. Julia held her breath.

'Christ, is this Hebrew or Japanese? It's certainly not French,' said the exasperated officer eventually and threw it away.

The search went on. In the bedroom they came across what was obviously a key piece of evidence indicating incipient revolution, Julia's ,22 pistol.

After a ridiculous exchange of words, during which the officer constantly kept brandishing the pistol threateningly, they finally took it. A few more gruff words and the squad left with several boxes of totally irrelevant information. In our flat we actually had enough evidence to have ourselves shot had we been in Leopoldville.

Fortunately we were not and just as fortunately the Belgian police seemed to have little idea what they were actually searching for so assiduously.

That same morning the homes of two hundred other Belgian Tshombists were raided throughout Belgium.

I was deeply shaken by the raids. Had our plans leaked? How much did Mobutu know? I flew to Madrid and conferred with Tshombe. We both knew that it was unlikely our plan had become known. More probably Mobutu had got wind of some other plan, heard a rumour or simply pressurised the Belgians into launching a series of cautionary raids.

We decided to press on . . . but warily.

Tshombe's HQ in Madrid had meanwhile unfortunately become the scene of a fair amount of internal bickering. For reasons best known to himself Tshombe had re-engaged an extremely suspicious Belgian by the name of Hamboursin who seemed to be in some sort of financial advisory position to Tshombe. In the first exile in Madrid he had apparently been given his marching orders after some unpleasantness. His reappearance at such a delicate stage in our operation, was bitterly resented by a number of Tshombe's aides. In Madrid I rapidly realised that relations between Tshombe and Monga were becoming strained.

Back to Brussels again and several long meetings with Quintin who had by now arrived back from Rwanda. Schramme was very keen to settle matters and it was time the full details were taken to him and the date fixed.

'Will you go back a third time?'

'I'd rather not,' said the Belgian.

'Why?'

'Just a feeling about Schramme. I don't entirely trust him. There is something going on.'

'What?'

Again Quintin shrugged.

'On my last trip to Punia Schramme was very cooperative and polite as usual. Then one morning I walked into his radio room by accident. Schramme found me there and became furious . . . told me to get out and never walk in again without permission.'

236

I digested this and patted him on the shoulder.

'Look, perhaps he was a bit overwrought. It is a tense time for all of us. I don't believe there is any reason to distrust Schramme. He's got too much to lose by not supporting the coup.'

'I suppose so,' said Quintin, unconvinced.

'Maurice, I'm not forcing you to go back but if you pull out now it will set the plan back by months. The decision is yours.'

Next day he came to see me and said he would return. My conscience lives with that decision.

Two days later Quintin left for Kigali. We were never to see him again. We waited the usual week and no reply. Nine days, ten days. Still no word. After two weeks Tshombe called me.

'What's happened to Maurice?'

'I don't know, sir.'

'Could something have befallen him; Schramme perhaps?'

'Possibly sir. There is only one way to find out.'

'How?'

'I'll go and see Schramme myself.'

Tshombe considered this for a moment.

'It's dangerous.'

'I know.'

'I won't let you do it alone. Kalibiona will go with you.'

'As you wish, sir.'

I had only been out of Tshombe's office ten minutes when Monga came rushing up to me.

The Old Man tells me you and Kalibiona are returning to the Congo.'

'That's right.'

'I'm coming as well. The Old Man says he has no objection.'

I shrugged my shoulders. The more the merrier into the Devil's lair, I thought.

35

Final Touches

'Are you sure we want to involve ourselves again in the melee?' Julia's face was creased with concern as we sat in the lounge of our Springs' home.

'We've gone too far to go back, Julia,' I replied. 'We've had six years with Tshombe; six years of ups and downs, times when we have been within a hair's breadth of success. We can't just forget our principles and sell six years down the river. We must go on to success.'

My wife nodded slowly. She knew herself the inevitability of this step.

For Kalibiona the path was not that easy. Not exactly the bravest of men, on the day before our departure from Springs he lounged about with a lugubrious face and nervously restless hands.

'How can you be so calm about this?' he demanded of Julia on one occasion at the height of our pre-flight preparations.

Julia shrugged philosophically and tried to placate our concerned colleague. 'Why do you say we will die?'

The Katangese shook his head and looked despairingly out of the window at the sun dappled Springs street.

'Schramme will betray us. He has already killed Quintin.'

'How do you know that?' Julia and I demanded sharply.

Kalibiona shrugged and turned away.

Alone later, Julia and I scoffed at his fears.

Only days before Monga, Kalibiona and I had boarded an airbus to Gatwick from Majorca and from there had caught a regular flight to Salisbury. I had already telephoned Malloch to say we were arriving and to prepare the Heron for us.

We had hardly arrived in Salisbury when we had hit the first snag. Malloch had dug his heels in and said the Heron would not make it to the Congo.

'Sorry, Jerry boy. Just won't make it on its range. No point in crashing, hey?'

What the motives were for his reluctance, I never found out. Vainly I had pointed out that it would be the easiest thing in the world for us to fly to Henrique de Carvalho in Angola and from there hop across to the Congo. Malloch had not budged.

Eventually, frustrated and angry, we had boarded another flight for South Africa and landed at Jan Smuts airport . . . me and my two black French speaking friends

238

— both without visas. Fortunately I had telephoned ahead and the usual magic doors were opened. Customs and immigration had waved us through and there we were in the heart of apartheid South Africa.

Kalibiona, Monga and I spent several days at Springs where Julia was now resident, furiously discussing the plans, conjecturing about our mission, about the whole project and always, about the fate of Quintin.

I began with the necessary steps to acquire an aircraft and while we waited for the final arrangements to fall into place it was a pleasure to take my two Congolese friends on a guided tour of my hometown. Despite the strong taboos, social and statutory, against mixing of races, we three musketeers wandered the streets unchallenged if not exactly unobserved. We visited my mother's shop in a nearby complex, spent several hours talking, greeting neighbours and friends. Springs was a small town and I can easily believe that our strange little ensemble was the cause of a spate of speculation.

The money for the aircraft was soon forthcoming from Spain and within days we had an Aztec fully fueled and waiting for us at Pietersburg in the northern Transvaal. Our plans were settled; we were on our way.

The twin engined Aztec droned west on the long hop to Texeira da Sousa, Angolan town and airfield, our host in the first exile and a convenient staging area for our next jaunt into the volatile Congo.

As the Aztec bumped to a halt at the little airstrip Monga pointed in the direction of the airfield building. A military jeep was streaming towards us in billows of dust.

'Friend or foe?' I said sardonically.

I recognised the stocky little figure standing in the passenger seat, firmly gripping the wind shield. My old PIDE contact, Rochas, our mentor during the first exile and my colleague in Munongo's intelligence section.

Our welcome at the dusty and all too familiar airstrip in Texeira da Sousa was ambivalent; surprise, pleasure and suspicion.

'What the hell are you doing here?' Rochas demanded as we climbed out.

'How did you know we were arriving?'

'I didn't. I thought it was somebody else. Stop avoiding the question. What are you doing here in this God forsaken place?'

'Passing through', I said airily waving at the vast scrub land stretching north east of the town. The PIDE agent gave a sardonic grin and shoved a finger under my nose.

'Up to mischief again.'

Rochas grabbed me by the arm and started pushing me towards the jeep. He beckoned Kalibiona and Monga to follow. Seconds later we were spinning through the dirty streets of the town to PIDE HQ.

'Now we get down to business', said Rochas grimly.

My heart sank.

But business it was. Litres of ice cold Portuguese beer, garlic sausages, cheese and coffee. Occasionally the agent would delicately probe my reasons for arriving. Never did he press the point.

Late that afternoon we were driven to our aircraft and given a rousing farewell as we took off and headed towards Portugalia, another Angolan town in the north east. Our reception was equally hospitable. Several PIDE agents escorted us back to their mess and we were put up for the night. Beer, the famed prawns peri peri and lots of banter.

Our Portuguese hosts were burning to know what our visit portended. They knew of my close associations with Tshombe, they knew my background, inevitably they must have deduced that things were moving across the border.

Early next morning we were taxiing down the runway and climbing smoothly into the still chill morning air. A wide sweep to port and we crossed the border at two thousand meters.

Below us the vast panoply of jungles and rivers unfolded in its primeval magnificence.

Back in the Congo, back in the intrigue and excitement. Almost visibly, I shook with the excitement and possibilities that I believed could flow from our mission; possibilities for a great and stable country.

Besides me, Kalibiona and Monga were lost in their own thoughts.

Pensive? Excited? Fearful?

I felt it was wrong to break the fragile silence. Just over three hours later we passed Kindu on our starboard bow.

So far so good.

No enemy aircraft and lots of clear blue sky.

Thirty minutes later we were above Punia; Schramme's Punia.

Below was spread the visible proof of the Belgian's industry; good roads, bridges, a proper landing strip, wide plantations starting out of the thick jungle; all Schramme's work, and that of his Simba prisoners.

We circled the airfield and I took the aircraft in. I glanced at Monga. His face was alive with excitement and anticipation. Across to Kalibiona. I recognised real fear in the taut lines of his face; the man really believed that we were flying to our death.

It was only as I taxied the aircraft towards the dispersal tarmac and saw the jeeps loaded with grim faced Katangese troops that I felt the icy claws of fear tugging at my stomach.

Christ, perhaps Kalibiona was right.

The two jeeps pulled up alongside the aircraft. I recognised the mercenary sitting in the lead jeep, a massive Walloon who had been in the Congo since the Simba rebellion.

I remembered a story I was once told about the man. During the Stanleyville operation he managed to accumulate a batch of about thirty Simba prisoners. While his Katangese troops had lined them up on a bridge he had proceeded down the line cutting their throats one by one with a fiercely honed bush knife. Bleeding corpse after corpse fell into the river until only the mercenary was left, literally dripping with blood.

And this was the man Schramme kept to greet visitors.

The Walloon immediately recognised me and let out a roar of greeting and as I leapt out the Aztec he fired a welcoming shot into the air from his FN rifle. Several of the Katangese followed suit as they saw Monga and Kalibiona. We were back in the Congo all right and it hadn't changed much. I began to breath more easily.

Cautiously we entered the air control tower which had been turned into a comfortable restaurant while the Walloon went to telephone Schramme. We sprawled on the chairs in the cool interior of the building.

Ten minutes later a jeep cruised to a halt and out jumped Schramme; the same old Schramme . . . dapper, precise, intelligent. He bustled forward and we shook hands.

A snap of the fingers and a servant came out of a side room with frothing beers.

Kalibiona's expression lightened slightly. At least we weren't going to be shot out of hand.

We gathered around a table.

'You know why we're here, Colonel?' I asked.

'Yes. To make final arrangements for the coup. I trust my observations and comments have been relayed to you by M Quintin?'

There was a brief silence. The subject of Quintin later, I thought.

'They have indeed, Colonel, I would like to present the broad plan in its final form. We would value your comments.'

Kalibiona spread out the maps and I began to explain my plan, as approved and modified by Tshombe. I explained the attacks on Bukavu and Kindu, the need for speed and surprise. Schramme took it all in, occasionally asking pertinent questions. At the end of the briefing he looked up.

'You have forgotten something surely, Puren?'

'And that is?'

'Denard.'

Again a tense silence.

Kalibiona leaned forward. 'M Tshombe was adamant that Denard not be included. He is to be left out altogether.'

Schramme shook his head violently. 'Do you seriously expect me to leave Denard on his own in Orientale Province to the mercies of the ANC once we revolt? Never.'

The mercenary's voice was hard and unyielding. I could see there was no point in arguing but still feared bringing in the unreliable Denard.

'Tshombe says no.'

'Then you will have to tell Tshombe that I will not co-operate. Denard must come in. It is as simple as that.'

I tried to explain our doubts about Denard, but Schramme was adamant. No Denard, no coup. In the end there was nothing I could do but accede.

'This will mean a substantial altering of the plan,' I said.

'Not too serious. Instead of X Commando striking out on two axises, Bukavu and Kindu, we now attack in three columns. I send one column to Stanleyville to RV with Denard's VI Commando and to give them sufficient strength to break out. I will arrange for Denard to meet us there. Then the plot follows through as planned. The Stan column falls back on Punia, RVs with the Bukavu column and the two then strike for Kindu.

As he spoke Schramme pointed out the details on the map.

I thought about it and nodded. As a diversion I promised to bring a small number of South African and Rhodesian mercenaries to stage with loyal militia at Baudouinville for an attack on Elisabethville.

'There are two major points; one, we must not dissipate our strength towards Bukavu or Stanleyville and, two, we must maintain speed. Speed in attack, speed in regrouping and speed in going south to Katanga. Speed, speed, speed.'

Schramme nodded and said he would plan the finer details. We returned to Denard.

'Do you think he will join us?' I asked.

Schramme looked down at his beer.

'Actually Denard has already suggested that we revolt. I met him in Obokote only a few weeks ago and he told me that he had been instructed to disarm my Commando. He suggested then that VI Commando and X Commando revolt. We have already drawn up plans suggested along the lines of M Tshombe as presented by M Quintin. I have not told Denard you or M Tshombe are involved.'

So that was it! Denard had been in the know the whole time. Even if we had wanted to keep him out it was too late. I prayed that for once his natural inclinations would not betray him . . . and us, too.

It was time to broach the burning question of Quintin.

'Colonel, we are concerned about the whereabouts of our courier, Maurice Quintin. We knew that he was coming to see you and that's the last we have heard or seen of him. He has disappeared.'

Schramme shot me a surprised glance.

'Quintin? But he left here three weeks ago. He said he was going back to Rwanda. I haven't seen his since then.'

'I see . . .'

'Perhaps he's found other work or . . .' Schramme tailed off and then quickly changed the topic.

Kalibiona beamed me a significant stare.

Only one thing remained to do; settle the date for the coup.

'When do we go?'

Schramme thought for a moment and then said, 'July.' He held up one finger. 'July 1st.'

We stood up and said our farewells. Monga remained behind with his beloved Katangese troops and Kalibiona and I bounced the Aztec down the runway and into the sky.

Below us a small group of Katangese Gendarmes waved and we saw Schramme's jeep batting along in a cloud of dust.

Kalibiona pointed to the wide jungle surrounding the marching plantation ranks.

'Somewhere in there he killed Quintin. I know for certain.'

36

The Go

The surrounding bush country of Portugalia was softened by the gentle colours of evening when we made our final pass over the tiny airstrip. Again, waiting to greet us, were the PIDE agents. It required no mathematical genius to work out that where there had once been three of us in the aircraft, there were now only two.

'Where's Monga?' demanded one official, moustache bristling with curiosity.

'Dropped him off along the way', I said vaguely and pointed in the direction of the east. With that he had to be content.

Next day was an early hop to Texeira da Sousa and right into the arms of my friend Rochas.

Deftly we parried the agents' questions until the frustrated Rochas instructed us to return to Luanda for interrogation by PIDE HQ. Kalibiona exploded with indignation but I managed to quieten him. I could sense Rochas would not press the issue but thought it best to play along.

'Okay, okay. We'll go', I said with mock resignation.

Kalibiona gave me a dirty look and shrugged his shoulders.

We refueled, climbed aboard the Aztec and took off. I circled the airfield and then set off on a general course west to Luanda, much to the satisfaction of the agents on the ground.

Ten minutes later I banked sharply towards the south east and droned towards Botswana; no time for bloody tomfoolery with the PIDE in Luanda. We landed at Maun in Botswana and then it was a short hop to Jan Smuts.

That evening Kalibiona was on a flight to Madrid and I was back at home with Julia in Springs.

'God, I'm happy to see you', she said with her face still buried in my shoulder.

'What's the excitement?'

'We were pretty worried about the delay. We didn't know what had happened.'

Julia handed me a telegram that had arrived several days earlier. It was from Tshombe in Madrid and dated May 30 1967.

'*Cables urgent si famille se porte bien — Grand-Pere.*'

The Old Man had obviously panicked over our long absence and feared that we had gone the same way as Quintin. I had not thought that our delay with transport and the PIDE in Angola would have been taken so seriously by Tshombe and Julia.

'You had better telephone him and break the news', I said.

Within minutes Julia was on the 'phone to Madrid and in fluent Swahili she told the relieved Tshombe of latest developments.

Two days later on June 2 1967, I was back in Madrid and in constant consultation with Tshombe. Now the tempo was speeding up. Last minute calculations, arrangements and consultations. Tshombe was deeply concerned about Denard's involvement but I explained that it was inevitable.

We altered a few of my original projections and added one or two of his modifications. As more intelligence became available we changed the plan, dropped some operations and included others.

And then it was ready. The plan that would topple Mobutu and return Tshombe.
Phase One:
Schramme's X Commando would seize Stanleyville, Bukavu and Kindu simultaneously.
Phase Two:
Denard's VI Commando, reinforced by elements of X Commando would retire quickly from Stanleyville to Kindu while Noddyn's Commando with elements of X Commando would break out at Bukavu and fall back on Kindu.
Phase Three:
A staging of the combined X and VI Commando and all other Katangese units at Kindu followed by a thrust into Katanga.
Phase Four:
The mercenary and Katangese column would link up with prepared units of former Katangese Gendarmes and a contingent of loyal Bahembi tribesmen near Kongola. The Rhodesian and South African mercenary contingent, airlifted in a few days earlier, would lead the five hundred ex-Gendarmes in an attack from Baudouinville.
Phase Five:
The combined task force would push into Katanga to reinforce the Elisabethville attack group, draw popular support from the Lunda tribesmen and take the whole Katanga Province within a matter of days.
Phase Six:
An ultimatum to Mobutu to abdicate, failing which a thrust towards Leopoldville.

I spent tense hours painstakingly covering every detail of the plan. Whichever way I looked at it we could not fail. Its strength lay in its simplicity and flexibility.

Once Schramme, Denard and Noddyn all managed to stage at Kindu the plan would follow through.

Even if the Kongola force failed to stage or the Elisabethville attack force did not get off, the impetus generated by the mercenary and Katangese column pushing south from the Maniema should be enough to overcome all ANC opposition.

The ANC were no match for us and Mobutu was in no position to rely on popular support.

It must work.

It would have to work.

June 10 and I arrived in Salisbury en route to Jan Smuts. My first stop was at Jack Malloch's office at the airfield.

'We want the Heron and the DC4 for an operation towards the beginning of the month', I stated baldly.

'Problems with the DC4's one engine, but it will be ready for you', Malloch replied.

He knew better than to ask questions.

Then it was on to Jan Smuts airport and to Springs.

In a fever of anxiety I waited for days to drag towards A-day, reappraising the key points, weighing up the personalities in the deadly game on which we were about to embark. Whichever way I looked at it, the success of the plan hinged on two elements; speed and surprise.

I had been in South Africa two days when I hard via *Radio South Africa* of a development that could have jeopardized our whole plot. Tshombe had recruited ten white civilians in the Congo to perform acts of sabotage in southern Katanga in an effort to distract attention from the real theatre of operation.

The target chosen was the rail bridge at Lubudi over which Katanga's vital copper resources flowed to Angola and the world markets. Destruction of the bridges would have had two effects, temporarily sabotage the Congolese economy and fool Mobutu into believing that the main well of opposition would stem initially from Katanga, not the east.

Unfortunately the ten civilians acted precipitiously.

They destroyed the bridge totally, impressively and entirely prematurely.

We learnt later that Mobutu had found out about the plan and, rather than retire without completing their task, the saboteurs had blown the bridge. Also, unfortunately, their escape precautions were not as effective as their sabotage skills. Within a few days four men in the team were rounded up and hideously tortured; fingers and ears cut off.

When I heard the news report in the dry and correct tones of the *Radio South Africa* broadcaster, my mind raced through the possible implications of their capture of our plan. A telephone call to Tshombe reassured me that the team had been completely uninformed about the details of the coup.

Still, Mobutu was now surely on his toes.

There remained one thing to do in South Africa; test the attitude of the South African Government. Through contacts I knew that the South African intelligence and security agencies had found out about my visit to Schramme. Time to put my cards on the table. This time I was determined to see the top dog; General Hendrik van den Bergh, Head of the Bureau for State Security and a close confidant of John Vorster, the Prime Minister.

Van den Bergh was an austere, bespectacled and neat man. He spoke quietly and listened attentively. He was also totally noncommittal.

As soon as I was settled in his office I launched into my spiel.

'General, there are certain forces based in Europe which are working for the overthrow of General Mobutu and the establishment of a Government under Tshombe.'

Van den Bergh inclined his head in acknowledgment. It was obviously no news to him.

'Planning has reached an advanced stage which means a coup is imminent. I would like to ask you your attitude to such a coup?'

'I am in no position to express an attitude one way or the other.'

'Would you be prepared to support such a revolt?'

'I cannot do that, Colonel Puren. My hands are tied.'

'Will the South African Government recognise a government under Tshombe?'

'Again I can express no opinion.'

I realised it was pointless continuing and rose to leave. He held out his hand and we shook.

I walked glumly from his office and through the security checks on the way out. The South African Government had obviously renounced all interest in the central African country. Missing the boat again, I thought bitterly.

On April 15, Julia had delivered one of the finest going away presents imaginable; a bouncing baby daughter. In another time and place my happiness would have known no bounds but as I saw my daughter's tiny face, I could only think of the cruel forces of circumstance that obliged me to leave my wife so soon.

June 19 was my last day in South Africa before leaving for Rhodesia. Julia, the children and I spent a quiet day at home. Soberly my wife and I discussed the prospects of success. We were confident that we would win but beneath it all there was that lingering uncertainty; a fear that perhaps we would never see each other again.

We made last minute arrangements. Julia contacted Tshombe and it was agreed that a telegram signed jointly by Marc Kalibiona and Julia would herald the beginning of the actual coup.

'What are the code words?' I asked.

Julia smiled, *'Commence la Melee.* What else?'

It was agreed.

It was a slow and poignant day, the lull before the storm. Next morning Julia drove me to Jan Smuts airport and we quickly kissed goodbye.

Once in Salisbury I went straight to Jack Malloch. More headaches. The engine was changed but there was no money for fuel. A quick 'phone call to Julia and instructions for her to contact Tshombe. Within a few days money arrived.

Now for my mercenary contingent. I spoke to Malloch and he put out feelers. In six hours I had my Dirty Dozen; tough, adventurous former Congo mercenaries. They were pulled in from all corners of the Rhodesian capital, from bars, dead end jobs, from responsible employment and from doss houses.

They knew absolutely nothing about the coup. All they knew was that they were returning to the Congo, that there would be fighting, and that there were good prospects for money and loot.

It was enough to draw them from their humdrum lives.

We waited in a fever of anticipation. The July 1 deadline was marching on.

As any old soldier knows, its the period of waiting that is the worst. If one does not keep one's mind constantly occupied, the doubts, the queries, the fears, begin to raise their heads. I resolutely fought self doubt.

On the afternoon of June 27 I received a telephone call from Julia in South Africa. She spoke in French.

'Grandfather has just telephoned from Majorca. He says you are to go to Luanda. He will give you further instructions from there. Do you understand?'

'Perfectly.'

I was relieved to hear that Tshombe would be coming with us. It would have had a tremendous impact on the morale of the troops.

There was a pause, then Julia spoke again.

'I love you and take care.'

It was hard to keep my voice calm as I replied, *au revoir*.

37

Loss and a Decision

We assembled near the DC4 a few minutes after midnight; Jack Malloch, myself and my 'Dirty Dozen'. The mercenaries were casually dressed, clutching much travelled kit and duffel bags, vaguely quizzical but otherwise perfectly at ease.

'All set, Jack?'

The Rhodesian gave a thumbs-up sign.

'Right, gentlemen, Luanda here we come.'

The mercenaries filed into the belly of the aircraft and sat on the seats we had bolted into the fuselage. I pushed my way to the cockpit. It was a chilly winter's night and we constantly rubbed our hands to keep the blood circulating. I looked at my watch, 03h00.

The DC4 lumbered to its hold position, the engines turning over as we waited for permission to take off. The radio crackled, Jack pushed the throttle forward and we were climbing steeply into the pitch dark African sky.

After a while I went back to the flight deck and lay down on the bed; enjoying for a while the gentle rocking of the aircraft in the air currents, listening to the muted crackle of the radio.

I sighed deeply. So this was it. We were finally on our way after weeks of tension and uncertainty.

And then I prayed harder than I have ever prayed before. I prayed for success, for Tshombe, for the people who would die, for a coup as bloodless as possible and for a just and lasting peace for the suffering people of the Congo. Minutes later I had drifted into a restless slumber.

Shortly before dawn we put down at Luanda airport and were guided to a deserted part of the airfield. Two men in civilian clothes were waiting for us. I climbed out of the aircraft and one of the men came forward.

'De Silva, PIDE,' he introduced himself in perfect English.

I guessed he was a very senior officer. Christ, surely there were not going to be difficulties over our last visit. My fears were dispelled.

'The arrangements have all been made. We will begin loading the aircraft tomorrow. Your men will be accommodated in The Fort and I am instructed to take you and your pilot to meet M Thoma Tshombe at the Kate Kero Hotel.'

I raised my eyebrows; Moise's brother in Luanda but no mention of the former Prime Minister.

In the hotel we were directed to an executive suite where we found Thoma ensconced. The chubby little man seemed distinctly harassed.

'Where's Moise?' I asked immediately.

'He's still in Madrid. He has some things to sort out and then he'll be arriving.'

'I had been given to understand that he would be here and ready to go into the Congo with us. It's essential for morale that he be with us.'

I was very angry.

Thoma held up a placatory hand.

'He's coming, he's coming. Don't worry. You take arms and ammunition into the Congo as arranged and then come out and pick up my brother.'

I muttered darkly.

'There is one other thing, Jerry.'

'Yes?'

'My brother has decided to scrap the Baudouinville attack group. Everything is to be concentrated on the Kivu operation.'

'That's not part of the plan.'

'I know, but that's what Moise wants.

I was forced to accede and in an angry frame of mind I stomped off for a few hours sleep.

Next day we were back at the airfield. The Portuguese were still loyal protectors of virtually the entire Katangese armoury and as we watched, truck after truck began arriving at the air base with the same material I had helped ship out so precipitiously in those last hasty days before the Katangese secession ended in 1963.

As we watched, a platoon of perspiring Portuguese troops in olive green fatigues obligingly hefted crates into the belly of the aircraft; FN rifles, rocket launchers, machine pistols, 30 cal machineguns and boxes of 7,62 mm ammunition.

At dawn on June 29 we took off from Luanda in the heavily laden DC4. The mercenaries, who kept out of trouble and sober in The Fort and Luanda, were now crammed in with the tons of armaments we were carrying. As we crossed the border my heart took an involuntary leap. It was actually all coming together, the precious plan was unfolding. Malloch kept a wary eye open at the wide blue Congo sky. A chance discovery by one of Mobutu's fighter aircraft would mean an abrupt and bloody end to our involvement in the coup. We were sitting ducks in the lumbering DC4.

Good fortune was with us, however, and we made Punia after an uneventful trip. The strip itself was actually ridiculously small for the gorged bird now hovering above, but Malloch, an exceptionally good pilot, easily brought the aircraft trundling down to a steady landing and a short stop.

Schramme was there to greet us as was Monga and an excited group of Katangese troops. Our mercenaries filed out and stood in a small knot waiting for instructions.

A truck arrived and they were spirited off to be kitted out.

Squads of Katangese soldiers descended on the DC4 and began carting out the crates of weapons and ammunition before Schramme's approving gaze. One of his biggest problems had been how to accumulate sufficient ammunition to initiate a revolt without rousing Mobutu's suspicion. My cargo had solved that particular dilemma.

Malloch paid his respects and, after promising to leave the Heron for us in Punia that afternoon, he turned the DC4, roared down the runway and climbed steeply towards the south and Salisbury.

Schramme and I clambered into a jeep and headed for the settlement camp Schramme had constructed on his rambling estates. The whole of Punia was alive with activity. Rows of jeeps under the trees, a number of them jacked up, mechanics swarming over, under and in them, piles of material standing beside trucks, being loaded into trucks, troops doubling around the base and hanging over the whole camp, that indefinable air of suppressed excitement that portends action.

I was shown to a bungalow and where I laid down for a short rest. Later that evening Schramme and I met on the wide colonial veranda of his bungalow and we discussed the plan.

'We are not going to make our July 1 deadline,' he said, and I agreed. Schramme went on: 'I met Denard on June 22 and he told me that Mobutu's 3rd Parachute Regiment are being sent to disarm X Commando. He said that he himself would not have the strength to take Stanleyville, but together we could do it.'

'Do you have any idea when we can move?'

Schramme shrugged his shoulders. 'I am meeting Denard again on July 2 at Laputu to discuss it. It will have to be soon though.'

I could understand Schramme's haste. With Mobutu's crack parachute regiment on the way the mercenaries would have a real battle on their hands if the coup didn't take off.

Cold beers arrived; Schramme hauled out a large scale map and we began going through the details. The mercenary leader told me that he was assigning one of his trusted officers, Noel, to attack Bukavu to bring out Noddyn and Kaniki. Another senior officer, Michel, had been detailed to command the attack on Kindu. Again I stressed the need for speed and surprise. Our forces were *not* to be dissipated towards Bukavu.

We sat up that night discussing all possible difficulties, testing our weaknesses, making contingency plans if any part of the operation failed. We did not for a moment concede that the entire operation could fail. In the hot and still Congo night, heavily scented with the shrubs that grew attractively and profusely around the base, we casually discussed the destiny of a nation. We were both aware of the immense gains for us and the Congo if we succeeded and of the fatal losses if we failed.

The next day was July 1, day after the anniversary of the independence of the Congo. At breakfast in Schramme's home I paused to remember that I had been involved with the Congo for nearly six years - a lifetime.

Alone at the table, I tuned into radio Brazzaville, a station popularly chosen by the mercenaries as the most reliable in view of the propaganda pumped out by Mobutu's radio news service.

Shortly after 07h00 the news transmission began.

The lead item had me choking on my scrambled egg and clambering to my feet. Tshombe had been kidnapped in midair during a flight from Majorca and was now being held in Algiers.

Events leading to the kidnapping of the former Congolese Prime Minister and aspirant president were confusing and shrouded with imponderables that have not been resolved to this day. All that I do know was that Hamboursin, the sinister wheeler-dealer bitterly opposed by the Katangese in Tshombe's entourage was involved, as was a French gangster called Bodenan.

The entire operation cost a great deal of money and I can only further assume that the CIA bank-rolled and plotted the snatch.

The operation had been accomplished with the minimum of drama high above the Mediterranean when Bodenan had produced a pistol and overpowered the two Spanish security guards protecting Tshombe. The pilot, too, it is understood, was in on the operation. He was a Wigmo old hand.

In retrospect I can only assume that somebody found out about our intended coup and decided to kidnap the popular Tshombe.

Who actually leaked the information I was never to find out.

Kalibiona?

Unlikely.

Certainly not myself.

Perhaps one of the mercenary leaders?

South Africa's Bureau of State Security?

One can only speculate.

More likely the huge financial undertakings involved in the bank-rolling of the coup was what gave him away to the intelligence agencies that relentlessly protected the interests of Mobutu.

In Tshombe's hotel room in Majorca, Spanish police later found nearly two million dollars in cash.

My suspicion of the Central Intelligence Agency was hardly allayed when, years later, Bracco recounted how he and Libert, well known to the CIA as strongly pro-Tshombe men and therefore threats to Mobutu, had been offered an Otter aircraft by a well known CIA operative to carry out a hare-brained rescue attempt on Tshombe, but both pilots were tipped off by a mechanic responsible for servicing the Otter not to ever consider flying the crate — she had been doctored.

On the eve of the coup we were thus deprived of a figure head, a rallying force in the revolt. The Congo had lost its finest statesman and I had lost a friend. I had still not absorbed the shock waves as I sat slumped in my chair staring at Schramme's ceiling.

Anger, despair, isolation, bewilderment, all battled for a place in the spectrum of emotions coursing through me.

Then the full implications sunk in.

Without Tshombe there could be no coup.

Without the lionized Katangese leader as a focus for revolt we were lost; our revolt would be construed merely as a mercenary power grab. We could not hope to win recognition or legitimation without Tshombe.

It was all over.

Reluctantly I dragged myself from the room and into the blinding morning sun. I found Schramme in a nearby office. He had also heard the news. As I walked in he looked up sharply.

I didn't mince words.

'So far as I am concerned the whole operation is off.'

Schramme shook his head but remained silent.

'We cannot go on without a popular figurehead. Besides, all that support that was promised to Tshombe by certain people will now dry up. We will have lost that financial backing.'

Again Schramme shook his head.

'We have enough material with which to begin the operation. Once we take Stan and Bukavu we will have even more.'

I hovered excitedly before Schramme's desk.

'This is madness. We can't start this operation without Tshombe. We must call it off. I'll take my mercenaries and leave in the Heron. We will go back to where we were.'

The mercenary leader rose suddenly and walked over to the window. Outside a number of Katangese Gendarmes were manhandling drums of petrol on to a truck. Behind that, four jeeps were drawn up in a row and troops were throwing kit aboard.

'I've made my plans. I am committed to go on. There is no chance that I will be able to pull out,' he said slowly. 'Besides, have you thought that when the coup succeeds we can install a caretaker Government that can demand Tshombe's release as nominated head of a sovereign country.'

It was a good point. If a *de facto* Congolese Government demanded the release of Tshombe there was infinitely more chance it would succeed.

Schramme returned to his desk and reached into a drawer. He pulled out a telegram and threw it down on the desk. I picked it up.

'*Commence la melee — Marc and Julia.*'

It had been sent late the previous day.

We looked at each other in complete silence, then I shrugged my shoulders and gave a weak smile.

'If you're going on with it then I might as well.'

We both burst out laughing.

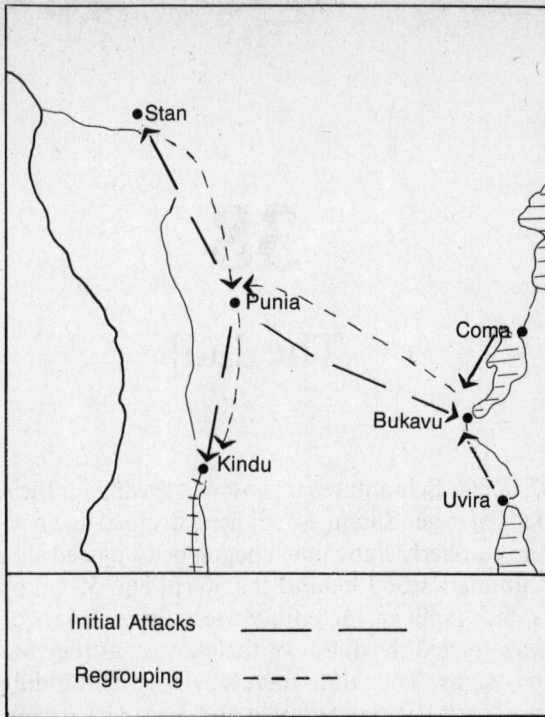

Initial Attacks ▬▬ ▬▬

Regrouping ▬ ▬ ▬

Theory

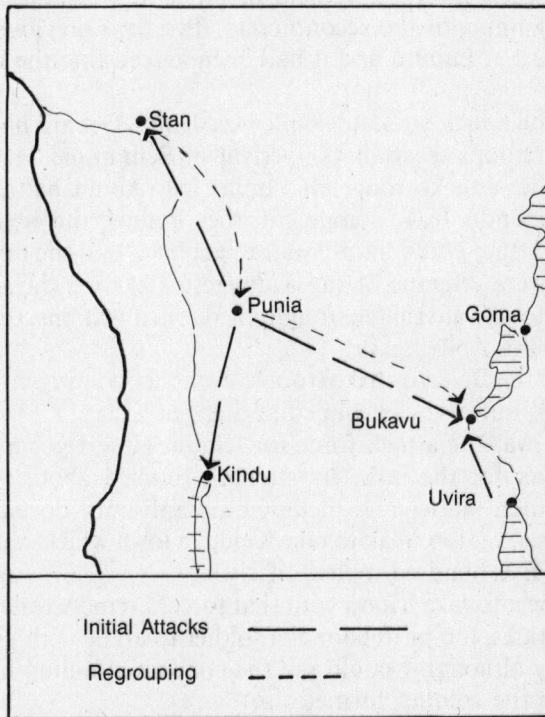

Initial Attacks ▬▬ ▬▬

Regrouping ▬ ▬ ▬

Reality

253

38

The Lull

Punia, July 4 1967, 06h00. Schramme's troops were leaving for their jumping off places. Truck and jeep loads of eager Katangese soldiers, weighed down with webbing, bulging ammo pouches and cavalierly slung machinegun belts, passed along the estates' roads. On the jeeps the gunners stood behind the 30 cal and 50 cal machineguns waving to the bystanders, faces split by incredibly wide smiles. Roars of approval from the knots of bystanders greeted the antics of the gunners as they waved berets and gave exaggerated victory signs. The white mercenaries smiled indulgently.

With common accord the mercenaries and Katangese were moving to liberate the Congo and their father, then held prisoner in a distant country.

It was the beginning of the second coup. Two days previously Schramme had again met Denard at Lubutu and it had been agreed that the revolt would begin on Sunday July 5.

H-Hour for the attack on Stanleyville was 06h00. Denard had promised to pull in his far flung troops to await the arrival of Schramme.

The Stanleyville attack group left Punia first. About battalion strength. The best of X Commando, lean, competent, they gunned the engines of their jeeps out of Punia as if they could hardly wait to get back into the thick of the fighting. Some of them were veterans of the Katangese secession days, professional and loyal soldiers who had alternately fought the United Nations, the ANC, the Simba rebels and now the ANC again.

Next out were the Bukavu strike troops; a smaller contingent under the Belgian mercenary Noel, but also disciplined and eager.

Finally, there was the attack force for Kindu. Here I got a shock. The group was far too weak for the task. Its strength totalled about two hundred men, Katangese and mercenaries and included my Salisbury dozen. At first glance I could see the force was too weak to take Kindu, a town which could only be reached by ferry across five hundred meters of river.

'You can't expect to take Kindu with that force', I remonstrated with Schramme.

Michel Hendricks, too professional a soldier to argue with his superior officer, stood silently by although I could see the concern clouding his face. Nervously he bit his lip as the column formed up.

254

Schramme dismissed my fears.

'It's big enough. No problem. Kindu won't be heavily defended and all we have to do is take the airfield and hold it for a few days until the rest of the column arrives. Of course that doesn't help', the Belgian mercenary said pointing an accusing finger at the form of one of my men collapsed under a tree.

I ambled over. It was Jimmy Mandy, one of the Dirty Dozen, a hardened former mercenary, ex-SAS, a real tough nut. He was paralytically drunk. Angrily I prodded him with the toe of my boot. He had been hired because of his Congo experience, not inconsiderable, but I was quite ignorant of the fact that he was a hopeless alcoholic.

Mandy turned his ruddy, veined face towards me and made a vague attempt at standing. I stared down at him in disgust.

'Can you fight?'

A gurgle for a reply.

'Can you walk?'

Another gurgle.

Several of Mandy's colleagues had come up and we looked down dispiritedly at him. Behind us the Kindu convoy was beginning to move. Several trucks and a jeep rumbled past. A mercenary officer shouted at our group in French.

'Throw the bastard on the truck', I said angrily and marched off.

One by one the vehicles pulled out of Punia and roared off to their target areas; north, south and east. Behind each column came the motley collection of civilian and military trucks carrying the families of the Gendarmes. Like most Third World armies the Congolese troops brought their families right to the front. The last of the vehicles disappeared and I was left with the dust, diesel fumes and the ghost town atmosphere of the now deserted estate.

Minutes later I was in the Heron and climbing quickly above the billowing dust clouds thrown up by the vehicles. I turned the nose of the aircraft north to Lubutu, my forward base situated half way between Punia and Stanleyville.

Once on the dusty little strip I set about preparing for any eventuality. After years of experience in the Congo I had learned that one had constantly to guard one's rear against the improbable or the unfortunate.

I appropriated eight drums of fuel from the dump at Lubutu and set about burying them from prying eyes. Again, from long experience, I knew the mercenary forces were likely to purloin anything they found, including petrol. With the help of a few plantation workers I covered the drums with builders timber and junk not far from the runway. So far, so good.

That evening I was entertained by the Portuguese planter on whose estate the airstrip lay, a grizzled, weathered old man who had spent a lifetime in the Congo. He had seen it all; the *Force Publics* mutiny, the Simba revolt, the ANC backlash. But still he clung on like a wild cactus, entrenched, adapted, roots deep into the economic well spring of the Congo.

His only concession to the fragility of his existence had been to send his family to Portugal to whom he frequently remitted large sums of money. The old planter and I sat on the veranda, drank beer and talked casually about the Congo, past and present.

At one stage he looked squarely at me and rubbed a horny hand across the stubble on his chin. On the night air it sounded like a carpenter's rasp against wood.

'You know, I would never have believed a single country could give so much blood in such a short while. In six years there has been enough blood lost to turn the lakes red. And why?'

I looked resolutely ahead.

'Power politics. International politics . . . international money. Support this side . . . support that side . . . give arms here . . . advice there. Those bastards could keep the Congo fighting itself for years to come.'

The settler drank deeply from his glass.

'You take a hundred different tribes and dialects and put them together; give them a government and a constitution and you expect them to govern themselves better than Belgium. Its foolishness. The real power is in the tribes and Mobutu only remains where he is because of the Americans. Without the Americans Mobutu would be 'phuut — gone.'

Here the colon put fingers to mouth and blew across them in a gesture of dismissal.

'And the Congo will continue fighting while Mobutu is there. It will fight until Mobutu is gone and the power returns to the tribes. I'm so tired of this fighting; not knowing if we'll get the next crop in or whether I will have to flee again. Tired, tired, tired.'

At that moment my host was quite unawares of the forces that were rushing through the same dark night in a thunder of engines and clash of gears, forces that would unleash another round of the fighting the planter despised. I kept my peace but silently prayed that my host would not have to flee again. I prayed harder that we would succeed and that the Congo could become stable and peaceful under an independent man of the people, somebody who understood the diffuse needs of the Congo. Somebody like Tshombe.

Next morning I was at breakfast in the dining room of the planter's house, alone except for an inscrutable manservant. I placed two portable radios on either side of the long dining room table. One I tuned to *Radio Stanleyville* and the other to *Radio Bukavu.*

It was exactly 06h10 on Sunday July 5 when I sat down to breakfast. *Radio Stanleyville* was playing light classical music and *Radio Bukavu* was broadcasting an interview with a visiting American anthropologist. The Portuguese settler joined me at the table.

Somewhere between the porridge and the eggs, *Radio Stanleyville* suddenly went off the air; complete silence in mid note.

The Katangese had seized the station.

'Stan fallen,' I said loudly and snapped my fingers.

The settler glanced at me in astonishment but did not press for an explanation of the cryptic comment.

On the last mouthful of toast, *Radio Bukavu* and the American anthropologist disappeared from the airways.

'Bukavu fallen,' I said and clambered to my feet.

It was time to tell my host of developments.

'Sir, I'm afraid blood is to flow again. This time, pray God, it will be for the last time. Perhaps this time we can create a Congo to which you will be able to bring your family again.'

And as the old man watched open mouthed, I excused myself, thanked him for the hospitality and sprinted for my aircraft.

39

Gains, Treachery

We ran into snags within the first hours of the operation; serious snags. Stanleyville first; Schramme's column had taken up their positions forty kilometers from Stanleyville on the night of the fourth as arranged and had waited for daybreak. Before the eastern sky was properly pink the columns of jeeps and trucks had snaked out from their camouflage positions and were racing against the sun to make Stanleyville by the 06h00 deadline.

The attack went exactly as predicted. Schramme's column crashed through into Stanleyville from the south east, small group deployed at key positions and the main body thrust straight at Camp Kitele where the ANC garrison was.

It was a massacre.

The garrison was to a man still recovering from the traditional Saturday night debauches and in hardly any position to stand . . . let alone fight.

Schramme's jeep raced through the main gates and began raking the barracks in a furious hail of fire.

In one corner of the parade ground a company of ANC troops were drawn up for inspection.

Three jeeps hared across the ground and at virtually point blank range cut down the stupefied ranks of troops.

Many of the remaining ANC troops did not even make it out of the barracks. Those that did were gunned down where they stood. Only a few made it to the safety of the encroaching bush.

Elsewhere in Stanleyville the mobile groups of the column quickly quashed the spontaneous outbursts of opposition.

Confused fighting, a few short fire fights and within fifteen minutes Stanleyville was firmly in our hands.

So far so good.

Schramme's men began casting around for the expected VI Commando.

Nobody!

Desperate searches in the outskirts of the town; no sign of the expected massed troops. All that was visible were several lone French mercenaries dressed casually or in Sunday best watching the fighting with open mouthed amazement.

The full enormity of the situation dawned on Schramme's assault troops. The surprise with which they had been greeted by the ANC was equalled only by the utter amazement of the VI Commando elements in the town.

Denard had not only failed to bring his troops in from the outposts . . . *he hadn't even told them of the coup.*

Absolute chaos!

Astonished French mercenaries watched as Schramme's jeeps wheeled into attack formations and in short vicious jabs, drove the ANC out of Stanleyville with a fearful loss of life to the defenders.

Schramme discovered Denard's duplicity even more dramatically. On the way into the attack that early Sunday morning, Schramme's command jeep came across the French mercenary hastening out of Stanleyville in the opposite direction. The two mercenary leaders pulled their vehicles to the side of the road and stared intently at each other.

'Aren't you in Stanleyville yet?' Denard asked in feigned astonishment.

'I will be at the appointed hour. Where are you going?'

Denard made some excuse but turned his jeep to face the way he had come. Schramme and Denard drove back into Stanleyville. It immediately became apparent that VI Commando had not staged.

'Where's your Commando?' Schramme demanded furiously.

'I don't understand it,' said Denard, disappearing ostensibly to find out what was happening.

The position was in fact worse than was at first imagined. Infinitely worse. Not only were Denard's troops still spread out at points as far north as one hundred kilometers, but the vast amount of transport for the groups was concentrated in Stanleyville.

Schramme's first move was to send an urgent all points radio signal to the outposts to fall back immediately on Stan. A number of groups were without transport and trucks had to be despatched.

It was quite clear that the speedy turn around we had envisaged for the Stan operation was now hopelessly out of gear. Bringing Denard's troops in would take at least three days, then several more days to group at Punia, then still longer to Kindu.

Meanwhile Mobutu's 3rd Parachute Battalion, already embarked to disarm Schramme, was hastening towards Stanleyville by way of the Congo River.

The element of surprise had gone and now it was only speed and boldness that could save the operation.

Denard's motives in not telling his troops to prepare for the coup are difficult to establish. One theory has it that Denard was hedging his bets. Had the paras arrived first Denard would have thrown his weight behind them. As it was, Schramme beat the paras to Stan and the French mercenary was obliged to join him. The concentration of VI Commando's transport at Stan strongly suggests that Denard was assembling further transport for the paras so they could attack Schramme at Punia.

Perhaps the paras were delayed and Denard took fright. Who knows? Others believed that Denard was simply too scared to tell his French mercenaries that he had contracted them into a revolt. This is probably more than just a rumour. He could hardly tell them that he had committed them to a coup without even warning them.

The situation highlighted the vulnerability of mercenaries in situations like this.

A decision to revolt against an employer would invariably have to be a consensual one. Denard had committed himself and then, when it had come to the crunch, backed out. It was a cowardly and foolish thing to do.

Still another theory has it that Denard was paid by a source to ensure the coup failed. It was well known that he was an agent of the SDECE, the French Secret Service.

As it was the French mercenaries were presented with a *fait accompli;* join the revolt or face the indiscriminate backlash of the ANC when they returned.

Reluctantly and bitterly the French mercenaries agreed to team up with the Belgians of X Commando.

It was an uneasy alliance of wary rivals thrown together in deadly peril by the actions of their leaders.

Be that as it may, what was intended to be a lightening raid and regrouping had turned into a shambles of failed communications and mutual distrust.

So much for Stanleyville.

At Bukavu, as expected, Noel's group roared into the scenic lake side resort with hardly a shot fired in opposition. On cue Bob Noddyn's group came up from Uvira and they rv'd the same day. Noddyn had at all times been fully informed of the coup and had in fact been personally contacted by Quintin.

Bukavu at least was a success.

And then we come to Kindu; our greatest defeat.

As planned Michel Hendricks had taken his troops to a staging area about twenty kilometers from Kindu on the eve of the attack. Early next morning he flung his advance sections against the jetty and seized the ferry on the north side of the Lualaba. Under light rifle fire the group crossed the river.

Then, as they hit the opposite bank, all hell let lose.

A concentrated fury of machine and rocket fire forced the group into cover in tight and dislocated groups.

The ferry was badly damaged and it was clear that reinforcements could not cross under the fire.

The Kindu strike force had run into a battalion of the ANC. Under the circumstances Michel did the only possible thing and gave the order to fall back to the banks of the Lualaba and try to recross the river.

As the first day of the coup wore on, the tiny group of mercenaries and Katangese held out against vastly superior numbers of ANC.

* * *

The sky was a searing blue with visibility easily one hundred per cent as I circled Stan that same July morning. Below me lay the neat streets and blocks of central Stanleyville spreading out to the maze of jumbled streets and alleyways that constituted the slums. I remembered the last time I had been in Stanleyville in a C-130, November 24 1964. Then the Belgian paras were busy throwing the Simbas out of the centre of the city.

The smudges of smoke now drifting lazily across the city reminded me of that day two years earlier. Stanleyville was again at war and this time the Katangese were fighting, not with the ANC, but against it.

While contemplating the Stan panorama, I happened to look out of the starboard ports and noted a Congolese DC3 in the circuit with me. A whole DC3. I licked my lips; just what we needed. I was still plotting how to get the aircraft on to the deck and into our hands when the radio crackled into life.

The pilot of the DC3 identified himself as from Leopoldville.

'Have you been calling up the control as well?'

'Yes, I have but there's no reply.'

'Why's that?'

'I suppose they have technical problems.'

There was silence again and the pilot of the DC3 called up again.

'What's all that smoke?'

'Oh, they're just burning some old tyres, I expect.'

'Looks like more than a few tyres.'

Again a silence.

'Are you going in?' demanded the DC3 eventually.

'Affirmative, follow me.'

'Roger.'

I smiled in anticipation.

I landed bumpily and taxied to the airport building at break- neck speed. Several Katangese troops were lounging around the machineguns in their jeeps. The Heron had hardly come to a halt before I flung myself out of the hatch and bolted towards the Katangese troops.

'Surround the DC3 and fast.' I shouted above the din of the aircraft's engines.

The troops galvanised. They revved their engines, squealed on to the runway and paced the DC3. I managed to scramble on to the back of one of the jeeps. The DC3 stopped and the main hatch slowly opened.

A cluster of astonished faces in the hatch found themselves confronted with a grim faced Katangese manning a ,50 calibre machinegun.

The passengers were a group of journalists come to cover the independence festivities in the Congo.

Some festivity.

'What the hell is going on here?' demanded one of them.

A hubbub rose and there appeared a danger of a sudden surge forward.

I leapt on to the bonnet of the jeep and authoritatively held up my hand.

'Gentlemen, I am afraid there is no point in getting excited. This airfield is now in the hands of the Katangese. It is the beginning of a coup that will return Tshombe to power.'

We ushered the indignant pilot and his buzzing passengers off the DC3 and into waiting transport where they were taken to see Schramme.

Later the party was confined to the Palace Hotel where they were eventually released by the ANC when we left. Those journalists got more of a story than they had bargained for when setting off from Leopoldville that morning.

Time to take stock of what we had at the airfield.

Three DC3s, three T26s and two Aztec Pipers.

A very nice haul.

It was while I was clambering in and out of our newly acquired air strength that I met an old French mercenary acquaintance.

His lugubrious face told me the story of exactly how the French mercenaries felt about the turn of events.

Early on a Sunday morning, on his way to church, he was confronted with jeep loads of Belgian mercenaries and Katangese riding around shooting up the ANC garrison. Worst still, he was then summarily ordered to join the coup . . . and there wasn't much choice in the matter anyway.

'Where is Denard?' I asked after listening to his catalogue of woe.

The mercenary shrugged, pointed an index finger at his own head and jerked the thumb in imitation of the actions of a pistol hammer. He clicked loudly.

'Shot himself?' I asked in amazement.

'No, somebody shot him. But not dead unfortunately,' and the mercenary spat on the ground.

One more complication. In trying to rally his men Denard had obviously encountered a bit of outraged opposition.

The next person I met at the airport was Monga. The young captain embraced me warmly and excitedly predicted that, despite the setbacks, we were going to win.

I hastily commandeered a jeep and drove to Stanleyville.

My first step was at the General Hospital where a quite unrepentant Denard was lying in bed in a private ward. His head was swathed in bandages covering the bullet wound that had scored a deep furrow across the back of his skull and missed killing him by literally millimeters. Only at this point did he discover my involvement in the coup.

At that stage I was still unaware of the depths of duplicity to which Denard had sunk and our conversation was reasonably relaxed. I promised him we would air lift him to Luanda and proper medical attention.

It was only when I met Schramme later that day that I heard the full story of Denard's despicable actions.

Schramme himself was convinced that Denard was playing a double game and was interested only on getting him out of the way.

All Denard's troops had been ordered back to Stanleyville from their outposts and now it was only a question of waiting.

Schramme was meanwhile pacing his command post like a caged bear, still smarting from Denard's betrayal.

Intelligence showed that Mobutu's Third Parachute regiment were almost on Stanleyville, ploughing up the Congo River by boat and barge, and we had not even grouped our element. I told Schramme of our haul at the airport and he eagerly agreed that I should return to Luanda for more *matériel*. That afternoon I was given a long list of essentials for the Commando.

Sunday night I spent in uneasy sleep at The Palace Hotel. In my mind I kept constantly flicking through the reports from the other fronts that had come flooding through that day.

Bukavu had fallen but Kindu was fiercely contested . . . VI Commando assembling . . . Mobutu's paras advancing . . . Denard wounded . . . Schramme furious . . . Tshombe kidnapped . . .

I fell into a restless slumber.

40

Losses

Schramme's radio officer, Captain Victor von Bucholz, had a face of thunder as I walked into the command centre next morning. He was angrily pacing up and down.

'*Merde, merde, merde,*' he muttered to himself.

'What's up?' I enquired.

'Disaster, that's all.'

'How so?'

Von Bucholz walked to a wall map and pointed at Bukavu, the town Noel had taken the previous day in order to bring Noddyn and Kaniki out from north and south.

'Point one,' said von Bucholz, 'Kaniki has refused to join us. He is staying where he is with his Katangese Commando. He is staying loyal to Mobutu, damn him!'

I swallowed hard. Kaniki's refusal to join us was not disastrous but it certainly cast a bit of a damper.

'Point Two. Noel and Noddyn have pulled out of Bukavu and are falling back on Punia. There was apparently some mix up with signals and, because of the delay here in Stan, they are returning to Punia.'

This was bad news. It was necessary to hold Bukavu until the Stanleyville group had a chance to form and retire on Punia. With Noel and Noddyn prematurely out of Bukavu, our eastern flank now became exposed.

'And Kindu?' I asked dispiritedly. Von Bucholz became even more serious.

'We have had no radio contact at all. The last we heard was that they were under heavy fire and trying to retreat. I think we must accept the worst. The Kindu force has been eliminated.'

Glumly I walked out of the command centre and drove towards the airfield. What an abortion! Kaniki reneged, Noel needlessly abandoning Bukavu, the Kindu force decimated and Schramme still trying to stage in Stanleyville with the paras breathing down our neck.

Truly, it was only speed and boldness that could save us now.

Schramme would have to reform quickly and strike determinedly for Katanga. Otherwise it was curtains.

I thought of Bukavu and imagined the column of olive green vehicles and crestfallen troops pulling out along the winding boulevards leaving a confused and frightened population behind.

And then Kindu; the reality worse than I even imagined.

As the first day of the attack had dragged on, the pressure against the attacking Katangese and mercenaries had increased. A second ANC battalion arrived later that day and then a third. By days end the original strike force of two hundred men was faced by a well equipped twelve hundred ANC troops.

The result of the engagement was predictable and tragic.

Under the relentless pressure of the ANC, the Katangese Gendarmes had cracked and a number of them, together with a few mercenaries, had been captured.

What followed had been Congo barbarity at its worst.

Legs and arms had been hacked off living prisoners, people forced to eat each other's flesh; the true horror of the ANC's unbridled savagery.

Michel had been killed as the handful of troops defended the airport against the overwhelming forces.

During the battle the Rhodesian and South African contingent had bunkered down in the shattered remnants of a building on the airfield and had kept up a withering fire in the direction of the ANC attackers.

As the day lengthened into night and the attacks had increased in ferocity, the isolated little band had sunk deeper and deeper into that terrible malaise caused by battle fatigue and depression.

The ANC were advancing, the attack force was melting on their flanks, and still the South African and Rhodesian mercenaries sat in the shelter of their houses, refusing to move.

Then came the hero of the hour, none other than Jimmy Mandy, the alcoholic adventurer I had ordered thrown on to the truck at Punia.

Completely sober now, calm and authoritative, he cajoled, bullied and ordered his colleagues into action.

Fighting a bitter rear-guard action under the determined command of Jimmy Mandy, the tiny group of mercenaries and several Katangese made it back to the banks of the Lualaba, located a barge and managed to push off into the river.

Elsewhere the demoralised mercenaries and Katangese were surrendering to the awful fate that awaited them at the hands of the ANC troops. The shattered hulk of the barge had drifted out into the middle of the stream, had withstood heavy doses of smallarms and rocket fire from the shore, the carnage watched by the baleful glare of mortar flares. Miraculously the barge had drifted against the northern bank of the river some three kilometers downstream.

The mercenary and Katangese group had leapt out and plunged into the jungle.

For the next four days the little band, dominated by the leadership of Jimmy Mandy, pushed their way two hundred kilometers north through hostile territory to RV back at Punia.

Behind them in shattered Kindu they left three of their company, Allan Gibson, his brother Dennis and another Rhodesian, John Kingston.

The next setback that bleak Monday July 6 wasn't long in coming.

Mobutu's paras arrived in Stanleyville. After leaving von Bucholz I had reported to Schramme and then, with a list of requirements, motored towards the airfield where ground crews were already refueling a Piper Aztec for me.

It was while we were thus engaged that the paras attacked suddenly and unexpectedly from the north west, just as the sun was beginning to send flaming tentacles through the trees.

Two Katangese and I were manhandling a forty-four gallon drum of fuel towards the Aztec when the first loud bangs distracted us. There was an instant returning clash of smallarms fire. Seconds later we picked out the swish of falling mortar bombs.

We all three buried noses in the dew soaked grass.

Involuntarily every muscle in my body cringed.

A palisade of dust plumes erupted in a line across the airfield, fortunately well away from the aircraft and us. Farther down the runway the individual raps of the automatic weapons had become blurred into a continuous chatter. We sprinted for cover behind a pile of rubble. To my disgust I found I had left my rifle in the Aztec but I at least had my pistol with me.

The sounds of battle reached head-thumping proportions.

I strained to see through the morning mist and into the haze of long grass, scrub and outright jungle fronting the end of the runway nearly a kilometer away.

The clatter of the rifles was overlaid by the harsher bark of the LMGs and the Brownings. Occasionally the crump of mortar bombs. I saw a bomb land roughly in line with us but far to the right and explode in a huge plume of smoke and gravel. Four trucks raced up to the building and disgorged two platoons of Gendarmes.

Monga led them.

Expertly he split the Gendarmes into two sections and they began leap frogging their way up the side of the runway, one section racing ahead thirty paces and then dropping into fire positions while the other section kept them covered.

My two Katangese and I tagged along and, step-by-step, ploughed our way from grassy patch to depression, to pile of rubbish towards the western end of the airfield, the jungle fringe and the fighting.

Once we passed an 81mm mortar section entrenched in a sandbagged emplacement. Unhurriedly and expertly the mortar men, one mercenary and two Katangese, were lobbing bombs into the jungle ahead according to the instructions crackling from their radios.

The same stylised routine of the section; number one hand over muzzle . . . number two bomb ready . . . number one hand away . . . number two bomb away . . . number two and three crouch on base plate.

Bang,

Number 3 hand . . . number two a bomb . . . number one hand over muzzle . . . and off again in a perfectly choreographed example of team work.

The air above our head had meanwhile become furious with the whistle and crack of stray bullets but we ploughed on.

Past another mortar section and then in front we could dimly discern the assault trenches dug by the Gendarmes and now packed with the furiously firing men.

Beyond them, we assumed, were Mobutu's paras.

And then suddenly the attack faded away.

The incessant chatter died like hail on a tin roof, drifted away into a few isolated bangs and then silence.

Somewhere to the left of me I heard a man groaning.

The smell of cordite and perspiration.

The paras had pulled back. The first of a series of such encounters with the probing paras; a grim little excuse-me-dance where the deadly suitor advanced and retreated in dainty steps.

The whole attack had lasted less then an hour.

We returned to the main hangar and began fueling the aircraft. Except for the few holes in a DC3 fuselage we had been untouched.

The drum of petrol we had been rolling had been hit by a tracer bullet and burned itself to a black heap. Plenty more where that came from.

The Aztec was refueled when the first casualty was brought in on a stretcher, a young Portuguese boy with shrapnel in his thigh and buttocks. A shard had neatly nicked a chunk off his left ear and this was constantly alluded to by the smiling casualty as a sign of the Virgin Mary's protection. He was heavily drugged with morphine and seemed quite at ease. The second casualty was also a Portuguese man, but this time far more seriously wounded. His torso was swathed in field dressings, a bandage already flowered crimson was around his head and on a hook by the side of the stretcher hung a plasma drip. He was unconscious but still breathing. Gently they were loaded on to the Aztec and I started the engines.

Before 07h30 the aircraft was climbing steeply away from the pitted airfield and the lazy puffs of ANC ground fire; myself, the wounded mercenaries and the wide blue Congo sky.

41

Wrong Turning

First stop was at Henrique de Carvalho. Portuguese army medics hoisted out my
casualties and spirited them away. The youngster was still fingering his ear and
babbling away about the Virgin Mary's mercy, but now he had a deadly pallor.
As for his companion, the medics took one look at him and pulled the blanket
gently over his face.

Rochas came bustling up to the aircraft with a message pad.

'Luanda wants to see you and this time no bloody nonsense.'

I nodded, took off and set course for the capital. Once there an official car
whisked me to PIDE HQ and Silva Pius, PIDE director general, but no relation
to Sapwe Pius of the Congo police.

We went into immediate conference over recent developments north of the border.
The Portuguese, and indeed the world, were completely confused as to what was
actually happening in the eastern Congo.

I had three specific requests for the PIDE officers. The first was Schramme's
list of essentials which I handed over and which was accepted without demur.
Second point was finding a successor and immediate substitute for Tshombe.

'The only person who will do is Godefroid Munongo. He's a Tshombist and
a respected figure with the Katangese.'

'Yes, but Munongo's fallen out of favour with Mobutu. He's under some sort
of arrest on the island of Bulabemba in the Congo River.'

'I know that, but that's where you people come in, get him out.'

'How?'

'A commando raid, whatever you like.'

Pius thought about it.

'I'll see what I can do.'

'Third point; now that the fun's starting in the Congo again all the adventurers
will start drifting into Angola hoping to get back into the action. We must recruit
them for better use. Can you help accommodate them?'

Pius nodded.

'We can put them up in the Castle, I suppose.'

I thanked him and left his office, elated at the cooperation of the Portuguese.

Wandering into the sunny streets of Luanda I had trouble adjusting to the fact that a few hours earlier I had been in the process of trading shots with Mobutu's troops on the overgrown western tip of Stanleyville airport.

I had not gone more than a few steps when I ran into Tshombe's old and trusted aide, Naweji. Bear hugs and big smiles as he told me that two other old Katanga hands, Bracco and Libert, were also in Luanda in the sure knowledge that they would be needed by me at some time. I grinned delightedly and we retired to the hotel accommodating my irrepressible comrades-in-arms.

'What brings you back?'I demanded facetiously of Bracco.

'The beer.'

It was a warm and friendly reunion with much serious discussion over the future of the revolt, its failures so far and our best course of action.

For some days at least the decision as what next to do was taken out of my hands as the Aztec I had arrived in proved to be quite unserviceable and badly in need of repairs. To my bitter frustration it turned out that there were no spare parts available and I would have to wait at least several days. Those days were spent hovering anxiously about the radio, PIDE HQ, the airfield and occasionally joining Bracco and Libert in a beer and prawn peri-peri feast. I believe those two would have been merry in the face of the Final Judgement.

It was July 8, soon after my arrival, that we heard the news via *Radio Luanda* and PIDE HQ that the thirty mercenaries doing administration work and some on leave in Leopoldville had been arrested by Mobutu's men, hideously tortured and eventually killed.

Only one man, an Algerian bodyguard to Mobutu, escaped the attention of Mobutu.

The fault for this fearful massacre had to be laid squarely at Denard's door.

The men were directly under his command and should by rights have been warned of the pending revolt. As it was the thirty hapless men were left high and dry by the actions of their colleagues hundreds of miles to the east. The ANC, unable to wreak vengeance in the field, found it easier to take it out on the clerks.

The massacres had several positive features though. It revolted international feeling and persuaded the mercenaries in the east that there was no possible alternative to victory or death in battle.

On July 10 the DC3, which I had captured at Stan, put down at Kariba airport in Rhodesia with Denard and several other wounded mercenaries on board. The aircraft was actually supposed to come to Luanda for us to use but Denard, from his stretcher, had forced the pilot to fly to Rhodesia.

As the wounded were being spirited off to hospital, rumours abounded that the whole operation had collapsed. Mobutu's clamp on news and Schramme's silence fueled speculation that the entire revolt had met a gruesome end at the hands of Mobutu's paras in some isolated part of the Congo wilderness.

Then on July 11 another DC3, one of the captured Stan ones, put down at Henrique de Carvalho with several grim faced mercenary officers on board.

Their mission was to convince the Portuguese of the dire need for assistance to Schramme who was still holding the paras off at Stan.

On July 12 we heard that Schramme had finally grouped his forces, swept the ANC aside and hit the road. For two weeks nothing was heard from him and I was praying that he was at Punia and preparing to strike south to Katanga. With the rest of the plan now in shambles there was still hope of success if Schramme could move into Katanga quickly and start a general uprising. In a fever of impatience I tried to arrange transport for us back to the Congo.

Then quite suddenly Jack Malloch returned to the scene. I was standing on the balcony of the Luanda airport building when I saw the Heron taxiing to a halt. At the controls was Jack.

'Where are you off to?' I asked him once he had disembarked.

He pointed north: 'Biafra.'

The civil war had just erupted and there were opportunities for relatively safe but well paid transport work to the secessionist state of Biafra. As usual the word was out and mercenaries from all points of the globe were converging.

'Look, you can't go back there now, Jack. Things are just warming up in the Congo.'

'They're warming up in Biafra as well.'

We argued for a little longer with Malloch saying he had no money for fuel to take me to the Congo.

'Don't worry about that,' I said expansively. 'The Portuguese will pay.'

Eventually after much arm twisting Malloch agreed to fly Naweji, Libert, Bracco and myself back to the Congo in search of the elusive Schramme column.

Next morning Malloch and his four passengers took off in the Heron, touched down at Henrique de Carvalho for refueling and then, in the best of spirits, we arrowed our way across the Congo wilderness for Punia and, we hoped, Schramme.

That was our first surprise. Schramme's rolling estates were deserted; empty of people, vehicles and certainly soldiers. But then the Maniema was like that. Through centuries of wars the local black civilians had learnt to quietly fade into the jungle at the first sign of trouble.

'Well, where's all this action you were talking about?' demanded Malloch.

I peered down anxiously.

'I can't understand it. Schramme should have been staging here now with the Stan and Bukavu forces.'

We flew over the airfield at Punia and saw the burnt out hulks of the two T28s astride the runway. I felt sick with despair. The two fighters could easily have been flown to safety in Angola but through ignorance or negligence they had been burnt to ashes on the ground by Schramme's forces.

There was obviously no point in wasting time flying over Punia.

'Better head south, Jack. There's only one possibility, he's already striking south for Kindu on his way to Katanga. If he moves his arse we might still salvage the situation.'

Dutifully Malloch turned the nose of the Heron and we scudded at treetop level south along the sand road leading to Kindu. Thirty kilometers later we noticed a billow of dust rising on the skyline.

'Bet my bottom dollar that's the Schramme column,' I shouted.

As we flew closer, the cloud of dust showed the column to be of considerable strength. My spirits soared. The Katangese were going home and God help Mobutu.

We swept closer and closer.

The sharp eyed Bracco was the first to voice his concern.

'That column is coming towards us. They're coming up from the south, not heading south.'

He was right. Seconds later we were overhead. Instantly we recognised them as an ANC strike force; jeeps, trucks and even a squadron of armoured cars. There was a sudden burst of fire below us and Jack banked sharply to starboard and away from the column. I tried to estimate the strength of the group; upwards of three battalions, around one thousand troops and a dozen Panhard armoured cars.

The implications struck home immediately. If the ANC column was coming up from Kindu it was clear that Schramme couldn't have gone down that road. If Schramme was not at Punia and not on the road to Kindu he could only have gone in one direction, east to Bukavu. I shook with rage. The whole column to Bukavu, dissipating our strength east, cardinal rule 1 broken, losing speed for the assault on Katanga, cardinal rule 2 broken, losing the advantage of surprise, cardinal rule 3 broken.

Christ, what was going on? The whole revolt was in jeopardy.

But in the aircraft we had even more pressing problems. Our fuel supply was critically low and it was apparent that we had a maximum flying time of thirty minutes.

No Schramme, no fuel, and the ground below crawling with ANC.

Charming!

'What now?' demanded Malloch.

'To Lubutu.'

'What's there?'

'A supply of fuel, hopefully.'

'And if not?'

'Then I doubt we will ever be getting back to prawn peri peri in Luanda . . . and you most certainly won't be going to Biafra.'

On the way to Lubutu I prayed the emergency petrol supply I had hidden was still untouched. With only minutes of flying time left we touched down at the Lubutu homestead and airstrip. It was deserted to the last dog.

Malloch gingerly put the Heron down and we taxied to the end of the runway. He turned the aircraft and left the engines running. With an ANC column in the vicinity, one couldn't be too careful. Everybody looked at me expectantly.

'Okay, okay, okay, I'll go,' I said and made to open the side hatch.

Bracco thrust his pistol into my hand and patted my shoulder.

'If you find a bank, let me know,' he whispered facetiously.

Much comfort.

I leapt on to the good earth of Mother Congo and was running like mad towards the rambling old settlers homestead no more than one hundred meters from the aircraft.

I pounded across the veranda and disappeared into the gloomy interior of the spacious house, pistol at the ready, safety catch off.

It was completely deserted; drawers pulled out, clothes strewn about, overturned furniture and a few broken ornaments; every sign of speedy departure. I allowed myself a pang of sympathy for the old settler. He would not be harvesting his crop this year.

Seconds later I was scrambling down the back steps and leaping over a low wall.

I loped across to the pile of builder's rubble. Frantically I pulled planks away to reveal the eight precious drums of fuel.

Safe!

As soon as my colleagues saw me battling to roll one of the drums towards the aircraft they bailed out and came to my assistance.

Together we manoeuvred the drums on to the aircraft, humped them on to the wing and pumped the life saving liquid into the thirst tanks. At any moment we expected to hear the roar of approaching vehicles, ANC vehicles.

We were possessed of super human strength that day as we levered the drums on to the wings. Within an hour we were finished.

The light was fading as we taxied across the runway and took off back towards Angola.

It was past 22h00 when our Heron finally put down at Henrique de Carvalho.

We had discovered nothing, achieved nothing. All we had to show for our troubles was a handful of Citronella grass I had plucked at Lubutu.

As we straggled exhausted from the Heron, the Officer Commanding Henrique de Carvalho, an aristocratic looking type, came out to meet me.

He looked sympathetically at our faces.

I said nothing; just handed him the handful of Citronella grass and walked away.

My carefully conceived plans for the overthrow of Mobutu were disintegrating about my ears.

42

Back in the Fray

The mercenary and Katangese revolt of 1967 wound a tortuous path towards annihilation; bogged down by personal animosities, indecisive leadership and rank treachery. It was to have its successes yet, even a few comic interludes, one or two masterful displays of initiative, but largely it became a saga of lost opportunities as the vision of a free Congo became more and more distant.

For the architect of the plan it was a galling experience, a disillusioning process. But back to Schramme.

By late July Schramme's two hundred mercenaries and one thousand Katangese were on the move and approaching the town of Bukavu accompanied by a convoy of civilian cars stretching for kilometers.

The civilian refugees, members of the Punia mining families, had requested protection from Schramme against what they believed would be a vicious ANC backlash once the mercenaries had left.

And it was in these ungrounded fears that Schramme found his excuse for not following up the plan and descending immediately on Katanga.

According to Schramme's later statements he felt morally obliged to escort the civilians to Bukavu where they could cross into neutral Rwanda.

A humanitarian gesture, he would have us believe — but I don't believe it.

When Schramme pulled out of Stan he left behind scores of white civilians who remained untouched by the ANC when they took the city. At that delicate stage Mobutu could not have risked another international outcry over treatment of prisoners, and certainly not white civilians. Also, Schramme could have ensured that some arrangements were made with the central Government to escort the refugees to safety away from the firing line.

A whole battle group redeployed, a revolution delayed because of two hundred white civilian refugees.

It is hardly creditable.

And even if concern for the civilians did initially take Schramme to Bukavu there was no excuse for his subsequent long stay.

I believe that Schramme's disregard of the plan was for an infinitely more sinister motive.

Be that as it may, Schramme's column was fast approaching Bukavu, recce jeeps out front, followed by trucks with troops and then the forlorn trail of dusty civilian cars packed with anxious families.

The whole world knew by this time that Schramme was heading for the sleepy little resort town . . . and so did Mobutu.

The General's position during this tense and confusing period was certainly unenviable. Despite inflated claims over his radio services of tremendous victories against the rebels he and his vast army were still unable to produce the body of a single 'ignoble' mercenary . . . except those massacred in cold blood in Leopoldville.

Mobutu knew the mercenaries were alive, that they were well and that they posed the gravest threat ever to his regime.

His humiliating inability to curb them was infinitely compounded by the fact that he had offered Leopoldville as the centre for the 1967 Organisation of African Unity conference. Opening date was scheduled for September 11 and Mobutu was determined by hook or by crook to quell the one thousand disenchanted troops among his fifty thousand man army.

The ever obliging Americans sent three C-130 transports to their protege to help air-lift the ANC troops from Leopoldville to Stanleyville and the battle areas.

And so, when it was reliably established that Schramme was actually on his way to Bukavu, Mobutu decided that they must be stopped and annihilated on the banks of the Ruzizi River as a signal warning of sovereign Zaire's ability to maintain its integrity.

Accordingly, his elite para battalions were dropped into positions in the rolling topography around the town, other troops and armour were rushed up from the south by road.

A solid cordon was thrown around Bukavu to block the rebels.

Mobutu's intention was finally, irrevocably to eliminate the troublesome mercenaries and Katangese to the last man. The mercenaries knew this. They realised there was no alternative to fighting their way out.

In those early August days then Bukavu had all the settings for a dramatic and bloody clash of two opposing armies, a spectacular show down at the OK corral, a final reckoning.

That, at least, was the way the international media saw it.

Press and TV crews flocked to somnambulist Rwanda and from the borders they watched and waited for the cataclysmic clash only a few hundred meters across the river.

Put bluntly, the world's eyes had come expecting to see the mercenaries get theirs; finally and bloodily.

By August 8 the clash was imminent.

In set book fashion the ANC had deployed along the escarpment fronting the main approach to Bukavu; redoubts built, assault trenches dug, armour positioned, mortar sections sited, observation posts erected and road distances marked for mortar bearings.

Quite obviously they expected the Katangese column to come thundering along the road fronting the brewery, home of the famous Primus beer, and dash themselves to pieces against the defences.

272

Equally obviously, the mercenaries were not going to do any such thing.

Schramme wheeled his column south just before the entrance to the town, split up into three groups and then drove in separate moving balls of fire and fury into the centre of the town.

By any standards it was a spectacular success and for the ANC an acute embarrassment.

Eye witnesses reported that the Gendarme machinegunners did not even bend down as they rode into the town by the three minor routes, one past the prison, another towards the centre of the town and a third in the direction of camp Saio.

These entrances were guarded by elements of the ANC. But they were no match for the mercenaries who were literally fighting with their backs to the wall. Using the tremendously accurate and concentrated fireforce so traditional to Congo engagements the ragged, bearded troops roared past the ANC positions, enfiladed them with murderous fire and then pushed straight into the deserted town.

Outflanked by the attackers, the carefully prepared defences of the ANC crumbled along the escarpment and within minutes the world through the TV cameras on the Rwanda side of the border were treated to the astonishing spectacle of Mobutu's elite red beret paras scrambling and jostling to make it across the bridge at Cyangugu and into neutral Rwanda.

Open mouthed journalists watched as the ANC fled into the town, handed over their weapons to the Rwandese and stood around in large demoralised groups.

In Bukavu itself Schramme's troops began rooting out the isolated pockets of resistance and setting up their own defences. Apart from the prestige, the mercenaries and Katangese achieved from their overwhelming victory, they also captured a mountain of equipment, ammunition, food and vehicles; easily enough for three months. It was like Christmas again.

As soon as the town had been secured the civilians began pouring across the bridge into Rwanda and so, unfortunately, did a number of the French mercenaries. Over the next few days more than eighty of them, among the finest and most experienced in the column, quietly slipped over the bridge, were interned at Cyangugu and then shipped home.

Their departure was understandable. They were from VI Commando and had been in the unfortunate position of having a revolt thrust upon them without warning.

Once it had begun they had been forced to join in to save their own lives, but now, only several hundred meters from neutrality, they saw no reason to stay.

A lot of their opposition sprang from the natural hostility that had existed from time immemorial between the French and Belgian mercenaries in the Congo.

With Denard invalided out the men had naturally fallen under the command of Schramme and his predominantly Belgian staff.

In the face of a common enemy they had co-operated and fought effectively and valiantly as ever.

Indeed, part of the Bukavu success can perhaps be attributed to the fact that the French simply wanted to shoot their way to safety. But now the party was over. Having reached sanctuary the mercenaries had deserted and in the way of all mercenary armies, there was nothing anyone could do to stop them.

That was one more cogent reason for Schramme to have struck to the original plan and taken the column straight to Katanga. The French would have stayed, they would have had no option, and would have fought desperately well.

Anyhow, by August 10 the shady boulevards of Bukavu and forested hills around it were firmly in Schramme's hands. The tables had been completely reversed.

Instead of Schramme being the hunted he was now quite clearly capable of becoming the hunter.

In keeping with his new status he invited the journalists from Rwanda to Bukavu and held a press conference.

To the astonishment of the world, the leader of the rag-tag one thousand man army, gave Mobutu ten days to resign or he would descend on Katanga or Leopoldville. And Mobutu knew he could do it.

To back his demands Colonel Monga, aide to Tshombe, announced in the same interview the formation of a provisional Government of Public Safety for the Congo until Mobutu stepped down.

Dressed neatly in camouflage uniform, a soldier President, Monga, read the declaration of a new Government over Radio Bukavu in slow measured tones.

'I address myself solemnly to all the Congolese people, to all the men, women and children of our stricken land; Congo. I address myself also to all the nations of the civilised world. I speak in the name of my ravaged country, in the name of the people, in the name of morality and justice. On this day August 10 1967 we proclaim the creation of a Government of Public safety temporarily based at Bukavu. The aim of the Government is to put an end to the civil war which has ravaged the Congo since the proclamation of independence on June 30 1960. Seven years of anarchy, seven years of civil war, seven years of trouble for the unhappy people of this country, has brought the Congo on its knees.

'A tyrant is trying to govern the Congo, the former sergeant major Mobutu. From today this man is branded a traitor to his country. He has truly betrayed the country, he has violated the Congolese constitution by becoming a traitor. The hands of the traitor Mobutu are red with the blood of the sons and daughters of the Congo. The members of the Bukavu Government insists that Mobutu should resign. He will later be judged by a popular tribunal. The Congolese people claim the right to judge the tyrant who has made the Congo, one of the richest countries in Africa, the most unhappiest. Just as a tree is judged by the fruit it bears, so will Mobutu be judged by the consequences of his rule. These consequences the Congolese people know all too well; famine, confusion, sickness, insecurity, war and so on. Mobutu has forgotten, because the sergeant major never realised, that a chief of state is a servant of his country. Mobutu has on the contrary exploited the trouble of the men, women and children of the Congo. Mobutu has ten cars, he has four houses, he has many mistresses who cost the Congo a great deal of money. He has robbed the treasury of our land of millions of Belgian francs which he deposited in Swiss banks. We have proof of this. But the traitor is not only a thief, he is also an assassin. He betrayed his brother in law, Lumumba. It was our Prime Minister who made Mobutu a colonel, yet Mobutu later had him arrested in Leopoldville and flown to Elisabethville after being tortured . . .'

And on it went, indicting Mobutu for corruption, bad Government and brutality; trenchant arguments as to why he should go.

274

The choice of a credible black leader for the group had not been an easy one. I had tried my best in Luanda to get Thomas Tshombe, Moise's brother, to return with me to the Congo but the man was adamant that he could not come. Attempts to rescue Munongo from Bulabemba island were a farcial failure. Monga, an educated graduate of the Belgian military academy, a loyal Tshombist and a true Congolese, was our only alternative.

His bravery at Stanleyville and on the road to Bukavu reinforced his claim to the post.

Back in Angola, meanwhile, I had been watching the coup unfolding in this unexpected direction. Beside myself with frustration I spent the days badgering the maintenance crew to hurry up and get the Aztec's spare parts and listening to every news broadcast about developments in the Congo. Then finally the spare parts arrived. I rushed off to find Bracco ensconced behind the ubiquitous glass of beer at the Kate Kero.

'It's all set. We can go', I told him happily.

'Go where?'

'Bukavu, you fool, where else?'

'Okay, I just thought we might be going to Biafra. But Bukavu sounds fine.'

'There's just one problem; the Aztec doesn't have the range.'

Bracco thought about this.

'I've got an idea', he said. We wandered down to the airfield. The plan was simple enough. We rigged two two hundred litre fuel tanks in the Aztec fuselage, ran a pipe system that would enable us to refuel in the air and then crossed our thumbs. A trial run showed the system was tricky but would work.

I knew that Bukavu had no airfield but I hoped that Schramme would have taken the trouble to immediately begin work on clearing a runway.

By this stage I was determined to return to the ground forces. Having started the whole exercise I could hardly let things drop without being there at the denouement.

Besides, I reasoned, Schramme still had a lot of punch left and a demoralised army opposing him.

There was no reason why he couldn't march on to Katanga as originally envisaged.

Bracco, Naweji and I were off early on August 10, one day after Schramme's steam roller success at Bukavu. Flying at maximum cruising speed we managed to make Bukavu by 11h00. Below us nestled the little colonial town in the enfolding arms of green forestry. The lake glittered in the hot sun. Inevitably there were a few drifting smudges of smoke that told of battle.

Bukavu had a fatal disadvantage and one that Schramme as a tactician should have known about. It was the only town of any size without an airfield. Our original intention had been to parachute Naweji out with the documents, but in our excitement we made a grave mistake. We forgot to take the side hatch off before leaving Luanda. Every time we tried to open the hatch the aircraft went into a banking roll and we had to hastily shut it. It was hopeless. We contented ourselves with crisscrossing Bukavu, lobbing out streamer messages.

Schramme had not taken steps to clear an airfield but as soon as we arrived over Bukavu, several platoons of Gendarmes were set to work furiously chopping down trees along one of Bukavu's boulevards in the faint chance that we could land. It was useless though. The road was too undulating and we would in all probability end up in the houses.

I was puzzling as to our next step when Bracco pointed to Cyangugu on the opposite side of the river. A smaller version of Bukavu, it also lolled alongside the river. More important, it had an airfield.

'We could put down there and try to sneak back into Bukavu,' he said.

I knew that Bracco had lived most of his life in Rwanda and that his father had been associated with aviation in that country for many years. Conceivably it might be possible to wrangle something through Government contacts.

'Do you know anybody at Cyangugu,' I asked.

'Only the Senior Air Controller,' Bracco replied as he guided the Aztec on the umpteenth pass over Bukavu.

'Who's that?'

'My father,' he replied dead-pan.

I could hardly believe our luck. The Aztec peeled off from the futile quartering above the town and we crossed the river into Rwanda air space. Bracco began calling up the Cyangugu control tower. No reply at first, then there came a crackling response. The duty air controller spoke with a pronounced African accent.

Bracco asked for permission to land.

There was a long silence as the controller obviously took instructions then he was back again.

'Negative, you can't land at Cyangugu and you are violating Rwanda air space.'

Bracco tried more forcefully and asked to speak to his father.

Another long pause and the the reply; 'Negative, M Bracco is unavailable to your call. Out.'

We shrugged shoulders and headed back to the Congo.

'Let's think this through,' I said to Bracco and Naweji. 'We want to land Naweji and I want to join the ground forces.'

'Check,' responded Bracco.

'There's not enough fuel to take us back to Angola.'

'Check.'

'There's no airfield at Bukavu so we can't land there.'

'Check.'

'We've been turned away from Rwanda.'

'Check.'

'Therefore there's only one alternative left. We ditch the aircraft in the drink and swim for the shore.'

'Check.'

We stripped to our underpants and I placed the radio codes in a plastic bag. My only regret was that we were losing an aircraft that would have been invaluable for communications with Angola.

Bracco slowly brought the Aztec down about fifty meters from the Congo side of Lake Kivu, cut back the throttle until she was almost stalling, dropped a few meters at a time and then, at snail's pace, belly-landed her on the water's surface. A sudden jar, the hatch was thrown open and Naweji, Bracco and I were swimming through the luke warm water like Olympic finalists. Behind us the Aztec sunk in less than a minute.

43

Bukavu

Bukavu itself was even more pleasant from the ground then from the air. In colonial times it had been a *Cote d'azur* of the Congo, a place of gracious streets, rambling houses and flotillas of small boats. The rolling country around Bukavu gave it a scenic quality. The war in the Eastern Congo had changed its face very little. True, fortifications had gone up along a twenty five kilometer perimeter, trenches, redoubts, sand bag emplacements and barbed wire coils, but still the resort had retained its old world unhurried charm.

All the white civilians had of course fled and the town was then entirely in the hands of the mercenaries and the Gendarmes. The only civilians, in fact were the wives and children of the Gendarmes who would have been expected to follow their men into the halls of hell itself.

And Bukavu had not exactly been destitute when the rebels had entered. The numerous hotels had thoughtfully left well stocked larders and wine cellars, the shops were still full of merchandise, civilian vehicles casually littered the streets and the invaders had the choice of a number of deserted homes from which to choose accommodation.

As soon as I arrived, in underpants and all, I could sense the mercenary's and the Katangese buoyant spirits. They had just decisively thrashed the ANC, had plenty of food, drink, ammunition. Just the time to get them back on the road and to Katanga.

I was taken to see Schramme in his command post and we shared a bottle of the finest champagne yielded by the town's cellars.

Schramme showed me a map of his defence perimeters and pointed out the six strongpoints. He gave details of ammunition reserves and said we could hold out for at least three months. He tapped a spot on the map near the lake side, Strongpoint Four, and said I was to take command of it.

I looked at him quizzically.

'But are we not preparing to move to Katanga?'

'Yes, yes of course, I'm preparing the column now, but we must be ready for a counter attack meanwhile', he hastened to assure me.

'We must move soon', I insisted. 'There is nobody out there to oppose us at the moment. At Punia, perhaps, but we can fight our way through.'

Schramme nodded again enthusiastically.

'Yes, of course.'

He leaned forward confidentially.

'In fact, it has been arranged with Denard before he left Stanleyville to launch a diversionary attack from Angola while we thrust from here.'

I had my own opinions about the likelihood of Denard launching his diversion. It seemed to me incredible that Schramme still placed any trust in Denard, then reposing with his head wound in a Rhodesian hospital.

My first day at Bukavu was spent stripped to my waist organising a squad of Gendarmes into a work party to build an airstrip. After two hand blistering days we had an eight hundred meter runway cleared atop the ridge and adjacent to the radio masts. The end of the runway faced Rwanda across the Ruzizi at cliff top.

About two weeks later the strip was to come in use when Libert arrived in a DC3 from Angola. The entire garrison turned out to welcome him.

To shouted encouragement from the onlookers Libert gingerly circled the makeshift runway, obviously made up his mind and came thundering down on to the landward side of the strip. He made a perfect approach and landing but under shot the runway and hit a large rock which wiped out his undercarriage. The DC3 roared angrily, slithered one hundred and fifty meters across the runway and, almost at a standstill, majestically toppled forward nose first into a gully.

Libert's stay was going to be a little longer than he anticipated.

Furiously we unloaded the DC3. Not a moment too soon. Two Congolese T28s dropped out of the sky and made a token attempt at destroying the already crocked aircraft.

As usual, they missed.

And so things settled into a pattern. I busied myself developing the fortifications at my strongpoint commanding the approaches to Bukavu from Goma in the north and also covering the harbour area.

Under my command I had eight surviving members of the Rhodesian and South African contingent together with a platoon of Gendarmes.

Our armaments consisted of a ,37mm cannon with solid and explosive ammunition, a ,75 recoilless rifle, a ,50 Browning machinegun and an 81mm mortar. This, besides the normal compliment of rifles and light machineguns, gave us a fairly formidable firebase that time and again sharply put the ANC back in its place.

We painstakingly dug assault trenches, a sandbagged redoubt for Sector HQ and communication trenches. Surrounding bush was cut down or burnt to give us a better field of fire and in a few strategic spots barbed wire was laid out. Along the whole perimeter at Bukavu the same preparations were being made for the group as we waited for the inevitable counter attacks.

They started within a few days; exploratory thrusts by the ANC against salients, all in other sectors. The quiet Bukavu hills would echo to the distant fusillade of shots and explosions. For the most part we contented ourselves with firing off our weapons with some of the vast amount of ammunition in stock.

Without boasting, I believe that with accuracy and dexterity and with our support weapons we could have taken on any standing army in the world.

There was an easy going routine in those early days at Bukavu. I was quartered in a splendid hillside residence overlooking the lake, a summer house belonging to some wealthy Congolese government officials which had been left intact since the town's capture; plush carpets, soft lighting and a comfortable bed included.

An average day would start before dawn with an inspection of my sector. Reports from the guard commanders would be taken in and then I would drive to Schramme's command post for the daily situation report and briefing with the other sector commanders.

These were always light hearted affairs with jokes, tomfoolery and plenty of idle chatter.

August 27 was my birthday and to celebrate, the French officers threw a party for me at a villa on the lake side. Champagne, *pate de fois,* white gloved waiters, the whole works. It was a night long affair with Monga and Naweji there as well as Bracco and a number of senior officers.

The rot had not set in then.

We were jovial and the mercenary officers basked in the stunning reversals their forces had inflicted on the ANC earlier that month.

Time for the toast.

The most senior officer present raised his glass and toasted my health.

Thirty glasses with the best French champagne, courtesy of a local hotel, were also raised.

Comrades.

Outside there was a brief mutter of gunfire in the northern sector.

For me that party was the highlight of our stay in Bukavu. Then we were still heady with success and convinced that soon we would be marching on Katanga and sweeping away Mobutu. The vindication of Tshombe.

But it was only time that marched on.

It became clear that no steps were being taken to move out.

Meanwhile, the ANC troops were being reinforced and we were wasting ammunition in inconclusive little encounters.

I brought the subject up at one of our situation reports late in August.

'Colonel, we seem to be easily containing the thrusts here at Bukavu but isn't it time that we began on the operation that we are here for; to attack Katanga and spark the revolt?'

The black officers and several white ones nodded in agreement.

Schramme held up his hand.

'I know how eager you are to move, but it would be unwise at the present. We still need to liaise with Denard in Angola. Also I am preparing for a column to move on Goma.'

There was a nod of agreement from von Bucholz, Schramme's faithful aide de camp.

'We can't just jump into this thing', he said.

'If we wait much longer we won't have a chance to jump anywhere except back across the Ruzizi', I said angrily.

'Have you stopped to think what would happen if we got to Katanga', von Bucholz demanded. 'The mercenaries would desert immediately and cross the border into Angola.'

'If they all deserted then it would make no difference. By that time the revolt would be taking off on its own impetus and we wouldn't need mercenaries. Besides, if they want to desert they can do so here quite easily.'

I knew inwardly that bickering was useless.

In August we lost one of our South African contingent; young Colin Taylor.

Early on a Monday morning I had sent a patrol out to recce ANC positions to the north west. Colin was point man and the rest of the patrol of seven Katangese spread out behind him. Out along the shore road they walked, across a road, through a gully and on to a twisting path running through thickly wooded slopes. Colin was a professional and highly competent soldier, but even the best can fail at that crucial moment to read the signs correctly. As the patrol passed a particularly dense copse of trees, there was a burst of gunfire from the right.

Colin dropped dead with a bullet in the head.

The rest of the section melted into the bush along the path, returned fire and began a step by step disengagement.

Two of the Katangese were wounded but they all made it back.

As soon as I heard the news I called for volunteers to help bring Colin back. Eventually I picked a section with several of the previous ambushed party included and we retraced our steps.

We located Colin's body in a trench alongside the path where he was almost completely covered in foliage.

He had fallen sideways off the path and out of sight when the bullet had struck. Just as well. I shuddered to think what the ANC would have done to the body of a mercenary.

Gently we lifted his body out and carried it back to our sector. Early next day a proper funeral service was held. Dressed in newly starched clothes my platoon stood braced as I read a prayer, a few words from the Bible and a short eulogy. The grave had been dug on the neat lawn in front of the clubhouse, overlooking an impressive sweep of the lake. The platoon came to attention and we lowered the shrouded form into the grave.

A Katangese guard of honour fired a volley into the air.

Afterwards we carefully covered the burial site and allowed the grass to grow over it. No doubt Colin is there to this day.

The death of our comrade was a signal warning to us that revolts are costly.

The first air attack on us had all the elements of high comedy. Shortly after noon on a blindingly hot day we picked up a faint drone from the south of the town. Two specks hovered in the sky high over the wooded hill tops. I stood outside my redoubt and trained my field glasses on the approaching dots, T28 fighters.

Closer and closer they came until they were across the southern end of the lake at one thousand meters and quite plainly heading straight for the most obvious target, the promontory on which stood the clubhouse and our redoubt.

'New developments; take cover,' I ordered and dived for a slit trench.

From the trench overlooking the lake I heard the drone of the fighters engines. But then, instead of dropping into a strafing run at some reasonable height, they carried straight on at that ridiculous altitude.

What were they up to?

Perhaps one kilometer south of our strongpoint, still at one thousand meters, they let rip with their rockets. Open mouthed we watched as the rockets trails whooshed overhead across the promontory at about two hundred meters, continued down the lake and arrowed into a thickly wooded hillside on the opposite side

280

of the lake . . . Rwanda to be exact.

'Christ, have they declared war on Rwanda?' one of my mercenaries shouted and went into paroxysms of mirth.

Second and third strafing runs by the aircraft were no more successful.

In time to come the air attacks were to prove more an amusement than a threat to us, unlike the mortar fire from the ANC ranks which became more accurate and intense as time wore on. By the end of the siege I estimated more than three hundred mortar bombs alone had hit our sector.

The rumour, probably quite correct, quickly spread through our ranks that Israeli instructors were assisting the mortar men.

From the middle of September it became quite clear that Schramme had no intention of moving and that it was in fact too late to move.

By then an estimated fifteen thousand troops were ringing us and break-out would be too costly in terms of lives and ammunition. My frustrations turned to resignation and I realised the only thing left to do was concentrate on staying alive.

Unhappily I had come to concede that our forces had failed Tshombe, had become static and impotent. Everywhere the momentum for revolt was running out.

Also from the end of August the ANC pressure began increasing day after day. The original skirmish at platoon level had escalated to company and battalion attacks. For several hours at a time fierce firefights would rage at some point or the other along the perimeter before slowly fading away. Because we were facing the lake and not outwards, we did not come in for ground attacks at all, our left flank being protected by another sector. But often enough on tours with Schramme I saw the advancing lines of ANC broken up by the mercilessly accurate mortar fire of the mercenaries.

The attacks would inevitably start in the same way.

A furious rocket and mortar bombardment from the ANC that would have little effect on the heavily entrenched defenders but would serve to give ample warning of an attack.

More Gendarmes would be drafted into the threatened area.

The barrage would lift and then the deathly silence.

In the distance blurry and almost indistinguishable from the surrounding bush would come a line of ANC troops. Then it would be a series of small firefights with a largely invisible enemy. Invariably it would fade after a few hours and the ANC would drift away, crawling backwards, dragging their wounded and dead.

Once or twice an armoured car would trundle into the attack with a bevy of troops bunched close behind for cover.

It would be promptly despatched by a well aimed anti-tank rocket, the accompanying troops would split for cover and a number would be mown down.

Then suddenly another piece was added to the Quintin puzzle.

One morning, with time on my hands, I wandered down to the Camp Saio, former ANC base at Bukavu, and started nosing around through old files and records. It was an excursion prompted by idle curiosity.

I ploughed through the dusty diaries and files littering the administration office in the camp; requisition forms, military charge forms, progress reports, strength returns.

Then I started looking through the file of radio messages received by the base since Tshombe had fled the country. Very routine; unit orders, instructions from the *Etat Major* in Leopoldville.

Quite suddenly I noticed the date line on one of the messages was Punia, May 1967, the time when Quintin was on his third visit to Schramme . . . his final one.

I pulled out the folder and poured over the contents.

'Notification to all bases Kivu Province Stop Arrest Order on Belgian colon Maurice Quintin Stop Believed in Kivu Province Stop Arrest and detain Stop'

The message was from Schramme's camp.

It was short and succinct.

But what did it mean?

I crossed to the window and stared out at the sun smashed parade ground, deep in thought. Had Schramme caused Quintin to be arrested?

Why?

Why would he risk having Quintin fall into the hands of the ANC of all people?

I hastened with the message to Monga and Naweji. We discussed its implications and eventually we agreed that I should broach the subject to Schramme directly.

I found him on the veranda of a Bukavu Hotel immersed in a French magazine that had only just arrived from across the river. I showed him the message and asked what it meant.

Without a flicker of interest Schramme took it and read it through quickly. He handed it back to me with a straight face.

'I never sent that message and I don't know who did.'

He went back to his magazine.

It was the last time I was to discuss Quintin with Schramme.

282

44

The Final Days

We all knew it was a crucial meeting. Schramme was tense, constantly flicking glances towards his aide and confidant, Victor von Bucholz.

Among the other mercenary officers there was confusion and consternation. Monga and several other Katangese officers were plainly angry.

After six weeks at Bukavu the mercenaries were as divided as ever.

I addressed myself to Schramme.

'Colonel, why do we not move? If we wait here any longer we will be out of ammunition and at the mercy of the ANC. We must move quickly.'

For the third time that order group, Schramme waved the message from Luanda at the dozen or so mercenaries and Katangese.

'Here's the answer, Puren. Denard has told us from Luanda that he is preparing a diversionary attack into Katanga from Angola. Our task is to remain here and further degarrison the Congo of ANC elements, then he'll move. That's your answer.'

A young Belgian mercenary snorted.

'Denard, look what he did to us in Stanleyville. He won't invade Katanga. We're fools to wait for him. For Christ sake let's move on.'

In a conventional army it would have been unheard for a young junior officer to talk like that to the OC, but in a mercenary group everybody had a right to his say, especially when the chips were down. Schramme nevertheless glared at the fair headed man.

'This time he won't let us down. I think we should trust him.'

'Rubbish,' replied the rebel. 'Denard is working his own fiddle in Angola and we're not included in his projections.'

'Are we going to stay put?' I demanded of Schramme.

'Not entirely, I have some things up my sleeve.'

'Such as?'

'Such as a diversionary attack on Goma on the north side of the lake.'

Again the young Belgian snorted.

'Goma, Goma. You keep talking about Goma, Colonel, but we haven't taken a step in that direction so far . . .'

'What steps have been taken to prepare for the attack,' I interrupted the man.

'We're preparing a column', said Schramme.

'I haven't seen it.'

Von Bucholz jumped to his master's defence.

'It's in the planning stage, on paper. What we really need is some form of lake transport for an amphibious attack.'

Monga, who had been listening to the exchange with increasing impatience, now interjected.

'Colonel Schramme, we have been hearing too many stories about raids on Goma and attacks from Angola. Nothing has happened. Meanwhile, the ANC are getting stronger and stronger and our ammunition reserves lower and lower. We must act now or never.'

There was a murmur of agreement from a number of the officers present. I entered the debate.

'We don't even have to attack Kindu. There is a road that bypasses Kindu on the east. If we had gone on that road a month ago it would have taken us five days to reach Katanga. Even now we can probably do it.'

Schramme hesitated.

'What's the opinion?'

Seven out of the dozen officers present opposed any immediate moves.

'Right, that's settled. We stay where we are for a while', he said with not a little indication of relief.

But Monga was not finished.

'In the mountains to the south west there are a number of rebel tribes who have been there for years. I can easily make contact with them and we could possibly join forces with the rebels against Mobutu.'

Schramme started in his chair.

'What you are suggesting, Mister President, is that the Gendarmes go into the mountains and wage guerrilla war.'

'Quite correct, Colonel. I am not asking the mercenaries to come with us but at least let me take my people to a place where they can be more effective.'

The Belgian mercenary leader was obviously not very happy at the suggestion.

'You can't pull out and leave us now, obviously. If the Katangese go the mercenaries will never be able to hold the town. And what happens when Denard's diversion begins. We will never have the strength to breakout of here to support him. We just can't afford to have the Katangese dispersed in the mountains.'

'Colonel, if there is any likelihood of a break out from here, we will stay. If not, if things continue as they are doing now, we will leave.'

'Who would go with you?' Schramme demanded, glaring at his officers.

Three black hands and one white — mine — shot into the air.

'If you could work something out by way of a meeting between myself and the rebels you mention, perhaps something can be done', Schramme said.

Schramme was obviously playing for time.

After the O group, Monga and I met at my redoubt.

'What are the chances of joining the rebels?' I asked.

Monga shrugged.

'If I take the Katangese out now the mercenaries will be massacred. Perhaps

284

it's best if we arrange a meeting between the rebels and Schramme first to see what we can do'.

Mid September was a low point in my Congo experiences. We were static, trapped, unmotivated, virtually without leadership. Plans were disintegrating, the mercenaries quarreling, lives being wasted, opportunities ignored. And then to cap it all I received word from Julia in South Africa. Things were not going too well for her.

Living in Springs with our three children, including a few months old baby, Julia was desperately short of money and continually plagued with worry about my safety.

Not one to sit back Julia began looking around for a job that would enable her to support the family. With her university education she found one easily enough — personnel officer for a large company in Springs.

The interview went flowingly and the post was assured. Then the manager asked for Julia's passport number and her permanent residency number. Here was the rub; she had her Belgian passport but had never applied for a South African permanent residency stamp. Reluctantly the manager said he would not be able to take her.

In desperation Julia turned to old contacts in civil and military security. One by one they turned their backs on her. The experience was a lesson in this type of covert operation. Reversals bring nothing but disclaimers from one's own governments. I wonder what victory would have brought us from the South African Government.

To compound the problem, even some of my old friends and Tshombe acquaintances, turned a blind eye to the misfortunes of my family. My greatest disappointment was Marc Kalibiona. Although he knew Julia was in financial straits and although he was holding the purse strings, he never saw Julia adequately provided for. It was only many years later that I was to discover Marc had also been sidelined and was himself unable to send money. As the news of my family's straitened circumstances dribbled through I became even more depressed.

I wasn't the only one. All seven of the remaining southern African contingent were by now also thoroughly depressed by the inertia at Bukavu. I decided it was time for a little action.

Schramme wanted lake transport and, by God, we'd provide him with Lake Transport. I focussed my binoculars across the Lake to where, four kilometers away, wallowed the shape of a one hundred ton steamer.

In happier days she had plied across Lake Kivu carrying peasants and visitors but the fortunes of war had decreed that the boat should now lie in no man's land, between the advance lines of the Gendarmes and those of the ANC. For six weeks she had been standing there, inviting and yet unattainable. My bored troops had long since nicknamed her *Titanic*.

I called my little contingent of mercenaries together. They gathered around; tanned dark brown by the Congo sun, grizzled, faded uniforms. Despite the boredom and insecurity they were as tough and alert as ever.

'Do you feel like some action?'

A ragged cheer as answer.

'Do you feel like a ride on the lake?'

A bigger cheer.

'Do you feel like liberating the *Titanic?*'

An even more enthusiastic reception.

I turned to the mechanics of the operation. First we needed an assault craft; enter the sleekest looking and most powerful cruiser we could find among the one hundred and fifty odd deserted boats littering the lake side at Bukavu . . . a cream and blue monster with two massive outboard motors.

Second we needed an assault group; enter seven tough but bored South African and Rhodesian mercenaries ready for a little action.

Third; we needed somebody to bring the boat back; enter mercenary Van Dyke, ex-Rhodesian car thief and self proclaimed wizard at mechanics.

Now was his chance to prove it.

I decided not to tell anybody else of the operation. The Belgians would get jealous, the French suspicious and the Katangese would insist on killing as many ANC as they could during the exercise, which could complicate things.

Just before sunset one evening we boarded all the equipment we needed in our boat, tools for Van Dyke, ammo pouches, torches. As the sun was setting over the Kivu hills we pushed off and cruised silently along the dusky shore line; past our perimeter and three kilometers to where the ferry wallowed against the jetty.

We were just short of the ANC lines.

Van Dyke expertly cut engines and the boat bumped against the jetty.

In a flash two of the assault group were pounding along the jetty with LMGs and dropping into defensive positions at the entrance. The rest of us shinned up the gang plank, two men forward, one aft and Van Dyke and I went down into the engine room of the ferry. The machinery stood indifferently in front of us. I held the torch and Van Dyke went to work. He was in his element.

Check water levels, injectors, oil levels. Nuts and bolts were loosened and tightened, taps opened and closed.

Apparently nothing organically wrong with the monster.

The Rhodesian gave a thumbs up sign, twiddled with a few levers and hand cranked the ferry's engine. It coughed into life. A huge toothless grin split Van Dyke's face.

Within seconds the two pickets were back on the ferry and we pushed off into the dark lake.

We were several hundred meters from the jetty when the ANC suddenly woke up to the fact that something was happening. A mortar flare burst high in the night sky and several lines of tracer bullets arced lazily out at us from their positions.

They did not have our range and the mercenaries laughed derisively.

We gently chugged back towards the promontory, The Congo night air was warm and enfolding. I sat on the bridge cradling my submachinegun and whistling contentedly.

The muted sounds of gunfire could be heard from the shore line where the Gendarmes were by now haphazardly returning the ANC fire which had initially been directed at us.

The brisk exchange lasted for ten minutes and then died away.

A little luck, a little planning, a little guts and a lot could be achieved in morale boosting satisfaction.

The *Titanic* nudged alongside a jetty below my redoubt. We berthed her and swaggered off our prize of war.

Early next day my field telephone rang at my redoubt. It was Schramme.

'What's that steamer doing below your positions?' he asked.

'We captured her last night.'

'For what?'

'For the attack on Goma, of course.'

'Oh,' said Schramme and rang off.

Attack on Goma, my foot.

The saga of the *Titanic* did not quite end there, though. As the weeks dragged on it became quite apparent that no Goma raid was going to materialise and the lake steamer was not actually going to serve any military purpose. It didn't take my little band of con artists long to put their heads together. One of the dirty dozen came to see me late one evening. He was a Rhodesian with three Congo contracts behind him.

'The men have been having a little discussion about the *Titanic*.'

'Well?'

'Well, we think she can be put to better use than just letting her sit there. She could be used for carrying strategic supplies.'

'Strategic to whom?'

'To us of course.'

'You mean loot, don't you?'

'Yes.'

I thought about it. My men were unlikely to be paid for their services, an uncertain fate faced them. Around them they saw the French and Belgians and Katangese plundering with gay abandon. Why not them? I nodded.

Thereafter the ferry began surreptitiously filling with stolen ivory tusks, booty from the town, anything saleable. By the end of two weeks possibly two hundred thousand dollars worth of goods were packed into the ferry. The mercenary spokesman came to see me again.

'Sir, we're ready to take the ferry out.'

'Who have you got to do it?'

'We've recruited a pilot, a steamer captain from Rwanda. He'll have to take it to a point fifteen kilometers up the river where we have arranged for some Greek treaders to meet her. All fixed up.'

'Well, good luck then.'

The mercenary grinned and walked out. Later that night the steamer pushed off and the captain picked a slow path up the lake towards the RV point. It could have made the mercenaries very rich men. It could have paid them enough each to set up their own businesses in South Africa. But it didn't.

Next day I found them in a mournful group in one of the redoubts.

'This hardly looks like millionaire's club,' I joked as I entered.

'It's not,' replied one bitterly.

'What happened?'

'That bastard pilot. He was so drunk he couldn't stand. Twelve kilometers out he put the steamer into the bank. The Rwandese have seized every last thing on the boat. The lot.'

I sympathised as best I could but I knew that such disappointments were the very essence of mercenary adventuring. There was not a Congo mercenary who did not have some tale of fortune made and lost by a quirk of fate.

Two days later the group were revived and cheerful.

In early October we received a message from Denard saying that a DC-4 would be making a parachute drop of supplies to Bukavu.

Good as his word, next day the DC-4 flown by none other than Jack Malloch, orbited the darkened Bukavu skyline at about 22h00 and began making runs over the city.

Instantly our VHF receivers picked up his signal and I guided him into the drop zone I had constructed with proper lighting. Very soon crates of supplies came drifting down, the chutes above them flapping like huge birds in the night.

On the third run the ANC around Bukavu woke up with a crash. A roar of gunfire echoed around the hills and tracer paths bored their way heavenward.

'Finding it a bit hot, Jack?' I enquired over the radio.

'Damn sight hotter than Biafra, anyway', he said.

He dropped the last load and then circled once more.

'Take a southerly route, Jack, and you'll hit less flak.'

'Roger.'

'Can you take a message for home. Tell Julia I am well and love her.'

'Roger.'

We heard the engines disappearing into the night.

It was the last friendly aircraft we were to see.

Next day at the same time two T28s put in an appearance in the obvious hope of catching Malloch on a return run.

In Bukavu the situation was now approaching critical proportions. The ANC pressure was increasing daily, the mercenaries were becoming unbearably tense and fighting was frequent.

The Belgian and French mercenaries, never noted for their abstemiousness, were drinking heavily. Although they were too professional to allow this to interfere with their fighting ability, the off duty hours were a series of bloody fist, knife and even gun fights between warring mercenary factions.

Schramme meanwhile had become more and more aloof.

All enquiries as to when we were moving were rebutted with a curt 'We're waiting for Denard.'

Relations between the mercenary leaders and their men became more strained. It reached breaking point in late October.

One of the mercenary officers had been continually needling Schramme. He had done it at that crucial O Group meeting. He never lost an opportunity to criticise Schramme. The Belgian leader took it in his stride but I could see he was approaching tolerance threshold. Then two days after the mercenary and Schramme had a blazing row the matter came to a head.

The young mercenary was playing a piano in the mess to the riotous amusement of the troops. Halfway through a number the door burst open and a young mercenary, also Belgian, shouldered his way through the crowd. He arrived at the piano, pulled out a pistol and, without a word, shot the pianist clean through the head.

52. Death crash — wreckage of a Wigmo T56 that crashed near Stanleyville. It claimed the lives of both crew members

53. Three Cuban-exiled Wigmo pilots — CIA men in Mobutu's service

54. Left — top — Wigmo pilots and their stumpy CIA supplied T56 fighter

55. Left below — Old Katanga hands — mercenary pilots Lt Roger Bracco and Captain Hedges — flying for the Central Government

56. Right — letter dated 7th December 1964 from Colonel Mobutu, President of Zaire, to Colonel Jerry Puren complaining about high profile mercenary leaders. The officer he particularly had in mind was Alistair Wicks

57. Below — The indomitable mercenary officer, Siegfried Meuller, on the road again

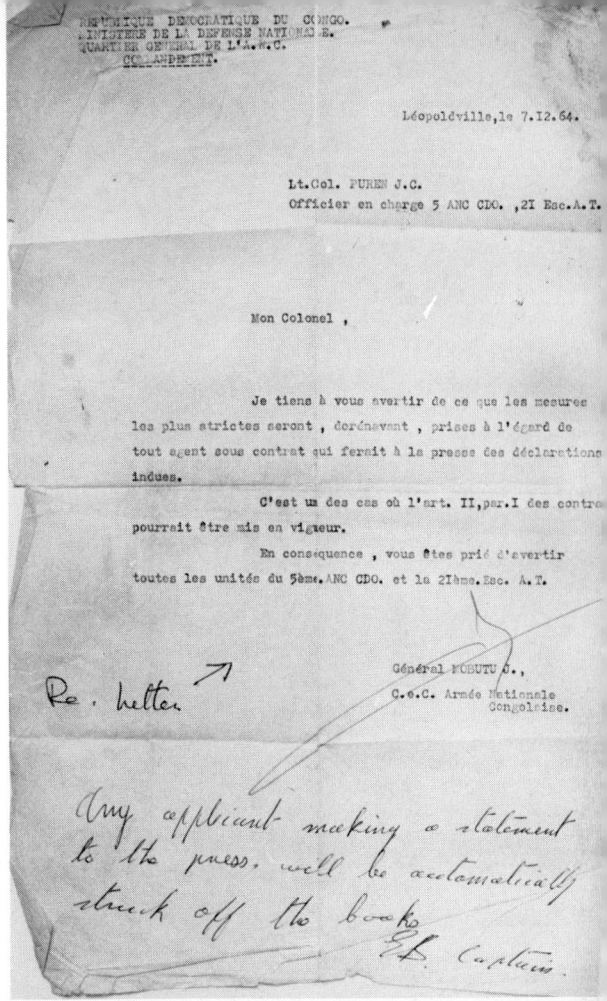

RÉPUBLIQUE DÉMOCRATIQUE DU CONGO.
MINISTÈRE DE LA DÉFENSE NATIONALE.
QUARTIER GÉNÉRAL DE L'A.N.C.
COLANDREST.

Léopoldville,le 7.12.64.

Lt.Col. PUREN J.C.
Officier en charge 5 ANC CDO. ,2I Esc.A.T.

Mon Colonel ,

Je tiens à vous avertir de ce que les mesures les plus strictes seront , dorénavant , prises à l'égard de tout agent sous contrat qui ferait à la presse des déclarations indues.

C'est un des cas où l'art. II,par.I des contrats pourrait être mis en vigueur.

En conséquence , vous êtes prié d'avertir toutes les unités du 5ème.ANC CDO. et la 2Ième.Esc. A.T.

Général MOBUTU J.,
C.e.C. Armée Nationale
Congolaise.

Re. letter

Any applicant making a statement to the press, will be automatically struck off the books

E.B. Captain

58. Left — Mercenary troops heading for Baraka on the Albertville ferry

59. Right — looking for enemy targets

60. The advance on Baraka 28th September 1965

61. Pushing the Simbas back. Mercenaries advance on foot into a rebel village — late 1965

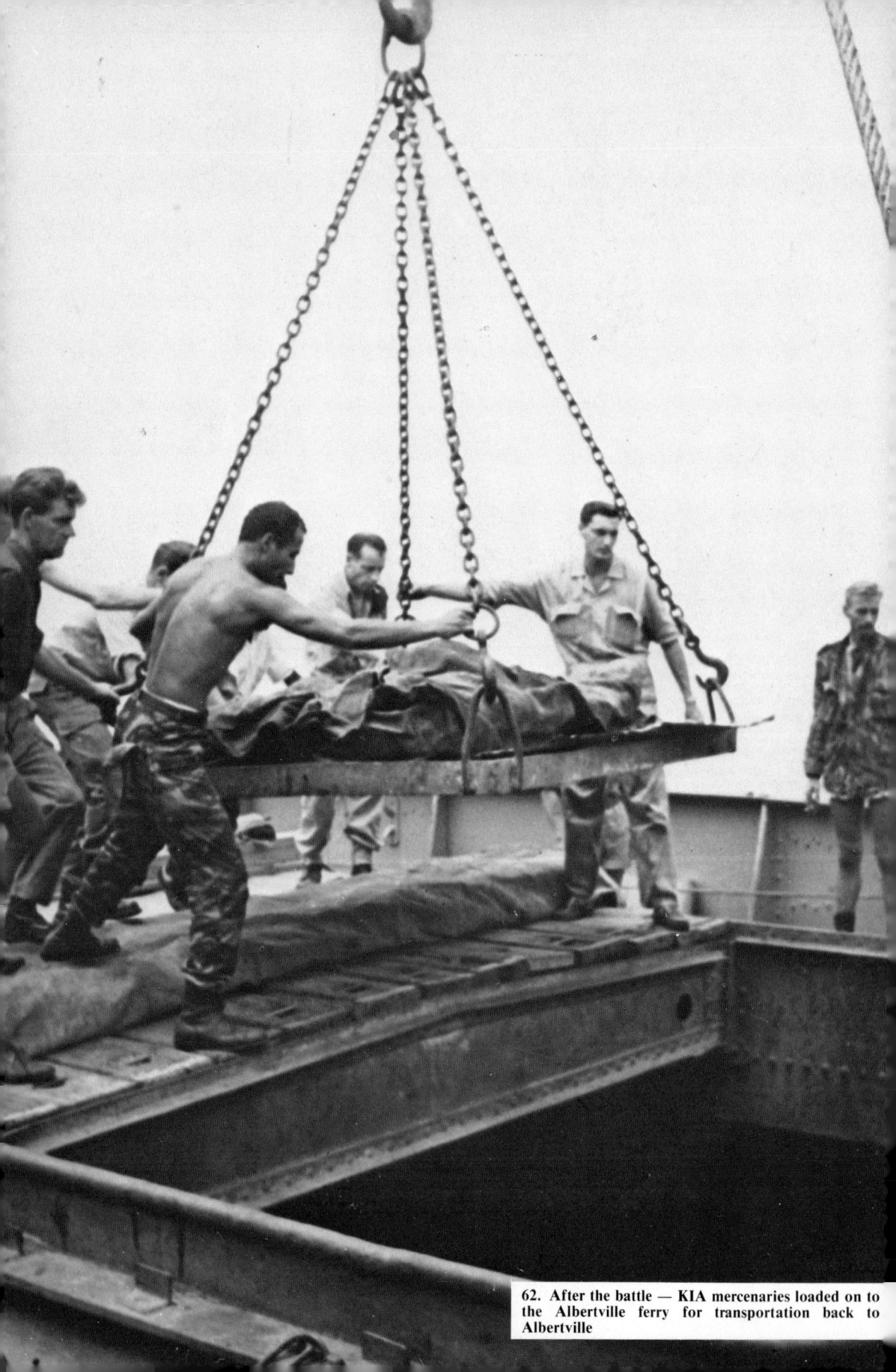

62. **After the battle — KIA mercenaries loaded on to the Albertville ferry for transportation back to Albertville**

Top right — the man they intended to reinstate — Moise Tshombe

Top left — the man they intended to topple — the CIA supported Colonel Mobutu Seso Seke, President of Zaire

66. Maurice Quintin (above), Moise Tshombe's personal emissary — destined to be killed in cold blood by 'Black Jack' Schramme in early 1967. Schramme was finally convicted of this murder in absentia in 1986

65. Bob Denard and 'Black Jack' Schramme (left), Congo warlords joined in an uneasy alliance during the second Katangese coup — 1967

Second Katangese Coup 1967

67. Left top — Bob Denard with Bob Noddyn (rt), a key man in the second Katangese coup attempt. The French mercenaries were tough and fierce, but totally unprepared and surprised by the rebellion

68. Left bottom — Mercenaries head for Bukavu

69-70. Above and left — 'Black Jack' Schramme's mercenaries roll into Bukavu

71. Below — Mercenary Camp at Bukavu

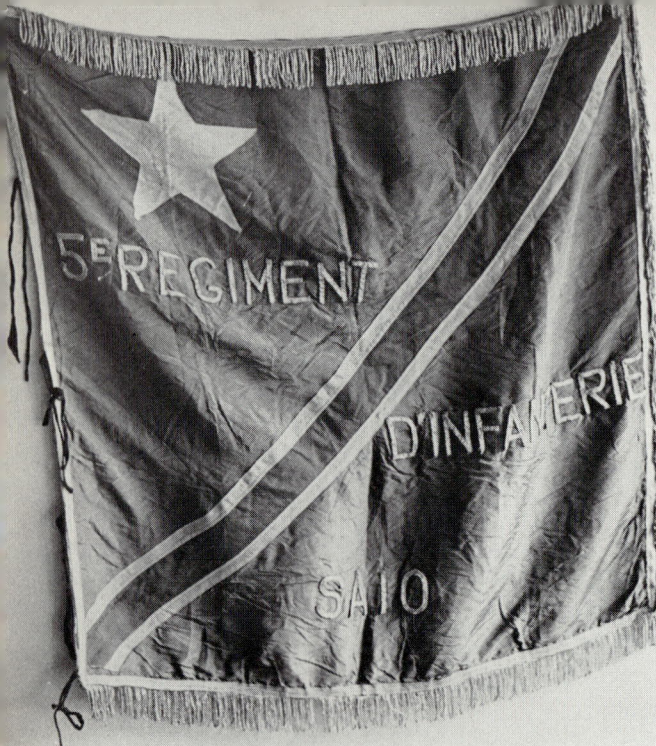

72. Blue and gold Zairean regimental flag captured by mercenaries during the fighting

73. Promised an amnesty on 14 April 1969 by President Mobutu, that was guaranteed by the OAU, through the Secretary General, Diallo Telli, Leonard Monga agreed to leave Rwanda with his 1,200 Katangese Gendarmes, their women and children. But all of them, man, woman and child, were treacherously butchered by Mobutu. Monga, himself, was finally executed at Camp Kokolo, near Leopoldville, on 14 April 1969. He died bravely

74. 'Black Jack' Schramme broadcasting from the Bukavu radio station

75. 'Black Jack' Schramme (centre) with a reporter and other white mercenaries in a Rwanda internment camp after the coup attempt had failed

76. 'Confidential' note sent by Puren in a bid to escape the Red Cross camp in Cyangugu, Rwanda, 1967 it was published in the press instead

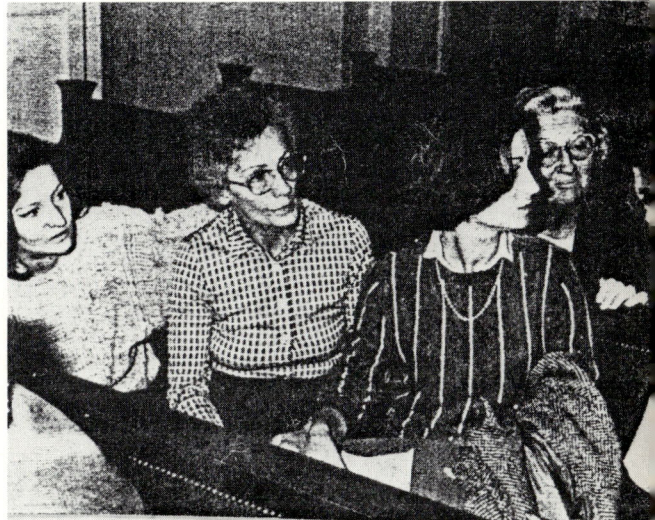

77. Maurice Quintin's family — the completion of a long but finally successful search for truth and justice — Brussels 1985

78. Former mercenary Rodrique in Mons, Belgium, court of law, protesting his innocence in the murder of Maurice Quintin — Brussels 1985

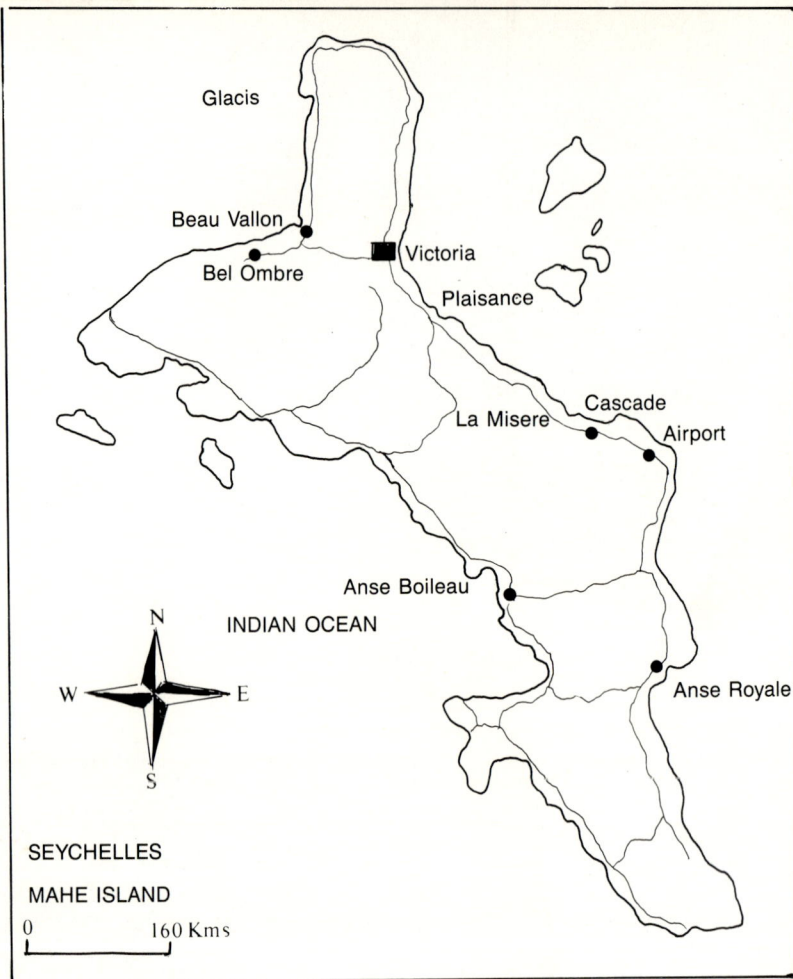

SEYCHELLES

MAHE ISLAND

INDIAN OCEAN

79. Some of the mercenary baggage containing arms, about to be loaded on the flight to Seychelles at Moreru Airport, Swaziland

80. The 'Frothblowers' arrive at Mahe

81. Right — mercenary Johan Fritz, killed by a comrade's accidental discharge

82. Countdown to disaster as mercenaries walk to airport building

**83. Mercenaries Aubrey Brooks and Roger England —
bruised and battered after capture and interrogation**

**84. Mercenaries Dolincheck, Puren and Carey at their
first court appearance**

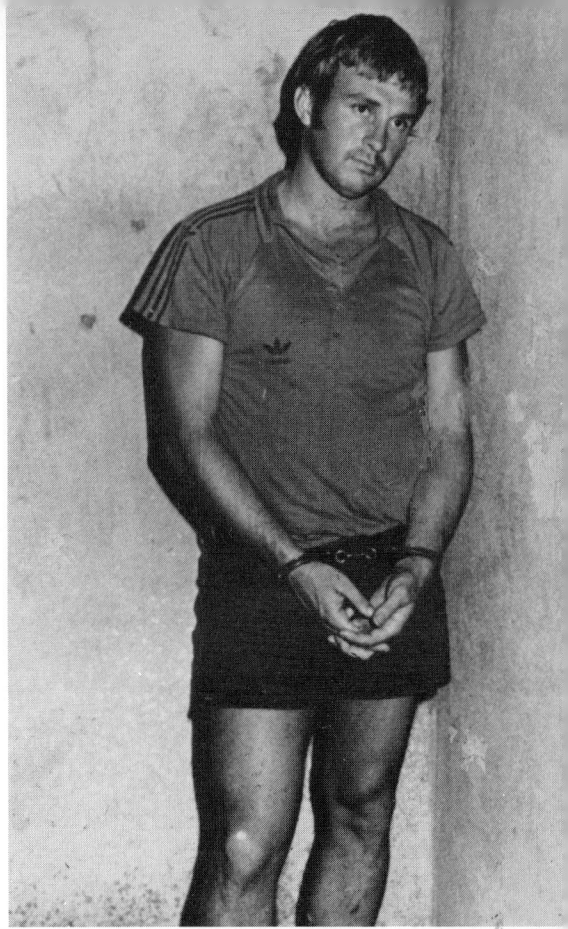

85. James Pillay, Commissioner of the Seychelles Police. Behind on the wall is pictured President René of the Seychelles — the man the mercenaries had intended to topple and probably kill

86. Right — Roger England in the punishment cell in Seychelles

87. Below — Dolincheck (rt centre), South Africa's man in the Seychelles coup

88. Arriving at court for their press conference (l to r),
England, Puren, Brookes, Carey — 1982

89. The deal which resulted in the condemned
mercenaries' release — press conference conducted by
Puren, Brookes, England and Carey in Seychelles
courtroom. Again President René looks benignly down
on the proceedings

The officer died in mid note.

The action was greeted with outrage by the other mercenaries; whether from a genuine liking of the victim or a fondness for his music I never found out.

The murderer was hauled before Schramme and the general expectation was that there would be a swift court martial and firing squad.

No such thing.

The man was secreted in quarters on the north side of town, in Bracco and Libert's house in fact, and the impression given that the culprit had been sent to Rwanda.

I never heard it suggested that Schramme had anything to do with the shooting, but . . .

It was perhaps as well that the assassin was a fellow Belgian and not a Frenchman. At that time the murder of a mercenary of one nationality by one from another would have sparked open warfare. Although several times I believe I antagonised the Belgians in general and Schramme in particular, no attempt was ever made to intimidate me; perhaps because my standing among my own Dirty Dozen and the Katangese was too good.

It was in these strained circumstances that the rebel leaders from the mountains north of us arrived at Bukavu. The group . . . perhaps a dozen neatly dressed men with ancient mausers . . . slipped easily through the ANC lines and into the resort town. Monga presented the men to Schramme.

After lengthy discussion it was agreed that Schramme would give them arms to start a diversionary attack from the mountains.

Monga struck a private deal that he and the leaders would keep in touch and, when the time was ripe, Monga would bring as many Katangese as he could, about four hundred men, into the mountains.

Schramme eventually dredged up one hundred and fifty old mauser rifles and presented them to the rebels.

It was perhaps a mark of their skills as guerrilla fighters that the dozen men managed to smuggle out the entire consignment of arms unaided . . . right through the lines of the fifteen thousand ANC troops encircling us.

Monga began making discreet enquiries as to which Katangese units would follow us into the mountains. The response was good.

Then events overtook us.

For some time Denard had been keeping up a constant flow of encouraging messages but his diversionary attack failed to materialise. We all knew that the showdown was approaching in Bukavu.

Night after night from our posts . . . I was now sleeping in the redoubt rather than my quarters . . . we could see the long columns of ANC trucks snaking down the coast road from Goma, flashes of headlights against the dark skyline, the rumble of engines. The ANC were preparing for a big push.

Schramme, eyes to his own interests, promptly ordered the banks of Bukavu to be opened and the money sent to Rwanda. The vaults were blown and an estimated 2,5 billion francs flowed across the Cyangugu bridge and it is reputed via the hands of Rwandese friends to Schramme's bank in Brussels. If he ever shared any of this windfall with others I never found out.

Certainly, no South African or Rhodesian received any money.

The big attack finally came on October 29 1967 in a fury of rocket, mortar and rifle fire from all sides. No probing attack this, it was the real thing.

Hour after hour the hills around Bukavu resounded to the crash of rifle, mortar and cannon fire until even the birds seemed to have left for safer pastures. The Katangese mercenaries held their positions with ease while the ANC took a fearful battering. But still they came on.

Schramme stayed at his command post and kept up a constant stream of instructions over his communication network, deploying reserves to the various sectors and seeing that ammunition flowed to the front.

And here was our problem.

The determined, concerted attacks were lowering our ammunition reserves dramatically and there were no replacements.

Enter the hapless Congolese Air Force again and another comic interlude.

Mobutu, disgusted with the inefficiency of his own pilots, hired several white mercenaries. Now mercenaries generally have a fairly strong objection to killing other mercenaries so when the first mercenary piloted T28s came on their missions, it did not take us long to establish air coms and convince them that it would be truly ignoble to kill fellow adventurers.

Obligingly we zeroed them on to suitable targets . . . empty houses for example . . . and dutifully they levelled them.

We were happy, they were happy and poor Mobutu, presented every day with fresh evidence of the destruction they were wreaking on the rebels 'positions', was also presumably happy.

Unfortunately we had no such luck in subverting the relentlessly directed mortar fire. Pressure grew and we knew the end was near.

Then on November 1 we had a dramatic O group with Schramme. The mercenary leader was excited. He showed us a radio message from Luanda.

'Second front opening today; Denard.'

'We can't fail to win. Katanga will rise and rescue us.'

I began to doubt the man's grasp of realities.

Denard did in fact launch his much vaunted attack from Angola into Katanga with one hundred and ten mercenaries and fifty Katangese. It was a horrible fiasco caused by inept leadership and rank cowardice. I doubt Denard actually intended to succeed.

After capturing Luashi with his mercenaries Denard split into platoons, couldn't make up his mind whether to attack Dilolo or Kolwezi, failed to seize an ANC armoury, was eventually ambushed by the ANC and retreated.

The most tragic feature of the whole operation was the fact that Katangese, at least two thousand of them, flocked to join his colours. Denard failed to give them arms although, with a little bit of cohesion, his group could have taken an ANC armoury.

A genuine popular revolt could have begun had it not been for his indecisiveness.

When he did finally pull out, he was accompanied by several thousand Katangese spoiling for another chance to have a crack at Mobutu.

The Portuguese, helpful as ever, put them up in camps in Northern Angola where they were indeed to have another chance at Mobutu. Much later . . . in 1977 and 1978 to be exact.

In Bukavu the fighting increased throughout the night of 2nd and 3rd November.

By 4 November the ANC were attacking in massed groups supported by armour. Our ammunition stocks had fallen disastrously low and the end was approaching.

At dawn on that day Schramme held a final O group in his command centre. It was short and to the point.

'Denard's invasion is a farce. We can expect no help from that quarter. Our ammunition stocks are virtually exhausted. It is now time to think of our safety and that of the Katangese and their families.'

A strained silence followed his words. The dozen or so officers remained mesmerised by the words which we had for so long expected and were now hearing. Schramme went on.

'I have made arrangements with the International Red Cross and the Rwandese authorities for us to be interned once we surrender our arms. What happens after that is in God's hands.'

Still silence from the gathered mercenaries.

'It must be understood that we are going to destroy every bit of equipment we cannot take with us. Nothing is to fall to the ANC.'

Schramme turned to the details. The various sectors were to fall back in phases to the Cyangugu Bridge. The women and children were to be the first across and then the Katangese troops. The mercenaries would be last out. He looked at his watch.

'We will meet again at 22h00 tonight at the old customs' house.'

That same day Schramme sent a message to Denard.

'Ici Schramme en Personne Stop Situation Sans Issue Stop N'Avons Plus de Munitions Stop Ne Savons Pas Encore Comment Cela Vo Finir Stop Reglerons Comptes Plus Tar Stop Vous Etes Des Assassins Stop et Fin.'

The mercenaries started pulling back through the rest of the night, slowly contracting their perimeter. That night the sector officers met on the road leading to the Cyangugu Bridge and watched the long lines of civilians, Katangese Gendarmes and mercenaries file past.

Next day, November 5, the last elements had pulled out of the battered town. Only my contingent, Schramme and I remained on the west bank of the Ruzizi. There was nothing between us and Mobutu's troops except empty streets.

'Okay, Jimmy, take them across,' I said.

The men formed up in a file and began moving across the river, several swaying with weariness. From Bukavu came the occasional mortar blast while eddies of smoke drifted above the tree line. Schramme and I looked at each other.

'Who shall be last out?' he asked with a wry grin.

'You can. The Congo has been your home longer than mine,' I said.

'Black Jack' Schramme shrugged.

'It is immaterial. We are both white Africans. Today I am being booted out of the Congo and tomorrow you will be booted out of South Africa.'

'Perhaps you are mistaken,' I remonstrated gently.

Again he shrugged.

'Perhaps. Anyway, let us go together.'

We walked across the bridge side by side as the first ANC armoured car came nosing down the road from Bukavu proper.

Neither Schramme nor I looked back.

45

Internment and Denouement

Our internment at Cyangugu came as a radical anticlimax to the last furious days of battle in Bukavu.

The weary mercenaries and Katangese queued to hand over their well used and cordite reeking weapons to the Rwandese authorities.

The trucks were reversed up and the mercenaries shuffled past reverently stacking their sidearms in the interiors.

I was one of the last in line.

Reluctantly I hauled out the only weapon I had, a 9mm parabellum pistol, and even more reluctantly I dumped it on the pile of weapons, my fingers lingering for a last few seconds on the comforting and familiar grip of the pistol.

Most of our war material had been destroyed before leaving Bukavu and the surrender of our own sidearms was more a gesture than anything else.

We gathered in loose and forlorn knots, hopelessly naked without the weapons that had become extensions to our own bodies over the last three months.

If we looked depressed, the Rwandese guards looked terrified as they surveyed the bleary eyed and ragged collection of black and white soldiers who had been doing battle with the pride of the Congolese army for nearly a hundred days.

Nervously they fingered their trigger guards as if waiting for us to suddenly erupt into ravening beasts prepared to tear them apart with our bare hands. We were ushered into a hastily constructed stockade . . . for the guards it was not unlike herding wild animals into a stockade . . . and then left almost entirely to our own devices.

Our surrender and internment had meanwhile been captured for posterity by the whirring TV and movie cameras.

In the stockade we found three large hangars in which we were all to live; mercenaries, Katangese and families, men, women and children.

I located my Dirty Half Dozen bunkered down in the corner of one of the hangars.

We remained in the stockade for one week.

Food was iron rations relieved occasionally with fresh produce; not imaginative but wholesome and plentiful. Water was fresh, we had access to Red Cross officials, received post and parcels and did not suffer unduly from the Rwandese guards' discipline.

More for the effect than anything, a huge hole was dug in the ground and our guards let it be known that anybody giving trouble could expect a few days par boiling under the African sun in the hole. To the French Foreign Legion veterans the discipline was entirely familiar and quite unimpressive. Anyhow, I doubt that more than two people saw the bottom of the pit in our six months imprisonment.

It was not that the mercenaries lived blameless lives in the camp. Far from it. Like all mercenaries in defeat, there was a flood of post mortems, recriminations and outright antagonisms; French against French, French against Belgian, Belgian against Belgian and white against Katangese. As the days lengthened the antagonism sometimes spilled over into running brawls.

Nobody, I am thankful to report, thought it wise to tangle with my brawny half dozen South Africans and Rhodesians.

The guards, perhaps understandably, preferred to leave *Les Affreux* to their own devices.

Then, three weeks after our arrival in the stockade the mercenaries were taken to a smaller and better protected camp right next door to our old camp. I do not believe that the Rwandese were proponents of apartheid and can only assume that the move was intended to neutralise our influence over the Katangese.

Once in the new camp the antagonisms and frustrations among the mercenaries became incomparably intensified. The whole camp was falling apart in an orgy of recriminations, self pity and rank insecurity.

We knew that Mobutu was demanding our extradition for trial in Leopoldville and we knew what that entailed.

We also learnt that the OAU countries had decided to refuse overfly rights to any aircraft carrying mercenaries so we were effectively sealed in Rwanda.

On the other hand Schramme, before our departure from Bukavu, had arranged with the Red Cross to assume responsibility for us in internment and we knew the organisation was fighting for our repatriation.

So were France and Belgium.

While the notes and negotiations progressed, we sat and prayed that our fate would not be in the hands of Mobutu.

Schramme, meanwhile, had renounced all concern in the camp or his position as leader of the men.

Day after day he sat outside his hut sunk in the deepest despair, rarely bothering to answer questions, preoccupied with . . . what???

His failure to follow the plan?

His future?

His Katangese troops?

Only occasionally did he rouse himself to rail against Denard for failing to support him.

Almost as soon as I arrived in the new camp I realised that boredom and apathy were my great enemies. I began to concentrate on keeping fit. Long runs around the camp, volley ball, pushing weights with makeshift objects, calisthenics and trips into the nearby woods to fell trees.

An indication of my determination to reach peak fitness was the fact that, at the end of our internment, I was felling and disposing into logs a tree a day, much to the amazement of the somnambulant guards.

I also arranged English classes for the French speaking mercenaries, intense little study groups under the trees with a piece of wood as a blackboard and charcoal as chalk. My classes never rose above a hard core dozen but every evening there would rise on the cooling African air the sound of twelve earnest voices engaged in conversations of broken English.

Two things occurred at this point to make me turn seriously to thoughts of escape.

The first was the repatriation of the Katangese Gendarmes, probably the most harrowing experience in my seven years in the Congo.

The first we knew about it was a rumour that Monga and Naweji had been promised amnesty via OAU representatives.

We heard Monga had accepted.

The news buzzed around the camp for several days gathering strength and colour.

Then we heard that Justin Bomboko, Zairean Minister of Justice, had been to see the interned Katangese and promised them amnesty. To back him up was Diallo Telli, Secretary to the OAU, who agreed to underwrite Mobutu's amnesty offer.

'Fools if they accept it,' spat the mercenaries and waited for the outcome.

It was confirmed that Monga had accepted and would be leaving with the first aircraft load. I could hardly believe the man's gullibility.

The crunch came early one morning in mid November. We heard the columns of Rwandese military trucks grinding along the dirt road leading to the adjacent Katangese camp. From vantage points in our own camp we peered through the wire as the drama unfolded.

On the first day a few of the Katangese were clearly eager to go. They and their families dragged their meagre belongings from the hangars and dumped them into the waiting trucks. They then clambered aboard and waited patiently. A ring of grim faced Rwandese guards with the Belgian officers surrounded the column.

More Katangese were propelled towards the trucks, this time at rifle point. Children and women began wailing. Little knots of Katangese Gendarmes hung back, obviously reluctant to board the trucks. We saw the Rwandese troops press closer, there was a slight tussle between several troops and Gendarmes.

A Belgian officer shouted an order and seconds later the Rwandese were wading in with rifle butts, batons and sticks.

Scores more Katangese came bounding out of the bungalows and a fierce fight raged between the two sides: the mercenaries all the while screaming encouragement and unit battle cries from the sidelines.

Eventually the Rwandese thought better of it and disengaged. The convoy with its handful of voluntary Katangese returnees roared away.

The next day was a different story. The Rwandese returned in force.

From our camp we heard the screams of the women and children, the sounds of blows and once or twice there were shots.

Struggling Gendarmes were bludgeoned towards the trucks, roughly thrown aboard, kicked and punched.

The screams of the men's families rose hysterically.

In our camp we watched helplessly as our former comrades were forced on to the trucks to what they knew was certain death.

Shouts of rage came from the mercenaries.

Past differences aside, they now angrily screamed abuse at the Rwandese troops and their white officers.

Several men grabbed the barbed wire and began tugging furiously.

Alarmed Rwandese guards scuttled down from guard towers and out of billets.

Within seconds we were faced with a scratch platoon of nervous guards all with cocked automatic rifles levelled at the enraged mercenaries. If the wire had given at that point I am convinced the Rwandese would have been torn apart with bare hands.

Then it was all over.

The last Gendarme was thrown on to the truck, guards scrambled up behind and the convoy rolled out and past our camp. We heard the mournful singing of the defeated and betrayed soldiers as they drove towards the Cyangugu bridge and their fate.

Monga went, as did Naweji.

It was a deeply unsettling event which plunged our camp into even deeper depression as our brave and resourceful former comrades in arms were taken away.

'That is the last we will hear of them. *Fini*', said one of the mercenaries bitterly.

His voice quivered with rage and sorrow.

During the whole episode Schramme had sat beside his hut and not moved. As the screams had reached him he had shut his eyes tightly.

Some people claim when the singing of the doomed men reached him he cried silently.

A short while after the South African contingent had even more reason for concern.

After lunch one day I was summoned to the camp administration building.

In a bare room I found Diallo Telli, Secretary of the OAU, underwriter of the Gendarmes betrayal, waiting for me.

There was not even the pretence of civility.

'The OAU does not recognise that South African mercenaries in this camp have any right of extradition. You will be held in detention forever.'

'I don't care a damn what the OAU recognises or doesn't recognise. We're in the hands of the Red Cross and not the OAU.'

The argument raged for a while longer and ended with Telli shouting that all whites had no place in Africa.

I walked out at that point.

I later learnt that he had been recording our interview on tape with the intention of distributing it among member states of the OAU to show exactly how courageous he was in dealing with the hated Congo mercenaries.

I wonder if he ever used the tape?

It was not with any special regret that I later learnt that Telli had been executed by his own Government, Guinea, for being a CIA agent.

At this stage the impulse to escape from what seemed like certain death entirely possessed me.

I called Bracco and Libert together and we plotted an escape. Within a few days we had hammered out a plan. There were two key figures; a black Katangese exile living in Rwanda and a Rhodesian pilot involved in charter work for the Red Cross.

Libert had made contact with the Katangese through Monga and I knew the Rhodesian pilot from old.

Phase One had Bracco, Libert and I passing out of the camp with a work party and then simply not returning. The terms of our confinement were in effect extremely lax. The guards realised, quite accurately, that even if we did escape from the camp we would have nowhere to go; not in the middle of a black state.

Phase Two was when we would meet the Katangese exile with transport and he would spirit us away for the night and later to the airfield at Cyangugu.

Phase Three involved sneaking aboard the aircraft which our friend was prepared to leave fully fueled and ready for us at the airstrip. Once aboard we were to fly to Angola and safety.

Libert and I pulled off Phase One perfectly.

We dropped behind a work party and melted into the jungle. We waited for Bracco. The Katangese exile arrived and we waited and waited. No Bracco. Eventually the contact got cold feet and disappeared. Libert and I managed to slip back into the camp via another work party where we angrily broached Bracco. We received no proper explanation of his failure to join us and for several days the atmosphere was icy.

Then to compound matters the pilot who had been in on the deal spilt the story to a South African journalist working for a popular magazine. Before I knew what was happening the story of our aborted exercise was all over South Africa.

And . . . with me still in the camp.

The days dragged on in uncertainty and confusion. Rumours abounded and then in April of 1968, it became quite clear that agreement had been reached and that we were about to be sent home. It would be difficult to describe the intense surge of relief that swept the camp. The mantle of depression that weighed so heavily fell away overnight, past quarrels were forgotten, thoughts only of the next adventure or home.

Early one morning in April 1968, I was as usual chopping wood, sublimating those gnawing doubts and fears in the rhythmical pleasure of hard, physical exercise. I sensed somebody standing besides me but carried on chopping. A person coughed discreetly. I slammed the axe resolutely into the trunk of the tree in arrogance and turned to face the intruder.

It was Rodrique, Schramme's chauffeur and loyal side kick, a powerfully built man with intensely Iberian eyes.

'Yes?' I sounded as foreboding as I could.

Since our internment I had had as little as possible to do with Schramme and his coterie. Steadfastly I had preferred not to involve myself in the collective post mortems on the operation; about which I had had enough.

'I wish to speak to you about that man Quintin', said Rodrique.

I raised my eyebrows quizzically.

'Do you know what happened to him?'

'Yes, Schramme and I shot him.'

It was said almost apologetically.

'Why are you telling me this?'

Rodrique shrugged his shoulders.

'It has been with me a long time. I know you were his friend. I want to . . . clear myself.'

'But why did you shoot him?'

I tried hard to keep an even tone as I thought of the energetic and fiercely loyal little settler, the victim of Schramme and his lackey.

Rodriguez shrugged yet again.

'Schramme actually shot him first. I don't know why.'

Then the story came tumbling out in a flow of words. Quintin, on his final visit to Schramme, had fallen out with the mercenary leader. Schramme and Rodrique had driven him into the jungle, lured him out of the car and, while he was walking a few paces ahead, Schramme had jerked up his FAL rifle and shot Quintin in the back. The doughty man was not quite dead. Schramme had indicated to Rodrique and he had executed the *coup de grace*. Together they had thrown the body into the Lowa River, itself no stranger to violent death and tragedy.

So there it was at last. Schramme had cold bloodedly executed Tshombe's emissary and thereafter had consistently lied about his deed. But why? The incident remains the single most puzzling event in my Congo experiences. It called into question all Schramme's actions, all his justifications for failing to take the bold and decisive steps that were demanded by the plan and the Congo.

The failure of the coup became no longer simply a litany of disobeyed instructions, indecisiveness and poor leadership, it began to show the inevitable hand of treachery.

46

Curtain Down and Personal Post Mortems

By 22 April 1968 it was confirmed that our agonies of uncertainty were over. We were instructed to gather our goods and prepare to return home. Early next day we were taken to Cyangugu airport and boarded two jets chartered by the International Red Cross.

It was a strange parting. The mercenaries were largely stunned into disbelieving acceptance that they were finally on their way home. Among a number of them the tensions and hostility that had built up during the previous eight months were too much to overcome: even in parting. There were simply surly nods of farewell.

For others there were genuine hard partings. I said goodbye to Bracco and Libert with a hard lump in my throat.

Others still, the more resilient ones, regarded it as simply a transient phase, the bridge between the old venture and the new; Biafra, South East Asia, Middle East, Chad.

We filed aboard the jet and then were winging our way north to Europe.

In everybody's passport was stamped the words 'Not valid for Africa', a relatively small price to pay for a failed coup.

One jet flew to Zurich and Paris and the others straight to a military airport in Belgium. In Zurich I and four of the southern African mercenaries disembarked and caught the next connecting flight back to Johannesburg.

My reception at Jan Smuts airport was emotional and ecstatic. Julia and I soundlessly clung to each other for a few moments. We broke and looked at each other.

'At least we tried', I said.

Julia burst simultaneously into tears and laughter. My children crowded around.

Later, much later, at home, rested and secure, my thoughts turned inevitably to the coup.

Where and why did it go wrong?

Why was the plan not followed?

Why did Denard procrastinate?

And the biggest question of all, why had Schramme acted the way he had?

Why had he killed Quintin?

Shortly after repatriation I was to learn that Schramme had been arrested by the Belgians and tried for the murder of Quintin under the Belgian law which protects any national of that country from an act of violence performed by another Belgian anywhere in the world.

At the trial Schramme's defence was simple enough. He conceded that Quintin had come to him with a plan for a coup against Mobutu. Schramme had told the court he had refused, Quintin had threatened to tell Mobutu that Schramme was involved in a plot, and in order to protect his troops and himself, the mercenary leader had been obliged to summarily execute Tshombe's emissary.

The Belgian judiciary apparently sympathised with Schramme's dilemma for they found him guilty of murder in a lower court and sent him to a higher court for sentence. Instead he was given a passport and when last heard of was living in Brazil, still awaiting sentence.

He had also taken the precaution of fathering a few Brazilian children thus ensuring him immunity from extradition.

The Congo ghosts, however, refused to die.

In the succeeding years Quintin's children ceaselessly sought to have justice done. In 1968 they had asked me to attend Schramme's hearing but the Belgian judiciary would not pay my flight and I was broke. I sent a sworn statement, however, and it had been read into the court records.

It was not until seventeen years later that they would make their first tiny breakthrough.

In mid 1985 I was out of the blue contacted by one of Quintin's daughters and asked if I would be prepared to be a witness at the trial of Rodrique. She claimed the Belgian judiciary had agreed to prosecute Rodrique and Schramme. I agreed instantly.

Thus it was in December of 1985, after last minute arrangements, I caught a Europe bound aircraft from Johannesburg's Jan Smuts airport.

It was to be a week of poignancy, reminiscences and renewed friendships.

I was collected from the airport and rushed immediately to Mons, the site of the ferocious World War-1 battles. There, in a sparse little courtroom, I caught up with the ghosts: Rodrique, leaner, greyer, than the Congo days; my old friend Bracco, now a successful publisher, and Christian Tavernier who so nearly disposed of Badger, my old comrade at arms, and, of course, Quintin's family, still determined to see justice upheld.

I managed to slip Rodrique a message: I was not there to victimise him, I was there to see that Schramme was extradited.

The case had proceeded smoothly until then: Rodrique had told the court that Quintin had been shot by Schramme after a drunken argument in Punia's officers' mess — Schramme had apparently drunk more than his daily ration of a bottle of whisky.

Rodrique had been ordered to carry out the *coup de grace* and had done so — he was merely a soldier — and then helped another mercenary carry Quintin's body to the Lowa River where they had consigned it to the crocodiles. It had been, conceded Rodrique ruefully, a strange time which made men do strange things.

For his part, he simply wanted to forget it all.

The other mercenary, Louis Otten, confirmed the story.

Dr Andre Gleviczky was next on the witness stand. He had been in Belgium on holiday from his medical practise in Ghana when he had read about the trial

315

and hastened to give evidence. In the bloody years under review he had been a company doctor in the Maniema. It was harsh evidence. Gleviczky claimed Schramme's 'pacification' programme was nothing other than a fullscale reign of terror in which thousands of people were arbitrarily executed under Schramme's direction as the mercenary warlord held absolute sway in an area twice the size o France and fourteen times the size of Belgium.

Not even the powerful mining houses in Maniema could intervene.

Under the gentle probing of the judge I gave my evidence: told of the coup plans, our suspicions about Quintin's disappearance, my encounters with Schramme and eventually Rodrique's confession.

Tavernier and Bracco also testified that I had told them in the Red Cross camp in Rwanda about the shooting and Rodrique's confessions.

My letter to the court from seventeen years earlier was produced and found to correlate almost exactly with the evidence I gave to the Mons' court.

I believe I made a good impression. A Belgian magazine described me as 'white haired, pink skinned, distinguished as an Indian major with nothing on the exterior to suggest an adventurer'.

The judge's findings about Rodrique were inconclusive and he was discharged. But the judge did dismiss the defence that Quintin was a double agent. Schramme was subpoenaed for retrial and in April 1986 the Belgian court sentenced him to twenty years imprisonment *in absentia*. The cumbersome process of applying for extradition through the Brazilian mission in Brussels began.

That is the one Congo ghost I would still desperately like to catch.

So much for the broad facts. Let's look closer at the whole puzzling incident of the Quintin murder which, I believe, is the key to Schramme's action during the coup.

Firstly, I have the strongest reservations about Schramme's justification for what was really brutal murder. Quintin visited Schramme twice before his tragic end. During that time arrangements for the coup had reached an advance stage. At no time had Quintin been led to believe that Schramme was opposed to the coup. And why should he be? Schramme had everything to gain by reinstating Tshombe and everything to lose by waiting meekly for Mobutu to disarm his gendarmes. Quintin was a perceptive man and fully aware of the dangers of the high stakes intrigue in which he was involved. If he had the slightest indications that Schramme was against the coup he would not have returned to the dragon's lair at Punia a second and certainly not a third time.

Until the third visit, Quintin, whose judgement I trusted implicitly, apparently remained convinced that Schramme was committed to the coup.

What happened on that last visit?

Did Schramme suddenly get cold feet and want to pull out?

That does not square with the facts. When we visited Schramme three weeks after Quintin's death, he was rearing to go. Again, when Tshombe was kidnapped, it was Schramme who insisted that the coup must continue . . . arrangements had been made, people committed.

Quintin was Tshombe's emissary and his loyalty was never called into question. He was also shrewd. Knowing Quintin I find it inconceivable that he would have been so crassly stupid as to threaten to betray Schramme while in Punia . . . surrounded by his Belgian troops and in the middle of his private empire.

No, Schramme certainly intended to join a revolt against Mobutu . . . but did he intend to finish it?

The key to the mystery lies in Quintin's third and last visit to Punia. Did Quintin threaten Schramme while in Punia or did Quintin discover something so important that Schramme was forced to take the radical step of killing a white civilian? Quintin's experiences in Schramme's radio room, the message I found at camp Saio; it all added up to the subterfuge and treachery on a grand scale.

But what could be behind Schramme's fear of discovery and Quintin's subsequent death?

Schramme knows but won't tell and Quintin is dead. It remains for us to conjecture.

Three possibilities come to mind.

Firstly, Schramme throughout his time in the Congo kept close contact with the Belgian military and security agencies. These agencies had played a double game with Tshombe and Mobutu in the early days of Congo independence; hedging their bets by supporting both secessionist Katanga and the central Government. With Tshombe out of the way in 1965 their support fell squarely behind Mobutu. The fact that the homes of pro-Tshombists were raided in Belgium by the Belgian security agents in the dark days of the first abortive Katangese coup against Mobutu was indicative of the extent to which Mobutu's interests were protected by the Belgians.

Then there was the CIA. Its involvement in the kidnapping of Tshombe is well established and its continual covert support for Mobutu under its Congo operations chief, Laurence Devlin, is now no secret. Devlin and his associates were reputed to have a wide range of dirty tricks in the Congo . . . including a proposed poison attack against Patrice Lumumba when he was still in power. Devlin was a sinister and constant figure on the Congo scene.

There were powerful western intelligence agencies in the Congo with Mobutu's interests at heart: and Schramme had close contacts with both of them.

Mobutu wanted the white mercenaries out and the Katangese dispersed but knew that whichever way it went he would have a fight on his hands.

So did the CIA and the Belgian intelligence agencies.

At this juncture we approach Schramme with a plan for a coup to depose Mobutu. Schramme takes instructions from his CIA and/or Belgian mentors and is told to join the operation but to ensure that it fails. Several birds would then be killed with one stone: the mercenaries would be expelled, the Katangese eliminated to a man and the exiled plotters exposed.

The coup began, Schramme attracted the dissident elements, fought a few sharp engagements and then obligingly led the whole rebel force to Bukavu where it could be surrounded, worn down and eventually dispersed.

The mercenaries are expelled, the Katangese returned to their fate and the exiled plotters indeed exposed and destroyed.

All according to plan . . . but not my plan.

Schramme's open hearted treatment by the Belgian authorities certainly bespeaks a certain *quid pro quo*.

Far fetched?

Stranger things have happened in the Congo.

The second possibility: Schramme knew and accepted that his fiefdom would come to an end at the hands of Mobutu's paras. It was probably safe to assume that he would have escaped untouched by the ANC; at that stage he was not in any way implicated in the rumours of insurrection. Inevitably though, his Katangese troops would be dispersed, possibly eliminated, by the paranoid Mobutu.

This eventuality would have proved unacceptable to Schramme on two counts: firstly he would be accused of deserting *his* troops and secondly, it didn't sound profitable enough.

Along comes a plan for a coup against Mobutu. Schramme looks carefully at the possibilities, ignores the ostensible motive of usurping Mobutu and sees the chance for some quick gain at the expense of the Congo. He accepts the plan but carries it only to the point of departure for Katanga and then, radically changing direction and intentions, makes for the Rwanda border seizing everything of value.

At Bukavu with easy access to Rwanda, he waits for his forces to be worn down, takes what loot he can and retires with his men.

The third possibility is the simplest and most appealing. Schramme's connection with the Belgian mining interests had already been remarked upon by Quintin and I have no doubt that his observations were substantially correct.

Supposing that both Schramme and his Belgian mining bosses accepted that the Katangese would eventually have to be disarmed by Mobutu in the interests of long term stability in the eastern Congo.

Suppose both Schramme and the miners knew that such a move would be bitterly opposed by the Katangese and that a clash between the Gendarmes and the paras would probably result in fearful destruction to the expensive mining installations in the Maniema, possible wilful destruction by the embittered Gendarmes.

For the miners then the solution would be to move the Katangese from the Maniema, away from the installations, to a cosy corner of the Congo where they could be disposed of with a minimum damage. What better vehicle to this end than our own proposed coup and what better driver than Schramme, ostensible leader of the Katangese.

The truth of the matter may one day emerge.

Meanwhile the human toll of the coup stands as testimony to incompetence or something worse of a single man.

More than one hundred Katangese died in the fighting and fifty five white mercenaries.

Mobutu lost seven thousand men.

Then there was Denard. The French mercenary had close and indisputable contacts with the SDECE, the French secret Service, but I doubt that he was motivated by instructions other than his own inner drive for self aggrandizement. If he was acting for the SDECE in deliberately failing the coup it is inconceivable that he would not have worked in tandem with Schramme and his masters. And this he definitely did not. Schramme's anger and surprise at not finding Denard's troops in place at Stanleyville was genuine enough.

Denard was quite simply the archetypical self seeking mercenary. He faded from the Congo scene but not from the world stage.

In 1977 Denard arrived unexpectedly with thirty rifle wielding men on the Comores Islands and seized them, installing his employer as President.

Denard became the head of the country's security forces and was dubbed 'Number 1 President' in the island lingua fraca and there, graver, leaner and more mellow he carved himself a niche among the amiable islanders. It lasted for two years until the Comores Island . . . under intense OAU pressure . . . asked Denard to leave. He surfaced briefly in Benin in 1978 in another coup attempt and then disappeared into obscurity . . . one step ahead of a French extradition order in connection with the Benin fiasco.

And for the rest of the soldiers and adventurers who came and went as threads in the tumultuous history of the Congo? A few settled down with their not insubstantial gains and became businessmen, restaurant owners, farmers or shopkeepers.

Mostly, though, they drifted away into dead end jobs in the capitals of the world or to new adventures in the hire of professional intriguers. Some became common criminals.

Libert and Bracco took off for new adventures in South America, Malloch flew in Biafra and then worked a sanctions busting route for the Smith Government in Rhodesia. He died in a crash in a refurbished Spitfire soon after Rhodesia became Zimbabwe. It reminds one of a Viking's funeral. Corporately they all remained bound by the ties of history and a shared experience in the dangers, excitement and rewards of mercenary soldiering.

Still they exist, numbers swollen by professional veterans from Vietnam, Angola, Mozambique, Rhodesia and South Africa, a restless strata always waiting for the next adventure, the next 'big one'.

The fate of the black Katangese, however, was infinitely more sombre. Their distrust of Mobutu's amnesty were fully justified. Rank and file Gendarmes were incarcerated in the old training camp of Ireba.

Immediately they were given a taste of Mobutu's forgiving nature.

Thirty men were shot dead and thereafter the remainder . . . all twelve hundred men, women and children, were systematically executed or starved to death.

On April 14 1969 Monga and Naweji were executed in Camp Kokolo near Leopoldville.

According to all reports they died bravely. But this was not the end of Mobutu's largesse.

Earlier in the year Kimba, former Congolese minister, and three other men were publicly executed in Leopoldville in the 'Easter Hangings' for allegedly plotting to overthrow Mobutu.

A little later, Pierre Mulele, former Simba leader, had been enticed back home to the Congo with guarantees of amnesty similar to the ones given to the Katangese.

After being royally entertained to dinner by Mobutu's aides, the hapless man was taken out and shot.

With a fine sense of propriety a Congolese court found him guilty of treason the next day and then sentenced him to death.

And then there was Moise Tshombe, betrayed by the CIA on the threshold of the coup, incarcerated for two years in an Algerian prison and eventually mysteriously dead.

He at least had no illusions as to whom he owed his misfortune.

As his hijacked aircraft landed at Algiers and he was hustled into captivity he said: 'The CIA has done this to me.'

And for myself the return home meant a difficult transition into the humdrum of a sedate commercial occupation. In retrospect my seven years of associations with the Congo constituted a long and hard road. I was not always understood or liked. This is not an attempt to grub sympathy but is a simple statement or fact. My guiding principles during the entire seven years was loyalty to Tshombe and the ideals he stood by.

I held these principles and actively fought for them when they were opposed by virtually the entire world community through the United Nations: I kept the principles even when opposed by the CIA and fellow mercenary officers: I was a Tshombist in the Congo at a time when people were dying for being precisely that and I remained faithful despite the desertions and betrayals.

My politics were suspect by the foreign forces involved in the Congo and my personal morality distrusted by my mercenary associates who sought no motives further than rank self interest.

Thus in 1964 *Time Magazine* could describe me as 'unpopular' in Leopoldville.

I accept that as a judgement on my politics at a time when the rest of the mercenary corps were nominally pro-Mobutu while I was avowedly pro-Tshombe.

In a Belgian magazine in 1968 Schramme was to label me an 'Agent of the arms merchants'. I accept this as a judgement by a mercenary who could not believe I would put life and limb at risk for a set of principles and loyalty to a black man.

Unlike Schramme, all that I had left, after seven years in the Congo, was a return air fare to Johannesburg, a golden medallion presented some years earlier by Munongo, and a host of doubts, disillusionments and unanswered questions.

Back in South Africa I was obliged to gracefully accept the violent and unnecessary deaths of close friends during the previous seven years, the lost opportunities for the creation of a great and stable nation in Africa, the wasted chance to mould circumstances and direct events . . . and to make history.

47

The Call

Adventure is addictive — it is that simple.

After seven years of the Congo — after the flood and near escapes, the drama and the failure — a common response for many people would be to throw anchor in the calmest waters. I tried and it did not work. Tough and restless, I returned from the Congo to the wonderful security of family and friends. My thoughts turned to ways of making a respectable living. A succession of occupations followed; farming in southern Natal, banking, insurance work and many others.

But it was not the restlessness that passed, only time.

The year 1978 found us settled in Durban on the South African east coast. Julia had a teaching post and I was partner in a highly successful used car business in the port city's Motor Town.

The children were at school and both Julia and I were tied up in a number of extramural activities.

Politics — always a passion of mine — had beckoned and I had become a prominent member of the New Republic Party's Bluff branch. I stood for city council in 1977 and for Province in 1981.

At the same time I was involved in the Lions' service organisation and was a member of the ex-servicemen's Memorable Order of Tin Hats.

The thoughts of the Congo were never far from my mind, however, and in 1977 after the Shaba secessionists thrust into Zaire I decided to commit my experiences to a book. It was a busy time of my life but underlying it all, beyond the comfort of home life and the greyness of civilian occupations, I knew within myself that adventure would again some day come my way. In Durban there was a large ex-mercenary contingent, interlocking with newer members of the profession who had come from Zimbabwe and Vietnam looking for other employment opportunities in the turbulent sub-continent. I kept in touch with them . . . and waited.

At first I found it hard to believe. After ten years of the humdrum, adventure did again call and its messenger was none other than my former comrade from the Congo days, Mike Hoare.

Since *those* days Mike and I had kept up a tenuous friendship. In the Congo he had been pro-Mobutu and I pro-Tshombe; the distinction was enough to keep us slightly distanced. I did not really get to know him again until about 1976 when I met him on the street and we got talking.

Later he was to come to an office cocktail party and then we began meeting on a more regular basis. Often we spoke of the Congo and people we had known. At that time Mike was living in the charming Hilton area near Pietermaritzburg, inland from Durban. He was an accountant, seemed to have fairly wide business interests and still kept an active interest in the old members of the *Wild Geese*.

I was thus not entirely surprised when Mike, looking older, leaner and sporting a whispy grey beard, came to visit me at my motor shop in Smith Street. It was a blustery May day and Mike came bundled against the wind. He sunk into a chair and I could almost feel the aura of excitement that surrounded him.

'I have something in mind which might interest you', he said with a half smile.

I took the 'phone off the hook, swept a pile of motor registration forms to one side and leaned forward intently.

He was, however, playing close cards. Elliptically Mike revealed he had been approached by certain people to organise a coup somewhere — would I be interested?

I was no stranger to conspiracy and knew Mike had his own reasons for being so vague at that point.

I nodded enthusiastically; ironically I seriously believed it had to do with Zaire because Mobutu had been hard pressed to handle the Shaba secessionists in 1977 and there had been talk of a 2nd Wild Geese Brigade being created to help out.

Mike left and I did not hear from him for another few weeks.

Then suddenly he was back in my office and this time I really knew things were beginning to move.

The old Congo hand told me he had been approached to overthrow President Albert René of the Seychelles and reinstall James Mancham, recently deposed President.

For a few seconds I remained stunned — the Seychelles had not entered my mind as a likely site for a mercenary coup although I instantly recalled that another old Congo hand, Bob Denard, had taken over the Comores only two years previously.

Mike pushed on.

The conspirators wanted a feasibility plan drawn up and were prepared to pay hard cash for it. After that there was the possibility of actually taking part in the coup.

Again he asked if I wanted in.

Again I nodded.

After Mike had left I had time to reflect upon the vast choices that were opening before me again; security and excitement, family and the unknown.

Mike's offer — made in the midst of the bustle and flurry of a normal working day in the salesroom — promised the familiar feel of impending action.

That night after supper I took Julia aside and told her of the offer.

She listened patiently as I summed up the arguments for and against involvement; the fact that we were not actually being called upon to undertake the coup but merely to see if it was feasible, the strategic importance of the Seychelles to the West and thus to South Africa, the merit in overthrowing a marxist regime.

'It sounds as if you've already made up your mind', she said when I had finished.

'I want to do it', I said.

There was a pause and then she smiled. I knew she could appreciate the excitement

322

that was welling within me at the prospects of another action; this one far from the Congo jungles and bushveld, on a tropical paradise island.

'Then go', she said.

Mike and I immediately fell to planning the visit.

We met either at his home at Hilton just outside Pietermaritzburg or he came to the garage in Smith Street where, in between my fielding telephone enquiries and seeing to clients, we saw to the finer details.

It was decided that Mike should go in disguise. As a Congo mercenary he had enjoyed and maintained a high profile — exactly the opposite to myself who had always preferred to work out of the limelight. The effect of this had been to propel Mike into the public eye while I was left with the reputation of an *eminence gris* in Congo politics.

It suited me that way.

And on this occasion it was to work in my favour because, while no snooping Seychellois security officer or customs man was likely to get excited by the name Jerry Puren in a passport, he might well do a double take if he saw Mike Hoare's name. In the event Mike grew a beard and secured a passport in the name of Thomas Boarel — the surname being achieved by adding one letter to his original name and changing another.

I began researching the history and politics of this tiny Indian Ocean Island state that we were plotting to subvert. Until then I had only been aware of the Seychelles, if at all, as a place where South African tourists went for tropical paradise holidays and where, occasionally, the Americans got huffy because of Soviet naval fleets using the port facilities.

It transpired the island had a population of sixty three thousand people living on ninety two islands in the Western Indian Ocean. The people spoke French, English and a Creole dialect and the main sources of income were tourism, fishing and copra exports. The island had been a British colony until June 29 1976 when it became independent within the Commonwealth. The first elected Prime Minister was James Mancham, a playboy type politician who drew most of his support from the business and conservative lobbies.

In June 1977 France Albert René, the opposition leader, carried out a successful coup with the assistance of Tanzanian forces and declared the islands a one party state with his Seychelles People's Progressive Party being that one party.

Although President René ostensibly adopted a non aligned approach there appeared substantial concern in western circles about his leaning towards the Soviets.

Mike let it be known he had also done his homework. He constantly hammered the theme that the Seychellois were desperately unhappy with the René Government and on the brink of revolt. Only the presence of the Tanzanian forces kept him in power. He told how the youth were being enrolled into the National Youth Service and that education above a certain level was being given only to people in the NYS. Even worse, René was favouring the Soviets and about to give them major facilities on the islands which would severely effect the balance of power in the Indian Ocean. The Marxist president, claimed Mike, was also as thick as thieves with Berenger's MMM party in Mauritius so it was likely those islands also would soon go 'Red'. And finally, it appeared as if there was offshore oil in the Seychelles which would be of vital interest to South Africa if only a friendly government ruled the islands.

When I asked details of whom exactly was behind the planned coup and who was putting up the money, he was slightly more reticent. All I gathered was that the key figure was sitting in London and operating through Seychellois dissidents living in Durban.

Finally we were ready for the reconnaissance operation. Mike telephoned to say the tickets were booked and that we would be leaving on Sunday. For security arrangements we were to travel separately and pretend we did not know each other. I was to meet Mike at Jan Smuts Airport. Arrangements had been made on the other side to meet certain unnamed dissidents who would give us more intelligence on the situation.

Julia took me to the airport. It had been eleven years since I had said goodbye to her knowing that I was heading into potential danger. She clasped my hand and squeezed it once. There would be no tears or drama in the parting — it had been like that in the Congo and it would be so now. I waved my last goodbye and joined the queue through the security checkpoint.

Then I was on the aircraft thundering down the runway.

I lay back in my seat and permitted myself a few moments to enjoy the irony of the situation.

Fifteen years earlier I had been instrumental in bringing Mike back into the Congo operations and now he was bringing me into the Seychelles action. Then we had been fighting marxist supported rebels in the Congo and now we were squaring up to a Marxist supported Government on an Indian Ocean island. But then we had been fifteen years younger.

48

Reconnaissance

The British Airways Boeing touched down smoothly at Pointe Larue airport on Mahe Island and taxied to the terminus. Travel weary passengers rose to stretch their legs; transit passengers to the left and disembarking ones to the right. Mike and I stiffened slightly in the oppressive tropical heat as we emerged from the air-conditioned aircraft. Then we were across the apron and into the airport buildings.

It had been a quiet flight during which I had spent most of my time reading. Mike, correctly, was taking security seriously.

We had agreed we were to be complete strangers to each other on the aircraft. We had only met surreptitiously for a few seconds at Jan Smuts — on the balcony of the departure hall. Mike had momentarily stood beside me and passed a folded newspaper. I opened it and there was a letter inside with the names of various Seychelles contacts. The *modus operandi* was clear enough. Mike would concentrate on an overview of the military situation while I, less public a figure, would make the main contacts with the Seychelles dissidents. Two names on the list caught my eye — Madam Marie Ange and Gerard Hoarau.

The passengers straggled off the aircraft. Customs and passport formalities were completed within minutes.

We sailed through as tourists Puren and Boarel with no problems.

I went to the car hire desk and claimed the car that had been left there in my name.

Mike, acting as if we had just met, came over and asked for a lift into town. I instantly agreed.

Half an hour later we had checked into adjoining rooms at the island's Reef Hotel. From my window I had a vista of the azure sea and startlingly white sands lined with palm trees. What an incomparably magnificent island, truly a paradise, I thought.

Mike entered and we began planning our day. Our transport problems had been solved with the hire of the little Mini Moke. In days to come it would see sterling action. With myself at the wheel and Mike in the passengers seat we were to crisscross that island for hours on end; ostensibly tourists enjoying the sights or, if really challenged, two businessmen sizing up the island for more tourist developments.

Methodically and professionally we checked all the key installations on the island; the army bases, the Tanzanian army camp in town which was later to become the headquarters of the People's Defence Force headquarters, the radio station and the police station.

We checked the approaches to these installations, possible fields of fire, measured out mortar distances, explored likely sites for road blocks and took careful note of the numbers of troops we came across, discreetly studied their weapons and tried to assess the indefinable something whereby a professional can tell whether the man he is facing comes from a disciplined force or a rabble.

By week's end we must have easily done six hundred to eight hundred kilometers.

We were careful to stay in the hotel in the evenings, however, as there were numerous roadblocks after dark. In the hotel even, we had to be cautious because we had been warned the bars were full of security agents in plain clothes, listening for talk of subversion.

It was towards the end of the week, however, that the most dangerous part of the assignment had to be executed.

We had to make contact with the dissidents and in particular with their leader. Mike had already decided that he should not be the one to make the contact and so I took the lead.

Mike gave me the telephone number of Marie Ange — the name I had seen on the list. The number was the central exchange of a bank and I was put through to the girl immediately; it was a lilting and youthful voice. I identified myself as a tourist and claimed we had a mutual friend who had suggested we should link up. We arranged to meet at Bon Vallon beach next day.

The next day I took the Mini Moke to the beach for the rendezvous.

I parked under the trees and waited. On cue a small car pulled to a halt nearby and a beautiful young girl climbed out. I knew it was our primary contact. The girl was dressed in a flowing sarong that could not hide the fine lines of her youthful body. She turned her head in my direction and with only the slightest hint of movement implied I should follow her.

I kicked off my shoes and, without looking as if I was in pursuit, tailed her.

Unselfconsciously she unhooked her sarong and revealed herself to be dressed in the briefest bikini. I was struck with admiration at the golden brown smoothness of her skin, the luxuriant glossiness of her black hair.

A moment's mirth seized me; in my mind's eye I saw myself as some less flamboyant James Bond and for a few seconds even contemplated introducing myself as such. Then instantly I gathered myself. We were not playing games.

The girl, Marie Ange, stopped walking and I caught up to her.

'You are, Mister Puren?' she said in flowing French.

I nodded.

'Good, we have been waiting several days for you. Please walk with me and pretend we are first acquaintances. M Hoarau is waiting to meet you farther up the beach. He is a prominent person here and cannot be seen contacting you openly.'

I nodded and we walked on in silence for perhaps another five hundred meters. Then Marie swerved off the beach and into the shade of some trees lining the coast. Our main contact was waiting for us.

Hoarau was a typical Islander, swarthy, good looking and casually dressed. Marie introduced us and we shook hands. In the first few moments of discussion I discovered why Hoarau had to be careful — he was chief of customs on the island and was known as a Mancham man.

We had half an hour's intense discussion together under the trees, both of us ceaselessly watching the movements of people around us, tense in case we were being observed. Hoarau quickly sketched the latest available information about troop strengths and dispositions on the island. He also gave me background on popular feeling among the Seychellois and endorsed what Mike had said about the dissatisfaction with René.

'The islands are ripe for revolt — it just needs the impetus to get them going and René will be out,' were his parting words.

I was not to see Hoarau again for some considerable time.

Next day I went to visit a distant relative, Frank Puren. Frank was a prominent stationer in Victoria and before that had held a senior position in the Island's parastatal bus company. We had a warm and wide ranging discussion about the island although Frank was quite unaware of the import of my visit. It was an enlightening chat because Frank had been a founder member of René's party and was in high party favour.

We also knew that an old Congo mercenary acquaintance of ours was on the island; none other than Bob Noddyn, who had taken part in the mercenary-Katangese revolt of 1967. After the Congo Bob had retired to the Seychelles, bought himself a restaurant and become a colonel in the island's top commando unit. After careful thought, however, we decided it would be better not to approach Bob at this stage; old mercenaries have an innate feel for the unusual or the conspiratorial and the last thing we wanted at this moment was to tip Bob off about our intentions.

At week's end we had done our work and found time for a little fun on the side.

As we filed back on to the jet I wondered when and under what circumstances I would again find myself back on the island.

Perhaps it was better that I did not know.

49

Planning

Back in the comfort of our homes Mike and I got down to the serious business of compiling a feasibility study for our employers. I made a relief map of the island and meticulously plotted all the major installations and dispositions on Mahe Island — the main island — while Mike began drawing up the report.

After hours of discussion on both Mahe and back at home we had come to the same conclusion; it was indeed possible to stage a coup that would overthrow President René and return James Mancham to power.

We worked from the basic assumption — provided by Hoarau — that the civilian population would support a coup and that there were elements in the police who would throw their weight behind us. The original five phase plan was a masterpiece of simplicity.

Phase One had us quietly infiltrate an advance party of about fifteen men on to the islands. They would secure a few safe houses and, over a few days, arms would be landed from yachts and cached at strategic points around the island.

Phase Two would see the same advance guard — at the given word - bringing the weapons in vehicles to the airport and then seizing the airport control tower. They would then guide in an aircraft loaded with mercenaries from a nearby jump off place — probably Kenya or the Comores Islands.

Phase Three begins when the mercenary force arrives, is armed and despatched to knock out the cannon above the airfield and neutralise the Tanzanian army base near the airport.

Phase Four sees other mercenary elements racing into Victoria and seizing the key installations, the President, his advisors and suspect senior police officers.

Phase Five involves the civilian uprising to mop up any points of resistance.

The total plan would entail about three million dollars and would require one hundred and twenty men. Mike remained cautious about revealing names of figures behind the coup attempt but I remained convinced that Mancham was being helped by the multi-millionaire arms dealer, Adnam Kashoggi.

Although I was deeply involved in the planning of the coup, I suddenly realised that I had actually very little knowledge of whom exactly was behind it. Mike was purposefully vague about the detail and — being an old Congo hand myself

— I accepted his reasons.

It was while we were still working on the details, however, that I had my first twinges about the standing of our employers. It transpired they had a battle scraping together the money they owed us for the feasibility study — small as it was. It also appeared they had even battled to get enough cash together for our trip to the Seychelles.

Kashoggi?

It began to look less likely. Not unnaturally I began to worry about where they were going to get the money for an actual coup but Mike placated me.

A second important question arose; where did the South African Government stand in all this? I asked Mike the question directly one day, pointing out that we would be foolish to become involved in something which did not have at least the indulgence of Pretoria.

Mike smiled widely and waved a placatory hand.

'The National Intelligence Service already know. They're taking a keen interest. Don't worry about them'.

Little did I know then that Mike had been in touch with the National Intelligence Service officer, Martin Dolinschek, alias Donaldson, based in Durban. He had sketched the outline of the plan to Dolinschek and he, in turn, had taken it to his superiors in the then Bureau for State Security. They had turned it down flat but Dolinschek kept contacts with Mike.

We completed the plan and Mike disappeared for a while. I received my money and sat back awaiting developments. They did not take long in coming and they were the last thing we expected or needed.

In November that year President René suddenly declared martial law, said he knew of a plot by Durban based mercenaries to overthrow his Government and detained about twenty islanders — including our friend Hoarau.

It was a bit of a shock to hear our plan had been rumbled so quickly but Mike assured me that the unhappy turn of events did not mean the whole thing was off. René, he said, had got hold of the wrong end of the stick.

It was not until nearly a year later that René was to release the detainees. Hoarau immediately made for South Africa and set himself up in Durban.

The plotting for the coup went ahead. With Mike's concurrence I began making some discreet enquiries about personnel. My task was to pull together the advance guard who would infiltrate the island as tourists and seize the control tower on A-Day. I did not have far to look. In the Assegai MOTH shellhole on the Bluff in Durban, my shellhole, there were a number of young policemen based on the Bluff who used to drop in for drinks. They were tough and responsible young men, well trained and disciplined. Cautiously I approached several of them and asked if they would be interested. The response was electric. Within days a half dozen had signalled their willingness to accompany me. Unbeknown to me, however, the men had taken the matter up with their station commander who had circumspectly indicated there would be no objection to them taking part if they agreed to do it in their own time. Also unbeknown to me — almost inevitably — the intelligence services picked up the news that I was recruiting policemen.

Dolincheck himself came to hear of it through a routine report and had immediately warned Mike of what he thought was a security breach.

Quite unaware of all this action, I went ahead and arranged a meeting between Hoarau and the policemen. It was a private occasion and the Seychelles conspirator left highly impressed by the calibre of men I would be able to deliver to the coup force.

But none of the policemen were destined to go to the Islands. There followed eighteen months of backwards and forwarding as the backers of the coup plot blew hot and cold about the idea. One minute the plan had been accepted and we were to begin recruiting more men. The next minute it would be off — the backers had pulled out. One day Mike would be promising action within days and the next he would be woefully admitting there was nothing happening. Always he would complain about the dissidents lack of resolve.

'I don't believe these people really want to overthrow René at all', he said once in one of his blacker moments.

I continued even keeled with the business of selling cars, keeping a watching eye on events, torn with hopes that it would go ahead and I could be in the action, and a sneaking wish that it wouldn't, so my comfort and security would not be jeopardised.

Once a week another of the Seychelles plotters, Gonzague D'Offay, dropped by the garage and, amid the flurry of daily business, we would find time to chat and speculate about the prospects of the coup coming off.

Often he would 'phone from our office to London for instructions and an exchange of information. His contact on that side was somebody called Eddie Camille who served in the Seychelles Foreign Office in London and whom I took to be one of the chief conspirators.

Slowly the core group in the coup plotting of that time crystallized; Mike, myself, Hoarau, D'Offay and Hoarau's brother, Owen.

Mike, being in Pietermaritzburg, was not always at the meetings.

On several occasions the Seychellois exiles suggested other leadership figures for the coup attempt.

At that stage it was still not a *fait accompli* that Mike would be leading the coup attempt. One name mentioned was George Schroeder, the former V Commando OC who had taken over for a caretaker three months after Peters had left. Schroeder was living in Cape Town and running a business. I counseled against Schroeder and urged them to stick with Mike.

But slowly my interest in the coup attempt began to wane. I told myself that it was highly unlikely that it would ever come off. As interesting as the chats were with the exiles I began to wonder if they were not really like so many scores of other exiled groups throughout the world; ceaselessly plotting the overthrow of their governments with little chance of success. I resigned myself again to the routine of running a business, accepted that my Seychelles 'adventure' was over.

50

We fly out

It was a Friday in November 1981 when it finally all came together. Mike arrived in a great hurry at the garage and asked if he could speak to me about the Seychelles.

The floor was full of customers. I had two 'phone calls on hold and a pile of paper work in front of me.

'It *is* that urgent. I owe it to you and I want you to come.'

I could sense his excitement and instantly I realised this was not just another wild goose chase — pardon the pun.

'I can't talk now, Mike. You can see the position. Julia and I are going to a convention in the mountains this weekend and I'll drop by your home on the way back.'

Mike nodded his agreement and left the office, bustling his way through the knots of customers and out into the late Friday afternoon rush. He looked like a person with a mission.

That weekend Julia and I attended a mini Lions' convention at the Drakensberg Gardens Hotel far in the country.

I was deeply preoccupied, wondering how the coup was to be arranged, who was going with us, what role I should have.

Julia sensed my mood but did not press me. She must have known it was the Seychelles thing again but kept her counsel. As always she knew that I would go to her for guidance and, again as always, she was prepared to wait patiently for that moment.

On our return to Durban on the Sunday we dropped by Mike's home in Hilton. With scant ceremony he hurried me through into his den and ushered me into a comfortable chair.

'It's on, Jerry. This time it is for real. The backers are there and the equipment is ready. I want you to come.'

So it had indeed come to fruition. All the planning and waiting had not been in vain. Again I was aware of the great division within myself; the desire on the one hand to be going into action and, on the other hand, concern for my family and security. It took several seconds to resolve.

'When?' I asked.

'On Wednesday this week,' replied Mike.

The time span momentarily took my breath away. After nearly thirty months of plotting and discussing it seemed inconceivable that it could all happen so suddenly, so immediately. My mind swam with logistical problems.

'I don't have a passport', I said.

'Then get one tomorrow', he replied.

I nodded agreement and we began discussing details. It became clear to me exactly how much work Mike had put into preparing for the attack.

'Where are the arms?' was my first question.

Mike waved his hands dismissively and said they were already cached on the island. I asked about manpower.

'There are fifty men who will be leaving with us and a large advance guard is already in place on the island. Together with civilians on the islands we can count on a hundred to one hundred and fifty men.'

'Where are Mancham and Hoarau?' I asked.

'They are waiting in Nairobi for us to accomplish the coup and then they will fly in and take up the reins.'

I asked what my immediate task would be. Mike held up two fingers.

'Your first job will be to take and secure the control tower at Mahe Airport when we go into action. The second will be to liaise with Bob Noddyn and Frank Puren to keep them out of circulation on the day we begin the operation.'

Quickly Mike explained the other details. We would be going as a sporting/social group to the Seychelles with the quaint name of the Honourable Ancient Order of Frothblowers.

I was designated Assistant Master of Ceremonies.

The Master of Ceremonies, Mike told me, would be Peter Duffy, a freelance photographer from Durban and a former Congo mercenary I had heard about but never met.

We were going to leave from Pretoria on Tuesday directly for the Seychelles. I immediately suspected connivance with the South African Government in the coup attempt. A refreshing change, I thought, from the timidity they had shown over involvement in the Congo affair all those years before.

Little did I know the subtle power shifts that had taken place in the preceding months. The advent of P W Botha to the post of Prime Minister had spelt the end of the primacy of the old BOSS — Bureau For State Security. It had been converted into an intelligence gathering unit under the control of the brilliant young academic, Neil Barnard.

In a complete reversal of what had happened during the Congo days, Military Intelligence (DMI) now gained primacy in the intelligence community and it was to these people that Mike's request for help was channelled and it was from them, steeped in the arts of clandestine warfare, that he had received assistance — allegedly on instructions from the top.

The assistance was to include AK-47 rifles, hand grenades, rocket launchers (which were not taken) and radios.

At one time a training area in the western Transvaal was also to be made available.

Mike thrust an air ticket into my hand, made out for Johannesburg. He also handed over one thousand rands in twenty rand denominations. The balance of fourteen thousand rands was to be paid on completion of the job.

'The whole thing should take about a week. Confirm your acceptance by Monday, Jerry', he said.

I nodded agreement. As I took the money I did not know the background to the offer Mike had made to me — his insistence that I went.

Later I was to find out that Martin Dolincheck had warned Mike against taking 'politicians' like myself. Whether it was Dolincheck's personal wish or the instructions of his employers that I be kept away I never did find out. Apparently when Mike broached the issue with the exiles they were adamant that I should accompany them. And in the end it was irrelevant because Mike did take me — with all the consequences.

Mike indicated that we should join the ladies for tea in the lounge. Throughout tea I sat in a fever of impatience. Julia sensed my mood and several times I caught her looking askance at me.

In the car on the way home I told her the whole story and broke the news that I would be going with Mike. She accepted it stoically although offering token opposition, principally, because of distrust of Mike's planning and expertise and the lack of a contingency plan. But from years of adventuring she knew that when I made up my mind there was little that could change it.

The next two days were a flurry of activity. I went to the Department of Internal Affairs in Durban and explained I urgently needed my passport renewed. By next day it was done. That Tuesday, November 23, I drove to the primary school where Julia taught and picked her up. Skillfully she drove through the mid afternoon traffic to Durban's Louis Botha Airport.

We said brief farewells, kissed and I was through the security check point. As a last gesture Julia pushed some bandages into my pockets. I smiled at the implied pessimism and then was swinging away through the security check point. A mad whirl of events seemed to be thrusting me forward.

At four that afternoon the aircraft touched down at Jan Smuts Airport. I gathered my holdall and walked outside to where, as Mike had instructed, I found a chartered bus.

The bus was surrounded by mercenaries — forty seven in all.

My first glance told me they were a tough and competent looking bunch. Most were youngsters, a number still serving members of crack South African Defence Force Active Reserve units such as the Reconnaissance and Parachute Regiments. There were a few old Congo hands as well like Tullio Moneta and Peter Duffy, and a sprinkling of former Rhodesian army specialists from units such as the SAS and Selous Scouts. The men, dressed casually in shorts and open-necked shirts, running shoes and sandals, seemed in high spirits.

Peter Duffy met me on the steps of the bus. He was a burly and exuberant man who thrust a book into my hands and asked me to take a nominal roll. As the men entered the bus I asked their names and ticked them off. Once it was completed I handed it back and he gave the signal for the bus to start. I did not know a single person on the bus.

It was only as we headed out of the airport toll gates that I found we were aimed not for Pretoria as suggested by Mike, but for Ermelo.

'And after that?' I demanded of Peter Duffy.

'Mbabane in Swaziland', he said.

At Ogies on the way to Ermelo the bus stopped at the nearest bottle store and our contingent of mercenaries poured off the bus, returning shortly afterwards loaded down with beer. I looked inquiringly at Peter Duffy and he shrugged.

From my Congo years I had learnt, often at my own cost, that serious soldiering and drinking don't go hand in hand.

The men clambered back on the bus and we roared off on the road to Ermelo. The party grew merrier and the men more boisterous.

We arrived at the Ermelo Holiday Inn to find Mike already booked in and awaiting our appearance. Our task force straggled off the bus and launched their first assault — against the ladies bar.

Drinks flowed freely and within a short time it was quite apparent that our disciplined group of adventurers were getting beyond themselves.

Mike came to my room with me and sprawled in a chair.

'Do you believe it is coming together now?' he asked at one point.

I smiled broadly and replied that I could see it was happening but I could hardly believe it.

We began discussing the coup. Mike told me the code word for Mancham would be *Cloudburst* while our group would be called *Fairy Queen.* Once the coup had been effected we would use the codes to call Mancham and his advisors in from Nairobi. There was also some vague talk of the Kenyan Government sending reinforcements once the island had been taken.

It was just before we made ready to go down to supper that Peter Duffy burst into the room.

'Problems downstairs', he said curtly. 'One of our people has punched a local in the face after a row over a girl.

Hoare was furious.

'What can we do to smooth things out? The last thing we need now is a criminal charge against one of our people.'

'I think the injured party will take money', said Duffy.

After some discussion it was agreed they would pay the man three hundred Rands for 'medical costs'.

Actually it was hush money.

I believe we explained our generosity by saying the club could not afford a scandal.

The incident left a nasty taste in my mouth and began raising some serious questions about the quality of some of the men we had aboard.

Dinner went off without a hitch and afterwards we all gathered in a conference room in the hotel.

Mike asked me to give a pep talk to the men and I filled them in with details about the Seychelles. I spoke of the free and easy lifestyle of the people, of the political situation, of the potential for revolt among the community and of our role. The group of mercenaries listened intently to what I was saying. Afterwards several came to ask questions.

Mike bustled around telling the section leaders that there was to be a meeting in my room because he had some important information to tell us all. I left early and before they arrived, I put a telephone call through to Julia in Durban.

'Where are you?' she asked.

'Ermelo, and tomorrow we go to Swaziland.'

There was a seconds silence and then she laughed.

'I told you I didn't trust Mike. You were supposed to be in Pretoria tonight.'

I tried to placate her fears. We talked a few moments longer and then said goodbye.

334

'I'll be back in a week', I said.

It was in fact to be nineteen months before I was to see her again.

There was a knock on the door and the section leaders began trooping into my room. I learnt the attack force had been divided up into four groups with different objectives.

Tullio Moneta, ex-Congo hand, was in charge of A Group which consisted of eighteen men and whose main task would be the securing of Pointe Larue army base.

I and two others were mustered in B Group whose task it was to take the air control tower and establish a radio comms system.

Mike Webb, ex-British Army, was in command of the sixteen man C Group whose job it was to take the radio station and the army camp behind it.

Group D was under Bernard Carey, then already on the island, consisting of six men whose onerous task it was to capture State House and the police headquarters.

Mike arrived and we got down to business.

It began with a bombshell.

'There has been a slight change of plan, gentlemen. We do not have the arms on the island so will be taking them in with us.'

The effect was electric. Consternation registered on everybody's faces and Mike was peppered with questions about how it would work.

Rather like a magician pulling a rabbit from a bag, he presented a sturdy looking holdall emblazoned with the badge of the *Frothblowers*. Deftly he unzipped a false bottom to the holdall and pulled it back to reveal a dismantled AK-47 nestling in carefully constructed polystyrene moulds at the base of the holdall. He zippered it up again and left the bag standing on the dressing table.

'No customs man is going to rumble that', he said.

I had to admit that the job had been extremely professionally done but within myself I knew the old adage that the more that was left to go right, the more was certain to go wrong. But it was too late a stage to argue the toss with Mike and I reluctantly let it go. Had we taken a strong stand there and then, how different might things have been.

It was while we were talking that my room telephone rang. Mike answered.

It was Hoarau wanting to get the latest details.

Mike told him that everything was going according to plan.

They chattered for a little longer — no apparent concern about using a public telephone to discuss the details — and then Mike returned the receiver to its cradle.

'Hoarau says they are waiting and ready for us to make our move.'

The section leaders were by now gingerly trying the holdall for weight and size. One by one they declared themselves willing to take the chance. Mike indicated that my holdall would not have a rifle but some hand radios. He also said we would be taking some other bags into the Seychelles which would be stuffed with toys — it would be a blind. Mike made it clear that our first intention was not to launch an immediate attack on the island but to infiltrate our party and await the word for him to act. He was unable to tell us exactly when that would be but most likely it would be within a few days of our arrival.

It had been a long day and one by one, the mercenaries excused themselves and turned in for bed. I lay awake for a long time thinking of the pending coup and hoping that the sudden changes of plan, lack of security and signs of indiscipline among the men would not presage greater problems.

I slept restlessly that night.

Early next morning the bus load of mercenaries were on their way across the Swaziland border and thundering towards Mbabane.

At the small Matsapa Airport we disembarked and began to board the sixty seater Swazi Fokker F28 on the apron. This was another shock as I had expected we would be going into the Seychelles on a bigger aircraft among more people. Here we were going in almost as a task force in our chartered aircraft with only a handful of other luckless fellow passengers.

Uneasily I watched as our precious Frothblowers' bags with their explosive contents were slung around by the ground handlers at the airport.

There was a moment of unendurable tension when Swazi security men with metal detectors advanced on the piles of luggage.

'Christ, no', I heard Mike say under his breath.

Incredibly, the officials ignored our heap of stacked bags and concentrated on the loose items of baggage belonging to the civilians. A wave of the hand from the security officer and the apron crews were slinging our bags into the hold.

Then everything was stowed and we were aboard, an excited and tense band of adventurers on a dangerous mission.

The aircraft had hardly cleared the Swaziland hills before the mercenaries were back into the booze. Mike came over and spoke confidentially to me.

'When we get to Mahe, Jerry, I want you to help take charge of the group and see they don't drink too much. I want them ready for action at a moment's notice.'

I took one look around at the amount of booze being drunk and suppressed a chortle. Did Mike think I was some sort of magic fairy that I could take forty seven bruising mercenaries under my wing and guard them from temptations on a Paradise Island?

I promised him, without too much conviction, that I would try.

Mike confided that he was not sure when the coup would actually take place; he first had to be briefed by the advance party already on the Island and then decide. As the next day would be a Thursday, it had been decided to give the men a free day. I urged him to make his move as soon as possible as I could foresee problems if the men really got in their cups on the island.

'My advance party will guide us on timing', he replied.

Little did I know then that Mike had in fact planned the coup for the November 25 when President René was going to be out of the country on a visit to France, but the drunkenness of the men had persuaded him that nobody would be in a fit state the next day.

And little did either of us know that our advance party — in fact no more than eight people — had been living the good life to such an extent that they had done very little effective intelligence work.

From the quality of the photographs they took of the key installations I can only guess that they were drunk most of the time.

Certainly there was a fair dent in the coup treasury by the time we arrived on the island.

51

Disaster

The Pointe Larue Airport on Mahe Island was oppressively hot as we clambered down the stairs from the Swazi Fokker.

Although the men had been drinking steadily during the flight they all suddenly became aware of the danger they were facing and became quieter and more intense.

We straggled across the apron and made for the passport and customs checkpoints. Passport control was a piece of cake. Soon we were walking through the customs sheds towards the exits.

Most people in their life have had occasion to try and smuggle a little something through customs and so are aware of the empty feeling as one walks ostensibly unconcernedly past the customs officials while all the time the contraband article snuggling in the luggage lies on ones thoughts like a mill stone.

Can you conceive what it was like to walk through a customs' check point with forty seven pieces of contraband carried by forty seven different people?

It very nearly worked . . . but not quite.

The advance party, Robert Simms, Mike Hoare's brother-in-law, and his girl friend Susan Ingles, Mike Hoare's sister-in-law, ex-Rhodesians Aubrey Brooks and Roger England, South African Desmond Botes, Britons Kenneth Dalgleish and Bernard Carey and American Charles Dukes, had arrived at the airport in several cars to await our arrival.

In the boots of the vehicles nestled the assembled AK-47s that the men had taken through Seychelles' customs a week earlier in a 'dry run'.

Also waiting at the airport to greet us was Martin Dolincheck, a South African National Intelligence Service agent, who was to serve as Hoare's intelligence advisor.

Dolincheck had come to the island under the name Anton Lubic and had promptly excited the interest of the Seychellois authorities with the way he scouted the islands strategic installations.

Nonchalantly the mercenaries sauntered through the customs exchanging ribald comments, looking for all the world like a slightly boozy rugby team.

Nobody was asked to open their bags.

One by one they clambered into the waiting hotel bus and found themselves seats.

Two customs officers were on duty. Unerringly I made for the younger one, placed my bag on the counter and smiled.

'Anything to declare?'

I shook my head and he waved me through.

One good turn deserves another — I pulled a little Frothblowers' lapel insignia from my pocket and gave it to the customs officer.

He smiled broadly and nodded his thanks.

As I moved off I cast a backward glance.

Only a few more to go and everything still sweet.

Out of the corner of my eye I noted one of our people, Beck, a tough former paratrooper.

He *looked* suspicious, I said to myself with a sinking feeling. He fidgeted and appeared uncomfortable. I had a last glance of him as he was weighing himself on a scale.

Then I was into the blinding sunlight and mingling with the mercenaries who were busy stacking their bags on the roof of the bus. Some had already taken their seats.

I exchanged a few words with the men and then climbed into the cool interior of the bus.

There was a tropical torpidness — a drowsiness that belied what was about to happen.

Suddenly the spell was broken.

Peter Duffy came bounding from the customs shed and on to the bus. His eyes were wide with concern, his voice taut.

'One of our people has had his baggage searched. They found fruit on one of the civilians and now they are searching all the bags. They've found the AK.'

Duffy's voice cut through the torpor of the day like a knife.

There was an instant stunned silence. And then the action shifted rapidly to the exterior.

From the bus window I saw Beck — it was his bag they had searched — come striding from the building, clutching his holdall with an angry customs officer in tow and a woman assistant.

The customs officer — he was the elderly one — grabbed Beck on his shoulder. Beck swung around and planted a blow squarely on the man's jaw.

His head snapped back and he collapsed on the ground.

The woman screamed.

The mercenaries stood transfixed. The bus was deathly silent.

Time stood in frozen frame.

The film suddenly turned from slow motion to double time. A police officer burst from a small office near the customs' office and began shouting for us all to get down and have our baggage searched again. He was fumbling with his holster as he shouted.

I knew the game was up; instinct and those years' experience in the Congo took over.

There was no time to hesitate or bewail events, because only speed and determination could extricate us.

'Get down boys, the game's up,' I shouted to the men in the bus, many of them still unaware of the drama that had just played itself out in the customs' hall.

The response was instantaneous.

The mercenaries poured off the bus while several others began slinging down the bags from the roof racks.

Without any panic the men quickly searched for their own numbered bags and unzipped the false bottoms.

For a few seconds the area around the bus was dotted with kneeling figures as they expertly withdrew their rifle parts and began assembling them. The lazy afternoon heat rang with the clicks of rifles being assembled, magazines inserted and cocking handles pulled. For those few moments there appeared to be a hiatus; the mercenaries assembling their weapons, the civilians and officials standing nearby stunned by the turn of events.

The lull was smashed suddenly with the crash of a single rifle shot.

I did not see who fired the shot but it transpired it was an accidental round loosed off by a fumbling mercenary, an American called Gribbon, as he tried to assemble his weapon.

As fate would have it, it was that single shot which would account for our only fatality. A young student and former paratrooper, Johan Fritz, was struck. By the time I reached him it was all over. Fritz was lying on his back in the customs' hall with two of our people bending over him — one of them a doctor whom Mike had recruited for the operation.

I had seen enough battle casualties to know the boy was finished. The bullet had entered his chest and blown the aortal part of the heart away. Blood was trickling from his nose and mouth.

There was another burst of fire and Esperon, as I discovered his name to be later, the elderly customs man who had rumbled the plot, staggered back with a wound in his shoulder.

Matters were slithering from bad to worse.

Desperately I looked around for Mike.

Nowhere to be seen.

And Duffy?

Again I could not find him.

There was nothing for it but to take charge.

Already the mercenaries were beginning to fire haphazardly, wasting ammunition and endangering innocent lives.

I detailed a section to push out along the Victoria Road and establish a roadblock in the direction of Pointe Larue. The perimeter was secured.

I noticed Mercenary Dunlop standing around without direction and told him to take some men to seize the control tower. This was done instantly.

The civilians were my next concern. I was determined that none of them should be hurt in what was to come. Quickly I rounded them up and herded them into a room in the airport building.

In the entrance hall, crowded on to a single bench and numbed with fear, I found our three little *Air Swazi* hostesses. Their eyes were fixed in horror on Fritz's body.

I apologised to them for what was happening and promised they would be safe. I beckoned them to follow and ushered them into an inner room at the airport.

A number of others were in the room, many sobbing quietly and I could see real terror on their faces. I tried to placate them but realised they were probably too shocked by the turn of events.

Much has since been made about us 'taking hostages'. Nothing could be further from the truth. I simply wanted to keep them in a place where they could not be hurt.

Rapidly I moved around the terminal building dousing the lights. Duffy and I held a hasty O group and dished out the hand radios to the roadblock and control tower parties.

Still no Mike Hoare.

It was getting dark when he eventually turned up.

By that time the mercenaries were standing-to around the perimeter and we were awaiting events.

As soon as the shooting had begun Mike had ordered the advance group, already in possession of their weapons in their car, to take out the Tanzanian Army base near the airport.

'Why the hell did you tell the men to get down from the buses?' demanded Mike.

It took me seconds to fill him in on the details, making it quite clear that we had no hope of brazening our way through a baggage check. Events had overtaken us and there had been no option but to take the offensive. And it was damned fortunate I had because nobody else had been around to take charge.

'More important, where have you been?' I demanded.

Mike replied he had gone down to the Tanzanian Army camp.

'Were any troops there?'

'None,' replied Mike.

Little did I know then that Mike had in fact detailed four men to seize the camp — and they had failed.

The four — Bernard Carey, Roger England, Aubrey Brooks and Charles Dukes — had got there in a car clutching their AK-47s.

On springing from the vehicle they had ordered the sentry at the gate to surrender.

The sentry, like a good soldier, did no such thing.

Instead he opened fire, forcing the retreat of the attackers.

The failure was partly Mike's fault.

He had at his disposal twenty three still serving citizen force members of an SADF recce unit; tough, experienced men who could have taken the sentry post out in seconds.

A few more men and the whole camp would have been rolled up.

Instead he sent men who had not handled rifles for months — in some cases years.

By the time a back-up force under Mike appeared the whole camp had been alerted and the mercenaries were immediately engaged in a fierce firefight.

Running low on ammunition Mike and his men had soon decided to retire to the terminal building.

At the terminal the tension was building by the second.

From the communications' room we could hear the radio chattering furiously as the word of the assault was broadcast to other units around the island.

I knew that within hours everything the Seychellois Government could pull together would be thrown at us.

340

Although confident we could hold them for a while I was desperately worried that our ammunition would run low. And, if they sent armoured cars in strength, I knew we had nothing to stop them.

It was time for decisions. I turned to Mike.

'What now?'

Mike panicked.

I find it painful to recount the behaviour of a former Congo comrade-in-arms and a friend in civilian life, but there is no other way to describe Mike's actions except as panic.

The unexpected turn of events had completely unsettled him.

It was immediately apparent he had no fall back plan and found difficulty in coping with the complexity of the problems thrust on him.

The first thing he did was tell me he had a 'hit list' of one hundred to one hundred and fifty names on him.

I advised him to destroy it immediately.

Then he said he had tapes in his suitcase from Mancham that were to be broadcast over Seychelles radio once we had taken the station.

They later transpired not to be tapes from Mancham at all but from Hoarau.

I told him to destroy those as well or put them in a safe place.

I again asked what we were going to do.

Mike thought for a moment.

'I'll wait until tomorrow.'

'You can't wait. If you wait now you are lost. There is plenty of transport available to get the men into town; buses, cars, everything. The whole island is in confusion and they don't know our strength. If we move quickly we can still pull it off,' I urged.

'I will go to town tomorrow,' Mike repeated doggedly. 'I will first regroup.'

'You've already regrouped,' I almost shouted.

For just a moment there flashed before me the memory of a time many years earlier when I had again tried desperately to make another mercenary leader in another coup attempt show boldness and determination in the face of crisis.

I tried another tack.

'What about the Tanzanians at Pointe Larue. Can't we take them out?'

Mike again shook his head. 'It will be too bloody an affair.'

'Well what then?' I demanded.

Mike pointed skywards and muttered that an Air India Boeing was scheduled to land later that night.

I let the words hang in the air and did not respond.

Intuitively I knew Mike was suggesting we use the Boeing to pull us out of our troubles but I had a personal deep aversion to putting civilians lives at risk.

I realised then that our only hope of salvation if Mike refused to go ahead with the coup was to try and extricate ourselves.

'If you refuse to move then let us try to make contact the Seychelles Government and make a deal.'

Mike thought about it for a moment and nodded his head.

Together Mike, myself, another mercenary and a Seychellois, Manuel Laluette, owner of a garage across the road from the airport who had been brought unwillingly in by our men while establishing their perimeter, left the terminal building and began to walk towards the filling station.

All telephones at the terminal building had been cut off — I had seen to it because I was afraid civilians there might try to communicate with the Government — so only Laluette's filling station had a working telephone.

Mike was later to claim in evidence at his trial he had caught a civilian trying to 'phone the Seychelles Government to make a deal.

What nonsense!

I was the *civilian* . . . I was telephoning in his presence . . . and with his blessing.

My first thought was the pilot of the *Air Swazi* Fokker that had flown us in. I was aware he staying at the Reef Hotel and it occurred to me he might be prepared to act as a link man for us.

With little difficulty I got through to him at the hotel. In a few short sentences I told him we were an attack group of mercenaries who had come to the island to overthrow the Government. We had secured the airport but now wished to make contact with Seychelles Government officials.

Could he assist?

There were a few moments of stunned silence on the other end as the pilot tried to decide whether I was joking or not.

Then he agreed to try.

Fifteen minutes later he telephoned back to say that nobody was interested in talking to us.

I tried another tack.

'Would you perhaps consider trying to fly us out then?'

It was clearly the last straw.

He became almost hysterical in his denunciations of us — all quite unnecessary I thought.

There was no point continuing the conversation so I rang off.

What now?

Mike told me, Manuel and mercenary Steyn, to remain where we were in reach of the telephone while he went back to the terminal building to assess the situation there.

He disappeared into the night and left the three of us exchanging uneasy glances. It was the beginning of the big wait.

Darkness had by then fallen on the islands and a slow but steady drizzle was coursing rivulets down the window panes, turning the foliage shiny and the tarmac slick. From the airport terminal building there was a silence broken only by the occasional mutter of gunfire. The building was mostly in darkness.

We waited for half an hour at the filling station.

Manuel and Steyn, the former an unwilling participant to begin with, began to get impatient.

In our light tropical clothes we were soon soaked. Icy rain water coursed a trickle down my neck.

Another half hour passed and the mercenaries began talking of leaving. There was a bizarre interlude. From the dark a youngish man dressed in jeans and a tee shirt emerged clutching an AK-47. He thrust the rifle into my hands.

'I'm not one of your people. I just joined in at the airport but I think perhaps I had better get out. Do you mind?'

I could hardly suppress a smile — talk about the lure of mercenarying.

'Not at all. Thanks for the help', I replied.

The last minute soldier of fortune melted back into the night and out of the story — never to be heard of again.

Thirty minutes more and I heard a faint voice calling from the airport.

'Jerry, Jerry'.

We made as to move but as if almost on cue we heard the ominous grumble of heavy engines from the direction of Victoria.

Instinctively we ducked down and watched from the safety of the garage wall.

Our worst suspicions were confirmed.

An armoured car emerged from the darkness and glided to a half no more than a hundred meters from us.

Its cannon bore on to the terminal building, there was a few seconds wait then suddenly the muzzle barked flame.

A corresponding flash and crash came from the terminal building.

A second bark.

Another explosion at the terminal building.

Obviously the armoured car was firing blind.

Moments later the mercenaries deployed around the terminal building returned the fire.

There were a score or more winking pinpoints of light in the dark and the flat, sibilant chatter of the rapid firing AK-47s.

From where we stood we were in the direct line of fire so we made rapid moves to extricate ourselves.

Just before we left I heard the high pitched whistle of escaping air from the tyres of the armoured car as the mercenaries' bullets slammed into the vehicle.

Later the car was to trundle into a ditch and become stuck and, later still, the mercenaries were to force the surrender of the crew by the simple expedient of smearing mud on its visors and pouring burning petrol into the interior.

The crew of the car were to suffer the only Seychellois fatalities of the engagement. Next day a young Seychellois officer, Antel, was found dead near the car. All the indications were that he had been executed.

Although nobody found out who had been responsible, the Seychellois' suspicions were to fall on Roger England, destined to be captured and suffer terrible maltreatment.

Manuel deftly guided us around to the back of the garage where a small pond lay. We huddled together for another ten minutes and then Steyn obviously got tired of waiting.

'I'm going', he said, pulling himself to his feet.

'Good luck', I wished as he began slowly walking along the road towards town.

It was the last I was to see of him. Later I learnt he had been intercepted by a mercenary roadblock and had joined the exodus with the rest.

Back at the filling station, meanwhile, the armoured car was slamming round after round into the terminal building and the mercenaries were still returning the fire.

To add to our problems, we came under fire from the northern end of the field, shells dropping dangerously near.

I realised we were now hopelessly cut off from the defenders in the terminal building and suggested to Manuel we leave the garage altogether and move into the cover of rocks immediately behind the building.

He agreed with alacrity.

It was clearly not to be my night. While moving through the pitch dark I fell over a precipice of twelve to fifteen feet and came thudding to earth. My knee was dashed against a rock and for several moments I was speechless with pain.

Manuel came to help me stand but I knew that I was going to be able to move only with the greatest difficulty.

'Go Manuel. There is no point in hanging around here', I said.

After initially rather nobly refusing he acceded, gratefully, and disappeared into the night.

I was now quite alone in a strange country, injured, armed with an AK-47 rifle, in unknown terrain and with not the slightest notion of what was happening to my colleagues.

The armoured car was still firing and a 75mm recoilless was peppering the area as I began crawling up the mountain and away from the action. It was an exhausting effort and every move brought pain flaming anew in my knee. After what seemed ages I reached a spot which I believed would give me cover and rest.

It was at that moment I heard a jet in the night sky.

I managed to locate the source of the sound and saw the fast receding port lights of what looked like a large passenger aircraft.

The *Air India* Boeing, I guessed, having arrived had rapidly assessed the situation and was flying away.

It never crossed my mind that the Boeing might have landed during the scrap because, from where I was, I would not have been able to see any aircraft landing from the south.

Shortly afterwards a fierce firefight developed near Pointe Larue army base and I wondered if the mercenaries were staging a counter thrust after all.

I only learnt later that jumpy patrols of Tanzanian and Seychellois troops had met in the dark and fired at each other under the impression it was the enemy.

After several hours a terrible silence fell over the whole airport and I became convinced that my colleagues had all been captured.

Painstakingly I began scrabbling a small trench in the hard mountain sand. I threw my AK-47 into the hole and covered it up.

I promised myself I was not going to allow myself to be caught like the rest. Little did I know there were precious few others left to be caught. The entire party that came over with me in the Swazi aircraft had escaped on the hijacked Boeing.

Only I and some of the advance party were left.

Our nightmare was about to begin.

52

Capture

By the first faint light of dawn I was able to establish my position. Not more than sixty meters from where I lay hidden behind rocks and bushes, but below me was the airport terminal building. I could see the bullet pock-marked building.

Many windows stared sightlessly from empty frames.

Of more immediate concern, however, were the scores of troops I could see deployed along the road immediately below me. Olive green army vehicles and several armoured cars were also spread out along the route. The whole area was an intense hive of activity.

It was time to weigh the options; stay in the bush with a badly damaged knee and hope to escape detection or give myself up and join my other colleagues I now firmly believed to be in the hands of the Seychellois authorities.

I decided on the latter.

Painfully I dragged myself to my feet and shouted in French to the nearest knot of soldiers that I wanted to surrender and that they should come and help me down.

Almost instantly, just below me a jeep careered to a halt and an officer in the driver's seat leapt out.

'We don't care a damn about capturing you . . . we just want to kill you', he yelled.

Seconds later there was a burst of gunfire from his crew.

He's direct if nothing else, I thought to myself ruefully as I burrowed for cover.

Death missed me that morning by millimeters and in so doing, shed a little good fortune. Ricochets from the bullets splattered the rocks and bushes around me. A tiny shard of metal struck my knee and clinically, almost surgically, the puffy balloon of fluid that had developed around my damaged knee was punctured. The fluid poured out and washed my leg, relieving both the pain and the pressure.

Not so pleasant was another piece of shrapnel that neatly furrowed a path down the outside of my right wrist and cut me to the bone.

Suddenly the firing ceased.

I pulled two bandages from my pockets, giving a silent prayer of thanks to Julia for insisting that I should take them along when I left home . . . which seemed like years before.

Deftly I wrapped one bandage around my wrist and the other around my knee and then waited for what I believed was my inevitable end.

Minutes later, when the expected assault by the Seychellois troops had not materialised, I poked my head cautiously over the rocks.

What the hell were they doing?

In seconds I had the answer.

The jeep had disappeared from below my position and its crew were now part of a long deployment of troops facing the airport.

Seconds later the Seychellois and Tanzanian troops attacked the airport terminal building.

Armoured cars forged ahead of the attacking troops firing round after round into the building.

The troops themselves kept up a constant fire on the building and surrounds.

Above the airport terminal building I could just see the tail piece of the Swazi Fokker shudder as cannon shells struck home.

Astonishingly, there was not a single return shot from the buildings.

Where were the rest of the mercenaries?

Within half an hour it was all over and the airport was looking a great deal more sorry for itself than it did before the attack.

I knew that I could not crawl away from my spot in daylight and prayed that the troops would not come back. But come back they did — well, sort of.

At midday a squad of troops in a jeep returned and began haphazardly firing in the general vicinity of where I had been sighted.

I kept my head down and prayed.

From the few short sights I had of them I rapidly became aware of the reason why their firing was so erratic and why they had so little interest in entering the bush to search for me — they were drunk out of their minds.

While retaking the airport building, the troops had clearly regarded it a tactical essential to neutralise the duty free liquor shop and they had done it with great efficacy.

Both myself, and, unknown to me, the other two other mercenaries hiding out in the nearby bush that day could indeed be grateful, because, had the troops captured us, then I am sure we would have been summarily despatched.

I spent the rest of the day skulking in my hidey-hole.

As dusk fell I thankfully got to my feet, tested my knee being delighted to find it much improved in the process, and crawled deeper into the bush.

Once away from the exposed rock face I collapsed, weak from lack of food, the returned dull pain in my knee and, worst of all, a bone chilling depression.

I believed I, alone, was the remaining free mercenary on the island.

Either the rest of the group were hiding in the bush or they had been captured and were probably, even at that very moment, undergoing terrible punishment and even death.

In my dank little jungle hidey-hole I thought of home and the children . . . the futility of it all . . . it was at that point I was my nearest to surrender.

Then, suddenly, an image flashed into my mind.

It was of a tiny group of mercenaries under furious fire; the building in which they were sheltering was shattered, two of their number were wounded, three others had been killed and hour by hour the opposing force grew larger and more aggressive. At their back was a river and on their flanks their supporting units were melting away or surrendering to the enemy to face unimaginable torture and terror.

On them, as well, the despair of defeat hung heavily.

It was hopeless.

There was an air of surrender.

The image crystallized. I saw Jimmy Mandy's weather and booze beaten face before my eyes. A man who in spite of alcoholism still had the spirit of the Special Air Service that had been imbued into him when he was so much younger, a spirit of 'Who Dares Wins' — a spirit that didn't countenance surrender.

I recalled reports of how he had angrily rejected talk of defeat, bullied, cajoled and threatened the survivors into action, laid down the covering fire as they retreated and ensured the capture of the craft that carried the bruised and exhausted mercenaries away from Kindu and over the river.

It was the same heroic Jimmy Mandy who had kept their spirits up as they trekked for two weeks through hostile Congo country to regroup with the other mercenaries at Punia.

The example — from another mercenary war fourteen years earlier — inspired me. I would not be captured on Mahe.

Like the Kindu mercenaries, I would survive.

The next fifteen days were to test my endurance and strength to the utmost. I lived in the bush without sight of humans, relying only on what food I could glean from the vegetation. By day fifteen that food totalled three pineapples and the juice of numerous coconuts.

I moved constantly during that time, afraid to remain too long in one place in case I was tracked.

Nights were a time of restless slumber, nerves taut for every sound, every snap of a twig. It rained several times and I was soaked to the skin.

I was having great difficulty in walking and eventually ended up hobbling around on a stick I had picked up in the bush.

I lost kilograms in weight. My wedding ring hung loosely on my finger. I removed it and attached it to my watch strap. Soon my watch was too loose to stay on my wrist and I had to remove that and bind it tightly to my silver bracelet.

On several occasions I dodged foot patrols of Seychellois forces — some of them with dogs. Once the dogs actually caught my scent and were straining at their leashes to drag their handlers into the bush after me. But it was dark and wet and the soldiers were bored and did not really believe anybody was there.

I scrambled away into the darkness and they never followed.

During that whole time the only thing that kept me alive and determined was the memory of my wife and children in Durban, recollections of the good times we had spent.

The disillusionment at the way things had turned out hung heavily.

By the fifteenth day, my earlier resolves to avoid capture at all costs had weakened considerably. I had lost weight, was feeling perpetually tired and unsteady and began to suffer bouts of giddiness.

Towards the end of the two weeks I began to hallucinate — at once beautiful and terrifying. It always had the same form, that of a silver garden enclosing a silver house. The first time it happened I was bowled over with the indescribable beauty of the garden. Wondrous plants and shrubs grew everywhere, enclosing patches of silver plated lawn. Everything had the regularity and form of stainless steel although the sense of the garden was one of warmth, not coldness. Then I saw the house; also silver and rising up from the surrounding shrubs and lawns. Along its front it had a wide colonnade — I saw it clearly — and behind the colonnade were rows of windows reflecting the warm glow of light. I stumbled towards the colonnade and tried to enter. There was a blur and I was suddenly outside on the lawn again. I tried a second and a third time. Each time the colonnades side skipped, the windows retreated and I found myself spread-eagled on the damp grass. Then slowly darkness overcame.

I awoke next day stiff, weak and lying in a small clearing in the jungle, a palisade of trees and shrubs enfolding me.

I knew I could not continue. It was time for decision again.

I resolved to turn myself in.

On the morning of December 10 I approached a household on the main road to Victoria and asked an old man if I could have a slice of bread with salt and a cup of water.

He knew instantly who I was but nevertheless courteously acceded to my request.

One of his youngsters was despatched to the nearby Cascades Police Station to tell them I was there.

Ten minutes later an army jeep with four soldiers arrived and I was hustled into the back.

It was the beginning of nineteen months incarceration.

53

Interrogation and Confession

It was with a deep sense of irony that I rode through the gates of Campe Pointe Larue that morning; the same camp that Mike's people had failed to take seventeen days before, the same camp that I knew we could with determination have seized with few problems. And here I was driving into it as prisoner of the men we had come to fight and — if necessary — kill.

The soldiers ordered me out of the jeep. Nobody struck or hurt me but there was a little shoving every now and then. I think they appreciated the fact that I was virtually crippled. Besides, it was fifteen days after the coup attempt and both the island's population and its security forces had calmed down after the initial shock. Other mercenaries captured more immediately, had been given a much more brutal treatment.

I was more fortunate.

At the army camp I was given a pair of shorts, bundled straight back into the jeep and driven to the Central Police Station. I was hurried upstairs and plonked down in a chair in an interrogation rooms. Mentally I geared myself for the contest that I knew was about to begin. I realised I was at a terrible disadvantage. I had no idea of what had happened to Mike or the others. Had they been captured and sung like canaries or had they got away. If they had got away I had a better chance of lying my way out but I needed to know that. I was acutely aware that anything I said could seriously affect them if they were being held.

The interrogation went badly. Three police interrogators used every technique of grilling they knew. Nobody hurt me or raised a hand but dozens of questions were fired. I was sworn at and dark threats issued.

Eventually I made my first statement.

It was a pack of lies.

I told them I had been a tour guide caught up in this terrible incident at the airport. I had taken fright when the fighting began and fled to the mountains. My fear that I would be associated with the coup attempt had led me to stay in the mountains.

The statement was dutifully taken down by the police.

Then they told me to my face that I was a liar.

As I was being taken away one of the policemen came up to me.

'You have got until tomorrow morning to change your mind — or else.'

For the rest of that day I stayed in my cell mulling over my options. I knew that if I admitted outright that I was part of the coup attempt it would be curtains for me. But if they could prove conclusively my story was a fabrication I was in even greater danger. Eventually I decided to stick with my original story.

Early the next morning a young police inspector came to me.

'Have you decided to tell the truth? Have you changed your mind?' he demanded.

I told him I had not changed my mind and was promptly born off to see Pillay, Commissioner of Police on the islands. He was civil but made quite sure I knew the gravity of the charge against me. I again denied complicity in the coup. Then he played his trump card.

'You do not want to co-operate with us it appears. I am afraid I have no option but to give you to the army. They have certain ways which I am sure will make you change your mind.'

I remained silent.

'You see,' continued Pillay, 'we do not do dirty work in the police but I am afraid I cannot say the same for the army.'

I still remained silent.

I was taken from his office and driven across town to Army Headquarters in downtown Victoria. It was a forbidding building and as I was rushed through the corridors in handcuffs, I noted the tough looking military police dotting the corridors.

With little ceremony I was thrown into a punishment cell for the night. The punishment cell was a peculiarly uncomfortable little device. It was about a meter square so that, although one could stand or sit, it was impossible to lie down. Inside it was inky dark with only a slight suffusion of light right at the top where the ventilation slit lay.

I remained cramped in that hole for the entire day during which I was not fed once.

Softening me up, I thought to myself, and concentrated hard on gearing myself for what I was sure would follow.

Early the next morning the door was opened and hands roughly jerked me out. This is it, I thought. The real interrogation is now going to begin. But it was not to be.

I was again hurried into a jeep where, to my amazement, two other white men were already sitting, their hands handcuffed behind their backs. I did not know them at all. Briefly we exchanged glances but on the journey back to police headquarters we did not say a word.

There was little point inviting a rifle butt in the back from the guards.

Only later was I to discover who they were; Martin Dolincheck, South African National Intelligence Service agent and Robert Simms, one of the 'large' advance party Mike had boasted about.

In complete silence we were taken to separate cells in the police station alongside the interrogation room.

Simms was the first to be taken — a small, whipper-snapper thin man looking more like a jockey than a mercenary. For ten minutes I heard the mutter of voices interspersed by Simms' high pitched squeak.

I could not hear what was actually being said.

Then Dolincheck was taken.

He was away for twenty minutes. Then, finally, a police guard came to my grill beckoned me to follow him.

In the interrogation room there were only four men, the Police Commissioner, Pillay, the Assistant Police Commissioner, Fonteyn and — strangely enough — two South African journalists.

One was Eugene Hugo and the other his cameraman.

I must indeed have looked a sight.

I had been eighteen days without food, I was still unshaven, I limped and was dressed in ragged shorts and *grasshopper* boots.

To my astonishment Hugo directed a number of questions at me.

I was astonished because he was a fellow countryman of mine and I had no idea what he was up to.

I wonder if the day will come when someone catches him in circumstances similar to mine.

He recalled he had interviewed me when I had come back from the Congo all those years before and claimed I had been interested in rescuing Moise Tshombe from Algiers.

'What has that to do with this situation?' I asked.

Hugo ignored me and, before the watchful gaze of the Commissioner and Assistant Commissioner, went on to falsely claim that I had been seen at the rifle range of La Mercy, north of Durban helping test the AK-47s we had brought with us.

I denied it emphatically.

The interrogation went on.

Hugo claimed he was a better South African than I was because I had got the country into a lot of trouble domestically and internationally with this coup attempt.

I could hardly deny the latter part.

As the discussion continued it rapidly became clear to me what Hugo was after — he wanted me to confess that the South African Government was involved.

I told him emphatically that I did not know where the arms came from or the money or the backers. It went back and forward and then suddenly I was overcome by a terrible weariness.

I told him to go to hell.

Hugo rose from his chair and told Pillay that once he got back to South Africa he would send the police a complete dossier of my past activities.

Then, adding insult to injury, he sanctimoniously asked if I wanted to give a message to my wife.

What a bloody hypocrite . . . It was the last straw.

I let fly at Hugo and told him not to go anywhere near my wife.

It was a stormy end to an unforgetable interview.

Pillay signalled for me to be taken away.

Before we left, however, I was allowed to go to the toilet — the first time since my capture. I thought of Hugo the whole time I was there.

Then it was back to the punishment cells for me and Unionvale Military Camp for Dolincheck and Simms. In the cell I was given my first meal since capture — a small portion of rice and fish.

That night I slumbered uneasily in my cramped quarters.

The voices began at about midnight.

From the next cell came an insistent sibilant voice calling 'Puren, Puren, Puren.' I tried to ignore it but the voice continued for what seemed like hours.

Eventually I answered 'Yes.'

Then began hours of diatribe from the unseen person; attacking me for being a mercenary, condemning South Africa for destabilising the countries on the borders, asking if I liked killing innocent men, women and children and wanting to know what the Seychelles had done that warranted our attack.

I was not the only one to get the same treatment.

One of the Seychelles conspirators, Jean Dingwell, was in the cell next to mine and, I learnt later, night after night was given the same hidden voice treatment.

Poor Jean had a rough time of it. He was sick and moaned continuously. Beneath his door flowed urine and excreta.

The stench was terrible.

During the entire time I was in those cells I managed — through good fortune — to ensure that I never once fouled them. Always when being taken out for interrogation or some other purpose I managed to find the opportunity to relieve myself.

On the third day the Tanzanians came for me again.

I was hauled from the cell and taken to a jeep. Some Seychellois troops joined us and we headed back to the airport and the mountains in which I had hidden for those long fifteen days.

I was told to find my identity documents which had got lost during my travail in the wilderness.

It was a tough day. Although I was not beaten or anything like that, I was forced to undertake some tremendously arduous physical exercise for which I was not fit or ready. Whenever I found it hard going to negotiate a hillside I was shoved or dragged.

Twice more the troops were to take me into the mountains and each occasion the going became rougher.

On one of the last trips a Tanzanian soldier displayed a surprising streak of compassion for my weakened state. He took my hand and ran with me to surmount a hill. When we reached the top I stopped, panting, and thanked him for the help.

He looked at me quizzically, not understanding

My condition continued deteriorating. In the first four days of detention I had two meals of fish and rice and some tea with iron ration biscuits. The debilitating walks in the mountains and the night time indoctrination talks slowly wore my spirit down. In all my years of mercenarying and adventuring I don't believe I had ever reached such a low point, physically and spiritually.

It was as if all my resistance was slowly crumbling. All the iron in my soul that had carried me through so many scrapes and tragedies before was melting to leave me alone, frightened, forlorn.

Rescue came in a singular fashion.

Late one night I was slumped in my cell when I heard a woman's voice outside my door. It was a woman guard — there is no sex discrimination in the Seychelles

People's Defence Force — and she was whispering.

'Mister Puren, look up, please.'

I lifted my head to where a faint suffusion of light came through the crack at the top of the door. There, suspended by two slender woman's fingers, was a banana. I scrambled to my feet and grabbed it.

'Thank you, thank you so much,' I managed to say.

There was a moments silence and then her voice again.

'Mister Puren, there are only a few of you left on the islands. All the rest have flown away.'

Her words had two effects on me. Firstly, the sheer compassion of her actions choked me with emotions and recharged my lowering resistance. Secondly, I knew that Mike had indeed hijacked the *Air India* Boeing as he had threatened.

A huge burden lifted from my shoulders.

If they had got away, there was no reason left why I should worry about getting them into trouble.

Early the next morning when the guard came to my door I told him to call the camp commandant. I wanted to make a statement.

The camp commandant was there within minutes and I was taken into a small, bare room to give my statement.

I told the whole story this time, about Mike coming to see me, the events leading up to our arrival on November 24, the people in our party — everything except my earlier recce visit to the island, two and a half years before. When completed the statement was put before me and I signed it.

It was the only one I was to make and it was used against me at my trial.

After fingerprinting I was again bundled into a jeep and whisked off to my new home — Unionvale Military Prison.

It was the tenth day of my detention.

54

Solitary

The vehicle slithered to a halt outside the main block of the Unionvale Prison.

A knot of inquisitive soldiers gathered around and began hurling insults and catcalls.

Gingerly I clambered out of the jeep, still handcuffed, to be confronted by Sergeant Victor, a huge Seychellois mulatto with a hardly benign regard for mercenaries.

More shoving and pushing and I was taken towards the cells.

Sergeant Victor studied my filthy condition and announced definitively: 'Showahs'.

I was taken to the ablution block where the magnanimous Sergeant Victor gave me four minutes to shower and use the toilet. I did my best and then stood waiting. A clean shirt and shorts were given to me.

Sergeant Victor took me to my new cell — it was a standard single cell with a bed and mattrass but after the punishment block it was luxury. The windows of the cell had been boarded up so that only a little light filtered through, hardly relieving the deep gloom. I lay on my bed — the first time in days I had been able to stretch out completely — and soaked in the luxury.

From then on I was also to receive regular but parsimonious prison food; a cup of tea and a slice of bread for breakfast, rice and fish for lunch and dinner. The rations were extremely frugal. I should have been gaining weight because of the inactivity but I actually remained constant. There was no doubt in my mind that it was a punishment diet.

Although still in solitary confinement I rapidly worked out by a process of deduction the number of people detained in the cells with me. I soon became convinced there were no more than five other mercenaries in Seychellois' hands — but I still did not know their identities. While walking from the cell to other parts of the building we sometimes passed each other, or I saw them looking out of their cells.

By the end of the month we had begun exchanging a few words.

My first night at Unionvale was not what could be considered restful.

Late that night the cell door burst open and a crowd of young Seychellois soldiers packed the threshold.

354

Drowsily I dragged myself to my feet and stared at the noisy group. This is it, I said to myself, they are going to beat me up.

Indeed, for a few tense moments it looked as if they were going to do precisely that. Suddenly the violent aggressiveness went out of them. Maybe I cut a pathetic and emaciated figure, maybe it was respect for age. I really do not know.

In the event they contented themselves with shouting insults about me being a 'white pig' and a 'colonialist' and demanded what had happened to Steve Biko, the black consciousness leader who died in the hands of the South African security police in 1977.

I tolerated it because I had no choice. Then they became tired with baiting me and made as if to leave.

One of them turned at the door and shouted, 'We will be back tomorrow night, Mister Puren, and then we will get you.'

I crawled back into bed and tried to sleep.

Sergeant Victor proved no less aggressive when the mood took him — and the mood seemed to take him mostly when he was a little tanked up with booze or with cannabis or with both.

The second night at Unionvale he came to my cell early in the evening and matter-of-factly told me they were going to shoot me at midnight exactly.

There seemed to be nothing I could say of any great moment so I kept quiet.

After he left I prayed silently that I would be able to see the dawn.

Deep within myself I could not believe that I would be shot out of hand; it made a mockery of the professional police approach which had been taken towards my confession and there had been constant references to 'the trial'. But I was still afraid that Sergeant Victor and some of the young bloods might take it into their heads to carry out a little vigilante vengeance.

At midnight exactly the door burst open and there was Sergeant Victor with a detail of troops. All of them clearly the worse for the drink.

He swaggered into the room and cocked his rifle.

'Get up Mister Puren, your time has come', he said in his rich patois drawl which, despite the seriousness of the situation, made the whole thing seem like a scene out of a bad comedy movie.

Wearily I climbed to my feet. Before me flashed a memory; that of a huge Gendarmes paratrooper surrounded by his rebellious men, pointing his rifle at me on a deserted Katanga road and gently squeezing the trigger. Local militia forces had saved me that day so many years before.

What would save me tonight, I wondered, almost academically.

In the end it was Sergeant Victor's own volition that saved me.

I suppose my face did not reflect the desired terror — by this stage of my detention I was calm and fatalistic.

The burly Seychellois roared in anger and advanced on me. There followed the one and only beating I was to endure in my detention.

Victor climbed in with his boots, fists and occasionally, rifle butt.

We swayed back and forward around the tiny cell. I saw every blow coming, as each fell I attempted to ride with it, each stab of pain I anticipated, reconciled and sought to conquer.

I did not scream, the only sounds were my grunts as the air was driven from my body by the blows.

It became an almost intensely personal thing, Victor doing his best to hurt me and myself concentrating exclusively on dealing with the pain. Almost everything else became irrelevant.

Then I felt blood trickling down my face.

Instantly Victor stopped. He called his men off and left — the whole incident had taken maybe three minutes.

Alone in the cell I realised I had been lucky. From the prospect of death I had been reprieved for what in effect was only a mild beating. I could live with it, I thought.

Next day an even bigger shock was in store.

After breakfast Victor came to my cell and actually apologised for the events of the night before.

I dumbly nodded my acknowledgement.

I was never to report the incident to the camp commandant and I think that made Victor unbend slightly towards me. I was later, in fact, to be taken from my cell and put in a more airy one with a view of Victoria and a constant cooling breeze.

The cell belonged to Roger England, another of the mercenaries, but the guards had taken such a dislike to him because of his constant cheeking that they had gladly thrust him into my gloomy hole of a cell.

Every now and then I was taken off to the Central Police Station for questioning about this or that aspect and then brought back to solitary confinement.

Things settled into a routine.

The days passed in preparation for 'the Trial' and again and again my thoughts kept turning to my family in South Africa and the stupidity that had driven me to embark on this operation without fully assessing the planning.

Bitterly I realised I had relied too heavily on Mike.

The solitary confinement lay heavily on me but very early on I had worked out a rigorous programme for keeping body and mind together.

I exercised regularly and methodically in my cell for a part of each day.

I also set aside time for what I called 'mind games' in which I would focus on a particular event that had happened in my distant past and then begin minutely reconstructing it. At other times I tackled mathematical problems, recited scraps of poems I had known from old, tried to recall the plots of books I had read and recounted to myself great events of history.

It all helped to discipline my mind and stave off the gnawing fears of the future and the great oppressive weight on the soul that is solitary confinement.

I think I came out of it fairly well but some of the others did not.

Roger England began talking to himself and often gesticulated wildly at apparently nothing.

The other person — the last I would have expected to be affected — was Dolincheck. He became quite paranoid and was convinced the Seychellois were trying to poison him. He complained incessantly about noises outside his cell.

After a few weeks reading matter began to arrive — first of all a Bible and then copies of the Seychellois newspaper *Nation*.

Miraculously I was allowed to sign a power of attorney for Julia in South Africa. We had several surprise visits while in detention.

One of the biggest was when the Tanzanian Minister of Defence, an army general, and his entourage arrived to visit us.

The Camp Commandant, Major Marengo, brought the general to my cell but before he could properly introduce us the general said affably: 'Thank you so much for the information you have given us. We find it very useful.'

I looked at him in amazement.

Marengo hastily butted in.

'No, sir, this is not Mister Dolincheck, it is Mister Puren, the one from the Congo.'

The General instantly recovered and I girded myself for the worst. It was to be nothing of the sort. He chatted amiably about his training experiences in Israel and told me he had been on the same paratroop course as President Mobutu Seso Seke. After a few more civil exchanges he bid me farewell and moved off to see the others in their cells.

I began to wonder at that point about the relationship between Dolincheck and the Seychellois.

Later, in a private conversation, Major Marengo was to tell me that Dolincheck had offered his services to the Seychelles but had been turned down.

The second surprise occasion came one morning. I was told I would be called upon to give evidence to the United Nations' commission set up to investigate the whole fiasco.

Better give them all assistance — or else — I was told by the Seychellois.

In fact the Commission's hearings, under its Panamanian chairman, Carlos Ozores, were conducted responsibly and politely.

I told them exactly what was in my statement to the police and expanded a little on my mercenary activities in the Congo.

I could not help but suppress a sense of irritation at the hypocrisy that allowed members of the Commission to appear shocked at the Congo actions when in many cases the countries from which they had come had themselves shown far greater examples of brutality in the recent past.

Days followed each other in a timeless, wasteful fashion.

Routine bored into my soul, desperation seized me.

Then, suddenly, the trial was upon us.

55

Preliminaries

Our initial brief appearance in court for formal remand was on January 5 1982. For the first time the captured mercenaries were brought together and I could get a clear sight of my comrades All of them, to a greater or lesser extent, had been through the same mill as I since that fateful November 24 day.

Aubrey Brooks was the one who had suffered the most physically.

The Durban based printer, a former member of the Selous Scouts and then the Greys Scouts of Rhodesia, had apparently come on the mission in an attempt to bale himself out of financial difficulties.

Brooks had been part of the advance guard. He had been at the airport when we landed and had been one of those unfortunate enough to have been detailed by Mike Hoare to launch the half-baked attack on Pointe Larue Camp.

In the firefight Aubrey had taken shrapnel in his thigh.

His buddies had helped him away and one had suggested he make his way back to the road to link up with other mercenary elements so he could get out of harm's way. En route Brooks passed out from shock and loss of blood. He fell into Seychellois' hands the next day and during the next few days was badly beaten.

The press pictures of his swollen face when he was first paraded for newspaper men told the tale.

Now he was standing tensely in the box with me.

Greying Briton, Bernard Carey, was there, too. He had served in the Congo and in other campaigns and had been pretty high up in the mercenary hierarchy.

Mike had contacted him about a month before the coup at his travel agency business in Pietermaritzburg. Carey had soon been roped into the plan and a few weeks before the operation had actually carried a rifle through Seychelles customs as part of a 'dry run'.

On November 21 he had returned to the Seychelles with Dalgleish, Brooks and Botes. Simms and Ingles were already in place on the island in the 'safe' house, but Charles Dukes and Roger England were to arrive later.

Carey had been one of those meeting us at the airport.

Together with the rest he had taken part in the battle at Pointe Larue and around the airport.

When the mercenary forces had been preparing to pull out, Carey had realised that Brooks was missing so he had volunteered to go back and find him.

The *Air India* jet left without him and the next day he was captured.

Under interrogation Carey was to let slip the name of one of the island's conspirators, Jean Dingwell, and he, too, was hauled into detention.

Blond, twenty six year old Roger England, like Carey, owed his unfortunate situation to an impulsive but noble decision.

When Carey returned to search for Brooks, England, then already walking out to the *Air India* jet, decided to stay behind and search as well.

Later when he realised it was hopeless to try and get through the surrounding troops, he ran across the runway and plunged into the sea.

He swam back to his hotel — taking most of the night — and went inside, trying to give the impression he had just arrived back from an early morning dip.

It did not work . . . he was arrested a few hours later.

These three were to take the severest beating from the Seychellois and Tanzanian troops. Indeed, Carey and Brooks, both suffering from bad injuries sustained during the fighting or from beatings, were at one stage threatened with execution in hospital and on another occasion were spirited away by enraged Tanzanian troops for even more beatings.

Robert Simms broke for his safe house the moment the shooting commenced at the airport. He, too, was later arrested, together with his girl friend, Susan Ingles, and the house searched.

Simms was a withdrawn character who never shared or entered into any true spirit of camaraderie. His and Ingles' amateurishness were also responsible for the sixth unfortunate adventurer being caught.

In a letter from Mike Hoare to Simms mention was made of Anton Lubic (Dolincheck's alias). The letter was never destroyed so Seychellois security had no problem in landing their biggest coup — the detention of a South African Secret Service agent.

Sandy haired Dolincheck preferred to keep himself distanced from us mercenaries, an approach that was later to earn him much approbrium from the rest.

Then there was, of course, myself. I was really the odd one out. I was variously described by the press as looking like a business executive, a grandfather or a senior sporting administrator.

It was also observed that I appeared to be a father figure for the other mercenaries. In a way I suppose they might have been right because I always conducted myself courteously and correctly. Where necessary I also tried to give encouragement and advice to the younger members of our party.

On our first court appearance we arrived barefoot, wearing shorts and shirts.

With successive court visits our appearances improved until by trial day we were all neatly turned out in suits.

Our next appearance was January 19 for another remand. Two days later — for the first time since being detained at Unionvale — my handcuffs were removed.

After that we appeared in court regularly every two weeks for remand.

Early in February we were told the exact charges.

We were all to be charged with treason — and we all knew the penalty was death.

Simms was to face two charges of treason, possession of firearms and acts preparatory to levying war against the Seychelles and, secondly, abetting persons in levying war against the Seychelles.

Susan Ingles was charged with acts preparatory to levying war and controlling funds in preparation of war.

Brooks, Carey and England were charged with levying war at the Pointe Larue army base and Carey and England were additionally charged together with me for levying war at the airport.

Dolincheck was charged with acts preparatory to levying war.

We were now faced with a dilemma. Should we plead guilty in the hope of protecting Simms and Susan Ingles or should we to go for a 'not guilty' plea and fight it out?

I decided to plead guilty and and place myself at the court's mercy.

The next problem was, of course, money, but it soon became apparent that *friends* would help us. We were given to believe that Mike Hoare had made twenty five thousand rands available for our defence. Later, too, I gathered that *Scope* magazine had contributed substantially — it was said fifty thousand rands — to the defence costs on condition that it had rights on the story.

Eventually *Scope* was to run a highly dramatised version of events over three editions in August and September 1982.

I passed my decision to plead guilty on to our instructing lawyer, Seychellois attorney, Shah.

At that time our defending counsel was to be Mike Hannon, a South African based lawyer. Hannon was to withdraw from the case because of a conflict of interests. It eventually fell to Mr Nicholas Fairbairn, a British MP and former Solicitor General of Scotland, to defend us. Fairbairn was a competent but over dramatic defence counsel; undoubtedly interested in both money and publicity as well as his clients.

On June 16 — I wondered to myself if the date had special significance for the Seychellois or were they just making a political point — we were all brought to court.

Chief Justice Earle Seaton took the bench.

In our neatly pressed suits we waited impassively as the preliminary matters of the trial were dealt with.

Fairbairn's immediate defence was that we could not be charged with treason because we were not Seychelles citizens.

Seychelles attorney, Bernard Rasool, argued that we could indeed be charged as Seychellois law resembled that of Zambia and not Britain — a 'person' in terms of their law could either be a citizen or a foreigner.

Judge Seaton's ruling was that we could indeed be charged with treason.

It was one against us.

The next day brought new developments.

Charges against Susan Ingles were dropped and she was released.

All of us, I believe, were pleased for the middle aged woman who had got herself in way above her head without realising what she was doing.

The second development was that Fairbairn argued before the court that it would be impossible to find an impartial jury to hear us as the United Nations' report which had already been published implicated us all in trying to overthrow the Seychelles Government.

There was another adjournment for the judge to consider this point.

June 18 came and Judge Seaton ruled that Fairbairn's argument about an impartial jury were not acceptable.

Two points against us.

Now came the moment for pleading.

Four of us pleaded guilty to the treason charge and the illegal possession of arms charge was dropped.

Simms pleaded not guilty to treason but guilty to the arms count. Shortly afterwards the treason charges against him were dropped.

Dolincheck, handling his own defence, first pleaded not guilty to the treason charge and then changed it to guilty thereby turning the court into a bit of a turmoil.

Judge Seaton ordered that his trial be separated from ours.

Dolincheck came up in court again on June 23. He attacked Mike Hoare for 'double crossing him', called me 'an old Congo renegade', and asked that sections of his diary written whilst on the island be censored because it might embarrass his family. He then went on to directly implicate the Kenyan Government in the coup attempt by saying that two aircraft loads of troops and police from there were scheduled to arrive at the island immediately after the coup to take over law and order.

In later evidence before the court and in a statement, Dolincheck condemned his former employers, the National Intelligence Services of South Africa, for failing to provide him with defence money. He then went into a long harangue against the evils of apartheid and the wickedness of the coup attempt.

He pledged to fight apartheid and declared our actions 'shameful'.

Now I can understand that Dolincheck was feeling isolated, but surely one of the risks any intelligence operator accepts, whether on authorised or unauthorised missions, is that if he is caught he is on his own. Those are the rules of the game and have been from time immemorial.

The fact that he should make such a song and dance is an indictment of himself as an intelligence operator and of the service that would employ such a man.

On July 5 the nine member jury took thirty minutes to find him guilty of aiding and abetting in the levying of war.

Our turn was not long coming. Two days later Fairbairn summed up our defence arguments. He submitted affidavits to the court saying we had been tortured into making our statements and in a dramatic delivery described us all as having been sadly misled by Mike Hoare. He also, which I thought was a bit impolitic, pointed out that the Seychelles Government had itself come into power by treason.

One by one, very briefly, we expressed our contrition.

Dolincheck, ever the dramatic, startled the court by asking that if he were sentenced to death it be carried out by a firing squad — so he could die like an 'officer and a gentleman'.

Judge Seaton took less than fifty minutes to think about it.

He returned from his chambers and we all arose to await sentence.

It was the longest moments of my life.

Judge Seaton first addressed himself to Brooks.

Unemotionally the words were read out: 'I sentence you in accordance with count five to suffer death in the manner authorised by law'.

There was a stunned silence in court.

Di Brooks, Aubrey's wife, suppressed a gasp from where she was sitting in the public gallery. She had been at the hearing all along — an immense tower of strength to her husband.

Roger was next.

Then me.

Finally Bernard.

We all responded in the same way.

'Thank you, My Lord'.

It was by then a matter of honour, of face, of dignity.

Inside me I felt the deepest and darkest pit open up and swallow my conscious thoughts, my emotions, my feelings. I sensed I was standing already at the edge of the trapdoor that would drop away and claim my life.

The rationalisations had gone.

I knew that nobody had been executed in the past twenty years on the island.

I knew René was faced with an enormous political problem if he executed us, and I knew that the fun loving Seychellois were three quarters of the way to forgiving us and quarter of the way to liking us.

But still, the words of Judge Seaton in their dreadful finality, swept the hopes and rationalisations away leaving me with nothing but despair, fear and resignation.

We were ushered out of the dock.

Like a dream I walked back to the jeep.

Is this me . . . am I really under sentence of death . . . am I really to die?

Dolincheck was given 'twenty years imprisonment' because he had been an 'accomplice' and had shown a sufficient spirit of contrition.

Simms got ten years for smuggling arms.

Fairbairn immediately gave notice that he would appeal against the sentence and the hearing was set down for September 20.

I resolved to pin my hopes on the appeal.

56

Appeal and Other Events

For us it was back to the cells and the task of keeping our sanity in the face of impending death and our spirits high amid the most dreadful monotony.

As the days passed the initial blank despair of our sentence began to lift and I allowed myself the luxury of hope.

Perhaps, after all, we were not to be killed.

On the outside, however, Fairbairn was waging an unrelenting war amid a blaze of publicity preparatory to the appeal. He produced the affidavits we had all made alleging torture — I told of being beaten up in my cell — and pledged to take the matter to the Commonwealth Heads of State, the United Nations and the British Prime Minister.

The stream of criticism and invective against the Seychellois Government, backed by the affidavits, profoundly disconcerted the René Government.

In my cell, meanwhile, I tried to convert unbearable boredom into endurable existence. As had happened to me so many times before in my life, a half learnt skill or amusement returned to help me through the darkest moments.

Ever since a child I had kept an interest in the psychic and dabbled — not entirely seriously — in things such as palm reading and tea leaf scanning.

My relations with the Seychellois guards was now more relaxed and one day, half in jest, I told Sergeant Victor that I could tell people's fortunes. I was astonished at the response. In short order Victor had his palm stretched before my face and was waving an empty tea mug in the air.

Slowly, with sufficient dramatic side effects, I began telling his past and his future. Now Victor and I had been in each other's company for some months and it was impossible not to pick up something about the man's past and his demeanour. I shamelessly embellished these and served them to the soldier as information from higher powers. I counted on Victor's simple nature and the Seychellois penchant for superstition.

It worked marvels.

Within a short time I had Clifford, another guard, come for guidance.

From conversations I had overheard between him and the other guards I gathered he was quite a swinger. I played heavily on this and warned him against adultery, gluttony and impulsiveness. He left impressed.

It was only the beginning.

Within a short while I began to receive a dribble of outside visitors on Sundays — all coming to hear their futures from the soldier of fortune from over the sea, the condemned man to whom the imminency of death had granted strange powers in detecting the affairs of the living.

It had a spin off effect, too. The visitors brought gifts of food and delicacies.

Clifford, who acted gate keeper with proprietorial pride, took his cut but I received enough in chocolates and sweetmeats to make life a little easier.

The fortune telling had another aspect which, had I perhaps been a little more attuned, could have given me even greater insight into the affairs of man and more particularly the dynamics of power.

As August dragged on I noted a deep moodiness in both Clifford and Victor. Their quest for the future — their own futures — became more insistent and intense. I dealt them the usual platitudes and they left dissatisfied and — did I imagine it — fearful. Only later was I to learn the reason for this pathetic search by the two men for their personal dispensation at the disposal of a higher hand.

Meanwhile in far away South Africa the rest of the cast were was getting different deserts from another judiciary. The charge they faced was one of hijacking. After hours of trial in Pietermaritzburg's old Victorian Supreme Court, Mike Hoare was sentenced to an effective ten years in jail. Duffy received an effective five years, Moneta five years, Dalgleish thirty months, Vernon Prinsloo 12 months, Charles Coatley an effective thirty months and Piet Dooreward an effective five years.

The remaining thirty four men got six months imprisonment each, with a further fifty four months suspended for five years.

The game was well and truly up.

57

The Deal

We had no idea what all the excitement was about. During the day of July 21 Sergeant Victor had paused before my cell door and in solemn tones warned me to be prepared to meet somebody 'big' later that day.

I took the news phlegmatically — another Government official, curious but influential member of the public or even, at a push, a journalist.

Towards evening the momentum began picking up.

Victor came booming along the corridor that we were to dress up in our 'best' and present ourselves at 19h00.

I pulled on my only suit and waited patiently.

At 19h00 sharp the doors opened to reveal Victor dressed in immaculately pressed battledress and wearing a side arm. His sidekick, Clifford, was likewise attired.

Both showed excessive courtesy towards me.

No pushing or shoving — just a courtly wave of the hand to indicate the path I should walk.

Outside in the courtyard I was joined by Brookes, Carey and England — the rest of the dead meat I thought grimly.

Two vehicles drew up.

We climbed in and the guards clambered up behind. Then it was a winding drive through the city's streets in the darkening gloom. Looks bigger than we imagined, I said to myself. My three colleagues were alert, a sense of anticipation suffused their beings.

As we approached Government House I decided we were going to see the Minister of Defence. But instead of making for the front door the two vehicles sloughed around a side entrance.

Almost furtively we were bundled from the vehicles and hastened up two flights of stairs — the sounds of a footfall echoing down gloomy and empty corridors, the only sound our breath and the occasional squeak of our guards' newly polished boots.

Suddenly we were before a white panelled door.

Victor knocked and we were admitted.

There were several chairs in the room, a desk and several side tables and a side lamp.

We stood in silence.

On all of us dawned the realisation that we were about to come face to face with the 'biggest' of all the islanders — the President himself.

Mentally I geared myself for the trauma of that first meeting — the hunters turned to the hunted, the eagle to the prey, the powerful to the helpless.

Minutes later the door swung open and Albert René, President of the Seychelles and commander-in-chief of its armed forces, was among us.

He looked shorter than I had imagined, had a clean-cut, youthful appearance, he was lean and alert.

There was a second's strained silence and then he bade us sit. Gratefully we took our seats and girded for what could be among the most unpleasant moments in our collective and not uneventful lives.

'Do you know who I am?' he asked.

'Yes, sir', several of us answered.

'I am the man you came to kill'.

An embarrassed silence.

What does one say? And what does one say when one knows that man now holds one's own life in the palm of his elegantly manicured hand? In the event nothing. One remains silent and prays harder than one has ever done before.

The President laughed gently and, almost chidingly, began recounting our coup attempt, giving startlingly accurate information about the planning and our own personal lives. We sat silently as he continued.

Then the preamble was over and he came to the point.

An appeal against sentence would be against our own best interests.

Fairbairn, he claimed, had been holding court in the Mariner's Arms telling exactly how he intended to arrange our pardon and had made serious charges against the Seychellois state — allegations of torture and worse.

The charges cast the Government in an extremely bad light and made it more difficult for the government to consider exercising clemency.

I saw Brookes, Carey and England shift in their chairs.

They knew they had been badly tortured. Yet they now saw their only hope of salvation would be to deny this ill-treatment. From their intent faces I saw the fierce conflict of emotions.

President René, no doubt, was also aware of the passions within the men, and pressed onwards.

He said the coup attempt and aftermath had been extremely painful to him and he wished for an honourable solution to the problem for everybody. Not that there was that much international pressure on him to release us, he added wryly.

'That pile of letters over there', he said, waving a hand to a side table stacked to overflowing with correspondence, 'is from people around the world begging me to help stop whaling in the Indian Ocean'.

'That pile there is from people asking for clemency for you'.

His elegant hand indicated another table on which there was a neat pile of ten letters.

Inwardly I permitted myself a wry smile. He certainly knew how to grind our noses in it.

The crunch.

'I am not offering a deal but if you withdraw the appeal', the words hung in the still evening air for what seemed like an eternity, 'you will be home by September'.

Our faces must have shown our emotions because President René paused for a moment to nod solemnly.

'I know what this means to you. I am not trying to torment you or make it worse. This is a genuine offer'.

There was absolute silence in the room as all of us weighed up the implications of what President René was saying. Had a deal indeed been struck? But with whom? Was it the South African government? Other countries? We knew the most likely reason for the offer was that René wanted to counteract Fairbairn's attacks on the Seychelles Government over their treatment of us prisoners. But here was a chance of reprieve. On the other hand, if we pushed ahead with our appeal it could, and most likely would, be turned down.

We saw the gap and took it, one by one we indicated we would withdraw the appeal.

President René slowly nodded his head in appreciation.

'I suggest — to formalise our arrangement — that you write to Fairbairn telling him you no longer need his service. I would like to see the letters'.

It was a subdued group who trooped out of his office and down to the vehicle. We all knew the risks we were taking.

Could we trust René?

What options did we have?

Was this wily statesman not trying to kill two birds with one stone — get us to withdraw the appeal and thus implicitly accept the burden of our guilt while at the same time taking the ultimate step of having us executed.

In all honesty, none of us had the right to expect anything else from him. I thought what Pretoria's response would have been if a group of Seychellois and foreign mercenaries had dropped on Church Square, Pretoria, in a bid to take out the Government.

Over the next week I carefully drafted my letter — withdrawing our appeal and repudiating Fairbairn. I had no personal grudge against the advocate although I had misgivings about the way he had handled our case and I took no particular pleasure in my put down of him. Still, it was my life against Fairbairn's reputation, which was not much of a contest.

A week later we were back in René's office. The same furniture, the same President.

The pile of letters from the whaling lobby was higher, those for our clemency unchanged.

Several of us were asked to read out our letters and René nodded his approval. We left again subdued having played the biggest card that had fallen to us since incarceration. Had we played it right?

The news of our abandoned appeal led to a spate of speculation in the press that a 'deal' had been worked out between the South African and Seychelles Governments. For us it was just survival tactics.

58

Coup — Again

I started from my sleep early that Tuesday morning, August 16, and instantly I was aware of two unusual events. In the first place my cell was in darkness — for the first time since my incarceration the lights were off.

In the inky blackness I felt totally disorientated.

The second thing was the unmistakable roar of heavy transport in and around the prison. I lay back and tried to put the pieces together.

What was going on?

Eventually I surrendered to drowsiness and slipped away into a restless slumber — punctuated every now and again by the renewed roars of vehicles passing beneath my window.

At dawn I was wrenched from sleep again — this time by the unmistakable sound of gunfire.

I scrambled to the slit that passed for a window in my cell and gazed down on the town, now slowly emerging from the gloom in the dawn's light.

It was deserted except for an occasional military vehicle. I had seen towns look like that before; in Katanga, in the Eastern Congo's Maniema area, in what was then Stanleyville.

There was a coup underway I said to myself and slid slowly down the wall, my mind furiously spinning through the options that could possibly be open to us.

An hour later — dead on normal time — the door opened and our Sergeant Victor came bustling into the cell.

'Only two minutes for washing and toilet today', he said brusquely and I made a dart for the ablution block.

On the way back to my cell he grabbed my arm and stared intently into my eyes.

'Do you know what is happening?' he demanded.

Puren is no fool and knows when to keep his mouth shut.

'I have no idea at all.'

I was shoved into the cell and the door slammed shut.

The sergeant's voice came from outside; 'Just now it will be on the radio and you will know everything.' I was never to see Victor again and as I had no radio I was never to know what it said.

But I had no need for a radio to guess what was going on. Below my window events were unfolding spectacularly. I saw several knots of soldiers advancing cautiously up one of the town's streets towards the prison. Every now and then they dropped into fire positions behind cover.

I started to get an empty feeling in my stomach,

Seconds later an armoured car came slowly grinding up the street.

It stopped and the cannon roared twice and then seemed to jam.

Christ, it had been shooting directly at the prison.

My worst fears were confirmed. A mutiny had broken out and the prison was caught right in the cross fire.

It seemed to be the story of my life.

Tea and bread arrived on time as usual although the guard serving it seemed anxious to get the chores done with as soon as possible. I knew better than to ask questions.

An hour later we had more problems.

I heard the crash on an exploding mortar nearby — damned near. Intently I listened for the departure report of the next shot and managed to locate the mortar's firing point as being somewhere in town to the right of my cell window.

The second shot came even closer.

I shifted uncomfortably. Only later was I to learn that loyalist troops were using our part of the prison block for their range finding.

The tense hours dragged on. The single mortar fired periodically, a report followed by a silence and then an explosion, some near, some far away.

I lay on my bed trying to think of other things as the fighting continued outside my window in a desultorily fashion.

I had no idea how the battle was going or even who was fighting or whether our prison was held by loyalists or rebels.

It was a bizarre situation.

Lunch — bully beef and rice — appeared by courtesy of the same harassed guard. Again nothing was said although at that moment a fierce smallarms firefight had developed almost outside the window of my cell. I tried to look as nonchalant as I could — as if being caught in the middle of a *coup d'etat* was an everyday event.

Ruefully, I had to admit that in my case it was almost becoming like that.

Little did I know that after lunch many of the defenders of the prison and surrounding camp, put off by the mortar attacks and having sustained a number of casualties, had fled.

We saw nobody until early evening when the whole confused situation suddenly, and dramatically, snapped into focus.

My cell door burst open and two young Seychellois soldiers stood on the threshold. They were strung as tense as piano wires. Both carried automatic rifles in the crooks of their arms, safety catches off. Sweat beaded their foreheads and they were covered in dust.

Faintly I caught the whiff of cordite on them.

The offer was straightforward.

'We are rebelling against the army chiefs of staff and invite you to join us. You will have your freedom and the opportunity to accomplish what you originally came for, one of them said in staccato French.

It was an offer I felt I could refuse and did. The youngster jerked up his rifle and we stared at each other intently for a second.

Then almost resignedly he said 'Okay', and slammed the door shut.

The key turned.

Each of the other mercenaries was approached with the same offer.

Each turned it down.

It was a spur of the moment choice for each of us and was taken, obviously, without consultation with the rest.

I believe most of us reasoned that whether René's troops or the rebels won we would still be in the same position — prisoners. But if we joined the rebels and they lost; well, it would be curtains. Besides, in a strange way, most of us felt some residual loyalty to René and believed that he was our best passport to freedom.

Night came and we began shouting at each other from our cells. There were no guards to stop us. I managed to call across to Roger England, now in my old cell, that he should try to force his way through the ceiling and release us. From my days studying it I knew it was very weak. He shouted back that he would give it a try the next morning.

We all turned in late that night; excited by the turn of events, apprehensive for the morning, in one way enjoying the relief from the monotony of our confinement and in the other deadly concerned about our safety. I don't believe any of us slept well.

Next morning the lone mortar spoke again.

I must say I had respect for the civilised way in which the Seychellois apparently only fought during office hours. Roger England managed to batter his way through the roof and into the orderly room upstairs. He found the keys and within minutes we were all standing outside our cells, swopping notes and wildly conjecturing about the strange turn of events.

Another mortar bomb exploded nearby, so we quickly vacated the top floor and made for the downstairs cells where the bombs would have less chance of penetrating. We unlocked one of the cell doors and marched in to find — to our astonishment — three Seychellois loyalists who had been captured by the rebels and locked up.

It was strange bedfellows indeed who settled down in Dingwell's cell that morning to await out events.

The Seychellois loyalists were apparently in dread fear that the rebels might kill them and so, to assuage their concerns, we quickly swathed them in bandages to make it seem as if they were injured.

We were not a second too soon, in fact, because several wild eyed rebel soldiers put in appearances during the course of that interminably long day. However, one glance at us pacifically sitting on the floor with the 'injured' prisoners and they would soon disappear again.

At lunch time we rustled up some beans and bully beef from the kitchen next door and then bunkered down quite cheerfully while the battle raged outside.

At one point, after we had become a little weary of the constant comings and goings of the rebels, we locked the door from the inside in the hope they would leave us alone, and they did.

It was later in the afternoon, that Lieutenant Maree, one of the captured Seychellois, decided he would make an attempt to contact the loyalists outside.

Dolincheck volunteered to go with him and quickly changed into a camouflage uniform.

They cautiously left the cell and disappeared.

Later we were to hear how the two had indeed managed to slip through to army headquarters to find — by a supreme twist of irony — our Sergeant Victor, dressed in red shorts with his hands cuffed behind him. He had been a leading light in the coup.

Dolincheck could not resist an aside or two to the crestfallen sergeant. Also at headquarters was the Russian ambassador, ex-Congo mercenary, Bob Noddyn, and some other dignitaries.

Those of us still in prison could only follow the course of events on the radio.

At first the rebels had succeeded in securing the radio station and for two days they had broadcast propaganda against the President telling of the great victories they were winning.

At the height of the coup the rebels claimed they were holding two hundred and thirty nine hostages — including us — and would begin to shoot us if their demands were not met.

Apparently they were demanding the removal of some top officers, but were not actually disloyal to President René.

Their threats to shoot us failed to cause us too much consternation because there was such visible disorganisation in their ranks that we doubted they would ever be able to find us again behind our locked door — let alone shoot us.

The drama was soon over.

Loyal troops quickly seized the advantage and the revolt was crushed. With the rebels surrendering everywhere the loyalist troops moved into Unionvale — which had been the seat of discontent — and found us patiently awaiting their arrival.

The coup attempt was a disaster.

It sprang from discontent among the rank and file over some of their officers, principally Major Marengo, and appeared in fact to have little to do with the President at all.

Marengo, in any other army's terms was a disciplinarian, but in Seychellois terms was a martinet.

I had sympathy for him, however, because the Seychellois soldier is no different from the Seychellois civilian; easy-going, fun loving and slack.

The chief conspirator turned out to be Marengo's secretary, a lance corporal, and a Sergeant Vito emerged as a key figure.

Marengo's secretary was wounded early in the fighting and was found in hospital by the loyalist troops. They claimed he committed suicide after his arrest but I believe he was quietly taken out to avoid future complications.

Whatever tragedy the coup offered for some — and lives were indeed lost — it was for us a great boon.

From the moment the loyal troops retook the prison and radio station we were never again to be locked up; we had become safe people. The night the loyalists arrived we were herded into a communal cell, for the first time all of us were together, and given our first decent meal in detention.

Jean Dingwell was also put in with us.

From then on our food and conditions of detention improved dramatically. From bread and tea for breakfast we jumped to eggs and bacon, from paltry helpings of fish and half cooked rice for the rest of the day we went to roast pork, salads and lentils To cap it all we began receiving early morning coffee and late night tea — with biscuits.

It was a touching display of gratitude to us for not jumping on the rebel bandwagon.

Meanwhile the rebels were being routed out and rounded up. More than a hundred were brought to the prison and put into our old cells.

Where we had one cell to a person, they were forced in four at a time.

And we thought we had had it bad.

59

Disappointment

Our greatly improved living conditions were thanks to the abortive coup of the Seychelles troops. But we were soon to learn that what we had gained on the merry-go-round of conditions of detention we had lost heavily on the swings of release.

Our September discharge date — promised by President René — dragged closer but already in discussions among ourselves we felt that the recent coup attempt must have had some effect on the release promise. It had and we were soon to be told about it.

In early September President René called us to his residence again and sombrely and straightforwardly told us it was out of the question to release us. He explained that complications had arisen because of the army revolt.

Although he did not spell it out we knew the problem.

René's Attorney General, Bernard Rasool, had declined to prosecute the rebel soldiers and had been fired.

Court cases for the rebels were coming up and the State was faced with the responsibility of confirming any death sentences that might be passed on the ringleaders.

It was a difficult and delicate time in the Seychelles and a sudden pardon of us by the President would have created enormous problems. Although bitterly disappointed I somehow had sympathy for the position in which the President had found himself.

He advised us to tell our families that we were well and to call upon them to use whatever influence on the South African Government they could to secure our release.

It was a sombre group of people who trooped from his office that day.

The one advantage, however, was that we had a chance to speak to our families. President René allowed us to telephone our people in South Africa.

Hearing Julia's comforting voice, so distant, struck me to the very core and for a moment I came close to losing the control I had maintained since the beginning of my detention. At that time we were talking about a January 1983 return date.

It was back into our communal cell. Although life was much easier for us and we were no longer burdened with the terrible isolation of solitary confinement it was, of course, not a bed of roses.

Sometimes tensions between the mercenaries sprang up, arguments, bitterness, sharpened by our disappointment at not going home.

People got on each other's nerves; Simms because he never shared food parcels, Dolincheck because he had a habit of turning important news items on his radio so low that only he could hear and England because he was cheeking the guards and creating problems.

Time hung heavily on all of us.

Weekends, especially, were a bore and sometimes even dangerous. Our Seychellois guards tended to hit the bottle at weekends and then the trouble would really pop. Automatic rifles would be fired into the sky for no reason, occasionally there would be a round or two of wildly erratic fire from the recoilless rifle outside the prison and once or twice some of them gave it a bash on a machinegun.

Our cell was quite exposed and not the safest place to be when the Seychellois troops got swinging.

Then suddenly there was another dramatic turn around in our fortunes on the Island.

It started when we heard a whispered rumour that there had been yet another coup attempt on the Island. We were staggered that anybody could think of taking on the Seychelles Government again after such signal failures on the two previous occasions. And because we had no details we were fearful that the new attempt would again delay our release.

The news came through in dribs and drabs. Two conspirators — a Mike Asher from Durban and an islander, Simon Domisse — had been blown up in their Kombi parked at a beach on Mahe.

Within days the Seychelles Government had the details — a botched and farcical coup attempt engineered partially in the back room of a butchery in Durban North and in a London hotel room which had been bugged by René's agents.

As soon as we heard the two conspirators had been blown up in their car, we, the imprisoned veterans, exchanged knowing looks.

Ostensibly it had been a badly primed bomb — their own — that had killed them. But it was not long before the guards began hinting at what we had suspected all along. The men had been arrested, interrogated and then blown up by the security forces; very neat, very terminal and without the immense political problems of two more conspirators . . . while still battling to get rid of the last lot . . . let alone the first consignment.

But the ill-advised coup attempt had a spinoff effect for us. Clearly President René thought it better to get us well away from the site of any further action.

Late one evening Major Marengo arrived and told us we were moving to new accommodation. We waited warily to find out whether it was going to be for the better or worse.

'I want you to take clothes and books for about two months. You will be back here on the mainland at the end of that time. Meanwhile, we are going to send you to an island where you will feel much freer than here.'

We cheered immensely.

Next morning we were taken in military vehicles to the airport where we boarded a Seychelles Air Force transport. Twenty minutes later we were circling Platte Island, a beautiful tropical spot surrounded by deep blue sea, skirted with sparkling white sands and lined with palm trees. To use an overworked expression — it was paradise.

All the bad vapours fell away from us as we trooped off the aircraft and were shown to the small house that was to be our home. To our delight we found we had two baths at our disposal.

In the camp area there were often groups of people from either the army or the National Youth, boys and girls aged sixteen to eighteen years, undergoing various forms of instruction.

The island was a training area for the Peoples Defence Force's raw recruits in the first phases.

Although the recruits were ordered to keep strictly away from us it was inevitable that we should meet and in some cases we became quite good friends with the young Seychellois.

During the hours of daylight we would be taken to the President's retreat — a very nice tropical summer house — and left to our own devices. We would collect shells, swim, laze around the beach and swop stories.

But soon the tensions of our close contact began building up again and often — distressingly often — it was Roger England who was the main cause of it. I am not sure what the problem was; whether it was his nature or just that the events since November 24 had badly affected him, but he was frequently fractious and difficult.

My first major row came soon after we arrived. Because of my age I was appointed by Major Marengo as senior prisoner and had the nominal responsibility of keeping some order among the little group.

Before we went up to the President's retreat I explained to everybody that we were on our honour, in a sense, and we should not go rooting through the house and getting into things which did not concern us.

It was a few days after this that I caught England going through the drawers in the house. We had a blazing row and I made it clear to him that if he wanted to take me on he would come off second best. He backed off a little but I had to watch him continually.

England was to have even more serious fights with others. He came to fisticuffs with Dolincheck, fought inoffensive Simms and once tried to climb into Bernard Carey.

We settled — apart from the occasional outbursts — into a deliciously comfortable pattern.

We would go to the beach for a swim before breakfast and have our first cup of coffee out there. By nine we were back at the camp for breakfast and then it was the beach again. Lunch was usually followed by a nap then it was more beach until 17h00 when we returned to the camp for supper and a cold drink.

When we first arrived we could get two or three cold drinks a day but this was later cut down — possibly because the troops guarding us complained about privileges we were enjoying that they did not even have. Of course coconuts and pawpaws grew in abundance. The physical effects of our early detention and ill-treatment rapidly wore off. We put on weight and became fit and tanned.

At night we were not locked up — we closed our own doors and windows.

Eventually our idyllic lifestyle became a bit too much for the troops who were sent to 'guard' us and they apparently claimed we should be looking a bit more as if we were paying for our temerity in trying to overthrow the President.

I had to admit I saw their point.

Anyhow, we were duly instructed to begin a vegetable garden near our house. This we did but again I must admit we hardly broke our backs.

We worked generally from reveille until breakfast time and then were free again for the rest of the day. Cabbages, peppers, lettuces thrived under our hands and I think most of us enjoyed the opportunity of putting in at least a little honest toil.

Occasionally Major Marengo would visit us with copies of telexes sent by President René to the South African Government appealing for clemency for convicted ANC members.

In 1983 when clemency was indeed extended to three ANC members sentenced to death our spirits soared. We remained avidly glued to the radio awaiting developments.

And thus the days slowly passed.

60

Reprieve and Pardon

The certainty that we were going to be released had built up slowly in our minds over a number of months. Although nothing official was said to us all the indications were that the Seychelles Government was keen to get rid of us. In discussions among ourselves we reasoned that René was in an uneasy dilemma; on the one hand our execution would alienate the sympathy the Government had won as a result of our botched coup attempt. On the other hand our continued detention was costing the Seychelles Government money. Besides, our release would be a magnificent public relations exercise for the Seychelles Government proving exactly how compassionate the President was compared to, for example, the heavy handedness of the South African authorities in executing ANC guerrillas.

Certainly, in their everyday treatment of us the Seychellois gave no indication of any residual feeling of bitterness or venality. Like true tropical islanders the heat and emotions of the first grim days after our coup attempt had all dissipated and we were treated with a mixture of curiosity and friendliness.

For me it was a wonderful living proof of how open and forgiving simple people can be.

Our first substantial hint that we were going home came in early July when a team of journalists from the British newspaper, the *Sunday Mail,* came to do a story on us.

Their interests were primarily in the two Britons, Roger England and Bernard Carey, but they spoke to us all in our little island paradise.

They gave us news that had us cartwheeling with joy.

President René had said we were very shortly to be repatriated.

At first I did not want to believe it but several days later we were picked up by the Seychelles Air Force Merlin and taken back to the mainland.

Everyone was talking of our imminent release.

We were put into our cells at the central police station but not locked up.

First class food was provided and we had a daily stream of inquisitive visitors coming to say their farewells.

One day we were invited to Commissioner Pillay's office and there the senior Seychelles police and the band of condemned 'desperado' mercenaries had drinks, chatted about their private lives, joked and pledged eternal friendship.

It could only happen in the Seychelles, I thought to myself as I watched Pillay and one of our party standing almost arms-about-shoulders swopping yarns.

That evening I was even able to palm read the fortunes of the Commissioner and his deputies.

Our time on Mahe inched by with all of us in a fever of impatience to return home. While waiting I spent my time writing letters to all who had befriended me during my incarceration.

Jean Dingwell, also released and rehabilitated, became a firm friend.

A planeload of journalists arrived and we knew that our release was imminent. But first we had to wait for President René to return from overseas as he wished to preside over what, not unnaturally, was a major diplomatic and humanitarian coup.

Then, suddenly, incredibly, the morning actually arrived and we trooped aboard the Boeing that was to carry us to South Africa. In an almost dreamlike state I endured the merrymaking of my comrades and the persistent questioning of the journalists aboard.

Then, finally, we were there.

Security at Jan Smuts Airport had allowed our close families into the customs' concourse at the airport. Di Brooks was there and Ina Dolincheck, Roger England's blond South African girl friend was there — and of course, Julia. Holding hands with her was my eight year old granddaughter Thandi.

We fell into each other's arms and for a few seconds I was beyond Jan Smuts airport, beyond the crowd, beyond conscious thought;

I was home with Julia.

We joined the rest of the disembarking passengers and moved into the main concourse.

It was chaos.

Newsmen and TV camera crews descended on us.

Through the crowd I found my parents-in-law Victor and my son and brother-in-law, Michel.

Newsmen peppered me with questions. One asked if I intended doing any more mercenary work.

'The only mercenary work I intend doing now is settling down and making a living for my wife and family.' I replied deftly piloting Julia towards the exit. And I meant it.

61

Reflections

I suppose in retrospect every conspirator who fails is obliged to say that it could have succeeded. But the coup attempt in the Congo in 1967 could, indeed, have worked. And I have no doubt the Seychelles coup attempt of 1981 could also have triumphed had the leadership been right and the planning more thorough.

The fault for the failure of that coup must lie squarely with Mike Hoare.

Cardinal errors were made in planning and execution. Perhaps the biggest and most obvious mistake was his attempt to smuggle the weapons of war through customs. Original projections had envisaged that the arms would be dropped off on the island before hand and the men would go through customs clean.

Cost cutting apparently persuaded Mike to scrap the hire of the yacht for the arms infiltration and take a more direct route. In so doing he gambled with his men's lives.

In the event, of course, it very nearly did work. Beck was the second last to pass through customs. If it had not been the eleventh hour discovery of his weapon we would would have cleared customs and been on our way to our hotels.

But a miss in the mercenary business is no less a miss even if it was so nearly a bullseye.

The second fault was that Mike failed to exercise determination and push through with the plot once the arms had been discovered. Although he took some elements to Pointe Larue military base he did not press home the attack.

Had he done so the island would surely have fallen into our hands.

Only later did we learn that no more than thirty Tanzanians were on the island.

Our reversal — and the fate of the coup attempt — was sealed not when Beck's AK-47 fell out of his bag but when Mike's men failed to roll up the Pointe Larue camp.

The collapse of the coup has meanwhile continued to exact a toll in human life as the *Movement Pour Resistance* extends its battle against the René government from exile.

On a bitterly cold December day in 1985 it took Gerard Hoarau's life.

The youthful Seychellois had just returned from an early morning visit to his doctor. As he approached his door in London's Edgeware district a swarthy man moved from the shadows and quickly approached. He drew a pistol from under his coat and pumped four shots at point blank range into Hoarau.

The conspirator, my friend, collapsed against his door bleeding furiously from head and neck wounds.

The assassin disappeared — clearly a professional who had carried out a contract killing.

First reports were that Hoarau had been the victim of a Libyan hit man. Scotland Yard's Murder Squad (Political) moved quickly.

Within twenty one days they had arraigned three 'security consultants' — William Underwood, David Coughlan and Dave Richards — on murder charges.

Rumours flew, the Hoarau family remained convinced the murder had been commissioned by a wealthy Italian businessman, Mafia connected and a close friend of René's, either with René's knowledge or on his instructions.

A correspondent of the South African *Sunday Times* meanwhile reported that Hoarau had confided to him shortly before his death that he was aware a contract was out on his life and he had already survived a Seychelles Government inspired assassination attempt in Cannes.

When I first saw news of Hoarau's death I froze. The thirty one year old Seychellois had got in above his head and, in the remorseless way of international intrigue, had drowned.

The islands, meanwhile, had lost a patriot.

I hold no grudges against Mike Hoare for the coup's failure.

Unlike Dolincheck I accept as part of the risks of adventuring that one must take the good with the bad. In a strange way my Seychelles experience proved both to me.

The bad was the monotony of incarceration, the loneliness of separation from my family, the agony of uncertainty caused by the death sentence.

The good was the firm friends I made on the island and the realisation, perhaps belated, that measured against the warmth of family ties, the rewards of adventuring are uncertain, dangerous and, ultimately, fleeting.

INDEX

381